GLOBAL PRODUCTION

Global Production

The Apparel Industry in the Pacific Rim

EDITED BY

**Edna Bonacich, Lucie Cheng,
Norma Chinchilla, Nora Hamilton,
and Paul Ong**

 Temple University Press / *Philadelphia*

Temple University Press, Philadelphia 19122
Copyright © 1994 by Temple University
Published 1994
Printed in the United States of America

The paper used in this publication meets the minimum requirements of American
National Standard for Information Sciences—Permanence of Paper for Printed Library
Materials, ANSI Z39.48-1984 ⊚

Library of Congress Cataloging-in-Publication Data

Global production : the apparel industry in the Pacific Rim / edited
   by Edna Bonacich . . . [et al.].
     p. cm.
   Includes bibliographical references and index.
   ISBN 1-56639-168-7.—ISBN 1-56639-169-5 (pbk.)
    1. Women clothing workers—Pacific Area.   2. Clothing workers—
Pacific Area.   3. Clothing trade—Pacific Area.   4. Women clothing
workers—Developing countries.   5. Clothing workers—Developing
countries.   6. Clothing trade—Developing countries.   7. Women
clothing workers—United States.   8. Clothing workers—United
States.   9. Clothing trade—United States.   I. Bonacich, Edna.
HD6073.C62P164   1994
331.4'87'099—dc20   93-36974

Contents

IV   The United States

Conclusion

Acknowledgments

This volume grew out of a grant from the University of California's Pacific Rim Research Program. The grant enabled us to call together two meetings of scholars studying this industry: an organizing meeting, in May 1991, and a conference, The Globalization of the Garment Industry in the Pacific Rim, to present final reports, in May 1992. In addition, the grant supported research assistance for the University of California faculty (Bonacich, Cheng, and Ong).

The grant was administered through the UCLA Center for Pacific Rim Studies, whose able staff (including Fauolegogo Tanielu, Sue Fan, and Scott Gruber) did all the organizing work for both meetings. In addition, they kept our books in order. The editing of the manuscript was organized by Leslie Evans of the Center and implemented by Patricia Ryan. We are grateful to all these people for their invaluable assistance.

Several people made important contributions to the conference, either as participants or as discussants. They include David Young and Steve Nutter of the International Ladies' Garment Workers Union, garment workers Ricardo Zalada and Alicia Zamora, and professors Elizabeth Petras, Roger Waldinger, Raoul Hinojosa, Eun-Mee Kim, and Nancy Wiegersma. We would like to thank all of them, particularly Betty Petras and Nan Wiegersma, who participated actively throughout the conference.

Introduction

Chapter 1

The Garment Industry in the Restructuring Global Economy

Edna Bonacich, Lucie Cheng, Norma Chinchilla,
Nora Hamilton, and Paul Ong

The apparel industry is one of the most globalized industries in the world. Some garment firms, such as Liz Claiborne, have their goods produced simultaneously in as many as forty countries around the world, including Hong Kong, Taiwan, South Korea, Singapore, the People's Republic of China, Thailand, the Philippines, Brazil, Costa Rica, Portugal, Italy, Yugoslavia, Turkey, and Hungary. Not all apparel firms have such an extensive scope, but nevertheless, we are witnessing the tremendous growth of production by apparel firms (including both manufacturers and retailers) in countries all over the world, and a concomitant rise in global trade.

This volume focuses on the globalization of the apparel industry in the Pacific Rim region. *Pacific Rim* usually refers to all the countries of Asia and the Americas that border on the Pacific Ocean. We have adapted this concept to the actual patterns of apparel production, and we focus on three areas in particular: Asia; the United States; and Mexico, Central America, and the Caribbean (hereafter referred to as the *Caribbean region*). Because the Caribbean is obviously not geographically connected to the Pacific, this choice requires some explanation.

Asia, the United States, and the Caribbean region form an important triangle in apparel production. In this triangle, the United States is the major market for production in both Asia and the Caribbean region. U.S. apparel firms are active in both regions, and Asian firms are increasingly active in the Caribbean region and the United States (see Chapter 2 for a full discussion). Although there has been a small decline in the dominance of the United States as the chief market, this basic pattern prevails and has shaped the development of all three areas. The Pacific Rim region, as we have defined it, thus forms a relatively integrated region of apparel production and distribution.

The most important omission in this picture is the western European industry. Italy, for example, was the world's second largest garment exporter behind Hong Kong in 1990. Indeed, six western European countries were among the top fifteen apparel exporters. Eighty-three percent of European clothing exports, however, went to other European countries. While 26 percent of western European garment imports came from Asia in 1990, 75 percent of North American garment imports derived from Asia. In 1989 19 percent of Asian garment exports were shipped to western Europe and 40 percent to North America (GATT 1992, 65–66). Asia is thus more integrated with the United States than with Europe, and the Caribbean region is even more so, as we shall see.

Nevertheless, it is important not to reify the Pacific Rim triangle. Firms scour the entire world in sourcing apparel and do not draw any special line around Asia and the Caribbean region. The autonomy and integration of this region is thus only relative and provides a convenient way to limit an already overwhelming topic.

The globalization of the apparel industry illustrates more general trends toward global production. Because the rest of the book focuses solely on apparel, in this chapter we briefly attempt to place the industry within this larger context.

Restructuring of the Global Economy

Global integration, a long-standing feature of the world economy, is currently undergoing a restructuring. Generally, until after World War II, the advanced industrial countries of western Europe and the United States dominated the world economy and controlled most of its industrial production. The less-developed countries tended to concentrate in the production of raw materials. Since the late 1950s, and accelerating rapidly in the 1980s, however, industrial production has shifted out of the West, initially to Japan, then to the Asian NICs (newly industrializing countries—namely, Hong Kong, Taiwan, South Korea, and Singapore), and now to almost every country of the world. Less-developed countries are not manufacturing mainly for the domestic market or following a model of "import substitution"; rather, they are manufacturing for export, primarily to developed countries, and pursuing a development strategy of export-led industrialization. What we are witnessing has been termed by some a "new international division of labor" (Fröbel, Heinrichs, and Kreye 1980).[1]

The developed countries are faced with the problem of "deindustrialization" in terms of traditional manufacturing, as their manufacturing base is shifted to other, less-developed countries (Bluestone and Harrison 1982). At the same time, they are faced with a massive rise in imports that compete with local industries' products, moving to displace them. This shift is accompanied by the rise of a new kind of transnational corporation (TNC). Of course, TNCs have existed since the beginning of the European expansion, but they concentrated mainly on the production of agricultural goods and raw materials and, in the postwar period, on manufacturing for the host-country market. The new TNCs are global firms that are able to use advanced communications and transportation technology to coordinate manufacturing in multiple locations simultaneously. They engage in "offshore sourcing" to produce primarily for the home market (Grunwald and Flamm 1985; Sklair 1989).

TNCs sometimes engage in direct foreign investment, but globalized production does not depend on it. They can arrange for production in numerous locations through other, looser connections, such as subcontracting and licensing. In other words, TNCs can set up complex networks of global production without owning or directly controlling their various branches.

The nation-state has increasingly declined as an economic unit, with the result that states are often unable to control the actions of powerful TNCs. The TNCs are supragovernmental actors that make decisions on the basis of profit-making criteria without input from representative governments. Of course, strong states are still able to exercise considerable influence over trade policies and over the policies of the governments of developing countries.

Some scholars have used the concept of "commodity chains" to describe the new spatial arrangements of production (Gereffi and Korzeniewicz 1994). The concept shows how design, production, and distribution are broken down and geographically dispersed, with certain places serving as centers within the chain. Power is differentially allocated along the chain, and countries and firms vie to improve their position in the chain.

Focusing on the geographic aspects of global production also has led to the concept of "global cities" (Sassen 1991). These are coordination centers for the global economy, where planning takes place. They house the corporate headquarters of TNCs, as well as international financial services and a host of related business services. These cities have become the "capitals" of the new global economy.

Another way to view the restructuring is to see it as the proletarianization of most of the world. People who had been engaged primarily in peasant agriculture or in other forms of noncapitalist production are now being incorporated into the industrial labor force. Many of these people are first-generation wage-workers, and a disproportionate number of them are women. These "new" workers sometimes retain ties to noncapitalist sectors and migrate between them and capitalist employment, making their labor cheaper than that of fully proletarianized workers. But even if they are not attached to noncapitalist sectors, first-generation workers tend to be especially vulnerable to exploitative conditions. Thus, an important feature of the new globalization is that TNCs are searching the world for the cheapest available labor and are finding it in developing countries.

Countries pursuing export-led industrialization typically follow strategies that encourage the involvement of foreign capital. They offer incentives, including tax holidays and the setting up of export-processing zones (EPZs), where the bureaucracy surrounding importing and exporting is curtailed; sometimes they also promise cheap and controllable labor. Countries using this development strategy do not plan to remain the providers of cheap labor for TNCs, however: they hope to move up the production ladder, gaining more economic power and control. They want to shift from labor-intensive manufactures to capital-intensive, high-technology goods. They hope to follow the path of Japan and the Asian NICs and become major economic players in the global economy.

Sometimes participation in global capitalist production is foisted on nations by advanced-industrial countries and/or suprastate organizations such as the World Bank and the International Monetary Fund (IMF), where advanced countries wield a great deal of influence. The United States, in particular, has backed regimes that support globalized production and has pushed for austerity programs that help to make labor cheap. At the same time, developed countries, including the United States, have been affected by the restructured global economy. Accompanying the rise in imports and deindustrialization has been a growth in unemployment and a polarization between the rich and the poor (Harrison and Bluestone 1988). This trend has coincided with increased racial polarization, as people of color have faced a disproportionate impact from these developments.

A rise in immigration from less-developed to more-developed countries has also accompanied globalization. The United States, for example, has experienced large-scale immigration from the Caribbean region and from Asia, two areas pursuing a manufacturing-for-export development strategy. At least part of this immigration is a product of globalization, as people are dislocated by the new economic order and are forced to emigrate for survival (Sassen 1988). Dislocations occur not only because global industries displace local ones (as in the case of agribusiness displacing peasants), but also because austerity programs exacerbate the wage gap between rich and poor countries (making the former ever more desirable). Political refugees, often from countries where the United States has supported repressive regimes, have added to the rise in immigration as well. Finally, some immigration results when people move to service global enterprise as managers, trade representatives, or technicians.

In the advanced countries, the immigration of workers has created a "Third World within." In this case, the newly created proletariat is shifting location. These immigrants play a part in the efforts of the advanced countries to hold on to their industries, by providing a local source of cheap labor to counter the low labor standards in competing countries.

In sum, we are seeing a shakeup of the old world economic order. Some countries have used manufacturing for export as a way to become major economic powers (Appelbaum and Henderson 1992; Gereffi and Wyman 1990). These countries now threaten U.S. dominance. Other countries are trying to pursue this same path, but it is not clear whether they will succeed. Meanwhile, despite the fact that the United States is suffering some negative consequences from the global restructuring, certain U.S.-based TNCs are deeply implicated in the process and benefit from it.

Contrasting Views of Restructuring

The new globalization receives different interpretations and different evaluations (Gondolf, Marcus, and Dougherty 1986). Some focus on the positive side; they see global production as increasing efficiency by allowing each country to specialize in its strengths. Less-developed countries are able to provide low-cost, unskilled labor, while developed countries provide management, technical, and financial resources. Together they are able to maximize the efficient use of resources. The result is that more goods and services are produced more cheaply, to the benefit of all. Consumers, in particular, are seen as the great beneficiaries of globalized production, because of the abundance of low-cost, higher-quality goods from which to choose.

Globalization can be seen as part of the new system of flexible specialization (Piore and Sabel 1984). Consumer markets have become more differentiated, making the old, industrial system of mass production in huge factories obsolete. To be competitive today, a firm must be able to produce small batches of differentiated goods for diverse customers. Globalization contributes to this process by enabling firms to produce a vast range of products in multiple countries simultaneously.

Another aspect of the positive view is to see the entrance of less-developed countries into manufacturing for export as a step toward their industrialization and economic development. Although countries may enter the global economy at a tremendous disadvantage, by participating in exports they are able to accumulate capital and gradually increase their power and wealth. Japan and the Asian NICs have demonstrated the possibilities; now other countries can follow a similar path.

Although workers in the advanced countries may suffer some dislocation by the movement of industry abroad, in the long run they are seen to be beneficiaries of this process. While lower-skilled, more labor-intensive jobs will move to the developing countries, the advanced countries will gain higher-technology jobs, as well as jobs in coordinating and managing the global economy. Thus workers in the advanced countries will be "pushed up" to more middle-class positions, servicing and directing the workers in the rest of the world. Moreover, as other countries develop, their purchasing power will increase, leading to larger markets for the products of the developed countries. Growth in exports means growth in domestic production, and thus growth in domestic employment.

Those who favor globalization also note its inevitability. The economic logic that is propelling global production is immensely powerful. Technology allows globalization, and competition forges it; there is really no stopping the process, so the best one can do is adapt on the most favorable terms possible. Nations feel they must get into the game quickly so as not to be left behind.

A favorable standpoint on globalization is typically coupled with an optimistic view of the effects of immigration. Like new nations entering the global economy, immigrant workers are seen as having to suffer in the short run in order to make advances in the future. Instead of being viewed as exploited, the immigrants are seen as being granted an opportunity—one that they freely choose—to better their life circumstances. They may start off being paid low wages because they lack marketable skills, but with time, they or their children will acquire such skills and will experience upward mobility.

In general, a positive view of globalization is accompanied by a belief in the benefits of markets and free trade. The market, rather than political decision making, should, it is felt, be the arbiter of economic decision making. This favorable and inevitable view of globalization is by far the most predominant approach. It is promoted by the U.S. government, by the TNCs, by many governments in developing countries, and by various international agencies. This position receives considerable support from academics, especially economists, who provide governmental agencies with advice. It is the dominant world policy.

There is, however, a less sanguine interpretation of globalization voiced by U.S. trade unionists and many academics who study development, labor, women, inequality, and social class (Castells and Henderson 1987; Kamel 1990; Kolko 1988; Peet 1987; Ross and Trachte 1990; Sklair 1989). In general, their view is that globalization has a differential class impact: globalization is in the interests of capitalists, especially capitalists connected with TNCs, and of sectors of the capitalist class in developing nations. But the working class in both sets of countries is hurt, especially young women workers, who have become the chief employees of the TNCs (Fernandez-Kelly 1983; Fuentes and Ehrenreich 1983; Mies 1986; Nash and Fernandez-Kelly 1983).

Some argue that globalization is part of a response to a major crisis that has emerged in the advanced capitalist countries. In particular, after the post–World War II boom, the economies of these countries stagnated and profits declined; stagnation was blamed on the advances made by workers under the welfare state. Capital's movement abroad, which was preceded in the United States by regional relocation, is an effort to cut labor costs, weaken unions, and restore profitability. Put generally, globalization can be seen, in part, as an effort to discipline labor.

Globalization enables employers to pit workers from different countries against one another. Regions and nations must compete to attract investment and businesses. Competitors seek to undercut one another by offering the most favorable conditions to capital. Part of what they seek to offer is quality, efficiency, and timeliness, but they also compete in terms of providing the lowest possible labor standards: they promise a low-cost, disciplined, and unorganized work force. Governments pledge to ensure these conditions by engaging in the political repression of workers' movements (Deyo 1989).

The disciplining of the working class that accompanies globalization is not limited to conditions in the workplace. It also involves a cutback in state social programs. For example, in the United States, under the Reagan-Bush administrations, efforts were made to curtail multiple programs protecting workers' standard of living; these tax-based programs were seen as hindering capital accumulation. The argument was made that if these funds were invested by the private sector, everyone would benefit, including workers. This same logic has been imposed on developing countries; they have been granted aid and loans on the condition that they engage in austerity programs that cut back on social spending. The impact of such cutbacks is that workers are less protected from engaging in bargains of desperation when they enter the work force.

This view of globalization is accompanied by a pessimism about the policy of export-led development. Rather than believing that performing assembly for TNCs will lead to development, critics fear that it is another form of dependency, with the advanced capitalist countries and their corporations retaining economic (and political) control over the global economy (Bello and Rosenfeld 1990).

Critics also note a negative side to immigrants' experiences (Mitter 1986; Sassen 1988). They see the immigration of workers as, in part, a product of globalization and TNC activity, as workers in less-developed countries find their means of livelihood disrupted by capitalist penetration. Immigrants are thus not just people seeking a better life for themselves, but often those "forced" into moving because thet have lost the means to survive. On arrival in the more-advanced economies, they are faced with forms of coercion, including immigration regulations, racism, and sexism, that keep them an especially disadvantaged work force. Especially coercive is the condition of being an undocumented immigrant. Critics point out that those who favor globalization promote the free movement of commodities and capital, but not the free movement of labor, in the form of open borders. Political restrictions on workers add to the weakening of the working class.

In sum, the critical perspective sees globalization as an effort to strengthen the hand of capital and weaken that of labor. The favorable view argues that the interests of capital and labor are not antagonistic and that everyone benefits from capital accumulation, investment, economic growth, and the creation of jobs. Critics, on the other hand, contend that certain classes benefit at the expense of others, and that, even if workers in poor countries do get jobs, these jobs benefit the capitalists much more than they do the workers, and also hurt the workers in the advanced capitalist countries through deindustrialization.

Where does the truth lie? One of the purposes of this volume is to assess this question in a detailed examination of globalization's effects on one industry in a variety of countries. As we will see, not only do countries' experiences differ greatly, but so do the perspectives and assumptions of the participants in this project. Some are firm believers in free trade, export-led development, and global capitalism. They see tremendous economic growth and the rise of previously underdeveloped countries into powerful actors in the world economy. Others view export-led industrialization as a dead end for some, although not all, countries. They focus on the pain and suffering of workers, especially women, as they toil in factories and in the underground economy spawned by global capitalism.

To a certain extent, one's point of view depends on geographic location. Generally, Asian countries, especially the NICs, appear to be transforming themselves from dependencies into major actors and competitors in the global economy, leading to an optimism about the effects of globalization. This optimism, however, blots out the suffering and labor repression that is still occurring for some workers in these countries, despite the rise in standard of living for the majority.

On the other hand, the Caribbean region generally faces a harsher reality, in part because the closeness and dominance of the United States pose special problems for these countries. They are more likely to get caught in simple assembly for the TNCs, raising questions about whether manufacturing for export will be transformable into broader economic development. Of course, some in these countries are firm believers in this policy and are pursuing it avidly, but there are clear signs that many workers are severely exploited in the process.

Similar questions can be raised about the later Asian entrants to the global economy. Will they find themselves under Japanese and NIC domination similar to U.S. domination of the Caribbean region? And if so, will they still be able to use this initially dependent position to develop economically and eventually to become global players in their own right?

Other confusing issues remain. For example, do women benefit from their movement into the wage sector (proletarianization) as a result of globalization? A case can be made that working outside the home and earning money gives women new-found power in their relations with men. It can also be argued, however, that these women remain under patriarchal control, but that now, in addition to their fathers and husbands, they are under the control of male bosses. They have double and even triple workloads, as they engage in wage labor, domestic labor, and often industrial homework and other forms of informalized labor (Ward 1990).

The two points of view lead to different politics. Those who hold the favorable outlook advocate working for the breakdown of all trade and investment barriers and to pushing rapidly ahead toward global integration. Critics are not trying to stem these forces completely, but rather, are attempting to set conditions on them. For example, globalization should be allowed only if labor and environmental standards are protected in the process. Similarly, the rights of workers to form unions should be safeguarded, so that business cannot wantonly pit groups of workers against one another.

The Apparel Industry

This volume focuses on one industry to examine the characteristics and impact of globalized production. Of course, apparel has unique features, although it shares many traits with other industries; concentrating on one industry thus offers only partial insight into the workings of the entire global economic system (see Chapkis and Enloe 1983 and Dickerson 1991 for an introduction to the global apparel industry).

The apparel industry stands out for several reasons. First, it is one of the most globalized industries in the world today; like the electronics industry, it has established a beachhead in virtually every country of the globe. Moreover, apparel is typically the entering industry for countries embarking on a program of industrialization, particularly export-led industrialization. In this sense, apparel production is the cutting-edge industry in the globalization process; it is pioneering global processing. We predict that many of the methods used in the globalization of apparel production will be followed by other industries, and thus the apparel industry may be a portent of things to come.

One of the reasons that countries aspiring to industrialization enter the apparel industry first is that aspects of the industry involve simple technology and hence low startup costs. The basic unit of production remains the individual sitting at a sewing machine. Although some technological strides have been made, sewing continues to be a labor-intensive activity that does not require formal education, so newly proletarianized workers can enter this industry without much advance preparation.

The image of the industry as entirely low-tech is false, however (Hoffman and Rush 1988). The designing, engineering, grading, marking, and cutting phases of production are becoming increasingly mechanized by computer technology, and the planning and coordination of far-flung production units requires highly developed communications and transportation technologies. Thus, a peculiarity of this industry is that it combines the most advanced technology with some of the least developed in the industrial world. The combination of high- and low-tech characteristics lends itself to a system of contracting out the low-tech, labor-intensive parts of production to less-developed countries. In this way, these countries become integrated into the global system of production by engaging in one aspect of the production process, namely, assembly. The electronics industry shares this characteristic with apparel, with labor-intensive assembly also sent to low-wage countries. In electronics, however, offshore assembly tends to be done in subsidiaries of TNCs from the advanced, industrial countries. In contrast, apparel is characterized by arm's-length relationships—especially contracting—in which the TNC neither owns nor necessarily has a long-term commitment to particular contractors or locations.

Because global apparel production can occur without ownership and commitment, the industry enjoys tremendous flexibility. TNCs can shift their production with relative ease to the places and firms where they can get the best deal. As a result, the labor market for this industry is truly the world, and all the countries of the world are put into competition with one another to obtain work in clothing assembly. Other industries may never be able completely to replicate the flexibility that the apparel industry has been able to achieve, but it surely stands as a model for their ideal system of production. Again, we see that the apparel industry may serve as a forecast of things to come.

Because this industry is often the first step in countries' entrance into export-led industrialization, it is also the industry that first encounters the process of proletarianization. Young women, often from rural areas, first encounter wage labor in this industry. The entire complex of problems that such a work force faces, including patriarchal domination, severe exploitation, lack of legal protection, continued domestic responsibilities, homework, and so on, is vividly in evidence in the apparel industry. By studying this industry, we are able to see clearly both the severe social costs of globalization, particularly for those who work at sewing, and workers' efforts to resist oppression. Garment workers exemplify the formidable challenge of finding ways for international labor to respond to international capital.

Just as the apparel industry represents a point of entry for countries and for their newly proletarianized workers, so it represents a point of entry for immigrant workers to advanced-industrial countries from the developing world (Green 1986; Hoel 1982; Morokvasic, Phizacklea, and Rudolph 1986; Phizacklea 1990; Waldinger 1986). Sewing jobs are often the first work immigrants can find, and conditions in garment-assembly factories in the advanced countries frequently mirror Third World conditions. The organizing of immigrant garment workers poses some of the same challenges as the organizing of garment workers in the developing countries, and both groups face the problem of intense competition among their employers for the assembly work offered by globe-scouring TNCs.

In sum, the apparel industry represents both the most advanced arm of globalization and some of its most negative effects, particularly for women. It is worthy of intensive study not only in its own right, but because it may well predict what lies ahead for many other industries. Therefore, we hope our study contributes to an understanding of globalization in general as well as to an understanding of this particular industry.

The unique feature of this book is that it examines a global industry from the perspective of different countries. We have included scholars from Asia and the Caribbean region, or scholars whose work has focused on these regions, along with those whose major topic of study is the United States. The diversity of vantage points enabled all of us to learn something of the tremendous complexity of the globalization process in this industry.

Although we are interested in the details of apparel production in each country, we placed special emphasis on the linkages between countries. Our guiding questions were: What role has the country played in the development of apparel trade in the Pacific Rim region? How has it been affected by trade regimes such as quotas and the encouragement of offshore processing? What is the role of foreign capital? What part have entrepreneurs from the country played in the apparel industry of other countries? Has the country sent emigrants or received immigrants connected with the apparel industry? What are the conditions of labor for garment workers?

In Part I we describe the globalization of the industry within the

Pacific Rim region and examine the role played by the United States in this process. Parts II and III concern the Asian and the Caribbean regions, respectively, and analyze the experiences of several countries within each of the regions. In Part IV we return to the United States to explore this country's response to the globalization process. Finally, we assess the impact of globalization on economic development and consider the prospects for international labor organizing among garment workers.

Note

1. Although the theory behind this work has received criticism, the description itself is accurate.

References

Appelbaum, Richard P., and Jeffrey Henderson, eds. 1992. *States and Development in the Asian Pacific Rim*. Newbury Park, Calif.: Sage.

Bello, Walden, and Stephanie Rosenfeld. 1990. *Dragons in Distress: Asia's Miracle Economies in Crisis*. San Francisco: Institute for Food and Development Policy.

Bluestone, Barry, and Bennett Harrison. 1982. *The Deindustrialization of America: Plant Closings, Community Abandonment, and the Dismantling of Basic Industry*. New York: Basic Books.

Castells, Manuel, and Jeffrey Henderson. 1987. "Technoeconomic Restructuring, Sociopolitical Processes, and Spatial Transformation: A Global Perspective." In *Global Restructuring and Territorial Development*, edited by Jeffrey Henderson and Manuel Castells, 1–17. London: Sage.

Chapkis, Wendy, and Cynthia Enloe. 1983. *Of Common Cloth: Women in the Global Textile Industry*. Amsterdam: Transnational Institute.

Deyo, Frederic C. 1989. *Beneath the Miracle: Labor Subordination in the New Asian Industrialism*. Berkeley: University of California Press.

Dickerson, Kitty G. 1991. *Textiles and Apparel in the International Economy*. New York: Macmillan.

Fernandez-Kelly, M. Patricia. 1983. *For We Are Sold, I and My People: Women and Industry in Mexico's Frontier*. Albany: State University of New York Press.

Fröbel, Folker, Jürgen Heinrichs, and Otto Kreye. 1980. *The New Interna-*

tional Division of Labour: Structural Unemployment in Industrialised Countries and Industrialisation in Developing Countries. Cambridge: Cambridge University Press.

Fuentes, Annette, and Barbara Ehrenreich. 1983. *Women in the Global Factory.* Boston: South End Press.

General Agreement on Tariffs and Trade (GATT). 1992. *International Trade 90–91.* Geneva: GATT.

Gereffi, Gary, and Miguel Korzeniewicz, eds. 1994. *Commodity Chains and Global Capitalism.* Westport, Conn.: Greenwood Press.

Gereffi, Gary, and Donald L. Wyman, eds. 1990. *Manufacturing Miracles: Paths of Industrialization in Latin America and East Asia.* Princeton: Princeton University Press.

Gondolf, Edward W., Irwin M. Marcus, and James P. Dougherty. 1986. *The Global Economy: Divergent Perspectives on Economic Change.* Boulder, Colo.: Westview Press.

Green, Nancy L. 1986. "Immigrant Labor in the Garment Industries of New York and Paris: Variations on a Structure." *Comparative Social Research* 9:231–43.

Grunwald, Joseph, and Kenneth Flamm. 1985. *The Global Factory: Foreign Assembly in International Trade.* Washington, D.C.: Brookings Institution.

Harrison, Bennett, and Barry Bluestone, 1988. *The Great U-Turn: Corporate Restructuring and the Polarizing of America.* New York: Basic Books.

Henderson, Jeffrey, and Manuel Castells, eds. 1987. *Global Restructuring and Territorial Development.* London: Sage.

Hoel, Barbro. 1982. "Contemporary Clothing 'Sweatshops,' Asian Female Labour, and Collective Organization." In *Work, Women, and the Labour Market,* edited by Jackie West, 80–98. London: Routledge and Kegan Paul.

Hoffman, Kurt, and Howard Rush. 1988. *Micro-Electronics and Clothing: The Impact of Technical Change on a Global Industry.* New York: Praeger.

Kamel, Rachael. 1990. *The Global Factory: Analysis and Action for a New Economic Era.* Philadelphia: American Friends Service Committee.

Kolko, Joyce. 1988. *Restructuring the World Economy.* New York: Pantheon.

Mies, Maria. 1986. *Patriarchy and Accumulation on a World Scale: Women in the International Division of Labor.* London: Zed Books.

Mitter, Swasti. 1986. *Common Fate, Common Bond: Women in the Global Economy.* London: Pluto Press.

Morokvasic, Mirjana, Annie Phizacklea, and Hedwig Rudolph. 1986. "Small Firms and Minority Groups: Contradictory Trends in the French, German, and British Clothing Industries." *International Sociology* 1:397–419.

Nash, June, and M. Patricia Fernandez-Kelly, eds. 1983. *Women, Men, and the International Division of Labor.* Albany: State University of New York Press.

Peet, Richard, ed. 1987. *International Capitalism and Industrial Restructuring.* Boston: Allen and Unwin.

Phizacklea, Annie. 1990. *Unpacking the Fashion Industry: Gender, Racism, and Class in Production.* New York: Routledge, Chapman, and Hall.

Piore, Michael J., and Charles F. Sabel. 1984. *The Second Industrial Divide: Possibilities for Prosperity.* New York: Basic Books.

Ross, Robert J. S., and Kent C. Trachte. 1990. *Global Capitalism: The New Leviathan.* Albany: State University of New York Press.

Sassen, Saskia. 1988. *The Mobility of Labor and Capital: A Study in International Investment and Labor Flow.* Cambridge: Cambridge University Press.

———. 1991. *The Global City: New York, London, Tokyo.* Princeton: Princeton University Press.

Sklair, Leslie. 1989. *Assembling for Development: The Maquila Industry in Mexico and the United States.* London: Unwin Hyman.

Waldinger, Roger D. 1986. *Through the Eye of the Needle: Immigrants and Enterprise in New York's Garment Trades.* New York: New York University Press.

Ward, Kathryn, ed. 1990. *Women Workers and Global Restructuring.* Ithaca: Cornell University, ILR Press.

PART I

Patterns and Linkages

Chapter 2

Mapping a Global Industry: Apparel Production in the Pacific Rim Triangle

Edna Bonacich and David V. Waller

The Pacific Rim region, defined here to comprise Asia, the United States, and the Caribbean region (including Mexico, Central America, and the Caribbean islands), represents an important triangle for apparel production. In contrast to apparel production in Europe, which is aimed primarily at the European market, production in the Pacific Rim is truly global, drawing all three regions into complex and constantly evolving relationships. The boundedness of this triangle is far from absolute, however, as transnational apparel and retailing companies trade and produce all over the world. In isolating the Pacific Rim region, we are dealing with a relatively coherent subsystem of global production. Its multifaceted relations encompass not only trade but also capital flows, globalized production, and labor migration. The basic links of the triangle, with numbers reflecting a rough chronological ordering of their development, are presented in Figure 2.1, which maps the emergence and implications of each of these links.

The Movement from the United States to Asia (Arrow 1)

The globalization of the apparel industry began when U.S. apparel firms first moved their operations to Asia in search of cheaper production (see Chapter 5 for a full discussion). Starting in the late 1950s, U.S. apparel firms moved first to Japan, then to Hong Kong,

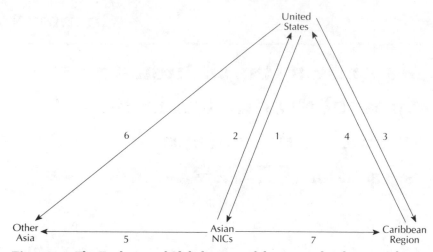

Figure 2.1 The Evolution of Globalization of the Apparel Industry in the Pacific Rim

and then to South Korea and Taiwan. Hong Kong, Korea, and Taiwan became three of the four Asian NICs (newly industrializing countries), using apparel as their first major export industry. U.S. apparel firms did not invest directly in Asia but engaged in contract manufacturing. Manufacturers and later retailers arranged to have their garments produced in Asia, even though they did not own the Asian firms.

At first, the main attraction was the low cost of labor. In 1975 the average wage for U.S. apparel workers was US$3.79 per hour, compared to US$0.75 in Hong Kong, US$0.29 in Taiwan, and US$0.22 in Korea. Hong Kong apparel workers were thus paid 20 percent of the U.S. wage; Taiwanese, 8 percent; and Koreans, 6 percent (U.S. Department of Labor 1990). In addition, severe measures were taken by NIC governments to keep workers subordinated and unorganized (Deyo 1989; Fuentes and Ehrenreich 1983).

The Asian NICs helped to augment their apparel industries as part of a development strategy to manufacture for export. Building on their advantage of low-wage labor, these countries established export-processing zones (EPZs) where foreign components could easily be imported and processed for export without undue bureaucratic interference. Workers in these zones were predominantly young women, who worked long hours for a fraction of men's wages (Currie 1985; ILO 1984). The NICs actively enticed foreign firms with promises of an abundant supply of low-wage, compliant labor, both inside and outside EPZs. Although low-wage, controllable labor was the initial attraction for U.S. firms, the Asian NICs quickly added other benefits, including the availability of quality textiles, flexibility of production, and, increasingly, high-quality merchandise. Even so, Asian NIC labor costs still remain below U.S. labor costs. In 1988 Hong Kong apparel workers were paid 31 percent of the U.S. wage; Taiwanese, 27 percent; and Koreans, 21 percent (U.S. Department of Labor 1990). The NICs thus offered the industry "value": that is, high-quality products at a relatively low price. In addition, as we shall see, they have developed as centers for organizing apparel production in other, lower-wage countries.

The Rise in Imports to the United States (Arrow 2)

A large proportion of apparel production in Asia was aimed at the U.S. market, leading to a tremendous rise in imports. In 1962 apparel imports were valued at US$301 million; by 1990 they had risen to US$21,931 million (Table 2.1), expanding especially during the 1980s. Though these imports did not all come from the Asian NICs, these three countries dominated U.S. imports in the early years and continue, along with the People's Republic of China, to be the major suppliers.

Garment imports took their toll on U.S. domestic production and employment. In 1980 the U.S. domestic industry provided 70 percent of the apparel consumed in the United States; by 1990 this portion had shrunk to 50 percent (AAMA 1991, 3). Employment dropped from 1,364,000 in 1970, to 1,264,000 in 1980, and to 1,029,000 in 1990 (AAMA 1991, 16).

Different types of garments have been differentially affected by imports. For example, the ratio of imports to domestic production of sweaters (measured in number of garments) was 3.35 to 1 in 1989. Underwear, in contrast, showed a ratio of 0.26 to 1. Heavily affected products included woven shirts and blouses, women's and girls' coats, and women's and girls' slacks and shorts. Less affected were dresses, men's and boys' suits and suit-type coats, and nightwear. To some extent the Asian NICs specialized in certain types of products. For example, in 1990 Hong Kong and Korea produced more sweaters

Table 2.1

Apparel Imports to the United States, 1962–1990 (in square meters [M²] and US$ millions)

Year	M²	US$
1962	397	301
1963	412	332
1964	469	375
1965	572	459
1966	650	518
1970	1,417	1,095
1971	1,754	1,342
1972	1,862	1,691
1973	1,747	1,923
1974	1,619	2,063
1975	1,736	2,263
1976	2,030	3,189
1977	2,062	3,611
1978	2,429	4,680
1979	2,233	4,834
1980	2,411	5,518
1981	2,622	6,514
1982	2,828	7,111
1983	3,240	8,277
1984	3,943	10,853
1985	4,279	11,887
1986	4,898	14,087
1987	5,458	18,038
1988	5,276	18,184
1989	6,049	21,046
1990	6,008	21,931

Source: AAMA 1991, 31.

than Taiwan, while Taiwan and Hong Kong produced more pants, shorts, underwear, and nightwear; by this time, however, China was the leading importer of every category of garments to the United States, as measured by number of garments (AAMA 1991, 32–34).

These imports were, in part, induced by sectors of the U.S. apparel industry. For example, according to Steele (1990):

The relationship of Hong Kong apparel producers with their Western customers is that of contract suppliers—i.e., they fulfill orders on behalf of the buyers acting for major distributors in which the buyers are largely responsible for determining styles, fabrics, patterns/colours, etc. The development of a native *couture* in Hong Kong capable of producing fashions acceptable to the West is in its very early stages.

Nor is it likely to advance very far, according to widespread belief, in view of Hong Kong's remoteness from the main marketplaces. Knitwear is a notable exception to this rule, however. (2)

In the same way, other NICs served as clothing producers for U.S. buyers, who still exercised considerable control over the production of apparel in the Far East.

Only some U.S. firms engaged in importing, however, and their activities put them at odds with local manufacturers, who found their products competing with much less expensive garments from Asia. The rise in imports led to a variety of reactions, including technological innovation, protection, the use of immigrant labor, and the encouragement of offshore assembly in Mexico, Central America, and the Caribbean (Arrow 3).

Technological Innovation

U.S. garment manufacturers enjoyed a major advantage in their market proximity, enabling them to monitor rapid changes in demand and respond to them with alacrity. Thus, the chief focus of technological innovation has been in the area of "quick response," or QR. QR was coupled with a recognition that the U.S. apparel market was becoming increasingly complex: demographic changes and the large number of working women have led to a diversification in demand. Consequently, there was a growing interest in the development of flexible specialization, involving small-scale batch production and rapid reorders, rather than mass production (Piore and Sabel 1984; AAMA 1988, 1989b).

QR information technologies are currently under development, with the potential to link the fiber, textile, apparel, and retail sectors, allowing the entire network to respond quickly to reorders. The key element is a computer-readable zebra label for retail products which can be used to activate the entire process of reordering (OTA 1987). A second type of innovation concerns modular production. While still relying on individuals working at sewing machines, the modular system replaces the old bundle system, based on section work, with teams of workers who complete particular garments. This system may not add to overall productivity, but it allows factories to produce certain finished garments more rapidly. It also encourages workers to develop an array of skills (AAMA 1988, 1989b).

Protection

The United States has a long history of attempting to control the growth of textile and apparel imports (Aggarwal 1985). Generally, these efforts have not involved halting imports or even keeping them at current levels; instead, such attempts have been aimed at controlling the rate of import growth, allowing sectors of the U.S. industry a chance to adjust before being hit by a sudden surge in imports (Nehmer and Love 1985, 241; Rothstein 1989, 45–46). A growth in the import share of the U.S. clothing market is accepted as inevitable, and policies are aimed at making that transition as painless as possible.

Efforts to control imports began in 1957 with a five-year agreement with Japan limiting cotton textile-product exports to the United States. Imports of cotton goods grew dramatically in 1959 and 1960, however, as new suppliers, especially Hong Kong, entered the market. This pattern of new entrants has continued, revealing the limitations of bilateral agreements (Nehmer and Love 1985, 239–40; Rothstein 1989, 45).

In 1961 the multilateral Short-Term Arrangement Regarding International Trade in Cotton Textiles (STA) was signed, followed by the Long-Term Arrangement (LTA) in 1962, covering a five-year period. The LTA was renewed in 1967 and 1970. Thirty-three countries signed, but cotton imports to the U.S. still grew dramatically. Moreover, noncotton goods, especially synthetic textile products, began to flood the U.S. market. Imports were increasing from both a growth in exporting countries and a diversification of products (Nehmer and Love 1985, 240; Rothstein 1987, 45–46).

In 1974 the more comprehensive Multifiber Arrangement (MFA) was negotiated, which, although it has been altered at each five-year renewal, is still in effect. As of 1993, we are operating under MFA IV. The MFA is a multilateral agreement negotiated under the auspices of the General Agreement on Tariffs and Trade (GATT) and endorsed by about fifty countries. It allows signatories to negotiate bilateral agreements regulating trade in textile and apparel. It also permits unilateral restraints, with consultation, against imports that threaten to disrupt a market (Nehmer and Love 1985, 241; Rothstein 1989, 45–47).

Under MFA I, the annual allowable growth rate in imports was set at 6 percent, far above the actual growth of the U.S. market (which is about 1 percent). Although subsequent MFA agreements have allowed for variances from this level, the 6 percent growth rate remains official policy, revealing the U.S. government's intention gradually to increase import penetration. Faced with growing political pressure to provide more protection and Congress's development of a trade bill that would have limited import growth to 1 percent a year, the Reagan administration began in 1986 to negotiate special agreements with Hong Kong, Korea, and Taiwan, limiting their annual import growths to 1.5 percent. China was given a special growth rate of 3 percent (Rothstein 1989, 47).

The United States has generally implemented MFA restraints by setting quotas on particular imported items. The exporting countries are then responsible for seeing that their quotas are not exceeded. Each exporting country has its own system of distributing quota production. In practice, the MFA has not been very successful in restricting apparel imports, as the trade statistics demonstrate. From 1984 to 1988 imports from all countries with which the United States had MFA agreements grew by 81 percent, or about 20 percent per year, as opposed to the mandated 6 percent (Rothstein 1989, 48).

There are several reasons for the weakness of MFA. The system depends on separate negotiations with each country over each product. Moreover, quotas cannot be negotiated before major import penetration and the resulting damage can be proven. The negotiations begin at the established base, often take months to conclude, and allow for 6 percent growth from the point of agreement (Rothstein 1989, 49).

Exporters are able to bypass quotas by slightly altering their products, thereby falling outside a particular product agreement. They can make small changes in the fabric or alter the type of garment. In one instance, shirts and skirts, with filled quotas, were sewn together as dresses that had unused quota and separated once in the United States. In another instance, jackets were made with zip-in sleeves and imported as vests, a nonquota category. Ramie, a fabric made partially from hemp, was invented simply to evade quotas (Rothstein 1989, 49–50).

Another weakness of MFA is that quotas measure imports by quantity, that is, pounds or numbers of garments, rather than value. This practice encourages exporters to produce higher-value goods in order to earn more from the quantities shipped within the quota limits and helps to explain why apparel has suffered from imports more than textiles have (Parsons 1988, 134–35).

Apart from the difficulties of MFA's structure, the United States has been especially weak at enforcement in comparison with the European countries and Japan. When faced with a surge of sweater imports from Korea, for example, Japan filed an antidumping suit and then signed an agreement in February 1989 limiting Korean sweater imports to 1 percent growth per year. Moreover, the Japanese demanded a minimum price structure for the imports. The half-hearted implementation of MFA by the United States is a product of the Reagan and Bush administrations' ideological opposition to trade restrictions of any kind (Rothstein 1989, 51). Under the GATT Uruguay Round, a ten-year phaseout of MFA has now been negotiated, to the consternation of many in the U.S. apparel industry.

Use of Immigrant Labor

Employing low-wage immigrant labor in an attempt to offset the low-wage competition in Asian countries is another tactic used to stem the rise in imports. Increasing numbers of Asian immigrants to the United States (Arrow 2) have accompanied the flow of Asian trade; some of these immigrants have become contractors and workers in the U.S. garment industry, along with immigrants from Mexico, Central America, and the Caribbean.

Offshore Assembly (Arrow 3)

Another U.S. response to the growth in imports is to have the labor-intensive aspect of the industry—namely, sewing—move offshore to areas where the cost of labor is lower. Although not invented for this reason, Item 807 of the U.S. Tariff Code (HTS9802.00.80 under the Harmonized Tariff Schedule) is used for this purpose. Item 807 allows U.S.-made components to be shipped abroad, assembled, and brought back to the United States with duty to be paid only on the value-added. Low labor costs mean a low value-added, so that the goods reenter with low tariffs.

Item 807 can be used anywhere in the world, but in practice, because U.S. components must be shipped to the assembly point, it is most prominent in nearby Mexico and the Caribbean countries, where transportation costs are not prohibitive (Rothstein 1989, 53). Maquiladoras—that is, in-bond or temporary importation enterprises that engage in offshore assembly—were developed to make use of the low-wage labor in these countries. The Border Industrialization Program with Mexico exemplifies the process (Fernandez-Kelly 1983). The apparel industry is not the only business to take advantage of this provision, but it is an important one.

The development of Item 807 trade serves other useful purposes besides countering imports. It provides development assistance and jobs to the poor nations surrounding the United States, thereby encouraging their political loyalty. It serves to counter illegal immigration, by keeping workers, who might come to the United States in search of jobs, in their native lands (Commission for the Study of International Migration and Cooperative Economic Development 1990). Because some of those immigrants work in apparel assembly anyway (in U.S. contract shops), the idea is to have them continue this work while avoiding all the social costs of undocumented immigration.[1] Moreover, labor standards are much lower in the countries of origin, allowing a substantial savings to U.S. garment manufacturers and avoiding the proliferation of sweatshops on U.S. territory. In sum, Item 807 kills several birds with one stone. It serves U.S. foreign policy objectives and reduces labor standards at the same time. Of course, this reduction has far-reaching implications for U.S. workers and the labor movement.

As in Asia, low wages and EPZs in Mexico and the Caribbean were a major attraction to U.S. garment capital (Bishop, Long, and St. Cyr 1990; Fuentes and Ehrenreich 1983; Grunwald and Flamm 1985; Kamel 1990). In 1984, for example, apparel workers in Mexico made an average of US$1.00 per hour, compared to US$7.00 in the United States. Workers in the Dominican Republic made US$1.24 per hour, whereas in Jamaica, Costa Rica, and Haiti, hourly wages were US$1.02, US$0.86, and US$0.43, respectively (Currie 1985). Wages have declined in this region in recent years, making it an even more desirable place to relocate.

EPZs also make Mexico and the Caribbean region attractive to U.S. firms that want to engage in overseas assembly. In Mexico the border region serves as a kind of EPZ, with maquiladoras performing the role of offshore processors for U.S. apparel firms. The Dominican Republic had at least twenty-six EPZs as of 1992, and the number of zones is growing there and in other Caribbean and Central American countries. As in Asia, Caribbean EPZ workers tend to be young women who work under especially onerous conditions (Bishop, Long, and St. Cyr 1990; Currie 1985; Starnberg Institute 1989).

Supplementing Item 807 is the Caribbean Basin Initiative (CBI), or Caribbean Special Access Program, created by the Reagan administration. The CBI includes a "Super 807" provision, allowing guaranteed access levels (GALs), or unlimited quotas for Caribbean countries—provided garments are assembled from textiles made and cut in the United States (Jacobs 1988; Rothstein 1989, 53). The CBI also encourages U.S. investment in the Caribbean apparel industry. Calculations of relative costs for particular garments show that Item 807 production in the Caribbean can meet and sometimes even better Hong Kong costs. The higher price of U.S. fabric and cutting is offset by the slightly higher cost of labor for sewing in Hong Kong, plus higher transportation and duty costs (USITC 1989, 6:4).

The U.S. government actively assists U.S. apparel manufacturers in moving their production to the Caribbean. It disseminates information, supplies business assistance, sponsors meetings, and provides an ombudsman to facilitate offshore assembly. The Agency for International Development (USAID) provides financing, helps Caribbean governments attract foreign investment, and runs management-training programs. The U.S. Department of Labor helps to develop training programs for Caribbean workers. As Rothstein (1989) states, "a domestic apparel producer can get far more U.S. assistance for contract garment manufacturing in Haiti than for manufacturing in North Carolina" (55).

In 1989 a "Special Regime" went into effect with Mexico, partially in response to Mexican concerns that too much of the quota was being filled by U.S. firms, leaving little room for Mexican apparel firms to gain access to the U.S. market. The Special Regime did not provide the same benefits to Mexico as the CBI did for the Caribbean in that it did not establish GALs. Assembly of U.S.-made and -cut fabrics was favored under the regime, but they still had to come in under a quota, with an upper limit of 6 percent annual growth. The agreement significantly raised the base level of quotas from 1987 to 1988, however (Jacobs 1988; USITC 1989, 6:7). The United States,

Canada, and Mexico have negotiated a free-trade agreement (NAFTA) that could drastically alter the structure of the apparel industry between the two countries (we return to NAFTA below).

The U.S. apparel industry is well aware of all the various attractions of Mexico and the Caribbean as a sourcing location. For example, *Bobbin,* a trade magazine, puts out an annual "807/CBI Sourcing" edition. For each of the Caribbean countries and Mexico, it lists the following features: language, population, labor force, unemployment, literacy, 807 exports, percentage of exports represented by 807, major ports, major airports, currency, adjusted hourly wage including fringes for operators, fringes as a percentage of hourly wage, average labor productivity as a percentage of U.S. labor productivity, market-level capability (e.g., budget versus better), frequent style-change capability, minimum order-requirement capabilities, industrial building rents, and industrial tax exemption. All these data enable U.S. firms to pinpoint the right country for them. According to the 1991 adjusted hourly wages for operators, including fringes, as developed by *Bobbin,* U.S. industry is poised to make use of every Caribbean island and Central American country as a place for overseas garment assembly (Table 2.2).

The Rise in Imports from Mexico, Central America, and the Caribbean (Arrow 4)

Item 807 imports have grown dramatically in the last decade. From less than US$500 million worth of garment imports in 1978, they shot up to more than US$2.2 billion in 1990. Item 807 accounts for about 10 percent of all apparel imports, a figure that has not changed much in the last few years. In other words, 807 imports have climbed along with overall imports and have contributed steadily to that growth.

The major countries involved in Item 807 production are shown in Table 2.3. The Dominican Republic is the biggest 807 importer, followed by Mexico. Guatemala, however, which is still a fairly small producer, shows the highest growth rate, at 48 percent between 1989 and 1990 (AAMA 1991, 35). Almost all 807 imports originate from Mexico and the Caribbean, with less than 10 percent coming from Asia and South America. The Philippines is an interest-

Table 2.2
Adjusted Hourly Wages, Including Fringes, for
Sewing Operators in the Caribbean and
Mexico, 1991 (in US$)

Country	Wages
Puerto Rico	4.85
U.S. Virgin Islands	4.50
Bahamas	2.50
Netherlands Antilles	2.23
Antigua and Barbuda	2.06
Barbados	1.83
Trinidad and Tobago	1.35
Panama	1.23
Costa Rica	1.09
St. Vincent and the Grenadines	1.07
St. Kitts and Nevis	1.00
Montserrat	0.92
St. Lucia	0.90
Mexico	0.88
Belize	0.85
Grenada	0.83
Dominica	0.81
Dominican Republic	0.75
Guyana	0.70
Jamaica	0.63
Honduras	0.60
Haiti	0.58
El Salvador	0.49
Guatemala	0.45

Source: Bobbin, November 1991, 48–49.

ing case, in that it falls more under the purview of the United States than of the Asian NICs.

Item 807 imports are dominated by a few products, including trousers, slacks, and shorts; body-supporting garments, mainly brassieres; shirts and blouses; and coats and jackets. Moreover, products differ greatly in the percentage of imports brought in under this provision (AAMA 1991, 36; USITC 1989, 6:7–8).

The offshore assembly "solution" to the problem of import penetration has created its own set of problems, as Item 807 imports have soared. Whereas Asian imports have hurt sectors of U.S. capital as well as labor, Item 807 has had a differential class impact. U.S. manufacturers were able to survive by investing and contracting in Latin

Table 2.3
Apparel Imports to the United States under Item 807 from Selected
Countries, 1990 (in US$ millions)

Country	US$	Percentage
Caribbean Basin		
Dominican Republic	581	26.3
Costa Rica	293	13.3
Jamaica	158	7.2
Haiti	148	6.7
Guatemala	117	5.3
Honduras	88	4.0
El Salvador	42	1.9
Belize	5	0.2
Other	27	1.2
Total Caribbean Basin	1.459	66.1
Other Countries		
Mexico	449	20.3
Colombia	113	5.1
Philippines	61	2.8
All other 807	126	5.7
Total 807	2,208	99.8

Source: AAMA, 1991, 35.
Note: Percentages are rounded.

America and the Caribbean, while U.S. labor standards were undercut and U.S. workers lost their jobs. This impact is sometimes ration-
alized by the claim that the U.S. industry suffers from a labor
shortage. Perhaps there is some truth to that in certain regions
(though not in Los Angeles), but the shortage, in large measure, is a
product of not paying competitive wages by U.S. standards.

The Movement of Asian NICs' Production to Other Asian
Countries (Arrow 5)

Partly as a response to the establishment of quotas by the United
States and other Western nations, the major Asian producers have
shifted their production to other Asian countries, including Thailand, India, Indonesia, Malaysia, Sri Lanka, Bangladesh, and especially China. A 1986 Congressional Budget Office report described
MFA as having created a "generation of apparel Marco Polos" roam-
ing the world in search of production sites with unused quota

(Rothstein 1989, 50). The movement of the Hong Kong industry to China can be seen as part of the same trend. Shifting production enables the major Asian producers to take advantage of the lack of quotas in these countries (Steele 1990). Avoiding quota restrictions is not the only reason for this movement. The cost of labor in Hong Kong, Korea, and Taiwan has climbed, reducing their competitive advantage in garment production. Meanwhile, other Asian countries, eager to engage in export-led industrialization, have offered their own low-wage labor for global production. In 1984, for example, average wages in apparel in the non-NICs included US$0.18 per hour in Indonesia, US$0.46 in Thailand, and US$0.35 in India and Malaysia. China, rising to become the premier clothing manufacturer in the world, had a wage rate of US$0.21 per hour in 1984 (Currie 1985). Once again, young women, often working in EPZs, serve as the chief apparel labor force.

The shift by NIC apparel producers to other Asian countries can be viewed, in part, as parallel to the movement of U.S. apparel makers to Mexico and the Caribbean. Hong Kong, Korean, and Taiwanese producers have engaged in their own offshore processing to reduce costs. Some of the lesser Asian producers, however, especially Thailand and India, have become major exporters of apparel in their own right.

Meanwhile, the Asian NICs are attempting to move to higher value-added production, either by shifting to more technologically advanced, capital-intensive industries or by moving upscale in apparel production. But they continue to be very active in world apparel production through sourcing in the less-developed Asian countries.

By 1991 the Asian NICs, now joined by China, still provided more than half (57%) of the garment imports to the United States (Table 2.4). Other Asian countries added another 26 percent, while Mexico and the Caribbean sent the remaining 16 percent.

The Movement of U.S. Production to Other Asian Countries (Arrow 6)

Some U.S. apparel producers have also become involved in shifting their production to the less-developed countries of Asia. U.S. retailers still tend to rely on the NICs either as direct sources of apparel

Table 2.4

Apparel Imports to the United States from Selected Pacific Rim Countries, 1991 (in square meters [M²] and US$ millions)

Country	M²	$	%M²	%$
Big Four				
Hong Kong	805	3,728	14.6	19.7
China	851	2,842	15.5	15.0
Taiwan	780	2,521	14.2	13.3
Korea	411	1,861	7.5	9.8
Total Big Four	2,847	10,952	51.8	57.8
ASEANª countries				
Philippine	337	999	6.1	5.3
Singapore	143	600	2.6	3.3
Indonesia	166	565	3.0	3.0
Malaysia	136	530	2.5	2.8
Thailand	132	515	2.4	2.7
Total ASEAN countries	914	3,209	16.6	17.1
Other Asia				
India	171	553	3.1	2.9
Sri Lanka	161	486	2.9	2.6
Bangladesh	209	440	3.8	2.3
Pakistan	87	208	1.6	1.1
Total Other Asia	628	1,687	11.4	8.9
Mexico	217	673	3.9	3.6
CBIᵇ countries				
Dominican Republic	311	910	5.7	4.8
Costa Rica	157	439	2.9	2.3
Jamaica	100	252	1.8	1.3
Honduras	71	196	1.3	1.0
Haiti	92	146	1.7	0.8
Other CBI	164	474	3.0	2.5
Total CBI countries	895	2,417	16.4	12.7
Total Pacific Rim Imports	5,501	18,938	100.1	100.1

Source: AMA, *Apparel Import Digest*, 1992 annual issue, Table lb.

ªASEAN = Association of Southeast Asian Nations.

ᵇCBI = Caribbean Basin Initiative.

imports or as indirect sources in the sense that the NIC producers are really getting their production done in other countries. Some U.S. apparel manufacturers also engage in this form of indirect production in the less-developed countries of Asia, with their Hong Kong office (for example) taking charge. Other U.S. manufacturers themselves contract for production in Asia's less-developed countries. Indeed, firms such as Liz Claiborne and The Gap source in multiple countries around the world.

Asian Involvement in the Caribbean (Arrow 7)

Asian garment producers have responded to U.S. efforts to counter-act imports in a variety of ways. As already suggested, quota imposi-tions can be bypassed by changing products and textiles, by upgrading the quality of goods to bring in higher-valued garments within the same quota, and by moving to other countries where quo-tas have not yet been set or remain unfilled.

Although much of the shifting of the industry has occurred within Asia, some segments of the Asian industry have relocated to the Ca-ribbean to gain easier access to the U.S. market (Steele 1988). Thus, Asian producers have taken advantage of unused quotas in Carib-bean countries, simultaneously benefiting from lower transportation costs. It is important to note that U.S. importers of Asian products have a joint interest in encouraging this type of movement.

Because Item 807 production depends on the assembly of textiles manufactured and cut in the United States, Asian producers in the Caribbean—who usually provide their own fabric—do not operate within the Item 807 framework. Imports from the Caribbean to the United States thus include non-807 goods. Non-807 apparel imports from the Caribbean quadrupled from 1985 to 1988, rising to US$327 million in 1988. Item 807 imports doubled over the same period (starting from a much higher base) to reach US$1.1 billion in 1988 (Steele 1988; USITC 1989, 6:2).

Asian investments are attractive to the Caribbean countries. In most cases, Asian projects contribute higher value-added, higher lev-els of investment, more development of skilled staff, and more jobs as compared to Item 807 firms. In order to maintain good relations with the United States and keep open access to the U.S. market, how-ever, Caribbean countries must be careful to avoid surges in Asian garment production and export to the United States. This fear has led to some discouragement of the growth of Asian investment in the Caribbean apparel industry (USITC 1989, 6:5).

Hierarchy of Production

The Pacific Rim triangle has produced a complex hierarchical net-work of globalized apparel production (Figure 2.2). U.S. retailers order clothing from both U.S. manufacturers and contract manufacturers (primarily located in the Asian NICs). Some U.S. manufacturers also arrange for production with contract manufacturers in Asia, though they are more likely to move to the less-developed countries of Asia. Many of them also produce in the United States, often using contractors who were immigrants from the garment-exporting countries. These contractors sometimes use subcontractors (not shown in Figure 2.2) or employ garment workers, many of whom are also immigrants. Some of the employees are homeworkers, the least protected of all workers (also omitted from the figure). U.S. manufacturers also engage in offshore production in Mexico, the Caribbean, and the Philippines. There contractors employ the local work force, sometimes using subcontractors and homeworkers.

The Asian NICs have their own factories, where they employ their own workers. They also engage in offshore production in less-developed Asian countries, employing another group of workers. Finally, the Asian NICs have begun sourcing in the Caribbean, making use of the work force there. Subcontracting and homeworking can add more layers to the network of production in these countries, too.

In all the countries engaged in garment production in the Pacific Rim triangle, a group of workers sits at the bottom of the hierarchy.

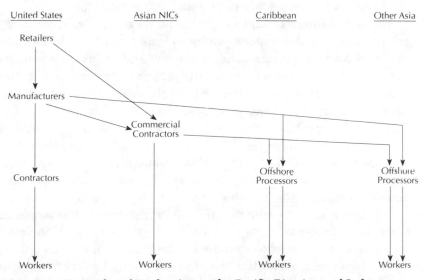

Figure 2.2 Hierarchy of Production in the Pacific Rim Apparel Industry

They are mainly women, often young, typically poorly paid, rarely unionized, and frequently working under onerous conditions. Although labor laws, wages, and other working conditions vary from country to country, and although the composition of the work force also shows variability, there is a commonality among all these workers. They are the people who do most of the labor on which this industry depends. And they are pitted against one another as the industry constantly shifts, seeking the most oppressed among them to employ.

Trade Liberalization

As mentioned above, the United States has negotiated the North American Free Trade Agreement (NAFTA) with Canada and Mexico, which went into effect January 1, 1994. The terms of this agreement are of great significance to the U.S. apparel industry. Importers, both retailers and manufacturers, do not want to place any restrictions on the free flow of trade. Manufacturers who do not import from Asia, on the other hand, want to be able to engage in offshore processing in Mexico and the Caribbean in order to compete with Asian producers. At the same time, they want to make it difficult for the Asian producers to take advantage of this trade liberalization.

This set of interests led to the negotiation of the "yarn-forward" principle, stating that apparel produced from North American–made yarn and North American–made fabrics would receive the benefits of trade without quota or tariffs. This principle protects U.S. textile manufacturers from competition with Asia, while allowing U.S. apparel manufacturers to engage in offshore processing in Mexico. Retailers and importers were not happy with these terms, because Asian imports would suffer a comparative disadvantage. Nevertheless, there is a possibility that illegal transshipments of Chinese-made goods, produced under the direction of Hong Kong firms, may enter the United States via Mexico after NAFTA's passage.

U.S. manufacturers who do offshore processing in the Caribbean have some concerns about NAFTA's potential effects on their arrangements with Caribbean producers; they fear that Mexico will be a more advantageous location than the Caribbean, leaving them with obsolete arrangements there. But this problem is a relatively minor wrinkle in the politics of NAFTA, compared to the larger Asian issue.

Meanwhile, U.S. garment contractors are left with the prospect of growing competition with Mexico, as some U.S. manufacturers shift to employing contractors there. Some U.S. contractors may shift their plants south of the border or open branches in Mexico. U.S. workers are especially likely to be affected by NAFTA as more jobs move south of the border and U.S. wages and working conditions erode to meet the competition of much lower standards in Mexico.

Conclusion

The relationships between the regions that make up the Pacific Rim triangle are far from static. They continually evolve as each reacts to the strategic moves of the others. But at the foundation of the system sits the garment workers, who labor under remarkably similar conditions wherever they are employed.

Notes

Acknowledgments: Thanks to Nora Hamilton and Richard Appelbaum for their helpful suggestions for revision.
1. Note that this viewpoint is controversial with some; Sassen (1988), for example, believes that overseas assembly actually stimulates emigration.

References

Aggarwal, Vinod K. 1985. *Liberal Protectionism: The International Politics of Organized Textile Trade.* Berkeley: University of California Press.
American Apparel Manufacturers Association (AAMA). 1988. *Flexible Apparel Manufacturing.* Arlington, Va.: Technical Advisory Committee, AAMA.
———. 1989a, 1990, 1991. *Focus: An Economic Profile of the Apparel Industry.* Arlington, Va.: AAMA.
———. 1989b. *Making the Revolution Work: How to Implement Flexible*

Apparel Manufacturing through People. Arlington, Va.: Technical Advisory Committee, AAMA.

Bishop, Myrtle, Frank Long, and Joaquin St. Cyr. 1990. "Export Processing Zones and Women in the Caribbean." Paper prepared for the 11th meeting of the presiding officers of the Regional Conference on the Integration of Women into the Economic and Social Development of Latin America and the Caribbean, Varadero, Cuba.

Commission for the Study of International Migration and Cooperative Economic Development. 1990. *Unauthorized Migration: An Economic Development Response.* Washington, D.C.

Currie, Jean. 1985. *Export Processing Zones in the 1980s.* Special Report No. 190. London: Economic Intelligence Unit.

Deyo, Frederic C. 1989. *Beneath the Miracle: Labor Subordination in the New Asian Industrialism.* Berkeley: University of California Press.

Fernandez-Kelly, M. Patricia. 1983. *For We Are Sold, I and My People: Women and Industry in Mexico's Frontier.* Albany: State University of New York Press.

Fuentes, Annette, and Barbara Ehrenreich. 1983. *Women in the Global Factory.* Boston: South End Press.

Grunwald, Joseph, and Kenneth Flamm. 1985. *The Global Factory: Foreign Assembly in International Trade.* Washington, D.C.: Brookings Institution.

International Labor Office (ILO). 1984. *Social and Labour Practices of Multinational Enterprises in the Textile, Clothing, and Footwear Industries.* Geneva: ILO.

Jacobs, Brenda. 1988. "The 807 Option: New Trade South of the Border." *Bobbin,* May, 26–33.

Kamel, Rachael. 1990. *The Global Factory: Analysis and Action for a New Economic Era.* Philadelphia: American Friends Service Committee.

Nehmer, Stanley, and Mark W. Love. 1985. "Textile and Apparel: A Negotiated Approach to International Competition." In *U.S. Competitiveness in the World Economy,* edited by Bruce R. Scott and George C. Lodge, 230–62. Boston: Harvard Business School Press.

Office of Technology Assessment (OTA). 1987. *The U.S. Textile and Apparel Industry: A Revolution in Progress.* OTA-TET-332. Washington, D.C.: U.S. Department of Commerce.

Parsons, Carol A. 1988. "The Domestic Employment Consequences of Managed International Competition in Apparel." In *The Dynamics of Trade and Employment,* edited by Laura D'Andrea Tyson, William T. Dickens, and John Zysman, 113–55. Cambridge: Ballinger.

Piore, Michael J., and Charles F. Sabel. 1984. *The Second Industrial Divide: Possibilities for Prosperity.* New York: Basic Books.

Rothstein, Richard. 1989. *Keeping Jobs in Fashion: Alternatives to the Euthanasia of the U.S. Apparel Industry.* Washington, D.C.: Economic Policy Institute.

Sassen, Saskia. 1988. *The Mobility of Labor and Capital: A Study in International Investment and Labor Flow.* Cambridge: Cambridge University Press.

Starnberg Institute. 1989. "Working Conditions in Export Processing Zones in Selected Developing Countries." Paper prepared for U.S. Department of Labor, Bureau of International Labor Affairs, Office of International Economic Affairs.

Steele, Peter. 1988. *The Caribbean Clothing Industry: The U.S. and Far East Connections.* Special Report No. 1147. London: Economic Intelligence Unit.

————. 1990. *Hong Kong Clothing: Waiting for China.* Special Report No. 2028. London: Economic Intelligence Unit.

U.S. Department of Labor. 1990. "Hourly Compensation Costs for Production Workers, Apparel, and Other Textile Manufacturing (US SIC 23), 24 Countries, 1975 and 1978–88." Bureau of Labor Statistics, Office of Productivity and Technology. Unpublished.

U.S. International Trade Commission (USITC). 1989. *Production Sharing: U.S. Imports under Harmonized Tariff Schedule Subheadings 9802.00.60 and 9802.00.80, 1985–1988: Formerly Imports under 806.30 and 807 of the Tariff Schedules of the United States.* Washington, D.C.: USITC.

Chapter 3

Power and Profits in the Apparel Commodity Chain

Richard P. Appelbaum and Gary Gereffi

The current restructuring of the global economy, in which commodity production and sales are spatially dispersed and integrated to an unprecedented degree, requires a reexamination of the ways in which surplus is extracted. In the traditional world-systems approach, core economic activities—defined as those in which a surplus is realized—were generally presumed to be located in core national economies. Similarly, peripheral economic activities—from which the surplus is extracted—were regarded as constituting peripheral national economies. Semiperipheral economic activities (and hence semiperipheral national economies) were thought to occupy an intermediate position, one from which surplus is both extracted (by core nations) and realized (from peripheral nations). Within this framework, nation-states were treated as the primary analytic units, providing an analysis of the global stratification of place based on the nation-state system (Emmanuel 1972; Wallerstein 1980; Smith and White 1990).

Global Commodity Chains and Economic Surplus

This traditional stratification system is being overlaid by the growth of core and peripheral relations within nations, as networks of global commodity chains alter the ways in which surplus is extracted and realized in a global economy. The notion of a global commodity chain offers a means of understanding production as a dynamic set of processes among firms, rather than as a static property of nations.

A *commodity chain* may be defined most simply as "a network of labor and production processes whose end result is a finished commodity" (Hopkins and Wallerstein 1986:159). The global commodity chain consists of "nodes," or operations that comprise pivotal points in the production process: supply of raw materials, production, export, and marketing—taking us "across the entire spectrum of activities in the world economy" (Gereffi 1992, 94). Each node is itself a network, connected to other nodes concerned with related activities. Such export networks are increasingly important in the contemporary global manufacturing system, resulting in a new logic of transnational integration based on geographical specialization and tightly linked international sourcing (Gereffi and Korzeniewicz 1990).

The global commodity chain approach argues that surplus accrues to different nodes in the commodity chain, depending on how they are organized and controlled, rather than accruing in a single (core) country. The analytic distinction between "core" and "periphery" might be more fruitfully applied to nodes in the global commodity chain than to countries in general. In this formulation, core activities in the commodity chain are those in which the principal surplus is realized; core nations (or, more likely, regions within nations) are those where the core activities are spatially concentrated. In examining the profitability of particular industries, one is then led to ask, Where does the global commodity chain "touch down" geographically, why, and with what implications for the extraction or realization of an economic surplus?

Buyer-Driven Commodity Chains and Flexible Production: The Case of Apparel

Global commodity chains (GCCs) have three main dimensions: an input-output structure comprising a set of products and services linked in a sequence of value-added economic activities; a territoriality that identifies the geographical dispersion or concentration of raw materials, production, export, and marketing networks; and a governance structure of power and authority relationships that determines how financial, material, and human resources, as well as economic surplus, are allocated and flow within the chain. Two distinct types of governance structures for GCCs have emerged since the early 1970s: "producer-driven" and "buyer-driven" commodity chains (Gereffi 1994).

Producer-driven commodity chains describe those industries in which large, integrated industrial enterprises play the central role in controlling the production system (including its forward and backward linkages). This type is most characteristic of capital- and technology-intensive industries such as automobiles, computers, aircraft, and electrical machinery, which are usually dominated by transnational corporations. *Buyer-driven commodity chains,* on the other hand, involve those industries in which large retailers, brand-named marketeers, and trading companies play the pivotal role in setting up decentralized production networks in a wide range of exporting countries, typically located in the Third World. This pattern of trade-led industrialization is common in labor-intensive, consumer-goods industries such as garments, footwear, toys, and consumer electronics.

Firms that fit the buyer-driven model, such as Nike, Reebok, Liz Claiborne, and The Gap, generally do not own any factories. They are "marketeers" (not "manufacturers") that design and market, but do not make, the products they sell. Such firms rely on complex networks of contractors that perform almost all their specialized tasks. "Profits in buyer-driven commodity chains thus derive not from scale, volume, and technological advances as in producer-driven chains, but rather from unique combinations of high-value research, design, sales, marketing, and financial services that allow the buyers and branded merchandisers to act as strategic brokers in linking overseas factories and traders with evolving product niches in their main consumer markets" (Gereffi 1994:99). Because buyer-centered commodity chains are highly sensitive to both changes in market demand and production costs, their manufacturing operations are likely to be located in areas where low-wage labor offers quick turnaround at the lowest cost. Such flexibility is often achieved through spatially dense contracting networks, permitting the manufacturer to select factories according to specific production requirements.

Contracting means that the so-called manufacturer need not employ any production workers, run the risk of unionization or wage pressures, or be concerned with layoffs resulting from changes in product demand. Through its own buying offices or commercial trading companies, the manufacturer can acquire the necessary production capability for a particular product run, externalizing many of the costs and risks associated with the labor process.

In the post-Fordist view, such "flexibilization" provides the manufacturer with a competitive edge, as a result of the externalities created by the physical presence of numerous suppliers and producers concentrated in geographically interdependent networks of small firms, factories, and specialized local labor markets (Porter 1990; Scott 1988; Scott and Kwok 1989; Storper and Christopherson 1987; Piore and Sabel 1984). Spatial concentration enhances the flow of information through family connections, personal relationships, and professional and community-based ties. "Flexibilization" also affects the distribution of the surplus, since the contracting nodes in the buyer-centered global commodity chains are likely to be those where the least amount of surplus is realized. In Marxist terms, contracting ensures that labor will truly remain variable capital, whose quantities and costs can be made congruent with the needs of the production process. In the language of world-systems theory, peripheral economic activities are externalized through contracting, while core economic activities remain internal to the firm. The districts where such contracting occurs are thus often relegated to the economic periphery, even if located within core countries.

The apparel industry is an ideal case for examining the dynamics of buyer-driven commodity chains. The relative ease of setting up apparel firms, coupled with the prevalence of developed-country protectionism in this sector, has led to the unparalleled diversity of garment exporters in the Third World. Furthermore, the backward and forward linkages from garment production are extensive and help to account for the large number of jobs associated with a flourishing apparel industry (Taplin 1993; Appelbaum, Smith, and Christerson 1994).

The apparel commodity chain is organized around five main segments: raw material supplies, including natural and synthetic fibers; the provision of components, such as the yarns and fabrics manufactured by textile companies; production networks made up of garment factories, including their domestic and overseas subcontractors; the trade channels established by export intermediaries; and marketing networks at the retail level (Figure 3.1). Each of these segments encompasses a variety of differences in terms of geographical location, labor skills and conditions, technology, and the scale and

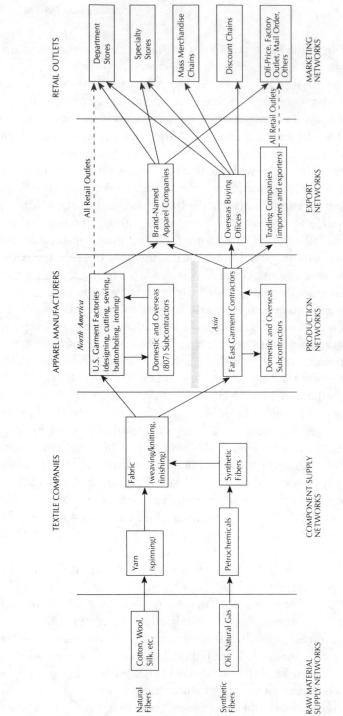

Figure 3.1 The Apparel Commodity Chain

types of enterprises. These characteristics affect the distribution of economic surplus throughout the commodity chain.

The Profit Squeeze: Recession, the Generation of Surplus, and Globalization

Concentration has become a fact of life in the once-fragmented U.S. apparel industry. In 1991 there were five billion-dollar apparel companies: Levi Strauss (US$4.9 billion), Sara Lee (US$4.1 billion), VF Corporation (US$3 billion), Liz Claiborne (US$2 billion), and Fruit of the Loom (US$1.6 billion) (Table 3.1). These five giants accounted for 23 percent of the U.S. apparel industry's total wholesale volume and for all its sales and profit gains, while the rest of the industry struggled through a second consecutive year of recession. Whereas net income in the apparel industry hovered near 5 percent of sales from 1987 to 1989, this figure plummeted to 3.4 percent in 1990 and to 3.2 percent in 1991 (KSA 1992c, 8). In the opinion of Kurt Salmon Associates, a leading consulting firm for the apparel sector, "a disproportionate amount of the profits needed to reinvest in the industry lies in the hands of only a few companies" (KSA 1992c, 1).

The fashion side of the apparel industry—that is, the women's

Table 3.1
Sales and Profitability of Top Ten U.S. Apparel Companies, 1991

Sales Rank	Company	Sales (US$ billions)	Gross Profit (percent)	Return on Sales (percent)	Return on Total Assets (percent)
1	Levi Strauss	4.90	NA	NA	NA
2	Sara Lee	4.10	NA	NA	NA
3	VF Corp.	2.95	30.9	5.5	7.6
4	Liz Claiborne	2.01	39.8	11.1	19.0
5	Fruit of the Loom	1.63	30.8	6.8	5.2
6	Leslie Fay	0.84	29.8	3.5	7.4
7	Crystal Brands	0.83	29.8	−3.9	−10.8
8	Kellwood Co.	0.81	17.3	1.5	2.6
9	Phillips–Van Heusen Co.	0.81	35.2	3.3	7.0
10	Russell Corp.	0.80	31.2	7.1	7.0

Source: KSA 1992c.
NA = Not available.

side—is especially vulnerable to market weakness. One of our respondents characterized the women's side of the industry as far more vicious, cut-throat, competitive, and exploitative than the men's side (Kurtzman 1992). The apparel recession has been accompanied by a retail recession, in which net income has declined steadily, from 3.3 percent in 1988, to 3.0 percent in 1989, 2.3 percent in 1990, and 2.0 percent in 1991 (KSA 1992b, 8). The current economic recession in both retailing and apparel highlights the downward "profit squeeze" in the apparel commodity chain.

As the market puts pressure on retailers' profits, the retailers respond by reducing the price they pay to manufacturers (or holding the cost at "price point," which, in an inflationary environment, amounts to the same thing). The manufacturers, in turn, hold the line on their contractors, reducing the margin they are willing to pay. That leaves the contractor with a simple strategy: reduce costs. Costs can be reduced by lowering standards (a simpler stitch, one fewer pocket) or by squeezing labor. Squeezing labor takes many forms: increased homework, a reduction in wages or piece rates, and further subcontracting to lower-cost factories. The third practice includes producing all or part of a garment "across the border" (Mexico in the case of Los Angeles, the People's Republic of China in the case of Hong Kong) or drawing on illegal factories that come and go with the night, leaving unpaid workers and unpaid rent. The very structure of the industry invites such abuses: virtually all physical labor is conducted through elaborate contracting networks, which shield the retailers and manufacturers from responsibility (and legal liability) for working conditions.

We review these points on the commodity chain, examining the nature of the profit squeeze at every step. We also consider other strategies, such as the elimination of overseas agents and buying offices (which take a cut of the surplus) or the consolidation of retailing and manufacturing (and hence the surplus generated by both) into a single operation. First, however, let us examine the impact of the current retail recession on the overall structure of the industry.

The garment industry has been aptly characterized as one of peaks and valleys. Stanley Hirsch, a major property owner in the Los Angeles garment district, expressed it graphically: "In the industry you can make a fortune or lose your ass. It's like a crap game. You either do something or float like a cork" (1992). The current reces-

sion has affected every company in the industry, enabling department stores to demand more quality at a lower price. This recession
is the third downturn in twenty years, and—as in the previous reces-
sions—it is leading to a restructuring of the industry.

The recession of the early 1970s forced many manufacturers offshore in search of low-cost contracted labor, fueling the growth of
the industry in Hong Kong, Taiwan, and South Korea. A decade later
the combination of recession, inflation, and oil shocks hurt manufacturers and retailers alike and contributed to a growing concern with
inventory control. The retailers that survived wanted smaller orders,
quicker delivery, and far shorter shelf life for garments. The move to
multiple fashion "seasons," as many as six per year for larger brand-
named companies such as Liz Claiborne, meant that racks might be
cleared in weeks rather than months. That, in turn, put enormous
pressure on manufacturers to find contractors who could quickly
and "flexibly" respond to changing fashions and fluctuating orders.

The current retail recession, which began at the end of 1990, contributed to the bankruptcy of major retailers, often the casualties of
excessive debt incurred as a result of leveraged buyouts. The present
economic climate has also reduced the willingness of banks and
other institutions to lend money (Morse 1992). For many manufacturers, there is thus a shortage of both demand from retailers and
investment capital.

Those manufacturers who survive are the ones that are able to
maintain quality at a given price, while ensuring reliable, on-time
delivery (Randall 1991). Paradoxically, shorter turnaround times often translate into a longer global reach in search of labor and quota.
As the vice-president and general manager of Manhattan Industry's
Hong Kong buying office put it, "I have to go farther and farther to
make [the buyer's] price point" (Ng 1991). Sometimes the trip is to
Latin America—to factories in Mexico, the Caribbean, and Central
America. Sometimes, particularly if manufacturers move down the
apparel chain, it is to such low-wage countries as Bangladesh or
Mauritius. And sometimes the trip is back home, to the factories of
Los Angeles or Orange County, where a growing supply of low-wage
immigrant labor, combined with the obvious response advantage of
being close to the home market, has proved to be increasingly attractive to American manufacturers.

Some informants stressed the "flexibility" of Asian production, in contrast to the mechanistic, standardized, "cookie-cutter mentality" of Europe and North America. Brent Klopp, senior vice-president for production and planning for Bugle Boy, contrasted this attitude with the "soldier mentality" of Asian producers, who "do what they're told to do, and don't ask questions" (1991). On the other hand, growing world competition for production in Asia, quota costs, fabric quality, and the difficulty of ensuring product delivery all encourage production closer to the home market.

Retailing: Strategies for Survival

There is considerable competition among diverse retail channels for growing shares of the U.S. apparel market. In 1991 department stores (Saks Fifth Avenue, Neiman-Marcus) accounted for 24 percent of U.S. apparel purchases; specialty stores (The Limited, The Gap), for 21 percent; national merchandise chains (Sears, J.C. Penney, Montgomery Ward), for 14 percent; discount chains (Wal-Mart, Kmart), for 19 percent; and off-price stores, factory outlets, mail-order houses, and so on, for the remaining 22 percent (KSA 1991, 4). The 1990s are expected to show further segmentation of consumer markets by age, income, geography, and other factors. By the end of the decade, retailers that are not solidly entrenched in one of three distinct niches—low price values, unique merchandise, or high service levels—are unlikely to survive (KSA 1990).

Discount and mass-merchandising companies account for the lion's share of retail sales in the United States (Table 3.2). But it was the apparel specialty stores in 1991 that turned in the highest gross profits (34.4%), operating earnings (6.3%), and return on inventory (18.7%) of any of the segments in the retail sector (KSA 1992b, 3). Nevertheless, the future seems to lie with the retail juggernauts. Between the early 1990s and 2000, Kurt Salmon Associates estimates that the ten big retailers (Wal-Mart, Dayton-Hudson, Melville, Price Company, The Limited, Costco, Dillard's, Nordstrom, The Gap, and Spiegel) will grow two to three times faster than the rest of the retail industry and take almost 60 percent of public-company sales (compared to 34% in 1991) (KSA 1992a). Obviously, this trend will increase the already considerable economic clout exercised by large retailers.

Table 3.2
Sales and Profitability of Top Fifteen U.S. Retailers, 1991 and 1987

Sales Rank		Company	Sales (US$ billions)		Gross Profit (percent)		Return on Sales (percent)		Return on Total Assets (percent)		Inventory Turns (number per year)	
1991	1987		1991	1987	1991	1987	1991	1987	1991	1987	1991	1987
1	3	Wal-Mart Stores	43.9	16.0	20.8	23.1	3.7	3.9	10.4	12.2	5.3	5.2
2	2	Kmart Corp.	34.6	25.6	25.0	27.6	2.5	2.7	5.4	6.2	3.6	3.5
3	1	Sears Merchandise Group	28.3	25.9	29.5	32.6	1.7	3.0	2.0	3.3	4.7	4.3
4	4	J.C. Penney	16.2	15.3	33.1	33.8	1.6	4.0	0.6	5.6	3.9	4.5
5	6	Dayton Hudson Corp.	16.1	10.7	27.1	24.3	1.9	2.1	3.2	3.8	5.4	5.5
6	7	May Department Stores Co.	10.6	10.6	30.9	27.2	4.8	4.2	5.9	7.2	4.4	5.3
7	8	Woolworth Corp.	9.9	7.1	32.6	NA	3.4	NA	-3.6	NA	3.2	NA
8	10	Malville Corp.	9.9	5.9	37.6	38.6	3.5	4.8	8.5	12.8	3.5	3.8
9	5	Federated Department Stores	6.9	11.1	NA	26.3	NA	2.8	NA	5.2	NA	5.6
10	NL	Macy's	6.8	—	NA	—	NA	—	NA	—	NA	—
11	14	The Price Company	6.6	3.2	8.9	8.9	2.0	2.3	7.3	8.8	20.0	20.2
12	12	The Limited	6.1	3.5	29.2	28.1	6.6	6.7	11.8	14.8	6.6	7.1
13	15	Toys R Us	6.1	3.1	30.0	29.8	5.5	6.5	7.5	10.1	3.2	3.4
14	11	Montgomery Ward	5.3	4.6	NA	27.8	NA	2.8	NA	3.5	NA	4.5
15	NL	Costco Wholesale Corp.	5.2	—	9.2	—	1.6	—	7.4	—	13.5	—

Sources: KSA 1988, 1992b.

NA = Not available.
NL = Not listed.

The retailer, as stated succinctly by Laura Paine, production manager for Gotcha Sportswear, "calls the price shots" (1991). It typically does a "keystone plus," doubling the price from the manufacturer and adding several dollars. The "plus" is then removed after a couple of weeks, leading consumers to believe they are getting a bargain. The large merchandising chains can afford to squeeze hard: they have the purchasing power and can always find copy-cat manufacturers who "knock off" low-fashion items. Stanley Hirsch provides an example: "I know a guy who makes pants to sell to Kmart for $6. Then Kmart comes to him with identical pants from Korea that cost $6 but also have a pocket, and says to him, either take a 25-cent cut for your pants, or add a pocket, or I'll drop you. The stores with big buying power can squeeze hard" (1992).

Hirsch offers a colorful commentary on recent changes in apparel retailing.

> The department stores fucked up, and they're eating it now. . . . When I bought Alex Coleman [a Los Angeles manufacturing company] in 1981, they were moderate. I bought it up when they were going broke. We produced for the May Company. One day the May Company comes to us and says they are trading up; they want more fashion in the store. They chased Alex Coleman out of the store, meaning that they lost all those customers. So those customers switched to Wal-Mart and Kmart. The shlubs from Harvard Business School raped the industry, trying to make more money for the CEOs. . . . Take Bullocks, once the epitome of a good department store; Bullocks used to be the best store in Los Angeles. They had a 40 percent markup. Then they chased out their customers, and offered higher CEO salaries. They kept offering sales: taking off, off, off from the price. The customers wised up and wouldn't buy at regular prices, and turned to the discounters. The customers no longer trust the department stores. The drop in sales is only partly because of the recession; customers have lost confidence because of this overly aggressive discounting in the department stores. . . . Retailers used to deal exclusively with particular manufacturers. Now the retailers aren't loyal. And the manufacturers don't trust the retailers.

The markup from manufacturer to retailer is typically 55 to 60 percent, although large-lot sales to a single retailer (thirty thousand units or more) may reduce this margin to as low as 30 percent or even less. Markups vary considerably with the item and the circumstances. Profits, which depend heavily on rapid turnover from manufacturer to retailer, also vary considerably; informants provided general estimates of 3 to 7 percent.

Despite the seeming diversity of fashion today, in recent years there has been a convergence of style, except perhaps at the very top. This trend is partly due to the growing oligopolistic power of the large retail chains and mass merchandisers, which "cherry pick" from the lines of different manufacturers to maximize their chances of moving goods off the floor (Klopp 1991). Whereas in the past a manufacturer might sell a wide variety of fashions to a single department store, now it is common to place a much narrower range of items in competing stores, with the retailers determining that range. Thus the same products are sold in a wide array of retail outlets, giving many department stores a similar look and feel. A second reason for fashion convergence, particularly in the youth market, is television: MTV was described as "the great globalizer," standardizing products across the United States and even the world (Klopp 1991). As George Randall, president of Yes! Clothing Corporation, put it, "there are no Japanese kids, German kids, or U.S. kids. There are only kids fifteen to thirty-five."

A principal survival strategy for retailers has been to cut out the manufacturer altogether, by taking over the manufacturing end and selling a private label. The Limited was the first major retailer to do its own manufacturing, a lesson that was quickly learned by other retailers, such as The Gap. The large chain department stores have also followed suit; Wal-Mart has been especially successful in eliminating the middleman. This route can be risky, however, because even major retailers are ill-equipped to deal with the complexities of global apparel manufacturing. Also, in the view of some industry insiders, the practice has been extremely bad for American retailing. David Morse, former managing partner of the California Apparel Mart, offers a somewhat different view of Wal-Mart: "Wal-Mart has been a big success, but they have killed Main Street. And they have squeezed out the middleman. Walton is seen as a hero by many, but I see him as having destroyed American business. Sam Walton is raping the land, changing the character of cities."

The Gap, the most popular and profitable specialty-apparel chain in U.S. retailing today, is an excellent example of a highly successful retailer-turned-manufacturer. Originally a Levi's outlet, The Gap was in economic difficulties in the mid-1980s. Levi's was not producing sufficiently diverse products to sustain consumer interest in the stores. After a corporate shakeup and restructuring, The Gap developed its own garment lines. The Gap is vertically organized, having internalized virtually all activities in the commodity chain, including its own retail outlets, except for direct labor. This strategy results in reduced risks, because The Gap controls much of its operations, ensuring on-time deliveries—an essential accomplishment, as Gap stores rely on high-tech just-in-time global production to change their inventory and "look" every six weeks (Mitchell 1992). Quick response is seen as vital to success in marketing today. In the words of James Cunningham, The Gap's Far East vice-president for offshore sourcing, "the best retailers will be the ones who respond the quickest, the best . . . where the time between cash register and factory shipment is shorter" (1991). It seems unlikely that these trends will reverse themselves; if anything, the buying cycle will likely continue to shorten in coming years (Morse 1992).

Manufacturing

While large retailers are price-makers, today's apparel manufacturers are price-takers. Wholesale prices have been flat since the late 1980s, despite rising production costs. Miguel Campos (1991), production manager for Bongo Clothing, a US$40 million company that sells moderately priced jeans and activewear, reports that a US$32 jean jacket wholesales for US$15, US$3 less than three years ago. Paul Tsang, former general manager of Unimix, one of Hong Kong's largest garment factories, laments that garments are no longer costed out in a negotiation between buyer and manufacturer; the latter simply gets prices (1991). He points out that a John Henry basic shirt has retailed for US$32 in the United States since the early 1980s, yet costs have gone up markedly during that same period. According to Tsang, even moving to Malaysia—which reduces his production costs 40 percent—did not substantially increase his profit margins, because retailers responded by lowering their prices to him. Despite these professed difficulties, it seems clear that apparel manufacturers continue to realize substantial surplus. The top executives and managers in garment manufacturing, along with their best designers, enjoy extremely high salaries if their products are successful.

Manufacturers respond in various ways to wholesale price pressures from retailers. Moving down the value-added chain is one strategy. The Gotcha Corporation, a US$60 million California active-wear company that specializes in tee shirts and the "beach look," has dropped its prices in an effort to reach a larger if somewhat lower-end market (Paine 1991). On the other hand, Bugle Boy, a Simi Valley–based company whose sales have grown to US$700 million in fourteen years, is determined to "maintain price point" even though its expenses and overhead have doubled since the company's sales took off.

Bugle Boy has pursued a second strategy, that of bypassing the retailer altogether and opening mall-outlet stores. The company has sixty-two of its own retail outlets, enabling it to display a much wider range of its products than would be possible in a department store (Klopp 1991). Some other major manufacturers have also taken this step (Van Heusen, Liz Claiborne), but for most manufacturers it is unlikely to prove viable (Morse 1992).

A third method for eliminating the retailer (one we have not pursued in our research) is the direct mail-order catalog. Spiegel, which pioneered the catalog sales of apparel 125 years ago, boasted nearly US$1.7 billion in annual revenue in 1989; J. Crew, a fast-growing newcomer, reached US$300 million in 1990. Other major mail-order apparel companies include L. L. Bean, Land's End, Eddie Bauer, Clifford & Willis, Tweeds, and Fingerhut. Even major retailers are beginning to sell by catalog; examples include Bloomingdale's, Saks Fifth Avenue, Bergdorf Goodman, Neiman-Marcus, I. Magnin, Victoria's Secret, Rich's, and Banana Republic.

A fourth strategy is vertical integration of fabric and clothing manufacturing, an approach favored by some Korean companies (as well as The Gap). Vertical integration enables the manufacturer to reduce costs and shorten turnaround times (Hirsch 1992).

A fifth method consists of revenue enhancement through licensing programs, allowing lesser-known companies to pay for the use of one's label. For example, Cherokee, a major Los Angeles manufacturer, boasts "a fabulous licensing program," accounting for a significant portion of its sales, under which such diverse goods as

watches, jewelry, swimwear, and luggage are sold under the Cherokee label (Glass 1991).

Finally, a sufficiently capitalized company can always branch out
of direct-apparel manufacturing, realizing a surplus through a variety of enterprises. The Hong Kong–based Wing-Tai Corporation is an
interesting example of an apparel company that has not limited itself
to apparel manufacturing. Wing-Tai is a self-described "diversified
multinational corporation," employing eight thousand people
throughout Southeast Asia in the production of more than thirteen
million garments annually. According to company literature, Wing-
Tai is seeking to build "a global apparel trading and manufacturing
network," involving more than twenty different apparel products
from nightgowns to heavy winter jackets (Wing-Tai Corporation
1991). The company has production facilities in Singapore, Malaysia, Hong Kong, and China, and it wholesales and distributes
through companies it has spun off in the United States and Europe.
Its recent acquisitions include British-based Polly Peck, as well as a
30 percent share of the European-based Campari. A short-lived joint
venture with Mast Industries, a subsidiary of The Limited, was to
have provided Wing-Tai with access to The Limited's US$5 billion
U.S. apparel market. Finally, Wing-Tai boasts substantial real estate
operations in Hong Kong, Singapore, Malaysia, and the United
States. These include large-scale housing developments (such as a
three-thousand-family project in Malaysia), architectural and engineering consulting; project management; construction; manufacturing, distribution, and marketing of building materials and office
furniture; and "venture-capital schemes."

Contracting

Contractors are the intermediary between the manufacturer and the
human hands that produce the garments, effectively shielding the
manufacturer from responsibility for labor conditions. As Mitch
Glass, vice-president of production for Cherokee, candidly states, "I
only deal with licensed contractors; I'm not the sheriff" (1991).

We have no direct data on the surplus realized by contractors,
although our impressions are that the retail recession has severely
cut into contractors' profits, increasing pressures on them to reduce

labor costs further. This profit squeeze, predictably, has contributed to a variety of labor abuses in the United States, as well as exploitative practices in countries where labor standards are either not enforced or nonexistent. In Hong Kong, for example, regulations exist concerning fire, ventilation, first aid, and working conditions that might lead to illness; their administration, however, is carried out through a nongovernmental organization (the Health and Safety Council), which is funded by the businesses it is supposed to oversee. Enforcement, needless to say, is minimal. "Health and safety is very backwards" (Leung 1991). There is no minimum wage in Hong Kong, no employment security, no pension plan, and no unemployment compensation. There is no legal right to collective bargaining; even in a fully unionized factory, the employer need not comply with the unions' demands.

The contracting system, which maximizes the flexibility of manufacturers, is often based on friendship and kinship networks that reduce the workers' sense of the need for an explicit contract. This situation is particularly a problem with subcontracting from one factory to another, or for homework, a practice that appears to operate with equal force in Los Angeles and Hong Kong (Lui 1991). Hong Kong factories, for example, frequently subcontract for cuffs, collars, and similar items that can be produced at home and brought into the factory for final assembly (Leung 1991). Interestingly, Hong Kong garment factories are in decline, just as Los Angeles's factories seem to be on the increase. The Hong Kong garment industry currently employs some two hundred thousand people in about nine thousand factories, many with fewer than ten workers; the total manufacturing labor force dropped from 40 percent of the work force in 1971 to 27 percent in 1991, although in absolute terms (because of population growth) the number of manufacturing workers has dropped only from nine to seven hundred thousand workers (Sung 1991).

Hong Kong's largest garment factories are rapidly laying off employees as production shifts to China and other low-wage countries. The Unimix factory, for example, employed three thousand workers when it was acquired by Wing-Tai in 1987; that work force has been cut to two thousand and is slated to "lean out" at fifteen hundred (Tsang 1991). Los Angeles, on the other hand, has as many as one hundred twenty thousand workers employed in five thousand factories, if we include estimates of the underground economy. According to official California Employment Development Department (EDD) estimates, employment in apparel grew by nearly one-fourth (23.2 percent) from 1985 to 1990, reflecting a sharp acceleration in an uneven growth pattern going back at least two decades (Bonacich and Hanneman 1992).

Tales of hardship abounded in our interviews with factory managers and owners in both Los Angeles and Hong Kong. Lawrence Ma, who owns the Ridewell factory in Hong Kong, suggested, "If you want to take some revenge against your enemy, try to convince him or her to have a garment business in Hong Kong" (1991). Ma claims that more than ten of his friends have lost their factories in recent years, particularly those specializing in large-sized, standardized orders, for which Hong Kong—with its rising labor costs—is no longer competitive. Ma attributes such problems to China's open-door policy, which has left Hong Kong with the quota but without cheap labor. Unimix, drawing on its size and capital resources, has thrived by moving into higher value-added products, "to higher and higher floors of the department store" (Tsang 1991). Whereas Unimix used to make for jobbers on London's cut-rate Commercial Street, it now sells high-end items to Calvin Klein, the Chelsey Group, Horne Brothers, the Burton Group, Structure, British Home Stores, Marks and Spencer, The Gap, Yves St. Laurent, Perry Ellis, and Nino Cerrutti. The Gap, whose reliance on a global network of more than five hundred factories arguably presages one future for the industry, employs a research and development staff that generates a waiting list of "tested" potential factories; "we pull the trigger when we're ready" (Cunningham 1991). Production can be shifted virtually anywhere, any time that the requisite mix of labor, quality, and turnaround time can be found.

Foreign Trading Companies and Offshore Buying Offices

Foreign trading companies are responsible for purchasing garments for manufacturers and retailers. For some, their "claim to fame is their address book" (Cunningham 1991). They are solely import-export offices. They generally do not perform design services, employ sewers, or manufacture fabric. They make their money strictly on commissions and quota, charging the factory price (plus commission) to their clients. This strategy works well for manufacturers who cannot afford to open offshore offices.

Offshore buying offices, on the other hand, are typically subsidiaries of U.S. retailers or brand-named apparel companies whose job is to source production for their parent companies. They may contract directly to factories for production, or they may contract to foreign trading companies for services. Although the latter strategy adds the trading company's commission to the cost of production, it also enables the U.S. company to avoid the costs and difficulties associated with quality control, which are assumed by the foreign trading company.

Both foreign trading companies and offshore buying offices, like the entire industry, are under increasing profit-margin pressure, because more and more U.S. manufacturers now maintain their own presence in the principal offshore regions where they contract. Foreign trading companies are learning that access to an offshore "address book" is no longer sufficient for many U.S. retail and brand-named apparel companies. "Everyone today knows manufacturers [factories]; why pay money to know a manufacturer?" (Cunningham 1991). Today buying agents must be able to handle such things as product development, sourcing, and identifying emerging sites for production.

Conclusion: Future Prospects for the Garment Industry

The commodity-chain perspective sheds light on a variety of economic agents in the Pacific Rim that knit together the manufacturing, trading, and marketing functions in the global apparel industry. Economic surplus appears to be concentrated in those nodes of the commodity chain where market power is greatest. On the retail side, giant discounters, national merchandise chains, warehouse clubs, and other large buyers now account for the lion's share of the orders in the U.S. apparel market. They use their leverage to exact compliance from domestic as well as overseas apparel manufacturers.

Unlike producer-driven industries, in which supply factors largely determine the nature of demand, in the buyer-driven apparel commodity chain the decisions made by big buyers shape global production networks (Gereffi 1994). It is important to realize, however, that the most profitable segments of the apparel commodity chain can and do change over time. In the 1960s and early 1970s—when export-oriented garment manufacturing was expanding in East Asia—U.S. garment companies, East Asian factories, and importers all made a lot of money. As the quotas and other protectionist policies of developed nations proliferated in the 1970s, the overseas factory owners and traders who manipulated these quotas (so-called quota brokers) garnered substantial windfall profits. In the 1980s market power in the apparel commodity chain began to shift toward integrated textile companies and large retailers, with garment manufacturers caught in the middle. As garment manufacturers were squeezed, they turned up the pressure on their contractors to make clothes with more fashion seasons, faster turnaround times, lower profit margins, greater uncertainty about future orders, and frequently worse conditions for the workers.

No segment in the apparel commodity chain guarantees high profits: there are bankruptcies and failures at every level. The current retail recession has forced a further restructuring of the apparel industry, with new emphasis on regional realignments in production and trade networks. East Asian garment manufacturers are becoming retailers, with an eye toward exploiting the vast potential of China and Southeast Asia as markets rather than export platforms. Similarly, the North American Free Trade Agreement is altering the calculations of retailers and manufacturers alike about the global sourcing game, as Mexico, Central America, and the Caribbean are tied more closely to the vicissitudes of U.S. consumer demand. In this context, economic surplus in the apparel commodity chain is less likely to accrue to those who make garments than to those who market them, although today, as in the past, the gains from this industry probably will not remain in any one place for very long.

References

Appelbaum, Richard, David Smith, and Brad Christerson. 1994. "Commodity Chains and Industrial Restructuring in the Pacific Rim: Garment Trade and Manufacturing." In *Commodity Chains and Global Capitalism,* edited by Gary Gereffi and Miguel Korzeniewicz, 187–204. Westport, Conn.: Greenwood Press.

Bonacich, Edna, and Pat Hanneman. 1992. "A Statistical Portrait of the Los Angeles Garment Industry." Department of Sociology, University of California, Riverside.

Campos, Miguel. 1991. Production Manager, Bongo Clothing, Los Angeles, California (interview September 18).

Cunningham, James P. 1991. Vice-President for Offshore Sourcing, The Gap Far East, Hong Kong (interview November 28).

Emmanuel, Arghiri. 1972. *Unequal Exchange: A Study of the Imperialism of Trade.* New York: Monthly Review.

Gereffi, Gary. 1992. "New Realities of Industrial Development in East Asia and Latin America: Global, Regional, and National Trends." In *States and Development in the Asian Pacific Rim,* edited by Richard P. Appelbaum and Jeffrey Henderson, 85–112. Newbury Park, Calif.: Sage.

———. 1994. "The Organization of Buyer-Driven Global Commodity Chains: How U.S. Retailers Shape Overseas Production Networks." In *Commodity Chains and Global Capitalism,* edited by Gary Gereffi and Miguel Korzeniewicz, 95–122. Westport, Conn.: Greenwood Press.

Gereffi, Gary, and Miguel Korzeniewicz. 1990. "Commodity Chains and Footwear Exports in the Semiperiphery." In *Semiperipheral States in the World Economy,* edited by William Martin. Westport, Conn.: Greenwood Press.

Glass, Mitch. 1991. Vice-President for Production, Cherokee, Sunland, California (interview August 14).

Hirsch, Stanley. 1992. President, A.C. Sports, Los Angeles, California (interview February 5).

Hopkins, Terrence K., and Immanuel Wallerstein. 1986. "Commodity Chains in the World-Economy Prior to 1800." *Review* 10(1): 157–70.

Klopp, Brent. 1991. Senior Vice-President for Production and Planning, Bugle Boy Industries, Simi Valley, California (interview October 11).

Kurt Salmon Associates (KSA). 1988. "The KSA Retail 100: Financial Profile for 1987." *KSA Perspective,* June.

———. 1990. "A Survival Course for the Nineties." *KSA Perspective.*

———. 1991. "Soft Goods Outlook for 1992." *KSA Perspective* (November).

———. 1992a. "Dancing with Juggernauts." *KSA Perspective* (January).

———. 1992b. "Retail Profile for Fiscal 1991." *KSA Perspective* (June).

———. 1992c. "Apparel and Footwear Profiles for 1991." *KSA Perspective* (June).

Kurtzman, Sally. 1992. Former head of Sportclothes Ltd., Los Angeles, California (interview March 3).

Leung Wing-yue (Trini). 1991. *Asia Monitor,* Hong Kong (interview December 3).

Lui, Tai-Lok. 1991. Lecturer, Department of Sociology, Chinese University of Hong Kong, Shatin, N.T., Hong Kong (interview December 4).

Ma, Lawrence. 1991. Owner, Ridewell Fashion and Sportswear Ltd., Hong Kong (interview December 5).

Mitchell, Russell. 1992. "Inside The Gap." *Business Week,* March 9, 58–64.

Morse, David. 1992. Former Managing Partner, California Apparel Mart, Los Angeles, California (interview January 7).

Ng, Ringo. 1991. Vice-President and General Manager, Manhattan Industries (Far East) Ltd., a division of Salant Corporation, Hong Kong (interview December 3).

Paine, Laura. 1991. Production Manager, Gotcha Corporation, Irvine, California (interview August 15).

Piore, Michael J., and Charles F. Sabel. 1984. *The Second Industrial Divide: Possibilities for Prosperity.* New York: Basic Books.

Porter, Michael E. 1990. *The Competitive Advantage of Nations.* New York: Free Press.

Randall, George. 1991. President, Yes! Corporation (interview August 12–13).

Scott, A. J. 1988. "Flexible Production Systems and Regional Development." *International Journal of Urban and Regional Research* 12:171–86.

Scott, A. J., and E. C. Kwok. 1989. "Interfirm Subcontracting and Locational Agglomeration: A Case Study of the Printed Circuits Industry in Southern California." *Economic Geography* 65:48–71.

Smith, David A., and Douglas R. White. 1990. "Structure and Dynamics of the Global Economy: Network Analysis of International Trade, 1965–1980." School of Social Science, University of California, Irvine.

Storper, Michael, and Susan Christopherson. 1987. "Flexible Specialization and Regional Industrial Agglomeration: The Case of the U.S. Motion Picture Industry." *Annals of the Association of American Geographers* 77:104–17.

Sung Yun-wing. 1991. Senior Lecturer in Economics, Chinese University of Hong Kong, Shatin, N.T., Hong Kong (interview December 4).

Taplin, Ian. 1993. "Strategic Reorientations of U.S. Apparel Firms." In *Commodity Chains and Global Capitalism,* edited by Gary Gereffi and Miguel Korzeniewicz. Westport, Conn.: Greenwood Press.

Tsang, Paul C. M. 1991. General Manager, Unimix Ltd., Hong Kong (interview November 28).

Wallerstein, Immanuel. 1980. *The Modern World-System II.* New York: Academic Press.

Wing-Tai Corporation. 1991. *Annual Report, 1991.* Hong Kong: Wing-Tai Corporation.

Zeigler, Greg. 1991. Vice-President for Production, Quiksilver, Costa Mesa, California (interview August 15).

Chapter 4

U.S. Retailers and Asian Garment Production

Lucie Cheng and Gary Gereffi

Beginning in the 1980s, changes in demography and lifestyles led the American mass market to fragment into distinct, if overlapping, constituencies. This development has set in motion a transformation of the retail institution. The traditional department stores and mass merchandisers have lost their hegemonic position, while a wide variety of specialty stores and large-volume discount chains has gained in importance. Measured by their overall sales, the discount chains of Wal-Mart and Kmart surpassed Sears as the largest U.S. retailers in 1991, and the specialty stores have the highest ratio of sales per square footage of any U.S. retail establishments (Gereffi 1994).

Frequent transnational movement of people and the efficient dissemination of ideas have contributed to the universalization of fashion taste and consumer demand. At the same time, consumer segmentation has been spurred by an increasing emphasis on individual expression. These two parallel trends led to the formation of an international market for a variety of product lines. Fashions created by designers of different nationalities in any world city are produced for specific customers found throughout the world. These concurrent developments have a definite relationship with the emergence of new production patterns in the global economy.

The Organization of Global Sourcing by U.S. Buyers

Although U.S. garment production is far from dead, more than 50 percent of apparel on the country's retail market is produced elsewhere. The organization of garment consumption in the United States is clearly stratified by retail institutions that target distinct income groups in the population. There are several types of retailers: swapmeet stalls; street vendors; small-volume, low- and medium-priced stores; large-volume, low-priced discount stores; mass merchandisers; department stores; and fashion boutiques or upper-end specialized retailers that deal exclusively with international and national brand-named products (see Table 4.1). The different categories of retailers establish distinctive relationships with importers and overseas manufacturers. As one moves down this list of retailers, the quality and price of the goods sold increase and the requirements of their international suppliers are more stringent.

U.S. buyers obtain their goods through the export and marketing networks they establish with overseas factories and trading companies. Increasingly, these networks span countries and even regions, depending on the wage factor and the stage of development of the apparel industry in each country.

Retailers and brand-named designers/merchandisers have different strategies of global sourcing, which in large part are dictated by the client bases they serve (see Figure 4.1). Fashion-oriented retailers that cater to an exclusive clientele for "designer" products obtain their expensive, nationally branded goods from an inner ring of premium-quality, high-value-added exporting countries (e.g., Italy, France, the United Kingdom, and Japan). Department stores that emphasize "private label" (i.e., store brand) products as well as national brands will source from the most established Third World exporters (the East Asian newly industrializing countries [NICs]), while the mass merchandisers who sell lower-priced store brands buy primarily from a third tier of medium- to low-cost, mid-quality exporters

Table 4.1

Organization of U.S. Retail Garment Industry

	High Price	Medium Price	Low Price
High Volume		Department stores Specialty stores	Discount stores Mass merchandisers
Low volume	Fashion boutiques	Small stores	Small stores Street vendors Swapmeet stalls

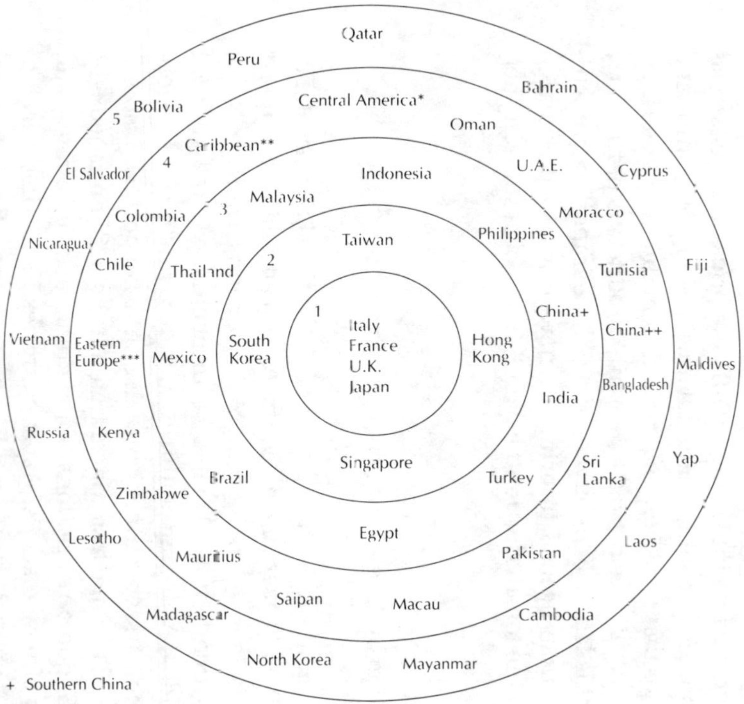

Retailers and Main Sourcing Areas

Fashion-oriented Companies
(Armani, Polo/Ralph Lauren, Donna Karan, Gucci, Hugo Boss, etc.)

- Rings 1, 2

Department Stores and Specialty Chains
(Bloomingdale's, Saks Fifth Avenue, Neiman-Marcus, Macy's, Liz Claiborne, The Gap, The Limited, etc.)

- Rings 2, 3, 4 (generally better quality and higher priced goods than those sourced by mass merchandisers and discount stores)

Mass Merchandisers
(Sears Roebuck, J.C. Penney, Woolworth, Montgomery Ward)

- Rings 2, 3, 4

Discount Stores
(Wal-Mart, Kmart, Target)

- Rings 3, 4, 5

Small Importers

- Rings 4, 5

+ Southern China
++ Interior Provinces of China
* Guatemala, Honduras, Costa Rica
** Dominican Republic, Jamaica, Haiti
*** Poland, Hungary, Czechoslovakia

Source: Gereffi (1993).

Figure 4.1 Production Frontiers for Global Sourcing by U.S. Retailers: The Apparel Industry

(Brazil, Mexico, low-end producers in the NICs, plus the People's Republic of China and the ASEAN [Association of Southeast Asian Nations] countries of Thailand, Malaysia, the Philippines, and Indonesia). Large-volume discount stores that sell the most inexpensive products import from an outer ring of low-cost suppliers of standardized goods (China, Bangladesh, Sri Lanka, Mauritius, the Dominican Republic, Guatemala, and others). Finally, some importers are like industry "scouts," who operate on the outer fringes of the international production frontier and help develop potential new sources of supply for global commodity chains (e.g., Vietnam, Burma, Saipan).

Several generalizations can be made about the production frontiers identified in Figure 4.1 (Gereffi 1994, 113). As one moves from the inner to the outer rings, the following changes are apparent: production costs and manufacturing sophistication decrease, while the lead time needed for deliveries increases. Therefore, the high-quality, multiple-season "fashion" companies, as well as the more upscale department and specialty stores, tend to source their production from the two inner rings, while the price-conscious mass merchandisers and discount chains tolerate the lower quality and longer lead times that characterize production in the two outer rings. The "industry scout" role played by certain importers is particularly important for this latter set of buyers, since these importers are willing to take the time needed to bring the new, low-cost production sites located in the fourth ring (and beyond) into global sourcing networks.

The Organization of Asian Production for Export

Most Asian garment production for export is for the U.S. market. For example, in 1989, 76 percent of North American clothing imports came from Asia, and 40 percent of Asian exports went to North America. Both trends now seem to be in decline. As the garment industry in "old" developing countries matures and "new" developing countries embark on garment production for export, U.S. sourcing activities will become less concentrated in Asia. Simultaneously, because of U.S. quota restrictions, unfavorable exchange rates, and the emergence of new markets, Asian countries increasingly seek to diversify their export destinations. With some exceptions, U.S. retailers typically do not deal directly with the final Asian producers, but go through several layers of contractors and agents.

Asian production for U.S. retailers is organized into two large categories. One involves a hierarchical structure headed by large, semi-official trade associations and the buying offices of major U.S. retail chains. Asian states have encouraged their establishment and in some cases have played an active role in their support. Another category consists of a variety of smaller traders, including importers, exporters, and wholesalers, who accept orders from U.S. buyers and arrange for Asian production and delivery, or who actively seek orders on behalf of the Asian producers. Each of these organizations has a specific production relationship with local factories and workshops. Some have exclusive arrangements with specific producers; others contract under a "free market" situation with small to medium-sized production firms or large garment factories; and many are subsidiaries or branches of vertically integrated conglomerates involving textile and chemical industries. All have their own networks of producers reaching into rural households.

The garment producers are involved in "specification contracting" relationships with the buyers who place the orders. Specification contracting is the production of finished consumer goods by local firms, whose output is distributed and marketed abroad by trading companies, retail chains, or their agents. This type of arrangement is the major export niche filled by the East Asian NICs in the world economy. East Asian factories, which have handled the bulk of the contract manufacturing orders from U.S. retailers, tend to be locally owned and vary greatly in size—from giant plants in South Korea to myriad small family firms that account for a large proportion of the exports from Taiwan and Hong Kong. Taiwan and Hong Kong have elaborate domestic subcontracting networks that include some large firms that produce key intermediate inputs such as textiles, medium-sized factories that do final product assembly, and many small factories and household enterprises that make all or part of the garment.

It is common for a developing country embarked on world trade to make maximum use of its most valuable resource: cheap and abundant labor. As a labor-intensive industry, garment production for export has been the choice of many countries at the early stage of national development. This choice soon met with resistance from the more developed destination countries in the form of quotas. Therefore, making good use of limited quotas became a concern of several Asian countries with strong state-guided development programs. Japan, Taiwan, and South Korea, at various times and under direct state initiative, have formed semiofficial trading associations to allocate quotas to producers. The existence of these associations allows the state to implement industrial development strategies, phasing out inefficient production as well as facilitating particular programs of development. The institution also provides a fierce battleground for firms jockeying for allocations and a warm bed for corruption.

The Overseas Buying Offices of U.S. Retailers

When U.S. retailers began knocking on their doors, Asian governments set up semiofficial associations and commissions to promote garment export and actively encouraged the formation of trading companies. In response, U.S. retailers began to organize their global sourcing efforts in some new ways. One example is the Associated Merchandising Corporation (AMC), which represents more than forty department stores in the United States. The AMC is a nonprofit service organization owned by its member firms. It is "the world's largest retail and merchandising organization, and a major importer with 31 offices on five continents" (Moin 1992, 7). The AMC has recently restructured to cut costs and provide more individualized services to its shareholders. Although more than 10 percent of its product-development program has been dropped, the AMC strengthened its worldwide sourcing and delivery services by establishing a research and development team to investigate changing sourcing opportunities globally (Moin 1992, 7). AMC shareholders are U.S. stores such as the Broadway and Bloomingdale's. Not all U.S. stores are represented by the AMC. J.C. Penney, Kmart, and Macy's, for example, have their own buying offices in Asia and buy their own private-label merchandise.

The AMC serves as a link between the U.S. consumer and Asian factories. Fashion trends, mostly European, are fed into the AMC headquarters in New York. Using consumer response, sales figures of the previous year, and suggestions from the local AMC offices in foreign countries, the headquarters develops a line for the new year and works with stores and merchants to establish objectives. A development trip to the AMC overseas offices is made to review samples and to visit vendors for further sample development and for price, quota, and delivery negotiations. To meet the objectives, local AMC offices find factories to produce samples, which are tested before they are shipped to headquarters for approval and forwarded to store buyers for approval or modifications. Orders are then confirmed, revised, or canceled. If they are confirmed, local offices arrange for production and shipping. The entire process takes a total of twenty-nine weeks, or slightly over seven months.

Foreign AMC offices compete as well as cooperate with one another. Orders may be switched from one locale to another because of price, color, fabric, quality of work, quota limitation, and so on. The local AMC office must be very familiar with the capacity of the factories in its area in order to be successful. Taiwan, for example, has about 1,000 "vendors" (factories), mostly small to medium sized, and the local AMC uses about 100 to 120 of them. Vendors are located throughout the island, primarily in suburbs and small towns. AMC production managers visit vendors frequently to obtain up-to-date information concerning the progress of orders and any potential labor problems. Their trips are also intended to cement personal ties with vendors, which are necessary for the stability of supply networks and quality control.

Workers interviewed at factories in Taiwan producing for the AMC are fairly satisfied with their pay and conditions. In fact, some experienced workers are so highly valued that the vendor shuttles them back and forth between the factory and their homes several times a day. Vendors complain that they have to do a lot to keep these workers but consider losing them a catastrophe. Many of the workers gained their experience from working at large factories. They switched to smaller factories in order to stay closer to home. Women workers have been socialized to accept the double burden of wage work and domestic responsibilities (Cheng and Hsiung 1991).

Because of rising labor costs in Taiwan, some medium-sized vendors are hiring foreign workers illegally. Tsai Kuang-chi, president of the Taiwan Garment Industry Association, blamed the 1990 fall in exports on the shortage of labor: "Garment factories have taken steps to contend with the labor shortage by improving productivity through new equipment and technology. Even so, the labor problem is so deep it has extended well beyond general laborers to the technician and management levels" (*Free China Journal,* August 31, 1991). In October 1991 the government lifted its ban on labor imports to "remedy Taiwan's serious labor shortage" (*Free China Journal,* June 1, 1993), and since then it has implemented several quotas for selected industries, including textiles and, to a much smaller extent, apparel.

Local AMC officials mention the high cost of Taiwan labor as the reason for losing production contracts to Hong Kong, Thailand, and more recently to Indonesia and the Philippines. They feel that Taiwan will become a center for technological and managerial services to garment factories in the region rather than merely being a production site. An official of the AMC in Taiwan explained: "Stores in the U.S. are relying more on us to provide market information, design, and fashion trends. Now that people in Taiwan have more money to spend, they buy more clothes. Also they prefer to buy American brands, not knowing that they are actually made here." Far from being a simple one-way relationship, the trans-Pacific linkage between retail and production is multifaceted and interactive.

AMC does not invest any capital in local firms. Although there are no long-term contracts and each order is independent, there is an ongoing relationship based on past performance. Typically, an order is too large for one firm and has to be split among several vendors. AMC frowns on subcontracting because of difficulties in quality control. It prefers to deal with the vendors directly. Although the production price is fixed, markup varies by store in the United States. Taiwan informants claim that standard markup is about 400 percent.

In addition to member-owned, large sourcing units such as the AMC, some major U.S. retailers have their own buying offices abroad. There are three types of overseas buying offices. Some companies, such as Sears and May Department Stores, do their own centralized sourcing. Others, such as The Limited, are retailers that are supplied through wholly owned subsidiaries, in this case, Mast Industries. Lark and Inchcape, on the other hand, are independent sourcing agents that meet the need of a wide variety of clients.

There is a symbiotic relationship between the overseas buying offices of major retail chains and the role played by importers and exporters. The overseas buying offices of major retailers purchase a wide assortment of products, typically grouped into "soft goods" (such as garments and shoes) and "hard goods" (such as lighting fixtures, kitchenware, appliances, furniture, and toys). Obviously, it is difficult for these buyers to develop an intimate knowledge of the supplier networks and product characteristics of such a diverse array of items. As a result, retail chains depend heavily on specialized importers and trading companies that continuously develop new product lines with the local manufacturers and provide retailers with valuable information about the popular items and sales trends of their competitors. By maintaining permanent representatives in the Asian producing countries, U.S. overseas buying offices can exercise better quality control (ESCAP/UNCTC 1985, 35).

U.S. retailers visit garment and fashion shows in Asian countries. Some countries, such as China, stage regular trade fairs where deals between U.S. visitors and Chinese producers are made. In Taiwan the Fangcuhui, or Textile Industry Promotion Association, and the Foreign Trade Department sponsor periodic exhibitions to attract foreign buyers. They also organize trade expeditions to the United States. Both organizations provide trade information to local manufacturers and exporters. The Fangcuhui is responsible for quota allocations. Since competition for orders is intense, U.S. buyers are generally wined and dined in Asia. Many Asian firms see entertainment as a very important activity in their business relationship with visiting U.S. retailers.

Generally, then, the overseas buying offices of major retailers tend to work with importers and trading companies in the fashion-oriented and new-product end of consumer-goods industries, while purchasing the more standardized, popular, or large-volume items directly from the factories in order to eliminate the importer's commission on these items. These factories in turn subcontract with smaller factories or household producers.

Smaller U.S. retailers often seek to establish long-term relations with end producers. Many "adopt" entrepreneur-producers and sponsor their children to study in the United States. This pattern of stabilizing a trading relationship is especially pronounced when buyers and producers belong to the same ethnic group.

Traders

Traders may be located in the United States or overseas. There are many categories of exporters and importers. General trading companies and exporters handle a wide assortment of products and sometimes help finance the production of their vendors. Importers and wholesalers are the intermediaries between retailers and their production subcontractors. Most of the leading apparel companies, such as Calvin Klein, Polo/Ralph Lauren, and Liz Claiborne, market their own exclusive designs or brand-named products but rely heavily on importers to ensure that quality standards and logistical schedules are met. Specialized importers deal only in garments or even in specific product niches within the garment industry.

As the garment market becomes more competitive, importers and wholesalers are finding themselves at the short end of bargains with respect to big U.S. buyers. The latter often insist on a buy-back arrangement for unsold garments. Some Asian importers and wholesalers have bought retail stores in the United States or developed other outlets such as the swapmeet to help absorb their buy-backs.

Big Production Firms

Since Asian governments have long facilitated the development of big firms that can monopolize domestic markets, medium-sized and small firms have been forced to find their niche in export-oriented production. Any production firm with more than three hundred workers is generally considered a big firm. Some large companies are foreign-owned, but the majority are set up by local capital. Frequently, the big firms are part of larger conglomerates. The factories are operated mainly by young women workers, although in Taiwan the workers tend to be older, between thirty and forty-five, and married.

As mentioned earlier, experienced workers are in high demand and therefore are in a better position to negotiate with local capital for higher wages and more benefits. Labor struggles in 1988 over benefit payments for childbirth resulted in the first women garment workers' union in Taiwan (Zhang Shenglin 1989). In response to labor demands, some big firms in Korea and Taiwan have closed permanently or have moved to other, less-developed countries such as

Thailand, Indonesia, and Guatemala. Managers of big firms claim that they have more orders than they can fill but are reluctant either to increase the work force or to subcontract out. This development has created more space for the growth of small and medium-sized firms.

U.S. retailers do not generally deal with big firms directly. Some companies have their own brands and labels, and others produce for large U.S. manufacturers. Asian firms gain access to the U.S. retail market for their own brands through exporters-importers, who until recently were mostly Asian American entrepreneurs.

Some of these entrepreneurs reported that although they import clothing from Asia, they prefer to use Jewish salespeople in the United States. One Chinese American importer-exporter explained: "They are more aggressive and skillful in sales work. There is also still a lot of prejudice against Asians selling Asian goods. We want the boutiques that cater to [white] Americans to buy Asian labels. It is more successful to have other Americans sell to them."

Small and Medium-Sized Producers

Small and medium-sized production firms constitute by far the largest group in the Asian garment industry dealing directly with U.S. retailers. Some of the firms are satellites of other firms. These companies may have, in addition to their own employees, a network of homeworkers, but only a few can claim an exclusive relationship with them. The preferred homeworkers are those who formerly worked for the big firms. U.S. retailers are linked with these firms in several ways. One way is for the local firms to serve as subcontractors to the main vendors of U.S. retail buying groups such as the AMC. Another method is for the firms to directly contract with traders or U.S. overseas buying offices. In a third way, Asian firms play an active role in soliciting orders from the United States.

Asian manufacturers are narrowing their gap with U.S. retailers. These firms are increasingly showing their products in U.S. trade fairs; inviting customers to visit; buying advertising spaces in international magazines, newspapers, and trade journals; and sending catalogs to overseas customers (e.g., Tang 1989). Many visit the United States regularly, calling on potential customers with samples of clothing. They tend to be very flexible and will make almost any

modifications. A few firms have Asian American designers as partners or employees. In fact, some Asian American designers in Los
Angeles trace their experience in the garment business to Asia before
immigration. Again, the spatial linkages between U.S. retail and
Asian production are more complex than simply a division between
marketing and producing activities.

Triangular Manufacturing: The Role of China

The imposition of U.S. import quotas, the rising cost of labor, and
currency appreciations in the Asian NICs led to the search for new,
preferably quota-free and labor problem–free, production sites in the
Pacific Rim. Each Asian NIC has a different set of preferred countries
where it sets up new factories. Many of the chapters in this book
have identified this process of "triangular manufacturing," described by Gereffi (1994):

> U.S. [or other overseas] buyers place their orders with the NIC manu-
> facturers they have sourced from in the past, who in turn shift some
> or all of the requested production to affiliated offshore factories in one
> or more low-wage countries. . . . The triangle is completed when the
> finished goods are shipped directly to the overseas buyer, under the
> import quotas issued to the exporting nation. Payments to the non-NIC
> factory usually flow through the NIC intermediary firm. (114)

Economic reform in China opened up a vast potential site for production. Geographic proximity, common cultural and linguistic heri-
tage, and abundant and cheap labor made China a favorite link in
the manufacturing triangle for Taiwan and Hong Kong (see Chen
1994). A 1991 survey of Hong Kong manufacturing companies reported that the number of garment workers employed by these companies in China was eight times the number employed within the
Hong Kong territory (Hong Kong Trade Development Council 1991,
3). Taiwan does not have similar statistics; however, the authorita-
tive Textile Industry Annals for 1992 included an entire chapter on
China's role in Taiwan's apparel industry (*Zhonghua Minguo Fangzhi Gongye Nianjian* 1992, 113–20).

By all accounts, traditional garment manufacturing has declined
in Taiwan. Employed garment and accessory workers in registered
factories dropped from 140,000 in 1987 to 82,000 in 1991, while the

number of establishments increased from 2,124 to 2,806 (*Zhonghua* 1992, 286). Factories are getting smaller, and an increasing number of garment workers, mostly women, are in the informal economy (Bo 1993). Although there are still barriers in Taiwan-China economic interactions, trade and investment have grown steadily, and transactions go through third countries, mostly Hong Kong. The Taiwan government reports that among those in the textile industry that have invested in China manufacturing, the garment firms makes up the largest share: 48.6 percent, or US$34 million (*Zhonghua* 1992, 62). Taiwan government and industry officials are promoting a division of labor between China and Taiwan to avoid retardation of industry upgrading. The plan suggests that China specialize in low-technology manufacturing, leaving to Taiwan the high-tech and high-value-added products. Taiwan is to be responsible for foreign buying orders, design, quality control, and overseas marketing, while China is to handle production processing (*Zhonghua* 1992, 116). China is unlikely to accept this division of labor, however, on any but a short-term and limited basis. Chinese officials are more interested in developing high value-added industries in their economic pursuit.

The China angle is not without risk. The constant threat of losing most-favored-nation (MFN) status has led to a general hesitation by Hong Kong, Taiwan, and other foreign entrepreneurs to rely on China for garment production. If China were to lose MFN status, tariffs on apparel would increase from about 20 to 90 percent, which would make it impossible to compete (*Women's Wear Daily,* June 17, 1991). U.S. buyers are still placing orders in China but are actively seeking alternatives. Hong Kong and Taiwan are diversifying while continuing to invest in China. For Hong Kong, which will be incorporated into China in 1997, the lure of China for apparel firms is twofold: as an integrated production base and as a booming market, especially for mid-priced branded apparel being developed by Hong Kong specifically for Asian consumers (see Gereffi 1994, 115, 115n.34).

Asian Immigration, the Changing Retail Market, and Garment Production in Asia

The growth of the Asian American middle class in the past two decades has brought about a change in American merchandising behavior. In the early 1980s it was nearly impossible for an Asian American woman of a body type typical of her group to find moderately priced and fashionable clothing that would fit without alteration. Recently, however, large department stores have greatly expanded their "petite" or "Club 5'3" sections to meet her needs. Similar adjustments have been made by shoestores and other businesses. Asian American models also have begun to appear more frequently in fashion magazines and sales catalogs, indicating a deliberate attempt to capture this burgeoning market. This phenomenon has contributed in part to the continued development of the garment industry in Asia, especially in the reconfiguration of the division of labor on both sides of the Pacific.

With the increase in the U.S. Asian population, the role of Asian Americans involved in the garment business has greatly diversified. Many are designers, wholesalers, buyers, and retailers. Their trans-Pacific linkage gives them an advantage in securing producers in Asia. One Chinese American interviewed claims to have eight small factories in Taiwan, Hong Kong, and China producing sweaters for him. His wife gets ideas from fashion magazines and by visiting boutiques in Los Angeles. They sell to stores in southern California, and the leftovers are sold in bazaars and swapmeets at reduced prices. Another Chinese American who has spent ten years in the business claims to have a corps of designers in Taiwan and Korea. He has factories in China and Taiwan and has about eight thousand boutique buyers all over the United States. Recently, he opened an outlet in downtown Los Angeles to absorb unsold goods and buy-backs. The heavy involvement of Korean Americans in the garment industry is also no longer limited to manufacturing but includes design and retailing as well.

Designers are no longer exclusively European or U.S., either in the ethnic sense or in spatial terms. Asian names such as Donna Hsu, Lin Chia-hwa, and Shiatzy are found in U.S. and Asian stores. Nor are there restrictions on the locations and ethnicity of producers, salespeople, and customers for the same garment design. U.S. linkage with East Asia in the garment industry has gone from a scenario of predominantly white designers, white producers, white salespeople, and white consumers; to white designers, Asian producers in Asia, white salespeople, and white consumers; to white, Asian, and Asian American designers, Asian and Asian American producers, and white and Asian salespeople and consumers in the United States and in Asia. Production, capital, and markets are globalized.

Although retailing in the United States structures garment production in Asia, Asian production also is changing retailing. Examples are the flourishing of swapmeets, street vendors, and boutiques in department stores, allowing greater diversification of lines. This trend is caused by overproduction and uneven distribution in Asia and by the buy-back policies imposed by large U.S. department stores.

As in other economic institutions, the organization and operation of the garment industry cannot be understood in purely economic terms. Socially embedded factors determine how the industry operates in various countries and how linkages between functions, agents, and organizations are formed. Some factors relate to the dominance of the state, which plays an active role in the promotion of particular forms of industrialization. An example is the set-up of "living-room factories" promoted by the Taiwan state to facilitate decentralization of industries within an export-led growth program of development. The living-room factories succeeded because the measure is consistent with family ideology and gender discrimination. The nature of garment production lends itself to labor-intensive activity, flexible work, and segmented time. All are characteristic of female labor (Cheng and Hsiung 1991).

U.S. retailers play a significant role in the structuring of Asian garment production, but the relationship is quite complex. As Asian immigration has increased, various roles in the garment industry have become ethnically diversified. Requirements of Asian customers in the United States and in Asia are linking the retail market on both sides of the Pacific. In a similar way, the appearance of Asian designers in U.S. cities is reconfiguring the traditional division of labor in garment production between the United States and Asia.

The current increase of women wage earners in the United States means that they need and can afford to buy more clothing for themselves and their families. There is a link between U.S. women consumers and Asian women workers in the garment industry.

Conclusion

We are witnessing a changing configuration of roles in the garment industry within the Pacific Rim. Spatially and ethnically, retailers, consumers, designers, and producers have shifting social identities and are engaged in overlapping networks that blur the boundaries between previously distinct functions in the industry. While U.S. retailers are a major factor in determining the organization of overseas production, Asian producers are buying U.S. retail outlets and are seeing both the United States and Asia as viable markets for their goods. Regional centers have emerged. In the Asia Pacific Rim, Taiwan, Hong Kong, and Korea have become service and financial centers for garment production, and Indonesia, the Philippines, Thailand, and China have become production sites. This particular configuration will no doubt shift as individual countries struggle for economic survival and vie for better positions in the capitalist world system.

References

Bo, Lanzhi. 1993. "Jingji zai jiegou zhong de funu jiuye bian quien" (Women's employment in economic restructuring). Master's thesis. National Taiwan University, Taipei.

Chen, Xiangming. 1994. "The New Spatial Division of Labor and Commodity Chains in the Greater South China Economic Region." In *Commodity Chains and Global Capitalism,* edited by Gary Gereffi and Miguel Korzeniewicz, 165–86. Westport, Conn.: Greenwood Press.

Cheng, Lucie, and Ping-chun Hsuing. 1991. "Women, Export-Oriented Growth, and the State: The Case of Taiwan." In *States and Development in the Asian Pacific Rim,* edited by Richard P. Appelbaum and Jeffrey Henderson, 233–66. Newbury Park, Calif.: Sage.

Economic and Social Commission for Asia and the Pacific/United Nations Centre on Transnational Corporations (ESCAP/UNCTC). 1985. *Transnational Trading Corporations in Selected Asian and Pacific Countries.* Bangkok: ESCAP.

Federation of Hong Kong Industries. 1992. *Hong Kong's Industrial Investment in the Pearl River Delta: 1991 Survey among Members of the Federation of Hong Kong Industries.* Hong Kong.

Gereffi, Gary. 1994. "The Organization of Buyer-Driven Global Commodity Chains: How U.S. Retailers Shape Overseas Production Networks." In *Commodity Chains and Global Capitalism,* edited by Gary Gereffi and Miguel Korzeniewicz, 95–122. Westport, Conn.: Greenwood Press.

Hong Kong Trade Development Council. 1991. *Survey on Hong Kong Domestic Exports, Re-exports, and Triangular Trade.* Hong Kong.

Moin, David. 1992. "AMC Tailors New Strategy." *Women's Wear Daily,* July 23, p. 7.

Spekman, Robert E. 1991. *U.S. Buyers' Relationship with Pacific Rim Supplies.* Los Angeles: IBEAR.

Tang, Fuzang. 1989. "Garment Export Strategies and Conditions." Taiwan Jingji Yuce yu Zhengee 20(2): 111–19.

Zhang, Shenglin. 1989. "Kongjian fengong yu laogong yundong" (Spatial division and labor movement). Master's thesis. National Taiwan University, Taipei.

Zhonghua Minguo Fangzhi Gongye Nianjian (Annals of the textile industries). 1992. Taipei: Taiwan Economic Research Institute.

Chapter 5

The Role of U.S. Apparel Manufacturers in the Globalization of the Industry in the Pacific Rim

Edna Bonacich and David V. Waller

The massive growth of apparel imports to the United States is often interpreted as resulting from the actions of firms and governments in other countries seeking to develop their U.S.-targeted export industries (Arpan, de la Torre, and Toyne 1982; Cline 1990; Ghadar, Davidson, and Feigenoff 1987; Hamilton 1990). Though there is certainly some truth to this interpretation, it overlooks the primary role that U.S. firms have played in developing imports. In the apparel industry, both retailers and manufacturers engage in importing. U.S. retailers are the primary importers in this industry, but in this chapter we focus on the role played by apparel manufacturers, both in charting imports and in continuing to develop them.

What obscures the role of U.S. firms in the import process is that many of them do not own the firms from which they import. Foreign direct investment is of relatively small importance in this industry (Oman 1989; United Nations 1987). Much more common are arm's-length transactions, such as contracting and licensing. International contracting takes two main forms: either the contractor is responsible for the full production process and often purchases the textiles (sometimes called commercial contracting), or the contractor engages only in the assembly (sewing) of already-cut textiles (offshore processing).

In this chapter we try to make sense of the role of U.S. apparel manufacturers, first, by examining the history of the involvement of U.S. apparel manufacturers in Asia, then by considering the role the U.S. government has played in promoting international contracting by U.S. apparel firms, especially in the Caribbean region, and finally by examining the annual reports and 10-Ks of some of the leading U.S. apparel manufacturers in which they describe their global operations.

Historical Evolution of U.S. Involvement in Asia

When U.S. apparel makers began moving to Asia, they had already made a first move within the United States, from the Northeast (New York, Pennsylvania, New Jersey, New England) to the South, taking advantage of the cheaper, nonunionized labor to be found there. This trend began in the 1950s and, according to one source, almost annihilated the U.S. apparel industry; only firms with strong brand names survived.[1] The South produced private label (i.e., store brands) for large retailers, such as Sears, J. C. Penney, and W. T. Grant. The first U.S. importers went to Japan in the mid-1950s. At that time, Japanese products were considered in the United States to be of very low quality. According to an industry expert: "People would spit on the merchandise. They would wonder if the sleeves would fall off." There was also political resistance to purchasing them, with demonstrations and picketing; resistance was effective because the products were not desirable anyway. This situation changed with the development of the highly popular, portable transistor radio—the first technological product made by Japan—giving Japan a new credibility and encouraging Japanese manufacturers to focus on higher-quality goods. By the mid-1960s Japanese products' reputation in the United States had begun to improve.

The Far East was to the southern United States what the South was to the Northeast: an opportunity to cut costs. The early apparel importers worked almost exclusively with the large Japanese trading companies, especially Mitsui. U.S. importers would take sample products they had either bought or made themselves and have them made in Japan at a lower price. As one source put it, "We taught them how to make the garments, about thread tension, how to pack a carton, etc."

Five U.S. companies made the move to Japanese production. Known in the industry as the "big five," or the "founding fathers," they were Regal Accessories (Irving Alpert), Republic Cellini (Hy Katz), Marlene, Spartan Mayro, and CBS (Jack Clark). These firms were all southern U.S. manufacturers, producing for the low end of the domestic market. Four of the five were in women's wear.

The shift to Hong Kong began in the late 1950s and 1960s. Entrepreneurs who left China with Chiang Kai-shek settled in Hong Kong and began producing goods for the founding fathers. Japan quickly became comparatively expensive and shifted to high-tech production. By 1970 Hong Kong was a premier producer; in the mid-1960s South Korea and Taiwan entered the market. They were developed as alternatives to Hong Kong between 1965 and 1975 and had achieved major producer status by 1980.

According to a Los Angeles manufacturer who was a member of one of the big five firms:

> The role of the United States was mainly that it was just a willing market, willing to pay obscene prices for the work they had done in Asia. We didn't think they were obscene because they were four or five times lower than U.S. prices, but relative to the local standard of living they were. We paid 25 cents to put a flap on a pocket, and 25 cents to sew on a collar. And 50 cents was a day's wage there! We didn't make the correlation. It would be like someone coming to America to buy Fords, and paying $100,000 a car. It provided so much excess capital that they could go into anything.

Quota was another source of financing for Asian companies; it negated the need for U.S. financing: "The United States, in its infinite wisdom, created quota and then gave it to Asian countries. So we don't own the quota we established. The Asians weren't stupid and made a commodity of it."

Another source reported his observations of Hong Kong: "I remember we would negotiate a deal with a person who didn't have any capacity for production. We would bring a sample, arrange the deal, and then they would go out and buy the machines to produce it." In those days most of the textiles were from Japan. The Hong Kong producer was responsible for buying what was needed. "We would open an L/C [letter of credit] to him, and he would open a child L/C to purchase the textile. He would be responsible for making the goods from scratch and delivering the finished product."

In the United States of the 1960s the Far East was still viewed, according to one source, as mysterious, and U.S. citizens were consequently reluctant to go there. They had difficulty understanding Asian business methods, such as the role of trading companies. Thousands went over, looked, and came back deciding not to do business there, leaving the field open for the founding fathers, who became very powerful. Retailers would pay them a premium simply for introductions to Far Eastern producers. There was also considerable corruption on the Asian end, with kickbacks paid to the U.S. importers from producers and from freight and steamship companies. The big five made a great deal of money until their customers, the retailers, went directly to the Far East and cut them out. The big five all died in the 1970s—as did their principals—after a twenty-year run.

A new group of importers emerged in the 1960s: U.S. manufacturers who designed their own goods and contracted production in the Far East. U.S. retailers joined the act in the early 1970s, deciding that they could take over manufacturers' profits; they chose to bypass the middleman altogether, producing the goods directly in the Far East and importing themselves.

U.S. retailers developed several strategies for entering importing. At great cost, some imported directly themselves and gradually— after about ten years of trial and error—were able to master the art. For example, Macy's created an entire importing line. It had twenty-five labels that looked like brands; it designed and created images and began manufacturing. Another strategy was used by The Limited, a specialty-store chain. Rather than learning to import, it bought an importing firm, Mast Industries, which served as its major buyer in Asia.

Retailers became the primary importers from Asia. They contributed to rising import prices because they could pay more than manufacturers. Instead of pricing goods according to their cost, retailers priced them according to the U.S. market. We were told the following story by a manufacturer:

There were two guys from The Gap in Taiwan, wanting to produce a chambray shirt. They reckoned they wanted to retail it for $28, and to allow a percentage to be used for promotion at $20 retail. They told the Taiwan producer they wanted to buy the shirt for $69 a dozen, even though the actual cost was $47 a dozen. The Taiwan producer smiled and said he could do it for $69.50. It was a $4 shirt but they paid $6.50 for it. This is the way retailers drove up prices. They set their prices by what they thought the customer would bear. Manufacturers don't work that way; they bargain over the true cost of production. This Taiwanese producer passed the word along, and soon no one would produce chambray shirts for less than $6.50. The retailers drove the market up. They could afford to be sloppy because they were getting such a big markup.

This process drove the manufacturer out, because, at US$6.50, it could no longer sell through retailers and make a profit.

The next shift occurred when companies started to import for markets other than discount and began to act like brand names. One major example was Britannia, which imported jeans more costly than Levi's. Britannia jeans had very labor-intensive patchwork, involving the kind of work Levi's could not afford to do in the United States. The success of Britannia encouraged other brands to follow, starting in the early 1970s. Now imports were no longer cheap goods, but goods that provided better value to the consumer. For example, high-fashion sweaters began being imported from Korea in large numbers during this period.

Like other importers, retailers are engaged in knocking off (copying styles); one source thought 90 percent of imports were knockoffs. "I've seen buyers from department stores take trips through Europe, buy clothes there, and hand them over to their Far Eastern suppliers to copy. They are able to save money by cutting out the middleman. They act like manufacturers. The distinction between manufacturers and retailers is disappearing."

Today, we were told, most of the big buyers in Hong Kong are retailers. Other importers either have moved back to the United States or have moved out of the major Asian producing countries to second-tier producers, such as Indonesia, the Philippines, and the Middle East. U.S. retailers do not go to these countries because they consider doing business there too risky.

One informant described his personal experiences with importing: "I was working for a New York firm that is no longer in business. I went to Hong Kong six years ago [1985] to run their Hong Kong business. We manufactured all the Jaclyn Smith goods for Kmart— about $100 million FOB. We were making skirts, blouses, slacks, etc." His home office sent him types of fabrication they were considering; his office in Hong Kong would research them and present the results to Kmart. He would then receive samples, duplicate them in Hong Kong, and negotiate prices. He would buy the piece goods, supervise production, inspect and correct, and ensure that the goods were sent off on schedule. "I had a staff of sixty to seventy-five people. We produced in Hong Kong, China, Bangladesh, Sri Lanka, the Philippines, Korea, Taiwan, Saipan, Zimbabwe, and India."

According to this source, the big U.S. manufacturers, such as Leslie Fay and Jordache, have their own offices in the Far East, but the smaller ones use trading companies. There are Chinese, British, and other trading companies, as well as some large U.S. ones. Two of the biggest U.S. trading companies are Lark International, whose principal is Ira Kay, and Wishbone, whose principal is Bobby Shamus. These firms deal in the hundreds of millions of dollars.

The latest phase in the development of importing, starting in the 1980s, was Asian apparel companies' attempts to penetrate the U.S. market more directly, bypassing U.S. firms' ability to control brands and distribution. Hong Kong companies began purchasing U.S. companies and going into direct competition with the U.S. brands. They also acquired some retail specialty stores, such as Foxmore and Aca Joe. Even this phase of importing is being aided by U.S. business. For example, the California Mart has an officer whose charge is to spearhead a program to help foreign importers and manufacturers ship their products to the United States and market them under their own label. The Mart teaches firms how to import correctly and how to deal with U.S. customs regulations. In sum, for a period of more than thirty years, U.S. apparel firms and related businesses have played an active role in the development of clothing imports from Asia.

The Role of the U.S. Government in Globalization

Although some U.S. government policies stimulated U.S. apparel firms' move to Asia, there has been more encouragement for movement to the Caribbean region (including Mexico and Central America). The motives for this assistance are complex; they include geopolitical concerns, as well as efforts to contain Asian countries' rising economic power. The government aims to help U.S. firms become "more competitive" by easing their access to cheaper Caribbean-region labor; in the course of doing so, the state clearly reveals its tendency to side with the interests of capital as opposed to labor. The survival of U.S. apparel firms may be enhanced by their ability to engage in offshore assembly, but U.S. workers are faced with unmeetable wage competition, and their unions are decidedly weakened by capital's easy move offshore. Businesses and the state argue that U.S. workers will, in the long run, benefit from the creation of higher-tech jobs supporting the remaining manufacturers, but the reality of this prediction—let alone its likely benefit to the workers who are actually displaced—remains highly questionable. The main mechanisms the U.S. government has used in encouraging offshore assembly are trade policies, financial assistance, and state-to-state aid.

Trade Policies

As described in Chapter 2, the United States has several trade policies encouraging offshore assembly by U.S. apparel firms and the subsequent importing of garments to the U.S. market. They include Tariff Item 807 (HTS 9802.00.80), the Caribbean Basin Initiative (CBI), the North American Free Trade Agreement (NAFTA), the Enterprise for the Americas Initiative (EAI), and the phasing out of the Multifiber Arrangement (MFA) under the General Agreement on Tariffs and Trade (GATT).

Item 807 dictates that tariffs apply only to the value-added of products assembled abroad. Thus, if U.S. apparel firms cut their garments at home and have them sewn offshore, they need only pay tariff on the value added by sewing—which can be very little, given low wages. Although Item 807 has been used in Asia, it is much more commonly used in Mexico and the Caribbean region, because of their proximity and the political clout the United States exercises over its neighbors.

At first, the CBI, passed in 1983, excluded apparel from the duty-free treatment of certain imports from the region. In 1986, however, the Caribbean Basin Textile Access Program (known as CBI II) was passed; sometimes known as 807a, or Super 807, this program established a two-tier quota system for participating countries. Guaranteed Access Levels (GALs) ensured unlimited U.S. market access for Caribbean apparel products assembled from fabric formed and cut in the United States. Designated Consultation Levels (DCLs) or Specific Limits (SLs) were set for garments not meeting this criterion, and they were subject to quantitative restrictions (U.S. Department of Labor 1990).

The North American Free Trade Agreement (NAFTA) should encourage a similar movement to Mexico. Item 807 has already caused some movement of apparel assembly to Mexico; NAFTA will only aid the removal of whatever tariff barriers remain. Still, NAFTA's passage might motivate those companies that have been hesitant to contract offshore. NAFTA increases the attractiveness of Mexico relative to the CBI countries, raising concern among the latter—and among those U.S. apparel fiems that have invested there—that Mexican production will undermine them.

On June 27, 1990, the Bush administration launched the Enterprise for the Americas Initiative. EAI is an elaborate program involving trade, investment, and debt concessions for all of Latin America. Implementation of EAI is a long-term process; the United States is negotiating bilateral treaties with individual countries, and some are moving more quickly than others. Like NAFTA, EAI poses a potential threat to the CBI countries in the short run. Nevertheless, it seems likely that, following NAFTA, an effort will be made to bring all of the Western Hemisphere into a single trade regime.

CBI, NAFTA, and EAI aim, in part, to enable U.S. firms to compete more effectively with Asia's lower production costs. In the case of the apparel industry, the goal appears to be to use the Caribbean region as a low-wage production center while maintaining the industry's design, engineering, and marketing aspects in the United States.

In contrast, the phasing out of the GATT's Multifiber Arrangement will lead to the end of quotas in the apparel industry and to a free-for-all global competition. Capital from all the major producing countries is likely to be attracted to the lowest-wage developing countries, such as India, Pakistan, Sri Lanka, Malaysia, Bangladesh, and especially the People's Republic of China.

Financial Assistance

Apart from trade policies that manipulate access to the U.S. market, the United States aids in the movement of U.S. capital abroad by offering financial assistance to firms that invest overseas. In particular, the U.S. government, through the Overseas Private Investment Corporation (OPIC) and the Agency for International Development (USAID), provides investment and project financing and investment insurance.

OPIC assists U.S. capital in four principal ways: by providing insurance against political risk, by financing investments through direct loans or loan guarantees, by organizing investment missions in the United States and abroad, and by supplying information services to potential investors. Examples of some apparel projects for which OPIC provided insurance in the early 1980s include the assembly of women's blouses by Judy Bond in Haiti in 1983 (a total investment of US$10 million); the manufacture of infantwear by Baby Togs in the Philippines in 1984 (US$2.5 million investment); the manufacture of men's and women's jeans by Gulf and Western in Haiti in 1983 (US$1.4 million investment); and the assembly of women's undergarments by Bestform Foundations in St. Lucia in 1982 (US$50,000 investment).

Direct financial backing is supplemented by government supports for U.S. overseas investors; U.S. embassies, as well as officers for the U.S. Department of Commerce, provide assistance. Commerce officers monitor relevant economic and political developments in host countries and communicate this information to other governmental agencies and to the private sector. The network of Commerce Department officials is often the first line of contact with host countries for potential investors.

State-to-State Aid

State-to-state assistance by the U.S. government to host countries helps to deepen the institutional environment favoring investments and offshore production in the Caribbean region. USAID plays an especially important role in this regard; through it, the U.S. government supports investment and export-promotion organizations with operations in the United States. These organizations include FUSADES in El Salvador, FIDE in Honduras, JAMPRO in Jamaica, CINDE in Costa Rica, CAEM in Guatemala, IPC in the Dominican Republic, and PROBE in Haiti, among others. According to Charles Kernaghan, the U.S. government has put US$290 million into funding these agencies, which, among other functions, actively assist

U.S. businesses in developing contacts and obtaining financial assistance for investments (1992, 17–18).

Much of the U.S. investment in the Caribbean region goes to export-processing zones (EPZs), where, in addition to various incentives such as tax holidays and infrastructural support, a strict labor regime can be enforced. Kernaghan found evidence that EPZs in Honduras and El Salvador maintained blacklists of workers who had shown any interest in forming unions (1992, 54–62). In other words, the U.S. government was helping to finance agencies actively engaged in preventing unionization.

These facts were dramatically revealed to the U.S. public in two television shows, "60 Minutes" and "Nightline," in late 1992.[2] They showed that USAID and other agencies had aggressively targeted U.S. businesses to shift their manufacturing to Central America, by advertising in U.S. trade journals and wining and dining U.S. business executives. From Central American EPZs U.S. businesses could import the finished goods back into the United States with reduced tariffs. The clear implication of these programs was that the U.S. government was using taxpayers' money to export U.S. jobs and then to set the conditions for the further erosion of those jobs through import competition. The resulting outcry embarrassed the Bush administration and led the U.S. Congress to cut funding to USAID.

Kernaghan listed thirty U.S. apparel manufacturers with investments in El Salvador, Honduras, and Guatemala (some having investments in more than one country) and sixty-eight U.S. apparel manufacturers and retailers that outsource production in these three countries (1992, 36). These companies, he argued, were ultimately encouraged to move by the U.S. government, and thus U.S. taxpayers are funding job losses for U.S. workers. Certainly a case can be made that promoting offshore production is in the broader interests of the United States, both economically and politically. Whether or not one makes such an argument, U.S. government polices actively encourage the globalization of U.S. apparel production, which in turn leads to an increase in apparel imports.

Company Reports

We reviewed the annual reports and 10-K forms of the major, publicly held U.S. apparel firms to see what they revealed about the firms' Pacific Rim activities.[3] For the purposes of this study, we decided to limit our review to firms with sales volumes of more than US$100 million; thirty-three firms met this criterion. The wholesale value of U.S. domestic apparel production in 1990 was US$39 billion; imports were valued at another US$39 billion, for a total of US$78 billion (AAMA 1991, 4). Our thirty-three firms had a combined sales volume of US$24.5 billion, accounting for about one-third of the wholesale clothing market in the United States. We requested annual reports and 10-K forms from each of the firms, and most complied.

Liz Claiborne

Liz Claiborne is a very successful and fast-growing women's-wear firm, founded in 1976. By 1981 its sales had reached US$116.8 million, and by 1990, US$1.729 billion.[4] Here is how the company described itself in 1990:

> The Company does not own any manufacturing facilities; all of its products are manufactured through arrangements with independent suppliers. . . . A very substantial portion of the Company's sales is represented by products produced abroad, primarily in the Far East. During 1990, the Company's apparel and accessories products were manufactured by approximately 300 suppliers, of which approximately 115 were domestic suppliers, and the balance of which were located abroad, mainly in Hong Kong, South Korea, Taiwan, the Philippines, China, and Brazil. The Company continually seeks additional suppliers throughout the world for its sourcing needs. The Company's two largest suppliers of finished products each manufactured approximately 5 percent of the Company's purchases of finished products during 1990, with no other single supplier accounting for more than 4 percent of such 1990 purchases. . . . The Company does not have any long-term, formal arrangements with any of the suppliers which manufacture its products. The Company believes that it is the largest customer of many of its manufacturing suppliers. . . . Members of the Company's production administration staff monitor production at the facilities which manufacture Company products in order to assure compliance with the Company's specifications and the timely delivery of finished items. . . . With respect to foreign suppliers' operations, these tasks are performed by Company personnel based at Company offices in Hong Kong; Taipei, Taiwan; Manila, the Philippines; Shang-

hai, China; Singapore; Costa Rica and Thailand; as well as by independent agents performing services in Korea, Brazil, Portugal, China, Italy, Japan, Yugoslavia, Turkey, Spain, and Hungary. The Company plans to open offices in Brazil, Yugoslavia, Indonesia, Malaysia, and India during 1991 as well as move technical personnel into additional countries to supervise production and quality assurance.

Crystal Brands

Crystal Brands was originally part of General Mills—the General Mills Fashion Group—but was spun off in 1985. It is the sixth largest apparel producer in the United States, with annual sales in 1990 of US$868.5 million. Among other things, the firm makes sportswear, including the Izod and Izod Lacoste labels. The 1990 annual report describes the company's international operations:

> Approximately 67 percent of the Company's products are manufactured in the United States and Puerto Rico, both in its own facilities and by independent contractors. The balance of the Company's products are manufactured by independent suppliers in foreign countries, principally in the Far East. The Company operates a Hong Kong sourcing office to coordinate Orient apparel sourcing. The Hong Kong office includes production merchandisers and quality control specialists who contract among various manufacturers and inspect the Company's offshore sourced goods and product lines. In addition, the Company participates in several duty-advantaged, low-labor cost apparel sourcing ventures in the Caribbean and has established several domestic contractor relationships, which supply a portion of the Company's apparel lines.

Among Crystal Brands' properties are manufacturing facilities in Corozal and Dorado, Puerto Rico; and San Pedro and Santo Domingo, Dominican Republic. The firm also has leased and owned properties around the United States and listed three offices in Kowloon, Hong Kong.

Gitano Group

The Gitano Group and its subsidiaries make a diverse set of apparel for men, women, and children, under the labels Gitano, Gloria Vanderbilt, and Regatta Sport. According to the company, it ranked second among all brands of women's jeanswear in the U.S. market in 1990 and first in nondenim jeanswear. The firm aims at the middle-income consumer.

> During 1990, Gitano obtained products marketed by it from manufacturers located in approximately forty countries. Gitano has had repeated dealings with certain of these manufacturers over the past several years. Generally, no contractual obligations exist between Gitano and its manufacturers except on an order-by-order basis. During 1990, Gitano obtained products directly from manufacturers operating factories located in the Far East, South and Central America, the Caribbean Basin, the United States, Eastern Europe, and other areas. . . . The Company believes that no manufacturer supplied more than 5 percent of Gitano's products during 1990. Gitano regularly investigates and evaluates new and existing manufacturing sources. . . . Normally, each manufacturer agrees to produce finished garments at a specified time on the basis of purchase orders from Gitano, supported by a letter of credit. . . . Each manufacturer generally purchases all necessary fabric and other materials from various suppliers. From time to time, Gitano may negotiate with fabric mills for a bulk price for fabric, without incurring any contractual obligation to purchase such fabric. Gitano then arranges for its manufacturers to purchase fabric from such mills. Each manufacturer produces finished garments in accordance with production samples and patterns produced or approved by Gitano's technical production support staff. Utilizing employees based in twelve overseas offices in the Far East, South and Central America, India, and Eastern Europe, Gitano monitors production at each manufacturer's facility to ensure quality, compliance with Gitano's specifications, and timely delivery of finished garments to Gitano's distribution facilities.

In addition to sourcing and importing, Gitano operates its own manufacturing facilities, accounting for approximately 15 percent of its 1990 production. One of its subsidiaries, Noel Industries, has Jamaican subsidiaries that operate several plants in Kingston, leased for cutting and sewing. Noel also built a plant in Guatemala City in 1987 for cutting and sewing. In 1990 it leased a storage facility in Guatemala City, which it is in the process of replacing with a larger distribution center.

Gitano expressed concern over import restrictions and keeps a careful watch over changes in quotas negotiated under the MFA. The firm was especially worried about a possible change in the status of China but believed it could deal with such adverse legislation if it was enacted:

> Gitano monitors duty, tariff, and quota-related developments and seeks continually to minimize its potential exposure to quota-related risks, through, among other measures, geographical diversification of its manufacturing sources, the maintenance of overseas offices, allocation of production to merchandise categories where more quota is available, and shifts of production among countries and manufacturers. Gitano believes that its manufacturing operations in the United States, the Caribbean Basin, and Central America, together with the recent expansion of its manufacturing sources and foreign offices, may help mitigate the adverse effect that any increase in such restrictions would have on Gitano.

In other words, this company openly links its globalizing strategy to the quota system. It also expresses concern over "political instability resulting in the disruption of trade from exporting countries," as well as changes in taxes and duties, fluctuations in the value of the dollar, and restrictions on the transfer of funds. Gitano takes advantage of both the CBI and Item 807.

These and similar descriptions in other 10-Ks and annual reports illustrate the sheer scope of global production by U.S. apparel manufacturers. They maximize their ability to move wherever and whenever they choose, taking advantage of various tax, tariff, quota, and other arrangements. By these means they are able to minimize risk. On the other hand, they keep a tight rein on their contractors in terms of oversight and quality control. They manage, in a sense, without tying up capital or taking responsibility for labor relations.

Table 5.1 lists the major garment firms by sales volume, the countries in the Pacific Rim where they have production, and the kinds of arrangements they have there. In this table (and throughout the text) we have omitted the firms' reports of their activities in Europe, Africa, and the Western developed countries of the Pacific Rim, notably, Canada and Australia.

Even given the limitations of the data, we see that many of the major U.S. apparel firms are active, to various degrees, in outsourcing production to Asia, Mexico, the Caribbean region, and South America. Their involvements vary from full ownership of subsidiar-

Table 5.1

Activities of Major U.S. Garment Companies in Developing Countries of the Pacific Rim, 1990

Company US$ Sales 1990 Key Products and Brands	Location	Type of Activity
Levi Strauss $4,247,150,000 *Sportswear* Levi's Dockers Britannia	Manila, Philippines São Paulo, Brazil Mexico Guatemala Costa Rica Dominican Republic Brazil South Korea China Hong Kong Taiwan Macao Thailand Malaysia Singapore Bangladesh India Pakistan Sri Lanka Indonesia Philippines Saipan	Subsidiaries Contractors (600 worldwide)
Sara Lee $3,756,000,000 *Hosiery, knitwear* Haines L'Eggs Beefy T	No information provided	
VF Corporation $2,612,613,000 *Sportswear* Lee Wrangler	No information provided	
Liz Claiborne $1,728,868,000 *Women's apparel*	Hong Kong Taipei, Taiwan Manila, Philippines Shanghai, China Singapore South Korea Costa Rica Brazil	Independent suppliers

Continued on next page

Table 5.1—*Continued*

Company US$ Sales 1990 Key Products and Brands	Location	Type of Activity

Fruit of the Loom
$1,426,800,000
  Men's underwear
    Fruit of the Loom
    BVD
	No information provided	

Crystal Brands
$868,465,000
  Men's wear
    Izod
    Lacoste
	Confecciones, Dominicana, S.A., Dominican Republic
	Crystal Brands (Hong Kong), Ltd.
	Palm Sports (Hong Kong), Ltd.
	Corozal, Puerto Rico
	Dorado, Puerto Rico
	San Pedro, Dominican Republic
	San Domingo, Dominican Republic
	Far East (Hong Kong office)
	Caribbean
		Subsidiaries (100% owned)
		
		Independent suppliers
		
		Sourcing

Leslie Fay $856,768,000 *Women's wear*	Hong Kong Taiwan South Korea Malaysia Philippines Dominican Republic	Independent contractors (59% sales produced under contract and imported)

Gitano Group
$806,586,000
  Women's wear
    Gitano
    Gloria Vanderbilt
	Noel Industries, Kingston, Jamaica
	Guatemala
	China
	Taiwan
	Hong Kong
	Singapore
	Brazil
	Central America
	Caribbean Basin
		Subsidiaries
		
		Independent suppliers (in 40 countries)

Continued on next page

Table 5.1 — *Continued*

Company US$ Sales 1990 Key Products and Brands	Location	Type of Activity
Kellwood $779,866,000 *Diversified*	Smart Shirts, Hong Kong Taiwan Sri Lanka Costa Rica Saipan China Haiti	Subsidiaries and joint ventures (12 plants in 8 countries)
Phillips–Van Heusen $732,936,000 *Men's wear* Van Heusen	Brazil Guatemala Far East Guatemala Honduras Costa Rica Dominican Republic	Licensees Sourcing
Russell $713,812,000 *Athletic clothing and leisurewear*	No foreign activity	
Hartmarx $579,800,000 *Men's wear*	Robert's, Mexico Japan South Korea Taiwan Thailand Hong Kong Chile Colombia	Affiliate (sold in 1990) Licensees
Oxford Industries $550,434,000 *Diversified*	San José, Costa Rica Yucatán, Mexico Sonora, Mexico (3) Dominican Republic (2) Mexico Dominican Republic Hong Kong Singapore (other countries not specified)	Own plant Lease plants 807 from own and other firms Independent suppliers

Continued on next page

Table 5.1 — *Continued*

Company US$ Sales 1990 Key Products and Brands	Location	Type of Activity

Warnaco Group
$545,228,000
  Women's wear
    Olga
    Hathaway
    White Stag
    Speedo
	Warner's de Mexico
	Juarmex, Mexico
	Olguita de Mexico
	Ciales, Puerto Rico
	Cidra, Puerto Rico
	Alajuea, Costa Rica
	Grecia, Costa Rica
	La Romana, Dominican Republic
	Puerto Cortes, Honduras
	Juarez, Mexico
	Youca, Mexico
	Mexicali, Mexico
	San Luis, Mexico
	Far East
		Subsidiaries
		
		Leased plants (including 807)
		
		Sourcing, imports

Salant Corporation $411,680,000 *Diversified*	Mexico Other not specified	Own and lease factories

Marcade Group
$377,651,000
  Diversified
    Members Only
	No information provided	

Gerber Products
$366,872,000
  Children's wear
    Buster Brown
	Puerto Rico
	Costa Rica
		Subsidiaries

Tultex Corporation $355,377,000 *Fleeced knitted sportswear*	Montego Bay, Jamaica	Plant owned by subsidiary
Oshkosh B'Gosh $323,377,000 *Workwear and children's playwear*	Choloma, Honduras Far East	Subsidiary Sourcing

Bernard Chaus
$291,101,000
  Women's wear
    Chaus
    Josephine Chaus
	South Korea
	Hong Kong
	Taiwan
	Philippines
	Jamaica
	South America
		Independent suppliers (about 160; 96% Far East)

Continued on next page

Table 5.1—*Continued*

Company US$ Sales 1990 Key Products and Brands	Location	Type of Activity
Nike, Inc. $266,100,000 *Athletic wear*	No information provided	
Russ Togs $236,951,000 *Women's wear*	No foreign activity	
Cherokee Group $202,000,000 *Women's wear* Cherokee Code Bleu	Guatemala	Sewing contractors (10% of production)
Hampton Industries $166,884,000 *Men's wear*	Far East	Independent producers
G-III Apparel Group $161,921,000 *Women's wear*	South Korea Hong Kong South America	Independent producers and contractors (43)
Beeba's Creations $158,047,000 *Women's sportswear*	Jamaica Costa Rica Peru (18% of production) India (14%) Sri Lanka (13%) Hong Kong (12%) Costa Rica (8%) Jamaica (6%) Bangladesh (5.5%) Mexico (3%) Brazil (3%) Philippines (<1%) South Korea (<1%) Singapore (<1%) Macau (<1%) Nepal (<1%)	Minority ownership Independent contractors
Garan $145,337,000 *Diversified* Garanimals Rob Roy	San José, Costa Rica	Own plant
Oneita Industries $140,386,000 *Diversified*	No information provided	

Continued on next page

Table 5.1 —*Continued*

Company US$ Sales 1990 Key Products and Brands	Location	Type of Activity
Farah, Inc. $139,616,000 *Men's and boys'* *wear*	Chihuahua, Mexico San Juan, Costa Rica (2) Piedras Negras, Mexico (4) Juarez, Mexico Suva, Fiji	Own plants Leased plants 50% in joint venture
Genesco $134,200,000 *Men's wear*	No foreign activity	
Sanmark-Stardust $124,717,000 *Women's intimate* *wear*	Puerto Rico Mexico	Lease plant 807 production
Superior Surgical $123,002,000 *Work clothes*	No foreign activity	
Oak Hill Sportswear $118,224,000 *Women's wear*	Unspecified	Imports

Source: Company annual reports and 10-K reports.

ies to partial ownership, to importing from independent manufacturers, to licensing, to contracting out the sewing. Sometimes it is difficult to distinguish between the different kinds of production arrangements; in all cases, however, these U.S. companies are actively involved in, and exercising substantial degrees of control over, the overseas firms.

There is a regional pattern in these data. Virtually all the production in Asia, with the exception of that in the Philippines, involves arm's-length transactions. In the Caribbean region and Latin America, we find more direct foreign investment; these countries' government policies—and also U.S. policies pressing for borders more readily opened to U.S. investment—account for this difference. The Caribbean region is used more for simple offshore assembly (807 production), and though this assembly can also be done through contracting arrangements, some U.S. companies have decided to set up their own plants and subsidiaries.

Conclusion

Globalization by U.S. companies is a complicated and multifaceted business. Although production arrangements vary, U.S. apparel manufacturers, along with U.S. retailers, are not passive recipients of globalization. They are actively pursuing global strategies and are supported in doing so by the U.S. government. Thus the "crisis of imports" flooding the U.S. market is not simply the result of the actions of overseas producers. U.S. apparel businesses have played, and continue to play, a major role in creating imports.

Notes

Acknowledgments: Special thanks to Richard Appelbaum, Norma Chinchilla, Nora Hamilton, and Paul Ong for their helpful suggestions on revising this chapter.

1. This historical account was told to us, with variations, by several people involved in the Los Angeles apparel industry (see interviews in the References). We have developed a composite account by combining the various stories.

2. For another exposé of the U.S. government's role in supporting the export of the industry, see Rothstein 1989.

3. The list was derived from Kurt Salmon Associates (KSA), supplemented by two Los Angeles firms omitted from KSA's list (1991). Two of the companies, Levi Strauss and Warnaco, were not publicly held at that time, but they had been and were required to file a 10-K. We also interviewed some privately held companies in Los Angeles that engage in overseas production and found that their overseas contracting practices were similar.

4. Liz Claiborne's international activities are described in fascinating detail in a series of articles in the *New Yorker* (Lardner 1988).

References

American Apparel Manufacturers Association (AAMA). 1991. *Focus: An Economic Profile of the Apparel Industry.* Arlington, Va.: AAMA.

Arpan, Jeffrey S., Jose de la Torre, and Brian Toyne. 1982. *The U.S. Apparel Industry: International Challenge, Domestic Response.* Atlanta: Georgia State University, College of Business Administration.

Cline, William R. 1990. *The Future of World Trade in Textiles and Apparel.* Washington, D.C.: Institute for International Economics.

Fitzgerald, Thomas M., Jr. 1991. Senior Vice President International, CIT Group/Factoring, New York.

Ghadar, Fariborz, William H. Davidson, and Charles S. Feigenoff. 1987. *U.S. Industrial Competitiveness: The Case of the Textile and Apparel Industries.* Lexington, Mass.: Lexington Books.

Glass, Mitchell. 1991. Vice-President of Production, Sourcing, and Scheduling, Cherokee Apparel. Interview conducted with Rich Appelbaum and Gary Gereffi, Sunland, California.

Goldman, Shelly. 1989. Owner, Monarch Knits; former importer, Los Angeles, California.

Gram, Louis R. 1990. President, Operon Distributors; major apparel warehouser, Los Angeles, California.

Hamilton, Carl B., ed. 1990. *The Uruguay Round: Textiles Trade and the Developing Countries.* Washington, D.C.: World Bank.

Hochswender, Woody. 1991. "For the Fashion Industry, Nowhere To Go but Up." *New York Times,* April 8, 1(B), 7(B).

Hyman, Ed. 1990. Production Manager, Nancy Johnson Corporation; importer, now out of business, Los Angeles, California.

Kapler, William G. 1992. Kapler and Associates; industry consultant with experience in Asian production, Santa Monica, California.

Kernaghan, Charles. 1992. *Paying to Lose Our Jobs.* New York: National Labor Committee Education Fund in Support of Worker and Human Rights in Central America.

Klopp, Brent. 1991. Senior Vice-President for Production Planning, Bugle Boy Industries. Interview conducted with Rich Appelbaum, Simi Valley, California.

Krieger, Robert. 1990. Vice-President, Norman Krieger; customs broker and foreign freight forwarder, Los Angeles, California.

Kurt Salmon Associates (KSA). 1991. "Financial Report: Diversified Dominates." *Apparel Industry Magazine* 52 (July): 32–36.

Lardner, James. 1988. "Annals of Business: The Sweater Trade." *New Yorker,* January 11, 39–73; January 18, 57–73.

Oman, Charles P. 1989. *New Forms of Investment in Developing Country Industries: Mining, Petrochemicals, Automobiles, Textiles, Food.* Paris: Development Centre of OECD.

Rothstein, Richard. 1989. *Keeping Jobs in Fashion: Alternatives to the Euthanasia of the U.S. Apparel Industry.* Washington, D.C.: Economic Policy Institute.

Shapiro, Bruce M. 1991. Manager, National/International Key Accounts, California Mart, Los Angeles, California.

United Nations. 1987. *Transnational Corporations in the Man-Made Fibre, Textile and Clothing Industries.* New York: United Nations.

U.S. Department of Labor. 1990. *Trade and Employment Effects of the Caribbean Basin Economic Recovery Act.* Washington, D.C.: Government Printing Office.

PART II

Asia

The Development Process of the Hong Kong Garment Industry: A Mature Industry in a Newly Industrialized Economy

Ho-Fuk Lau and Chi-Fai Chan

Apparel is a mature product, meaning it has undergone various evolutionary stages. According to our study in 1991, the international movement of garment manufacture follows a trickle-down pattern — the flow of production has followed distinct stages in what we call a product's "life cycle," and "trickles down" from country to country according to varying levels of economic development.[1] We have labeled this theoretical framework "product life cycle and international production" and have used it to analyze Hong Kong's garment industry.

Globalization in manufacturing has become a world trend for many industries, particularly among those industries in the "maturity" stage of the product life cycle. The apparel industry has reached this level; there is little capacity for further growth. Because garment manufacturing is so labor intensive, innovation in machinery and production processes can only marginally improve productivity. In this chapter we follow the garment industry's path to maturity, by examining the underlying forces of its international movement.

"New" Theories of International Trade?

After four years of investigating varying levels of success for nations involved in international competition, Michael Porter concluded that national prosperity was created, not inherited; a nation's competitiveness depended on the capacity of its industries to innovate and upgrade (1990). He suggested four major attributes ("diamond" factors)—factor conditions, demand conditions, related and supporting industries, and industrial structure combined with cultural context—that determine a nation's ability to foster and sustain an industry's global competitive advantage. Although this formula provides a dynamic basis for analyzing competitiveness, the international movement of a product's manufacture must still be explained. To understand world trade and investment in the garment industry, we examine market orientation (the "internationalization process") and product orientation (the "international product life cycle").

Several studies have concluded that export-manufacturing firms attracted by a foreign market's sales potential generally increase their foreign involvement in an incremental process (Bilkey 1978; Cavusgil and Nevin 1980; Johanson and Vahlne 1977; Johanson and Wiedersheim-Paul 1975; Rugman 1980). In the early stage, these firms export goods to foreign clients. In time, some firms set up wholly owned subsidiaries inside these foreign target markets. These firms are involved in international trade during the early stages of their internationalization process and became multinational corporations.

Other studies found that the manufacture of some products moved from industrialized to less-developed countries in a predictable pattern (Vernon 1966; Wells 1968). To generalize this phenomenon, we can assume that a truly innovative product will be invented, produced, and marketed in an industrialized country during the introductory and growth stages of the product life cycle. Later, in an effort to reduce production costs, some firms (during the product's maturity stage) will transfer the product's manufacture to less-developed countries. It will then be exported back to the industrialized country where the product was invented. It is this quest for lower production costs that has created international trade. Some of these firms may want to internalize their comparative advantage by establishing manufacturing subsidiaries in a developing country (see Figure 6.1).

A Dynamic View of International Trade and the Formation of Transnational Corporations

For a developing country with a small domestic market, the internationalization process tends to follow the trickle-down, or waterfall, pattern of the "international product life cycle" (Keegan 1989). Firms in such countries typically do not have access to highly sophisticated technology and are therefore unlikely, if not unable, to invent truly innovative products. Instead, they acquire production knowledge for mature products from industrialized countries. Because of the limitations of a small domestic market, firms in developing countries need to sell their products abroad. When their production costs become less competitive in the global market, firms tend to transfer production to other countries with even lower production costs. Generally, when a product has reached the maturity stage in industrialized countries, it is still in the introductory stage in developing countries. According to Porter, firms whose main advantages in the global economy are lower-order advantages, such as low labor costs and inexpensive raw materials, are anything but unique and are easily replaced (1990, 49). When the product has

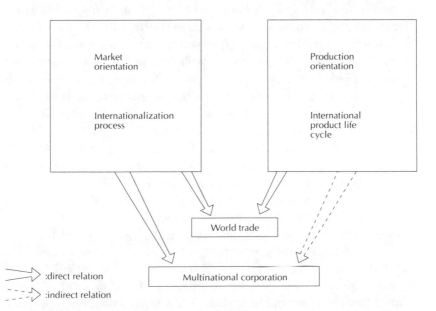

Figure 6.1 A Dynamic View of International Trade and the Formation of TNCs

reached the maturity stage in developing countries and its production has been transferred to less-developed countries, the product will then reach the growth stage in these countries. At the maturity stage, because of the lack of technological support, firms in developing countries tend to adopt one or more of the following strategies: improving production skills and moving "up-market" (making higher-end products), actively pursuing offshore production, moving to "downstream" value activities (marketing and services), and seeking production agreements for a new mature product (Table 6.1).

The Hong Kong Garment Industry

In the early postwar years Hong Kong was primarily an entrepôt for mainland China. The large influx of immigrants from China in the late 1940s brought capital and technology; the first cotton spinning mill was established in 1947 by a Shanghainese industrialist. The United Nations's 1951 embargo on China seriously disrupted entrepôt trade. Hong Kong began vigorously developing its manufacturing sector in the early 1950s, taking advantages of the skills and capital of the Chinese immigrants. Because of Hong Kong's many disadvantages with regard to industrial expansion—including a lack of natural resources, a relatively small domestic market, and a scarce supply of land for industrial use—its manufacturing industries have been involved predominantly in producing "light" consumer goods.

The manufacturing sector was the largest employer in Hong Kong until 1990, when it was overtaken by the wholesale, retail, import/ export trades, restaurants, and hotels sector. From 1960 to 1980 (except for a brief period in 1966) manufacturing accounted for 40 to 50 percent of total employment. By 1990, however, its share of total employment had fallen to 29.5 percent (Hong Kong Industry Department 1991a, 6). Manufacturing industries in Hong Kong consist of mainly small and medium-sized factories.

Because of increasing automation and the relocation of labor-intensive and lower-end production activities to China, the average number of employees in Hong Kong's industrial establishments dropped from eighteen in 1985 to fifteen in 1990. In 1990 86.1 percent of industrial establishments had fewer than twenty employees, and 94.7 percent had fewer than fifty (Hong Kong Industry Department 1991a). More than half the total manufacturing employment was concentrated in about 5 percent of all firms—the largest establishments, employing fifty or more workers. Many of the smaller operations have become subcontractors for the bigger factories. Approximately 90 percent of local industrial production is aimed at export markets (Hong Kong Industry Department 1991a). Since 1985 the major export markets for Hong Kong–manufactured products have been the United States, the People's Republic of China, Germany, the United Kingdom, and Japan. Hong Kong's main manufacturing industries are textiles, apparel, electronics, household electrical appliances, plastics, and metal products. In 1990 these industries combined employed 572,470 workers (71.3% of total manufacturing employment) and exported US$20.99 billion (at US$1 = HK$7.8) worth of goods (72.5% of total domestic exports).

In terms of export value and employment, apparel has been the largest of Hong Kong's manufacturing industries since 1959. Garment exports as a percentage of all exports have declined gradually since 1978 but have maintained a share of approximately 30 percent (Table 6.2). Garment-industry employment reached a peak of 299,934 workers in 1986 and then dropped to 251,746 in 1990 (Table 6.3). Hong Kong was the world's top exporter of garments during the periods of 1973 to 1977 and 1980 to 1985. Since Italy took the top spot in 1986, Hong Kong has remained the second largest garment exporter by value every year except 1988, when South Korea took second place (Hong Kong Industry Department 1991a, 35). If foreign-owned subsidiaries' exports are counted, Hong Kong has maintained the world leadership in garment exports for more than one decade (KSA 1992).

The Hong Kong garment industry can be divided into two broad sectors: cut-and-sew and knitting. In 1990 about 80 percent of garment workers were engaged in the cut-and-sew sector and 15 percent in knitting. In 1988 more than 80 percent of garment firms employed fewer than fifty people (Table 6.4). Garment factory employment has decreased since the mid-1970s; before that time, average garment-factory employment was more than forty workers. Such employment gradually declined throughout the 1980s, dropping to twenty-six workers in 1990 (Table 6.3). The average factory employment for the garment industry is higher than the average of the overall manufacturing sector, because of the labor-intensive work (Table 6.3); also,

Table 6.1

Product Life Cycle (PLC) and International Production

	PLC in Industrialized Countries		
Industrialized countries	Introductory Stage	Growth Stage	Maturity Stage
	1. Product innovation 2. Commercialization 3. Manufacture	1. Product improvement 2. Manufacture 3. Market expansion	1. R&D on improving product and production process 2. Innovate new product 3. Offshore production
	PLC in Developing Countries		
Developing countries	NA	Import	
	Introductory Stage	Growth Stage	Maturity Stage
	1. Acquire manufacturing skill 2. Manufacture for export	1. Improve manufacturing skill 2. Manufacture for export and local consumption	1. Improve technology and move up-market 2. Prepare manufacturing for another mature product 3. Offshore production 4. Move to down-stream activities (marketing and service)

Less-developed countries	NA	NA	PLC in Less-Developed Countries		
			Introductory Stage	Growth Stage	Maturity Stage
			1. Acquire manufacturing skill 2. Manufacture for export	1. Improve manufacturing skill 2. Manufacture for export and local consumption	1. Improve manufacturing process 2. Manufacture for export and local consumption 3. Prepare for another product

Table 6.2

Export Performance of the Hong Kong Garment Industry: Annual Growth
Rate and as a Percentage of Domestic Exports, 1973–1990

Year	Annual Growth of Garment Export (%)	Annual Growth of Domestic Exports (%)	Garment Export as % of Domestic Exports
1973	21.9	27.7	38.3
1974	17.4	18.0	38.2
1975	16.6	−0.2	44.6
1976	40.1	43.0	38.0
1977	−2.7	7.0	39.7
1978	13.0	16.0	38.6
1979	28.2	37.0	36.0
1980	15.5	22.0	34.1
1981	21.6	18.0	35.2
1982	1.9	3.0	34.7
1983	19.2	26.0	32.9
1984	35.9	32.0	33.9
1985	−3.9	−5.8	34.6
1986	16.2	18.6	33.9
1987	25.2	26.8	33.5
1988	3.0	11.5	30.9
1989	6.8	3.0	32.1
1990	0.4	0.3	31.9

Source: Trade Statistics, various issues.

Note: Based on export value of articles of apparel and clothing accessories, Category
842–848.

labor costs as a percentage of total production costs for the garment
industry are higher than the average of the manufacturing sector (Table 6.5). Labor shortages are a significant threat to the manufacturing
industries. In the clothing sector during the six quarters preceding
1992, approximately 6.4 percent of the industry's jobs remained unfilled. The industry has been permitted to apply for import labor, but
the quota is limited to fill only 16 percent of all vacancies in the
industry (KSA 1992, 14).

At the end of 1990 there were 122 overseas investments in the
textiles and clothing industry, with a total value of approximately
US$423 million (Hong Kong Industry Department 1991b). Among
these foreign investments, 30 were from Japan (US$115 million), 15
were from the United States (US$35 million), 24 were from the
United Kingdom (US$48 million), and 9 were from China (US$35
million). Japan has been the leading source of foreign investment in
Hong Kong's manufacturing industries. In 1990 total foreign invest-

Table 6.3

Number of Establishments and Persons Employed in the Hong Kong
Garment Industry, 1950–1990

Year	Number of Firms	Number of Persons Employed	Average Number of Persons Employed per Firm	
			Clothing Industry	All Manufacturing Industries
1950	41 (2.8)	1,944 (2.4)	47	55
1955	99 (4.1)	4,261 (3.9)	43	45
1960	970 (18.1)	51,918 (23.8)	54	41
1965	1,514 (17.5)	87,454 (25.6)	58	39
1970	3,491 (21.1)	158,025 (28.8)	45	33
1975	8,047 (25.9)	257,595 (37.9)	32	22
1980	9,499 (20.9)	275,818 (30.9)	29	20
1985	10,307 (21.4)	292,789 (34.5)	28	18
1986	10,392 (21.4)	299,932 (34.5)	29	18
1987	10,556 (20.9)	298,377 (34.1)	28	17
1988	10,412 (20.6)	286,659 (33.9)	28	17
1989	9,672 (19.4)	274,732 (34.2)	28	16
1990	9,746 (19.9)	251,746 (34.5)	26	15

Source: Hong Kong Industry Department 1991.

Note: Figures in parentheses denote the percentage share of all manufacturing industries in the respective year.

Table 6.4

Distribution of Hong Kong Garment Factories, by Employment Size, in 1988

Factory Size by Number of Persons Employed	Firms		Persons Employed	
	No.	%	No.	%
1–19	6,999	67.2	45,087	15.7
21–49	1,800	17.3	57,858	20.2
50–99	1,062	10.2	73,449	25.6
100–199	396	3.8	53,359	18.6
200–499	129	1.2	34,882	12.2
500–999	21	0.2	14,384	5.0
1,000 and above	5	0.1	7,640	2.7
Total	10,412	100.0	286,659	100.0

Source: Hong Kong Industry Department 1991a.

Table 6.5

Production Costs in the Garment Industry, 1981–1988

	Value in HK$ millions[a]				
	1981	1985[b]	1986	1987	1988
Consumption of materials, supplies, and industrial services	22,863 (68.3)[c] (73.9)[d]	29,156 (65.2) (69.0)	37,580 (66.9) (71.6)	47,170 (68.1) (72.6)	46,942 (68.0) (73.2)
Labor costs	7,534 (22.5)[c] (17.4)[d]	11,336 (25.3) (20.8)	13,357 (23.8) (19.3)	15,154 (21.9) (17.9)	15,397 (22.3) (17.2)
Other expenses	3,098 (9.2)[c] (8.8)[d]	4,240 (9.5) (10.1)	5,195 (9.3) (9.2)	6,914 (10.0) (9.5)	6,719 (9.7) (9.5)
Total production costs	33,495	44,732	56,132	69,238	69,057

Source: Surveys of Industrial Production, Census and Statistics Department.

[a]US$1 = HK$7.8

[b]The 1985 figures do not include one minor item, ISIC 3274—Hosiery.

[c]Figures in this horizontal row denote the respective percentage share of the column total (production cost of garment industry).

[d]Figures in this horizontal row denote the percentage of value of the manufacturing sector in Hong Kong.

ment, at original cost, was US$3,966 million: 32 percent came from Japan, 31 percent from the United States, 11 percent from China, and 7 percent from the United Kingdom. Nearly 60 percent of total overseas investments were concentrated in four industries: electronics (30%), electrical products (11%), textiles and clothing (11%), and chemical products (8%).

Major products of the garment industry are woven trousers and slacks; woven blouses; woven shirts; knitted sweaters, jackets, and pullovers; and knitted blouses and shirts; combined, they accounted for more than 67 percent of total garment exports during the 1980s. The United States, Germany, the United Kingdom, Japan, and Canada are the five major markets for Hong Kong garments. These five markets consumed about 70 percent of garment exports before 1990 and 80 percent of garment exports during 1985–91. In other words, Hong Kong's garment industry has relied heavily on a very few markets.

The Development Process of Hong Kong's Garment Industry

China's open-door policy began in 1978 (Mun 1979). Making the most of the tremendous benefits the new policy offered, Hong Kong's economy underwent a substantial restructuring during the 1970s. A recent survey indicated that approximately 75 percent of Hong Kong manufacturing firms had production facilities in China, including wholly owned factories, joint ventures, and outward processing plants. Approximately 3.2 percent of firms had factories in other countries (Hong Kong Trade Development Council 1991). A survey conducted during 1991 showed that among 1,256 responding manufacturers, 40.7 percent (511) had investments in southern China's Pearl River Delta region and 5.5 percent (69) were planning to invest there (Federation of Hong Kong Industries 1992). This movement to mainland China has become a popular trend in Hong Kong, particularly among labor-intensive industries.

The garment industry has undergone structural changes as well. The industry's process of development since 1950 can be divided into four stages: technology transfer, growth, early maturity, and maturity (Lau 1988).

Technology Transfer, 1950–1959

In 1950 there were forty-one garment factories in Hong Kong, employing 1,944 workers. Garment exports represented about 4.4 percent of Hong Kong's total exports (HK$162 million). Because of its status as a colony, Hong Kong benefited from easy access to the British market. Hong Kong's cheap labor attracted many foreign firms, especially from the United Kingdom, which was the largest market for Hong Kong garments during this period. After 1959, when the British government imposed quota restrictions on the importation of Hong Kong's cotton textiles, the United States became Hong Kong's largest export market—and is to this day (Luey 1969, 122–23).

In the 1950s Hong Kong's garment firms concentrated on learning the technology of manufacturing. Exported garments were cheap and of poor quality. Fortunately, there was not much competition in the international markets of the 1950s: Hong Kong's current major competitors, Taiwan and South Korea, were less active during this period. In 1955, for example, approximately 75.4 percent of Hong Kong's exports were from the manufacturing sector; for Taiwan and South Korea, the shares were 46.2 and 5.9 percent, respectively.

The garment industry enjoyed rapid growth during the 1950s; by late 1959 garment exports had risen to HK$793 million—five times 1950's exports—and accounted for 34.76 percent of total exports. For the first time, garment exports surpassed those of the textile industry. In 1959 there were 461 garment factories in Hong Kong, employing 28,985 workers (Hong Kong Census and Statistics Department 1969).

Growth, 1960–1973

In 1960 Hong Kong's major garment-export markets, including the United States, Canada, Italy, Norway, West Germany, and Australia, imposed export quotas on textiles and garments. In 1963 the United Kingdom redefined its annual quota by splitting the original four categories into thirty-four (Luey 1969, 124). To cope with the ever-increasing pressure from importing countries, Hong Kong manufacturers used four tactics during this period to increase their competitive edge: developing nonquota markets; moving production offshore (to use other countries' quotas); producing more costly, "up-market" items; and establishing fashion design departments (Lau 1988).

Early Maturity, 1973–1984

In early 1974 the establishment of the Multifiber Arrangement (MFA) placed Hong Kong's textile and garment exports under a highly structured monitoring system. At the same time, garment industries in other Asian countries, particularly South Korea, Taiwan, and mainland China, grew rapidly and became viable competitors in the global market. Hong Kong garment manufacturers tried to cope with the fierce cost competition and the increasing pressure of protectionism by using the tactics outlined above. In the early 1980s many Hong Kong firms moved production operations to mainland China, a trend that has continued. The industry reached the maturity stage during this period, moving its product focus from inexpensive, basic garments to more fashionable, higher-priced ones.

Maturity, Consolidation, and Internationalization, 1985–Present

In early 1985, in order to cut imports from Hong Kong, the U.S. government redefined the term "country of origin" for fabrics and sweaters, creating chaos in the Hong Kong garment industry for some months. The trend toward increased protectionism has continued, and with it the number of restrictions being imposed. Hong Kong's rising costs for garment manufacturing significantly affected its competitiveness; many firms relocated their manufacturing operations during this period to mainland China and other low-cost countries. Hong Kong had gradually evolved from a garment-manufacturing center into a garment-sourcing center. Transnational manufacturing became a common phenomenon.

A Mature Industry in a Newly Industrialized Economy

Results of this study confirmed the findings of Lau's previous research (1988) and also verified the product life cycle and international production framework. Hong Kong's garment industry is now in the latter half of the maturity stage; it is no longer a competitive production base for ready-made garments. Hong Kong's garment manufacturers and traders place orders to factories in China. Among the 180 responding firms in our survey, 78.4 percent subcontracted work to factories in China and 31.7 percent had manufacturing subsidiaries there (Table 6.6). Despite the fact that the majority of Hong Kong's garment exports are monitored by the MFA regime, garment firms have actively pursued establishing manufacturing subsidiaries

Table 6.6

Hong Kong Garment Manufacturing in China

Company Activity	Number of Companies	Percent
Producing garments in China		
With factories in China		
Manufacturing companies	52	28.9
Trading firms	5	2.8
Without factories in China		
Manufacturing companies	45	25.0
Trading firms	39	21.7
Subtotal	141	78.4
Not producing garments in China		
Manufacturing companies	23	12.8
Trading firms	16	8.8
Subtotal	39	21.6
Total	180	100.0

in China. About 43 percent of the responding garment manufacturing firms had factories there. This figure is, however, much lower than the manufacturing sector's average; a 1991 survey conducted by the Hong Kong Trade Development Council showed that approximately 75 percent of all manufacturing firms had production facilities in China. Reasons cited for transferring production to China included low production costs (cheap labor), an ample supply of workers, and cheap land (Table 6.7). Quota was never a motive behind the move to China, because they are more easily obtained in Hong Kong than in China (*t*-test significant level at 0.001 and 0.01 for garment manufacturers and garment traders, respectively). The study also indicated that Hong Kong's garment industry reached the late maturity stage by 1985; the majority of the FDI (foreign direct investment) of the responding garment manufacturing firms fell into this period. Forty-six firms (or 78% of the fifty-nine garment-manufacturing firms having FDI) set up their first offshore factory during this period (Table 6.8). China's Guangdong Province was the most popular choice for offshore production facilities; only seven of the firms with factories in foreign countries did not have plants in China (cross-tabulation was used to eliminate firms that had factories in more than one country).

Compared to China, Hong Kong has a more highly skilled labor force and a better supply of materials (Table 6.7). In order to main-

Table 6.7

Hong Kong Garment Manufacturing Firms' Satisfaction with Hong Kong and China as Bases of Production

Factors	Base of Production	Mean	Number of Cases	t Value
Cheap labor	Hong Kong	2.1889	90	−17.59**
	China	4.6111		
Ample supply of labor	Hong Kong	2.2111	90	−15.64**
	China	4.8333		
Cheap land	Hong Kong	1.9213	89	−16.09**
	China	4.7079		
Efficient labor	Hong Kong	3.8556	90	2.98*
	China	3.3222		
Sufficient managerial manpower	Hong Kong	3.8427	89	5.01**
	China	2.9663		
Better labor skill	Hong Kong	4.2299	87	5.29**
	China	3.4368		
Sufficient supply of materials	Hong Kong	4.5056	89	10.00**
	China	2.6292		
Low cost of materials/supplies	Hong Kong	3.2273	88	−0.28
	China	3.2727		
Ease of quota attainment	Hong Kong	4.0235	85	7.98**
	China	2.4353		
Potential of local market	Hong Kong	3.3333	78	1.11
	China	3.1538		
Good transportation network	Hong Kong	4.7303	89	13.24**
	China	2.8876		
Government efficiency/ support	Hong Kong	4.1136	88	10.84**
	China	2.4773		
Tax concessions	Hong Kong	3.9878	82	3.93**
	China	3.3537		
Political stability	Hong Kong	4.1977	86	7.11**
	China	3.0349		
Cultural affinity	Hong Kong	4.5000	86	7.46**
	China	3.5698		
Overall satisfaction level	Hong Kong	3.4588	85	−1.31
	China	3.6706		

Note: A t value of 1 = extremely unsatisfied; 6 = extremely satisfied.

** significant at 0.001 level.

 * significant at 0.01 level.

Table 6.8

Establishment of Hong Kong Garment Manufacturing Firms' First Offshore Factories, by Year

Location[a]	1960–1964	1965–1969	1970–1974	1975–1979	1980–1984	1985–1989	1990	1991	Total
China									
Guangdong Province	—	—	—	1[b]	4	31	8	1	45
Other provinces	—	—	—	—	—	1	—	1	2
Taiwan	1	1	—	—	—	—	—	—	2
Macao	—	—	1	1	—	2	1	—	5
Singapore	—	—	1	—	1	1	0	0	3
Malaysia	—	—	—	—	—	2	1	0	3
Philippines	—	—	—	—	1	1	2	—	4
Thailand	—	1	—	—	—	—	—	—	1
Sri Lanka	—	—	—	—	2	—	—	—	2
United Kingdom	—	—	—	—	—	1	—	—	1
Other	—	—	1	—	1	3	1	—	6

[a]Firms may have factories in more than one country. In China a firm may have factories in both Guangdong and other provinces.
[b]Established in 1979.

tain leadership, some Hong Kong garment manufacturers have diversified into other types of garments. Approximately 63 percent of the responding firms claimed that they produced more than one major product (27.5% produced two, 12.5% produced three, and 12.5% produced four). Further investigation into the relationship between different garment products showed that a manufacturer who produced more woven shirts (11–100%) would also produce more woven blouses (11–100%). Chi-square value was not significant for other combinations of products. Manufacturers of woven shirts were expanding their product lines to include woven blouses, a more value-added product. In addition, many Hong Kong garment manufacturing firms tried to upgrade quality and improve efficiency by introducing automatic machinery, computerized equipment, and new management techniques.

Because Hong Kong manufacturing firms do not possess the technology necessary to create new products or to improve existing ones, they have tried to improve their competitiveness by providing more services. Moving to the downstream value activities was one alternative. For instance, only 46.7 percent of garment manufacturing firms considered manufacturing their most important activity; 29.2 percent of firms cited sales and 16.7 percent cited trading as most important. In addition to offshore production, some garment manufacturing firms (26.7%) established sales subsidiaries in their major markets, switching their emphasis to selling directly to visiting buyers and foreign firms' buying offices (Table 6.9). By doing so, these firms provided more packaging and shipping services than firms selling indirectly through local trading agencies.

Conclusion

The garment industry is labor intensive and involves relatively low levels of technology; when the industry reached maturity in industrialized countries, it moved to developing countries. This international production movement follows a predictable pattern that we have examined through the different stages of the product life cycle in accordance with the economic development stages of the country. Garment manufacturing in Hong Kong took off in 1959 and reached maturity in late 1970s. Since then the industry has begun to move

Table 6.9

Distribution Channels of Hong Kong
Garment Manufacturing Firms

	Selling in Hong Kong					
	20% or Less of Firm's Sales		21–50% of Firm's Sales		51–100% of Firm's Sales	
	No. of Firms	%	No. of Firms	%	No. of Firms	%
Local exporters	31	25.8	20	16.7	18	15.0
Buying office of foreign firms	18	15.0	36	30.0	26	21.7
Buyers visit Hong Kong regularly	21	17.5	37	30.8	32	26.7
Others	3	2.5	N/A	N/A	2	1.7
	Selling in the Marketplace					
	20% or less of Firm's Sales		21–50% of Firm's Sales		51–100% of Firm's Sales	
	No. of Firms	%	No. of Firms	%	No. of Firms	%
Importers	18	15.0	23	19.2	5	4.2
Wholesalers	14	11.7	15	12.5	2	1.7
Retailers	13	10.8	14	11.7	2	1.7
Firm's foreign sales subsidiary	10	8.3	14	11.7	13	10.8

production processes to other low-cost, less-developed countries, despite the monitoring of the MFA regime.

Under the Sino-British agreement, Hong Kong will have its independent entity in GATT and the MFA after Britain returns Hong Kong to China on July 1, 1997. Therefore, Hong Kong garment firms can maintain their quota after 1997. They will diversify their production to countries where they can obtain quotas and at a lower cost. Large garment firms will maintain their headquarters in Hong Kong for production planning, sourcing, and financing activities. But smaller firms may need to relocate both their factories and their offices to mainland China in order to be competitive. Operating cost would become too high for small and medium-sized manufacturing firms in Hong Kong by the end of the 1990s.

By extending the concept of the product life cycle in international trade developed by Raymond Vernon (1966) and Louis T. Wells (1968), and by incorporating Michael Porter's (1990) argument on national "diamond" factors, we have developed the product life cycle and international production framework to explain this movement of a product's manufacture. One of the basic assumptions of this framework is that the technological gap between industrialized and less-developed countries still exists, though to a lesser degree than before. Thus, a truly innovative product will be invented, manufactured, and marketed in industrialized countries. Successful transnational firms may aim at more than one market in launching a global product, but the target markets will usually be industrialized countries. A second assumption is that in the early maturity stage in industrialized countries the product will be introduced to developing countries for manufacturing. The product, particularly in terms of its manufacture, will also go through the introductory, growth, and maturity stages in developing countries. When the product reaches the growth stage in the developing countries, it will be moved to less-developed countries for manufacturing. When the industry reaches maturity in the developing countries, it will be in the growth stage in the less-developed countries. This trickle-down approach springs mainly from production cost concerns. If an industrialized, major-market country's government imposes trade barriers, then the operating, or "landed," cost will determine the manufacturing location of the product. In other words, if trade barriers make production in less-developed countries prohibitively costly, then production will move back to an industrialized country.

This framework is useful in analyzing the movement of the manufacture of any products requiring, like apparel, labor-intensive work and low levels of technology, such as toys and shoes. The framework can be applied to Hong Kong's garment industry, but more studies are required to test the framework's applicability in other developing countries, in less-developed countries, and for industries other than apparel.

Note

1. A structured questionnaire was sent in early 1991 to two thousand garment companies registered with the Hong Kong Textile Controls Registra-

tion (TCR) in 1990. TCR is published annually by Hong Kong's government and includes firms (in both the manufacturing and trading sectors) holding quotas for textiles and/or garment products during that calendar year. Hong Kong is an export-oriented city, and the TCR list covers most of the garment-manufacturing firms there. There were 10,291 companies listed in the 1990 TCR. According to official statistics, there were 9,746 garment firms in Hong Kong in 1990.

There were 234 responses to the survey questionnaire. Among the 180 usable questionnaires, 55 were from garment-manufacturing firms, 60 were from garment-trading firms, and 65 were from garment-manufacturing and trading firms. Although our response rate of 11.7 percent was low (the response rate for this type of study in Hong Kong is typically very low [Chen 1985]), the number of usable questionnaires was large enough for statistical analysis. The responding companies represented a wide spectrum of the Hong Kong garment-manufacturing firms in terms of number of years in operation, garment sales turnover, and number of workers employed.

A systematic sampling method was used for this survey. Cross-tabulation was used to identify the companies that had offshore factories. Chi-square was used to test the relationship between men's woven shirts and other major garment products. Paired t-test was used to compare the reasons for manufacturing garments in China and Hong Kong.

References

Bilkey, Warren J. 1978. "An Attempted Integration of the Literature on the Export Behaviour of Firms." *Journal of International Business Studies* (spring/summer): 33–46.

Cavusgil, S. Tamer, and John R. Nevin. 1980. "A Conceptualization of the Initial Involvement in International Marketing." In *Theoretical Development in Marketing,* edited by C. W. Lamb and P. M. Dunne. Chicago: American Marketing Association.

Chen, Edward K. Y. 1985. "Multinationals from Hong Kong." In *The New Multinationals: The Spread of Third World Enterprises,* edited by Edward K. Y. Chen, 88–136. New York: John Wiley and Sons.

Federation of Hong Kong Industries. 1992. *Hong Kong's Industrial Investment in the Pearl River Delta: 1991 Survey among Members of the Federation of Hong Kong Industries.* Hong Kong.

Hong Kong Census and Statistics Department. 1969. *Hong Kong Statistics, 1947–1967.* Hong Kong.

Hong Kong Industry Department. 1991a. *Hong Kong's Manufacturing Industries, 1990.* Hong Kong.

————. 1991b. *1991 Survey of Overseas Investment in Hong Kong's Manufacturing Industries*. Hong Kong.

Hong Kong Trade Development Council. 1991. *Survey of Hong Kong Domestic Exports, Re-exports, and Triangular Trade*. Hong Kong.

Johanson, Jan, and Jan-Erik Vahlne. 1977. "The Internationalization Process of the Firm: A Model of Knowledge Development and Increasing Foreign Market Commitments." *Journal of International Business Studies* 8 (spring/summer): 23–32.

Johanson, Jan, and Finn Wiedersheim-Paul. 1975. "The Internationalization of the Firm: Four Swedish Cases." *Journal of Management Studies* 12 (1–3): 305–22.

Keegan, Warren J. 1989. *Global Marketing Management*. Englewood Cliffs, N.J.: Prentice-Hall.

Kurt Salmon Associates (KSA). 1992. "The Hong Kong Textile and Clothing Industry: A Techno-economic and Market Research Study." Report prepared for the Industry Department of Hong Kong.

Lau, Ho-Fuk. 1988. "Cooperation between Hong Kong and China Enterprises: A View from the Evolution of the Hong Kong Garment Industry." In *Enterprise Operations and Management Mechanisms*, edited by Shu-Liau Zhou and K. C. Mun, 184–91. Beijing: Economic Management Publishing Department, Chinese Academy of Social Sciences.

Luey, Paul. 1969. "Hong Kong Investment." In *Foreign Investment and Industrialization in Singapore*, edited by Helen Hughes and P. S. You, 112–39. Canberra: Australian National University Press.

Mun, Kin-Chok. 1979. "Hong Kong Investment in East Asia: Underlying Pattern and Motivation." In *Proceedings of the Academy of International Business*, 494–502. Asia-Pacific Dimensions of International Business, Hawaii.

Porter, Michael E. 1990. *The Competitive Advantage of Nations*. New York: Free Press.

Rugman, Alan M. 1980. "A New Theory of the Multinational Enterprise: Internationalization versus Internalization." *Columbia Journal of World Business*, spring, 23–29.

Vernon, Raymond. 1966. "International Investment and International Trade in the Product Cycle." *Quarterly Journal of Economics* 80 (May): 190–207.

Wells, Louis T., Jr. 1968. "A Product Life Cycle for International Trade?" *Journal of Marketing* 5 (July): 1–6.

Chapter 7

The Globalization of Taiwan's Garment Industry

Gary Gereffi and Mei-Lin Pan

Since embarking on the path of export-oriented industrialization in the mid-1960s, Taiwan has been firmly entrenched as one of the leading textile and apparel exporters in the Pacific Rim. Currently, Taiwan ranks behind Hong Kong and the People's Republic of China and before South Korea among the "Big Four" Asian exporters; the Big Four accounted for more than half of U.S. apparel imports from the Pacific Rim by volume and nearly three-fifths by value in 1991 (see Chapter 2). Taiwan's role in the global garment industry is changing dramatically, however. Like Japan, Korea, and Hong Kong, Taiwan has confronted rising wage rates, labor shortages, and sharp currency appreciations that have diminished its international competitiveness as an exporter of low-wage, labor-intensive consumer goods. Taiwan's aggressive move toward a more diversified and industrially upgraded export profile has had a profound impact on the thousands of workers and myriad firms that make up the island's declining apparel sector.

Taiwan is part of a new international division of labor in the Pacific Rim: Taiwan's garment shipments to developed countries are being replaced by its exports of textile inputs to successive waves of new Third World apparel producers, especially China. These trade patterns are linked to the multifaceted role of foreign capital in Taiwan's apparel industry. Although there has been some foreign direct investment in the garment industry in Taiwan, a far more important trend in recent years has been the rapid growth of outward investments by Taiwanese firms busily establishing production and export platforms in a multitude of Asian countries (as well as in various nations in the Caribbean Basin). These transnational "triangle manufacturing" networks are an essential feature of today's global apparel industry. Taiwan's erstwhile exporters are being transformed into intermediaries between foreign buyers and new producers in low-wage nations that have sufficient quotas to supply protected developed-country markets.

Overseas investments by Taiwan's manufacturers are only half the story of foreign capital in the apparel industry. Foreign buyers provide the vital link between Taiwan's highly efficient manufacturers and their ability to penetrate export markets. Taiwan's retail buying offices spread the country's triangle sourcing networks throughout the Pacific Rim. We found that China is surprisingly unimportant as a sourcing site for the apparel orders that come into Taiwan, because most retailers channel their China trade through their Hong Kong buying offices.

Globalization has had a significant impact on workers and industrial districts in Taiwan. As local production networks are dismantled because of the internationalization of Taiwan's apparel industry, employment patterns and working conditions in the industry have changed. This trend has had major implications not only for the kinds of jobs that will be available in the future but also for Taiwan's long-term development prospects.

The Growth and Shifting International Role of the Garment Industry in Taiwan

The expansion of the garment industry mirrors the evolution of economic development in Taiwan in the postwar era. Import-substitution industrialization (ISI) prepared the way for subsequent phases of export-oriented industrialization (EOI), in which exports evolved from simple, labor-intensive items to more sophisticated, high-quality consumer and intermediate goods (Gereffi and Wyman 1990). The industrial development of Taiwan's garment industry, and the corresponding changes in its international trade position, can be categorized into four periods.

Initial ISI, 1949–1965

The first period of Taiwan's economic development extended from the time the Kuomintang party fled mainland China and moved to Taiwan at the end of the 1940s, through the initial phase of ISI, to the termination of American foreign aid in the mid-1960s. The garment industry was given a high priority by Taiwan's government in the First Stage Economic Development Plan beginning in 1953 (Chen 1989). Using imported cotton and other raw materials, garment production mainly supplied domestic needs. A large component of the domestic market consisted of military and school uniforms, so the garments produced in these years were primarily standardized goods rather than fashion items.

Initial EOI, 1966–1973

The second period was the start of EOI in Taiwan. A key factor for the development of the garment industry in this phase was the establishment of Taiwan's upstream (synthetic fibers) and mid-stream (spinning, weaving, dyeing, finishing, and knitting) industries in the textile/apparel complex. These backward linkages ensured the supply of high-quality inputs for the manufacture of garments and accessories (stockings, neckties, gloves, scarves, etc.). Taiwan's apparel exports were predominantly directed toward the United States.

"Booming" EOI, 1974–1987

In 1974 the Multifiber Arrangement (MFA) was first implemented by developed countries to "manage" the international trade of garments (Yoffie 1983; Dickerson 1991). Within the MFA, individual quotas were negotiated in bilateral agreements that set precise limits on the quantity of textile and clothing products that could be exported from one country to another. Quotas did not stop Taiwan's garment exports, however; in fact, they had the opposite effect of stimulating industrial upgrading and export diversification in Taiwan and other East Asian nations. Apparel producers carved out specialized export niches and used their inexpensive labor to convert the apparent obstacles of the quota system into advantages.

The U.S. market grew in importance during this period. In 1980 61 percent (US$527 million) of Taiwan's total apparel exports went to the U.S. market, a substantial increase from 47 percent in 1970 (Moon 1987, 111–12). Labor costs in Taiwan began to rise sharply in the 1980s, however. State legislation known as the Labor Standards Law, dealing with workers' wages, health, and safety, was enacted in 1984, along with other policies to regulate business activities. To confront these changes, the garment industry extended its domestic subcontracting networks to sustain profits (Shieh 1990).

Expanding Overseas Investments, 1988–Present

The factors favoring Taiwan's garment industry have deteriorated steadily in recent years. Taiwan's exchange rate vis-à-vis the U.S. dollar plummeted from forty in 1985 to twenty-six in 1990. In the late 1980s the problem with quotas was not the limits placed on garment production, but rather the fact that total output in Taiwan fell short of the quota levels set in previous years (because the cost of apparel exported from Taiwan was becoming too high). Given the appreciation of the New Taiwan (NT) dollar, labor shortages, international protectionism, and competition from other developing countries, Taiwan's garment industry faced three alternatives in this period (the first two of which are not mutually exclusive): internationalization, industrial upgrading, or exit from the industry (bankruptcy or disinvestment). Extensive outward investments by Taiwanese garment entrepreneurs spread from China and Southeast Asia to Caribbean Basin countries (Mexico, the Caribbean islands, and Central America). Because of its cheap labor and geographical proximity, investments in China were well under way (usually passing through Hong Kong as a financial intermediary) before Taiwanese political officials approved these capital transfers in 1989.

The decline in Taiwan's garment sector is evident in production and trade data. In contrast to Taiwan's light manufacturing production index—which increased by more than 50 percent during the first half of the 1980s and remained stable in the latter half of the decade—the textile index fell by nearly 10 percent from 1986 to 1990, while the wearing apparel production index plummeted by 25 percent (CEPD 1991, 90). This decline coincides with the sharp appreciation of the NT dollar after 1986.

Trade statistics are even more revealing. Textile and clothing exports, as a share of Taiwan's total merchandise exports, fell from 25 percent in 1965 to 15 percent in 1990. The other members of Asia's Big Four experienced relatively smaller declines in the relative importance of their textile and clothing exports during this twenty-five-year period: Korea's textile/apparel products dropped from 27 percent of its total merchandise exports in 1965 to 22 percent in 1990; in Hong Kong the decline was from 52 percent to 39 percent; and China shifted the least, from 29 percent to 27 percent (World Bank 1992, 248–49). These trends do not necessarily reflect the peak years of textile and apparel exports in these countries, because they became major participants in the global industry at different times. The apogee for textile and apparel exports in Hong Kong was during the 1960s; for Korea and Taiwan it occurred in the mid-1970s; and in China the upswing has extended from the late 1980s into the 1990s.

The new role of Taiwan's textile and apparel industry in the Pacific Rim is highlighted by the changing composition of its exports since 1975 (see Table 7.1). From 1975 to 1986 Taiwan's exports of apparel and accessories represented more than 55 percent of overall textile product exports, yarn and fabrics comprised slightly over 40 percent, and textile fibers made up 1 to 4 percent of the total. In the

Table 7.1

Composition of Taiwan's Textile and Apparel Exports, 1975–1992

	Textile Fibers		Yarn and Fabrics		Apparel and Accessories		Total	
Year	%	US$ millions	%	US$ millions	%	US$ millions	%	US$ millions
1975	1.1	17	41.7	649	57.2	891	100.0	1,557
1980	2.5	109	41.4	1,791	56.1	2,427	100.0	4,327
1985	3.7	232	40.2	2,516	56.1	3,512	100.0	6,260
1986	3.6	278	40.6	3,102	55.8	4,264	100.0	7,644
1987	3.5	329	43.8	4,152	52.7	4,996	100.0	9,477
1988	4.6	448	47.4	4,638	48.0	4,704	100.0	9,790
1989	5.9	615	50.5	5,216	43.6	4,498	100.0	10,329
1990	5.9	603	57.5	5,912	36.6	3,772	100.0	10,287
1991	5.5	654	58.6	7,030	35.9	4,308	100.0	11,992
1992[a]	5.9	470	61.2	4,878	32.9	2,626	100.0	7,974

Source: Taiwan Textile Federation, *Statistics on Taiwan Textile and Apparel Industries,* various years.

[a]January through August.

next six years, however, the stable export profile of the preceding twelve years was radically transformed. By 1992 Taiwan's apparel and accessory exports had fallen to one-third the total for textile products, while yarn and fabrics had soared to 61 percent and textile fiber exports stood at 6 percent. In absolute terms, Taiwan's apparel and accessory exports reached their peak value of US$5 billion in 1987; this total fell to US$4.3 billion by 1991. Intermediate exports of yarn and fabrics pulled nearly even with overseas sales of finished apparel by 1988, and since that year textile intermediates have surged well ahead of finished apparel to lead Taiwan's exports of textile products.

In the international division of labor of the Pacific Rim's textile and apparel complex, Taiwan thus has shifted from exporting fin- ished apparel for developed-country markets (mainly the United States) to supplying intermediate textile products to China and, to a much smaller but increasing degree, emerging Southeast Asian gar- ment exporters. In 1991 63 percent of Taiwan's declining apparel exports (totaling US$2.2 billion) and 44 percent of its accessories (US$347 million) were still destined for the United States. In that same year, however, Hong Kong received the bulk of Taiwan's grow- ing exports of fabrics (46%, or US$2.4 billion), yarns (43%, or US$756 million), and fibers (36%, or US$235 million) (TTF 1992). Because Hong Kong is the primary trade conduit to China, Taiwan was indirectly supplying China's booming garment-export industry with these textile inputs. This impression is confirmed by Hong Kong trade figures, which show that reexports of textiles shipped from Taiwan to China via Hong Kong increased more than sixfold, from US$415 million in 1986 to US$2.6 billion in 1991 (TTF 1992, 64). Taiwan's new role as an intermediate goods exporter is clearly established by the fact that in 1991 Taiwan's US$2.6 billion of textile reexports to China through Hong Kong exceeded the country's US$2.2 billion of finished apparel exports to the United States.

Recent Trends in Foreign Direct Investment

Foreign capital in the garment industry in Taiwan comes from both overseas Chinese and foreign national investors. According to the Investment Commission of Taiwan's Ministry of Economic Affairs, there were 208 cases of inward foreign investment in the garment and footwear industries from 1952 to 1992, totaling US$82.3 million (MOEA 1992, 5). Overseas Chinese investors, almost exclusively from Hong Kong, comprise 62 percent of the cases but only 35 percent of the value of foreign capital in these industries. Japan accounts for the majority of the foreign national investments, by both volume and value. Although foreign direct investment in Taiwan's apparel and footwear industries grew by US$25.7 million between 1988 and 1992—virtually all of which came from foreign nationals—it remains an insignificant portion (far less than 1%) of all foreign direct investment coming into the economy. Furthermore, although 90 percent of the foreign-owned garment firms in Taiwan were set up to supply overseas markets, their export total accounted for only 4 to 7 percent of garment exports from Taiwan in the 1980s (MOEA 1990, 12, 60).

In terms of foreign capital, the most significant trend for Taiwan's garment industry has been the rapid expansion of outward flows of foreign direct investment in recent years. Overseas investment in low-wage countries is one of the main alternatives for Taiwanese apparel companies in dealing with high labor costs, an appreciating currency, quota restrictions, and shrinking profits. Overseas investment by Taiwanese capital is not a new story, although before the late 1980s most of these investments were disguised to escape Taiwan's strict controls on outflows of foreign exchange.

Asia has been the most popular location for Taiwan's manufacturers. According to official data, Hong Kong, Singapore, and Southeast Asian nations such as the Philippines, Indonesia, Thailand, and Malaysia accounted for more than 80 percent of the cases of foreign direct investment by Taiwanese garment and footwear firms from 1959 to 1991. Central American and African countries made up the remaining investments (MOEA 1992). Besides ample cheap labor to reduce production costs, these Asian countries also possessed the garment quotas needed to export to the United States and other developed countries adhering to the protectionist policies of the MFA.

China has become the top priority for Taiwanese overseas investors since 1988. The garment and footwear industries ranked third in popularity for Taiwanese investors in mainland China (behind plastic and rubber products and electronic and electrical appliances). In 1991 the number of cases and the value of Taiwan's outward investments in China exceeded the total amount of Taiwanese foreign direct investment in the rest of the world combined; in the first quarter of 1992 Taiwan's investments in China were twice the total for all other countries (MOEA 1992, 57–62). Abundant cheap labor is one of the main reasons for locating in China; the average wage rate there was only one-tenth that of Taiwan (Huang 1990, 21). When other production costs, such as raw materials, machinery, transportation charges, and taxes, are considered, a garment made in China costs about one-fourth as much as an equivalent item made in Taiwan. Net profits for Taiwanese garment manufacturers that export from China are around 15 percent, a rate much higher than what typically can be obtained by similar firms in Taiwan. If political relations between Taiwan and the mainland remain cordial, the importance of China for Taiwan's garment industry seems destined to be even greater in the future.

The Taiwanese firms in China retain strong links with Taiwan. As we already have seen in the discussion of trade flows, Taiwan's exports of textile products (fabrics, yarns, and fibers) to China via Hong Kong have skyrocketed in recent years. Many of Taiwan's exports to China are being used by Taiwanese firms located on the mainland. A survey of Taiwanese investments in China commissioned by Taiwan's Ministry of Economic Affairs found that 70 percent of the raw materials and 66 percent of the machinery used by Taiwanese garment companies located in China were imported by third parties from Taiwan. Furthermore, Taiwanese investors in the mainland are given special concessions by the Chinese government not offered to other foreign investors. Enterprises from Taiwan can be 100 percent Taiwanese-owned, 50 percent of their output can be sold in China's domestic market, and the firms are granted a discount for the usage of land in setting up factories (Huang 1990, 14–15; Liou and Chen 1992, 140). The privilege of selling one-half of their output to China's giant domestic market is especially important, because it increases the likelihood that Taiwanese entrepreneurs will make profits. Thus, China has become a critical offshore production base for Taiwan's textile exporters as well as for the garment entrepreneurs that have transferred many of their factories to the other side of the Taiwan Straits.

Overseas Buying Offices and Triangle Sourcing Networks

Although outward investments by Taiwanese manufacturers and the emergence of China as one of the world's biggest export platforms are central features in the globalization of the garment industry, the key role of commercial capital in the Pacific Rim has been relatively ignored. Today's integrated system of global production and trade initially led to a focus on the increased importance of international subcontracting in the world economy. As traditionally defined, *international subcontracting* is "the strategy whereby transnational corporations assign the most labor-intensive phases of production of a shirt, a car, or a semiconductor to countries where the labor costs are lowest" (Gereffi 1993, 69). This conception of a "new international division of labor," however, is to a large extent already outmoded in East Asia (Fröbel, Heinrichs, and Kreye 1980). It mainly applied to the early stage of EOI, in which there was an emphasis on low-wage, assembly-oriented production in foreign-owned factories located in specially designated export-processing zones.

By contrast, one of the most distinctive traits of contemporary East Asian EOI is that local private firms (not transnational corporations) are the main exporters of finished consumer goods. The Asian factories that make these products are involved in contract-manufacturing relationships with the foreign buyers who place the orders. In this form of "specification contracting," local firms carry out production according to complete instructions issued by the buyers and branded companies that design the goods; the output is then distributed and marketed abroad by trading companies, brand-named merchandisers, large retailers, or their agents. This type of production system, which has been called a "buyer-driven global commodity chain," is common in a wide range of labor-intensive, consumer-goods industries such as garments, footwear, toys, and consumer electronics (Gereffi 1994). Whereas domestic firms are in charge of the decentralized manufacturing stages, foreign capital tends to control the more profitable export and marketing networks.

The garment industry is an ideal case for studying the dynamics of East Asian EOI and buyer-driven commodity chains. The fact that the textile and apparel industries are the first step in the industrialization process of most nations, coupled with the prevalence of developed-country protectionism in this sector, has led to the unparalleled diversity of garment exporters in the Third World. In the mid-1980s clothing accounted for more than one-fifth of all Third World manufactured exports, with East Asian economies dominating the field. Together East Asia's Big Four accounted for nearly 75 percent of all clothing imports by value to the United States in 1980 and 60 percent in 1988, compared with a total share for Latin America (excluding Central America and the Caribbean) of less than 10 percent in both years (Gereffi 1993, 75). Why have East Asian nations been so much more successful than other garment producers in penetrating the world's largest market, the United States? The answer rests in large part on the effectiveness with which East Asian exporters have mastered the art of "specification contracting" by meeting (and anticipating) the needs of U.S. buyers.

Our analysis of this process in Taiwan focuses on the main companies that coordinate buyer-driven commodity chains: large U.S. retailers. In the early 1960s U.S. retailers bought almost all their merchandise from domestic manufacturers. With the growing availability of low-cost apparel from Third World producers, however, the ratio of imported to domestically made garments in the United States began to rise. Although the figures vary by product, the general trend is the same: from less than 10 percent of U.S. consumption in 1965, the share of imported apparel rose to 25 percent in 1975, 30 percent in 1980, more than 40 percent by 1985, and 50 percent by 1991. Given the growth of low-priced and increasingly high-quality garment imports, most of the larger U.S. retailers began to develop global sourcing strategies, especially for the fashion-oriented segment of the apparel industry.

Overseas buying offices were established by major U.S. retailers to purchase a wide assortment of products, typically grouped into "soft goods" (such as garments and shoes) and "hard goods" (such as furniture, lighting fixtures, appliances, kitchenware, and toys). Before the existence of direct buying offices overseas, importers were the key intermediaries between U.S. retailers and foreign factories. Sears, Montgomery Ward, and Macy's were the first American companies to establish buying offices in Hong Kong in the 1960s, mainly for hard goods. The really big apparel orders came when Kmart and J. C. Penney set up their Hong Kong buying offices in 1970, quickly followed by additional branch offices in Taiwan, Korea, and Singapore. By the mid-1970s many other retailers, such as the May Department Stores Company, Associated Merchandising Corporation (AMC), and Woolworth, had jumped on the direct-buying bandwagon in the Far East (Gereffi 1994).

Table 7.2 lists the top ten retail buying offices in Taiwan in 1992. Kmart and Wal-Mart, the two biggest U.S. retailers today, do the largest volume of business in Taiwan, with annual orders of US$500 million and US$300 million, respectively. J. C. Penney, AMC (a member-owned group buying office for forty different U.S. stores), Mast Industries (the major overseas sourcing arm of The Limited), Montgomery Ward, and Woolworth all purchase between US$100 and US$200 million in merchandise through their Taiwan offices, while Sears, May Department Stores, and Macy's do US$50 to US$75 million in business from Taiwan. Note that these amounts refer to the value of *orders* placed with the retail buying offices in Taiwan, not to the volume of *shipments* from Taiwan. Almost all the major retailers with buying offices in the newly industrialized countries (NICs) of East Asia (Taiwan, Hong Kong, Korea, and Singapore) split their orders into two categories: those they source domestically and those they source offshore. Offshore sourcing raises the issue of triangle manufacturing, a key feature of buyer-driven commodity chains in East Asia.

In triangle manufacturing, foreign buyers place their orders with Taiwanese or other East Asian NIC manufacturers from whom they have sourced in the past, who in turn shift some or all of the requested production to affiliated offshore factories in one or more low-wage countries (e.g., China, Indonesia, or Vietnam). These offshore factories can be wholly owned subsidiaries or joint-venture partners of the East Asian NIC manufacturers, or simply independent overseas contractors. The triangle is completed when the finished goods are shipped directly to the foreign buyer, under the import quotas issued to the exporting nation. Payments to the non-NIC garment factory flow through the NIC intermediary firm, usually via back-to-back letters of credit. Triangle manufacturing thus changes the status of the NIC manufacturer from an erstwhile production contractor for the U.S. buyer to a middleman in the buyer-driven commodity chain. The key asset possessed by East Asian NIC manufacturers is the trust they have established with foreign buyers, generated by numerous successful export transactions over the years (Gereffi 1994). These middlemen often have an ethnic or cultural

Table 7.2

Top Ten Retail Buying Offices in Taiwan, 1992

Company	Year Established	Value of Orders Placed in Taiwan (US$ millions)	Sourcing Channels[a]		Types of Merchandise	
			Taiwan (%)	Offshore (%)	Soft Goods[b] (%)	Hard Goods (%)
Kmart	1971	500	40	60	45	55
Wal-Mart[c]	1981	300	55	45	30	70
J. C. Penney	1971	200	70	30	50	50
Associated Merchandising Corporation (AMC)[d]	1973	180	60	40	65	35
Mast Industries[e]	1973	140	100	0	100	0
Montgomery Ward	1983	135	77	23	35	65
Woolworth	1975	110	80	20	46	54
Sears	1967	75	98	2	40	60
May Department Stores Co.	1974[f]	70	78	22	65	35
R. H. Macy & Co.	1986[f]	50	80	20	73	27

Source: Interviews in Taiwan by author (Gereffi).

[a]Combined total for soft goods and hard goods.

[b]The soft goods percentages are exclusively apparel, with the following exceptions: Kmart—apparel, handbags, and home fashions; Wal-Mart—apparel (70%) and footwear (30%); and Montgomery Ward—apparel and footwear (minimal).

[c]Wal-Mart's sole sourcing agent in Taiwan, and much of the rest of Asia as well, is Pacific Resources Export Limited (PREL). Although registered as a Hong Kong trading company, PREL is owned by Indonesia's Salim Group, one of the biggest industrial conglomerates in Asia.

[d]Associated Merchandising Corporation is a group buying office that serves about 40 different stores in the United States, including Dayton-Hudson, Federated Department Stores, Target, and Bradlees.

[e]Mast Industries is the main overseas sourcing arm and a wholly owned subsidiary of The Limited.

[f]R.H. Macy and the May Company bought jointly in Asia from 1960 to 1973. The following year, May Company set up its own buying office; Macy purchased through Linmark Services, an independent buying agent, until 1986, when Macy established a separate buying office.

linkage with the offshore factory owners that actually make and export the goods in triangle manufacturing arrangements. For example, Hong Kong and Taiwanese firms frequently hook up with overseas Chinese businessmen in Southeast Asia, a fact that hinders their Korean competitors, who lack this social network.

Table 7.2 indicates the degree to which U.S. retailers source from Taiwanese or offshore factories. All the top ten retailers, with the exception of Kmart, source the majority of the orders placed with their Taiwan buying offices from local factories. The merchandise managers in Taiwan's buying offices are responsible for monitoring the quality and delivery schedules of all orders filled in offshore as well as Taiwanese plants. That can be a monumental task, because the larger retailers work with two to four hundred different factories spread across Asia, Africa, and Latin America. Orders typically are placed three to six months in advance of the scheduled delivery date. Longer lead times are needed for countries that do not have the capability to manufacture their own piece goods (i.e., fabrics).

Because they do not want to be responsible for 100 percent of any supplier's output, most retailers eschew "exclusive factories." That is particularly relevant for seasonal goods such as apparel, for which orders may according to consumer buying cycles (e.g., lightweight clothes for spring and summer versus heavier outerwear sold only in the winter), because factories specialize in different types of merchandise. Nevertheless, retailers try to retain a relatively small number of core contractors that receive the bulk of their orders. One of the biggest retail buying offices in Taiwan, for example, deals directly with 250 factories, which in turn may use their own subcontractors. Of this total, there are thirty key vendors (i.e., factories) with an annual order volume of US$500,000 or more, while each of the top ten vendors supplies the retailer with over US$1 million worth of goods per year. All 250 companies are evaluated annually using a sophisticated vendor matrix that incorporates a variety of criteria, including on-time delivery and product quality (including styling). These vendor profiles inform decisions by the retailer's merchandise manager as to who will receive future orders.

Taiwan's top ten retail buying offices are about evenly split in terms of the predominance of hard goods versus soft goods in their sourcing activities (see Table 7.2). The discount chains and mass merchandisers (Kmart, Wal-Mart, Montgomery Ward, Woolworth, and Sears) give more emphasis to hard goods, while buying offices responsible for sourcing for department stores and apparel retailers (AMC, Mast Industries, May Department Stores, and Macy's) focus on soft goods, which are exclusively apparel. J. C. Penney gives equal weight to both kinds of merchandise.

Table 7.3 focuses on Taiwan's triangle sourcing networks just for apparel. There is a much wider range in the percentage of apparel orders that are sourced domestically versus offshore, compared with the combined figures for the hard-goods and soft-goods retailer sourcing channels found in Table 7.2. Whereas three retail buying offices (Kmart, Montgomery Ward, J. C. Penney) gave just 25 to 35 percent of their orders to local factories, six other retailers sourced 70 percent or more of their apparel orders in Taiwan. Mast Industries is exceptional because it places 100 percent of its apparel orders with

Table 7.3

Taiwan's Triangle Sourcing Networks in Apparel, 1992

	Source of Apparel Shipments	
Retail Buying Office	Taiwan (%)[a]	Offshore (Main Countries)[b]
Kmart	35	Indonesia, United Arab Emirates, Philippines, plus 10 additional countries
Wal-Mart	50	China, Indonesia, Sri Lanka
J. C. Penney	25	Philippines, Indonesia, Thailand, Bangladesh
Associated Merchandising Corporation (AMC)	70	Philippines, Singapore, Malaysia, Indonesia, Thailand, China
Mast Industries	100	None
Montgomery Ward	33	Indonesia, Thailand, Philippines, Chile
Woolworth	75	China, Indonesia, Sri Lanka, Bangladesh, Vietnam, Lesotho
Sears	92	Bangladesh, Philippines
May Department Stores Co.	80	Indonesia, Singapore, Philippines
R. H. Macy & Co.	85	Philippines, Indonesia

Source: Interviews in Taiwan by author (Gereffi).

[a]The Taiwan percentage refers to the proportion of each retail buying office's orders made in and shipped from Taiwan.

[b]Offshore shipments refer to orders received and processed by Taiwan's retail buying offices but transferred to Taiwanese-affiliated offshore factories for production and export under the quota of the designated countries. Offshore sources are listed in their relative order of importance to the buying offices in Taiwan.

Taiwanese factories and also is the largest apparel exporter from Taiwan. This case merits a more detailed analysis.

Mast Industries is the overseas sourcing arm for The Limited, the largest retailer of women's apparel in the world. Mast specializes in "speed sourcing." It is reputed to have the fastest turnaround time for garment sourcing in the business (thirty to forty days from order to shipment). According to Jack Welch, president of Mast Industries Far East Ltd., "Mast doesn't do anything different than anyone else, except that we keep the pressure on the factories to meet their deadlines and we ship by air" (personal interview, October 30, 1992). Whereas all the other leading retail buying offices do triangle manufacturing from Taiwan, Mast Industries in Taiwan does not utilize offshore production. "If we are going to make our shorter lead times," explained Beatriz Mi, vice-president of the Taiwan Branch of Mast Industries, "then we have to produce locally. We have no other choice" (personal interview, November 13, 1992). Although air shipping is four to five times more expensive than sea transport, air transport takes just two days instead of twenty. "The buyer decides whether he wants to ship by air versus by sea," said Welch. "Everything price-wise is done by percentages up." Taiwanese factories also are noted for their craftsmanship, an important selling point for fashion-oriented apparel companies. "Taiwan's garment industry has to do production involving very short lead times because it's higher quality work," said Lawrence Chu, sales manager of the Garment Division of the Tuntex Group, a large, vertically integrated textile and apparel firm in Taiwan. "This is the only way Taiwan can compete with Sri Lanka, Indonesia, and the Philippines" (personal interview, November 21, 1992).

The main countries where Taiwanese vendors have offshore sourcing networks are located in Southeast Asia (Indonesia, the Philippines, Singapore, Malaysia, and Thailand) and South Asia (Sri Lanka and Bangladesh) (Table 7.3). China is a major apparel supplier for only two of the top ten retail buying offices in Taiwan: Wal-Mart and Woolworth. That is in striking contrast to the importance of China both for Taiwanese garment entrepreneurs who moved offshore and for Taiwan's textile exporters. This apparent anomaly is accounted for by the fact that most large retailers centralize their sourcing of goods from China through their Hong Kong offices. As Jack Welch noted, "Hong Kong business is easy, and Guangdong province [in southern China] is too. There are ten thousand factories a taxi ride away." Another factor limiting the role of Taiwanese garment firms in China is the limited availability of quotas. Taiwanese companies were relatively late entrants into China, compared to Hong Kong businesses; therefore, they have not been able to get sufficient quota for exporting to the United States.

It is difficult to determine the total amount of Taiwan's apparel exports channeled through its retail buying offices. One of the few empirical studies of overseas buying offices estimated that about 20 percent of Third World–manufactured exports flow through this channel (ESCAP/UNCTC 1985, 35–36). The total value of orders placed by Taiwan's top ten retail buying offices in 1992 is US$1,760 million, of which approximately US$855 million was for apparel (Table 7.2). Taking the share of these apparel orders that actually were filled in Taiwan (see Table 7.3), we find that the total value of apparel shipments from Taiwan comes to nearly US$510 million. If we divide this figure by Taiwan's 1992 estimated apparel exports to the United States, US$2,115 million, we see that 24 percent of Taiwan's apparel exports were channeled through its ten biggest retail buying offices. Adding the smaller retailers with direct buying offices in Taiwan, plus the brand-named companies that do not own any factories but engage in substantial amounts of specification contracting (such as Liz Claiborne, whose 1992 apparel exports from Taiwan were in excess of US$50 million), it is likely that 35 to 40 percent of Taiwan's apparel trade with the United States is controlled by foreign buyers—that is, U.S. retailers and branded merchandisers.

Labor Conditions in Taiwan's Garment Industry

Taiwan's garment industry is characterized by three common working conditions: piece-rate wage labor, overtime hours, and an overwhelming preponderance of women in the labor force. The piece-rate wage paid to a garment worker in Taiwan is calculated by the amount of work completed; even if the wages are paid monthly, workers receive different sums according to the total hours put in and their productivity. The level of orders received from buyers is decisive in determining how long a worker is employed each month;

garment factories try to employ their in-house workers at least eight hours per day.

Overtime work is the typical means of coping with fluctuating demand in high seasons. If the orders cannot be finished in-house in a certain time period, they are subcontracted out to workshops or homeworkers. Thus, the fluctuation in monthly wages for an in-house worker depends not only on the individual's skill level, but also on the amount of overtime received. The earnings of subcontracted workers, on the other hand, are dependent on how much work they are given by the principal factories. The regular work schedule set by the Labor Standards Law is eight hours per day, not to exceed forty-eight hours per week. Workers in Taiwan's garment industry commonly are employed an average of ten overtime hours per month (DGBAS 1990, 523, 530).

The gender division of labor in garment production follows the principle that men are engaged in nonsewing jobs and women do the sewing. The sewing workshops tend to be established by married women who previously were employed in a garment factory. The nonsewing jobs are mostly done by men, although the dividing line here is not so rigid. Most of the bosses of principal firms or workshops doing nonsewing tasks are male. Although women account for the majority of the labor force in Taiwan's garment industry, they earn less than men in every functional category. In a survey of garment workers conducted in 1990, it was found that the average hourly pay of a female wage earner was only four-fifths that of a male worker (US$2.53 and US$3.09, respectively) (DGBAS 1990, 199, 523). The differences were even larger for the salaries workers in management and administrative positions. Homeworkers are usually paid lower wages than in-house workers.

The average monthly earnings of garment workers rank among the lowest of all manufacturing sectors in Taiwan. This situation has not changed in more than thirty years (DGBAS 1991, 146–47). In 1990 the average monthly earnings of garment workers in Taiwan were US$575, which was only 70 percent of the average wage for all manufacturing establishments in that year. Compared to earnings in other Third World countries, however, the wage rate for garment workers in Taiwan is relatively high.

The contrast between Taiwan and Indonesia is highlighted by

Sandra Lee, sales manager of Cannontex Industrial Company, a leading Taiwanese apparel manufacturer that closed all three of its factories in Taiwan between 1990 and 1992 and now has a wholly owned subsidiary in Indonesia that exports 90 percent of its garment production to the United States: "Indonesia is an ideal place for garment manufacturing. It has lots of land and a huge population. The wage rates are much lower than in Taiwan. The minimum wage in Taiwan is $600 per month, but you can't find workers for under $800 per month. In Indonesia, the monthly wage rate is $100, which includes a 20 percent increase over last year's wage. Inflation is growing in Indonesia because the economy has been booming" (personal interview, November 17, 1992). As in Taiwan, the official work week in Indonesia is forty-eight hours (Monday through Saturday, with Saturday afternoons off), but the employer is allowed three hours of overtime per day on weekdays. Thus the length of the actual work week is sixty-three hours. The down side of Indonesia from the manufacturer's point of view is its productivity. "The productivity of the Indonesian workers is much lower than in Taiwan," observed Lee. "In Cannontex's three Taiwanese factories, 1,000 workers produced 24,000 dozen woven garments per month. In Indonesia, 2,600 workers also make 24,000 dozen garments per month with the very same machinery as used in Taiwan."

Taiwan's garment industry began to confront the problem of labor shortages when the work force stopped growing. In the late 1980s the labor shortage rate was estimated at 20 to 35 percent, and the problem has become more acute since then. According to one estimate, the garment industry in Taiwan needs more than twenty thousand additional workers (Wu and Chang 1991, 39–41). Immigrant workers are considered one possible solution, and garment employers are looking to the government for help (Wu and Chang 1991, 73). But the Taiwanese government has been quite cautious on this issue. According to official figures, only 3,425 foreign workers were allowed in the textile industry in 1992, including in dyeing and ironing jobs for garment manufacturers. Moreover, this policy made it illegal for foreign immigrants to be hired as sewing workers. Thus the immigration of foreign workers does not appear to be a politically viable option in Taiwan.

Conclusion

The globalization of Taiwan's garment industry has brought with it not only new international roles, but also dramatic changes for the local economy. It has disrupted many communities that were organized around apparel factories and their dense domestic subcontracting networks. The real problem faced by this industry in Taiwan and other rapidly industrializing nations is that garment factories are not able to attract sufficient numbers of workers, given the low wages and difficult working conditions in the sector. Young workers are not entering the industry, and those that remain confront an unstable future. Apparel firms are cutting back their local manufacturing operations and setting up new production complexes in low-wage countries. Some of the more ambitious companies are trying to establish their own brand names to allow forward integration from manufacturing into retailing, with an eye on the booming China market. The jobs created by this kind of expansion require advanced skills and pay high wages, but they are few in number.

Overseas production by Taiwanese manufacturers has created a vertical division of labor in the Pacific Rim. Taiwan supplies the raw materials, machinery, and, most important, orders from foreign buyers. The workers in China and other low-wage Asian nations make the finished garments. Globalization of the garment industry in Taiwan helps to relieve some of the acute pressures felt by the textile and apparel companies, but it does nothing for the thousands of local workers who were employed in the industry. According to a recent survey of manufacturers (including garment firms), one-fourth of Taiwanese businesses investing in China have reduced or closed down their production at home (cited in Taiwan's *United Daily News,* April 5, 1992). China has become a strong competitor to Taiwan by copying its manufacturing methods but with lower production costs. The threat faced by Taiwan's garment industry is a hollowing out of its industrial base, while Taiwanese manufacturers become intermediaries for aggressive exporters elsewhere. As production levels in China and Southeast Asian nations grow, however, foreign buyers will be inclined to cut out the Taiwanese middlemen and deal directly with their major overseas producers. When that happens, employers as well as workers in Taiwan's garment companies will be looking for new jobs.

Acknowledgments: The research by Gary Gereffi for this chapter was funded by grants from Taiwan's Chiang Ching-Kuo Foundation for International Scholarly Exchange (United States), as well as the Arts and Sciences Research Council at Duke University. These sources of support are gratefully acknowledged. Thanks also go to Lucie Cheng, Lu-Lin Cheng, and Ok-jie Lee for their helpful comments on an earlier draft. Personal interviews cited in the text were conducted by Gereffi.

References

Chen, Ming-Chang. 1989. *Comparison of the Innovation Strategies between Taiwan, Hong Kong, South Korea, and Japan* (in Chinese). Taipei: Taiwan Garment Industrial Association.

Council for Economic Planning and Development (CEPD). 1991. *Taiwan Statistical Data Book, 1991.* Taipei: CEPD.

Dickerson, Kitty G. 1991. *Textiles and Apparel in the International Economy.* New York: Macmillan.

Directorate-General of Budget, Accounting, and Statistics (DGBAS), Executive Yuan, Republic of China. 1990. *Yearbook of Earnings and Productivity Statistics, Taiwan Area.* Taipei: DGBAS.

———. 1991. *Statistical Yearbook of the Republic of China, 1991.* Taipei: DGBAS.

Economic and Social Commission for Asia and the Pacific/United Nations Centre on Transnational Corporations (ESCAP/UNCTC). 1985. *Transnational Trading Corporations in Selected Asian and Pacific Countries.* Bangkok: ESCAP.

Fröbel, Folker, Jürgen Heinrichs, and Otto Kreye. 1980. *The New International Division of Labour.* Cambridge: Cambridge University Press.

Gereffi, Gary. 1993. "International Subcontracting and Global Capitalism: Reshaping the Pacific Rim." In *Pacific-Asia and the Future of the World-System,* edited by Ravi Arvind Palat, 67–81. Westport, Conn.: Greenwood Press.

———. 1994. "The Organization of Buyer-Driven Global Commodity Chains: How U.S. Retailers Shape Overseas Production Networks." In *Commodity Chains and Global Capitalism,* edited by Gary Gereffi and Miguel Korzeniewicz, 95–122. Westport, Conn.: Greenwood Press.

Gereffi, Gary, and Donald L. Wyman, eds. 1990. *Manufacturing Miracles: Paths of Industrialization in Latin America and East Asia.* Princeton: Princeton University Press.

Huang, Ching-Hui. 1990. *Discussions on the Origins, Processes, Results, Fu-*

tures, and Solutions for Taiwan's Businesses Investing in Mainland China—A Management Perspective (in Chinese). Taipei: Industrial Development and Investment Center.

Liou, Tai-Eng, and Dung-Li Chen. 1992. *The Development of the Textile Industry across the Taiwan Straits and the Possibilities of their Competition and Cooperation* (in Chinese). Taipei: Taiwan Institute of Economic Research.

Ministry of Economic Affairs (MOEA), Investment Commission. 1990. *Survey on the Business of Overseas Chinese and Foreign National Investments and Their Contribution to Taiwan's Economic Development (1988)* (in Chinese). Taipei: MOEA.

————. 1992. *Statistics on Overseas Chinese and Foreign Investment, Technical Cooperation, Outward Investment, and Outward Technical Cooperation.* Taipei: MOEA.

Moon, Chung-in, with Chull Ho Chang. 1987. "Trade Frictions and Industrial Adjustment: The Textiles and Apparel Industry in the Pacific Basin." *Pacific Focus* 2(1): 105–33.

Shieh, Gwo-Shyong. 1990. "Manufacturing 'Bosses': Subcontracting Networks under Dependent Capitalism in Taiwan." Ph.D. dissertation, University of California, Berkeley.

Taiwan Textile Federation (TTF). Various years. *Statistics on Taiwan Textile and Apparel Industries.* Taipei: TTF.

World Bank. 1992. *World Development Report, 1992.* New York: Oxford University Press.

Wu, Hui-Lin, and Ching-Hsi Chang. 1991. *A Study of the Labor Shortage and Foreign Workers in Taiwan* (in Chinese). Taipei: Chung-Hua Institute for Economic Research.

Yoffie, David B. 1983. *Power and Protectionism: Strategies of the Newly Industrializing Countries.* New York: Columbia University Press.

Chapter 8

The Korean Garment Industry: From Authoritarian Patriarchism to Industrial Paternalism

Seung Hoon Lee and Ho Keun Song

Because developing countries typically lack sophisticated technologies and great reserves of capital, they must choose export industries strategically. Many countries have chosen the apparel industry as an entrée into the global economy, because it is mainly labor intensive, with low-skilled and low-paid jobs. The export market provides an excellent opportunity, as long as the comparative advantage of low costs is maintained. The garment-exporting sector, nearly nonexistent before the 1950s, has grown rapidly in several developing countries as a major source of foreign-exchange earnings, employment, and economic growth.

The apparel industry's ability to generate capital accumulation, however, is another question. Since the 1960s the industry has played an important role in South Korea's economic growth; garments' share in the nation's total export revenue was 18.5 percent in 1967 and 13.6 percent in 1990. Although investment in apparel production has persistently increased, it has been relatively small compared to that in other industries. Moreover, massive state subsidies, including priority in credit rationing, low interest rates, and various tax credits, have contributed to the industry's profits. For example, the Korean government gave a subsidy value of 27 percent to garment exporters in 1972. For this reason, Korea's clothing exporters have often been charged with dumping. All this indicates that garment exporting has not been profitable in the normal sense; instead, government subsidies have compensated for losses and have maintained a minimum level of profit for garment manufacturers.

The purpose of the state subsidies has been twofold: development of foreign-exchange earnings and job creation. Since the early stages of Korean economic development, the garment industry has been the most important source of foreign-exchange earnings (although the export-construction industry gained prominence in the late 1970s). In 1991, when Korea suffered from a record-breaking trade deficit of nearly US$10 billion, the industry enjoyed a trade surplus. Although the export of clothing dropped sharply by US$400 million in 1991, apparel was still Korea's leading manufactured export.

As of 1990, the garment industry has accounted for an annual average of 5 percent of total manufacturing employment. The industry has absorbed a large portion of the working population that has moved out of the traditional rural sector. A significant proportion of the Korean labor force has been employed in garment production, but these workers have been paid minimal wages. Low wages were imperative for encouraging exports.

The Korean garment industry has been particularly vulnerable to market fluctuations. Until 1988 approximately 95 percent of garment exports were produced under contract to foreign firms, rather than under Korean-owned labels. After 1988, however, production of quality goods with their own brands increased rapidly because a strategic choice was made to use technological upgrading to meet worsening conditions of garment manufacturing. The United States and Japan are Korea's largest export markets, accounting for more than 70 percent of total exports (Table 8.1). This high degree of market dependence is detrimental to the stability of the garment industry's product and labor markets.

Korean economic development was predicated on the massive inducement of foreign loans. The Korean government has made strenuous efforts to earn foreign exchange in order to pay back foreign loans and to finance the importation of capital goods and raw materials. The garment industry has played a leading role in fulfilling these goals and in generating many jobs. To this end, labor repression has been pursued vigorously.

Table 8.1
Korea's Garment Exports by Country, 1989 (in US$ 1,000s)

Country	US$	Percentage
United States	3,735,915	40.6
Japan	3,113,361	33.8
West Germany	567,375	6.2
Canada	369,957	4.0
United Kingdom	310,302	3.4
France	144,527	1.6
Netherlands	132,919	1.3
Other	837,980	9.1
Total	9,212,356	100.0

Source: Korean Foreign Trade Association 1990.

The Employment System in the Garment Industry: The Development of Authoritarian Patriarchism

In contrast to workers under industrial paternalism (common in Japan), industrial workers in Korea are exposed to open competition in the labor market without legal and institutional protection. State welfare provisions are extremely weak, and production workers are typically excluded from company welfare benefits. The Korean labor system can be described as authoritarian patriarchism. It is characterized by labor repression, the absence of welfare programs, and the lack of labor-market institutions and legal provisions protecting workers (such as unions, minimum wage laws, and provisions for job security) (Song 1991). Korean authoritarian patriarchism developed in the garment industry.

Labor Force Composition

The textile industry has been the leading sector for job creation in Korea's economic development. It accounted for 15 to 30 percent of employment in the manufacturing sector between 1976 and 1989. The garment industry occupied a central place in the textile industry in terms of employment, accounting for slightly less than 60 percent of the textile labor force. The number of manufacturing workers increased annually until the 1987 labor dispute. The 1987 labor dispute was a watershed in Korea's industrial relations. It was a political challenge by discontented workers against authoritarian labor repression and a low-wage system. Although neither systematic nor organized but merely an explosion of worker resentment, the dispute caused the state to relax labor repression significantly and for years after to permit workers to have a high wage increase. Since then, however, rising labor costs have caused a decline in employment in the textile and garment industries. The decline has been accelerated recently by a labor shortage in manufacturing industries in general and the garment industry in particular. This shortage has been associated with a worsening of industrial conditions in labor-intensive industries, affected by the erosion of Korea's competitive advantage in the global market.

General characteristics of Korean garment industry firms and workers are summarized in Table 8.2. Most firms are small, undercapitalized, and located in three major cities.

As of 1991, the labor force was composed of unskilled (69%), female (65%), and poorly educated (50.3%) workers. Because these statistics include spinning and silk workers, who have a relatively higher human capital, the reality is worse in the garment industry (Uh 1991; Song 1989). More than 75 percent of the apparel labor force is female, young, and unskilled. More than half have worked in the industry for less than one year. Low wages and poor working conditions are associated with the low levels of human capital in this industry.

Hierarchy of Subcontractors

A sharp division of labor exists in this industry. Large garment firms in Korea concentrate more on marketing, allocating quotas, and acquiring raw material than on direct production, which is usually carried out in subsidiaries. Quota allocation is used as a powerful means of controlling subsidiaries. Thus, protectionism by other countries, as expressed in the setting of quotas, creates and reinforces the structural dependence of subsidiaries on parent firms (Aggarwal 1985; Cline 1987).

The industry forms a structure of hierarchical dependence. Subsidiaries are subordinate to the big firms, which benefit more than do the direct producers. In an interview conducted in Seoul in January 1991, one subcontractor operating a small firm with twenty

Table 8.2

Characteristics of Firms and Workers in
Korea's Garment Industry

Firm Characteristics[a]	
No. of workers	**Percentage**
under 19	52.3
20–99	37.3
100–499	9.6
more than 500	0.8
Capitalization (million won)	**Percentage**
under 100	85.5
100–499	14.0
above 500	0.5
Location	**Percentage**
Seoul, Taegu, Pusan	81.2
Kyonggi-Do	8.0
Other	10.8
Worker Characteristics[b]	
Skill level	**Percentage**
Unskilled	69.0
Skilled	8.5
Technician	4.3
Office	18.2
Gender	**Percentage**
Male	35.6
Female	64.4
Education	**Percentage**
Elementary	10.4
Middle	39.9
High	49.7

Source: Korean Association of Textile Industries, 1988,
1991.

[a]Based on survey data for 250 apparel firms in 1988.

[b]Based on survey data for 225 apparel, knitwear, spinning, silk, and dyeing firms in 1991.

workers lamented, "Of the 12 percent margin created from producing one jacket, 8 percent goes to the mother firm, 2 percent is reserved for financial costs, and the remaining 2 percent is for us, the direct producer." Thus, subcontractors must cover all their production costs, including workers' wages, with the 2 percent margin allocated to production.

In order to overcome their structural dependence, subsidiaries attempt to expand their subcontracting network into more firms and to develop their own products independently of the parent firms. Markets are already monopolized by big firms, however, and their control over managerial skills and information makes it difficult for small firms to penetrate the market.

Three types of subcontracting exist in Korea's garment industry; the important distinction lies in whether or not a firm possesses its own brand. Most large firms engaged in export production contract to produce the brand-named products of foreign firms. The first pattern of subcontracting involves large firms with production facilities of their own. They allocate jobs to subsidiaries, including small and medium-sized firms, or to producers in the informal sector. Large firms, with factories and production facilities of their own, are likely to produce their own brands. They may still produce nonbranded garments for foreign buyers, but they also produce brand-named goods for the domestic market. The second pattern of subcontracting involves general trading companies, which do not operate production facilities of their own. These companies engage only in dealing with markets, negotiating with foreign buyers, and allocating quotas, while their subsidiaries are responsible for direct production. The third type consists of medium-sized firms that control smaller firms and individual producers. Medium-sized firms sometimes work for firms of the two other types.

The complex subcontracting system has a tremendous influence on production and profit-making in garment manufacturing. First, the production of garments is absolutely dependent on quota allocation by big firms; quota allocations have been used to suppress unions in subsidiaries. Parent firms exclude unionized firms from quota allocation, fearing disruption of their production schedules. Second, the hierarchy of subcontracting within the industry determines profitability. The closer a firm is to the top of the hierarchy, the better its profits. Third, because some homeworkers are engaged in production at the lowest level of the hierarchy, the subcontracting system obscures the boundary between the formal and informal sectors. Parent firms allocate a large proportion of production to homeworkers, who are usually married women, as a means of reducing wages and avoiding worker organization. It is not uncommon for factory managers to keep lists of married women, former employees of that factory, available for homework when necessary. Thus, the subcontracting system is used to avoid unionization and maintain low wages in the garment industry.

Assembly Lines and the Labor Process

Korea's garment industry has concentrated on the mass production of low-priced goods for export markets, and this basic character has determined the system of organizing work. Most firms in Korea use the assembly-line system. Although it is well suited to the mass production of garments, this system is not easily adaptable to changes in the production cycle or to market fluctuations (Hoffman and Rush 1988). It does, however, enable employers to control labor intensity by increasing the speed of the conveyor belt.

In 1985 it was estimated that 80 percent of Korea's firms relied on the assembly-line system. A survey conducted by the Korean Association of Apparel and Garment Industries in 1988 found that only 41 percent of firms used assembly lines, while others combined assembly lines with the progressive-bundle system (Korean Association of Textile Industries 1991). These figures suggest that assembly lines were the main apparel production system up to the 1987 labor dispute but were gradually being replaced by the progressive-bundle system.

Work organization is also structured to facilitate the operation of assembly lines. For example, D Apparel, a large subsidiary of a Korean conglomerate, operates three separate factories near Seoul. Each factory, producing one or two garment products, has three production departments. Within each department is one cutting section and three production sections. The cutting section is usually filled with skilled male workers, while the production sections employ mainly unskilled female workers. Each production section is composed of about one hundred workers; the department head is supported by supervisors, who are responsible for production sections of about ten work teams, each made up of a team leader and five to ten workers. Altogether, thirty-two hundred workers, including two hundred office workers, are employed in the three factories. In sum, about three thousand production-line workers are regulated by high-level managers (three department heads and twelve supervisors) and low-level managers (team leaders). All managerial positions, including team leaders, are occupied by male workers. Most large garment firms have a similar structure of work organization.

Small firms are organized very differently. They are often found in the basements of four- or five-story buildings in and near industrial towns. They employ a small number of female workers, who use old-fashioned, secondhand sewing machines. Typically, a skilled male cutter regulates the entire work process; he is in charge of the production schedule, job flow, and activities ranging from job allocation to training newly recruited workers.

Labor Practices at the Workplace

In Korean garment factories, a figure pronouncing the daily production target (set in the department heads' managerial meeting) is pinned up on a notice board. Typically, this target is determined by the size of the order received from buyers, with workers' opinions and suggestions entirely ignored.

The production target, which is divided equally among the work teams, usually exceeds the regular eight-hour work day stipulated by the Labor Standard Laws and requires average overtime work of two hours. Garment workers take it for granted that they will have to work for ten hours or more every day. In seasons of high demand, overtime work continues through the night. Before the 1987 labor dispute, workers were willing to accept overtime, because it was the only means to increase their meager earnings. Garment workers have recorded the longest average work hours of any manufacturing industry in Korea. They reached 250 to 260 hours per month before 1987 and decreased to 240 hours thereafter.

It is relatively simple to calculate monthly wages for garment workers because the high turnover rate makes seniority and job tenure largely irrelevant. As of 1991, they typically worked ten hours per day and were paid a base rate close to minimum wage, plus overtime pay. Monthly earnings for a female, unskilled garment worker amounted to approximately 360,000 won (about US$475) in 1991.

The daily factory schedule helps us to understand the everyday life of workers. Workers arrive at factory at eight-thirty every morning and spend half an hour preparing themselves for work. The managerial meeting is held at this time, and the daily production target is posted. Regular work starts at nine o'clock and continues until noon. Workers are not permitted to go to the bathroom, because leaving their seats disturbs the flow of work and could result in defective products. (This rule is more rigidly enforced in electronics plants.) Lunch, which is served in a factory cafeteria from noon until one o'clock, is partially subsidized by the employer. The afternoon work schedule continues from one until six, the end of the regular work day; however, workers are provided dinner at six o'clock and then work overtime from seven until nine at night. In a high-demand season, most workers are assigned overtime work continuing until dawn. They also work Saturdays and Sundays but are permitted to have a break every other week.

Supervisors and work team leaders are responsible for the completion of the daily production target. Because work teams are the basic unit of production, leaders are assigned to do many jobs, ranging from the control of work speed to evaluation of workers under their supervision. More often than not, leaders abuse the limited power given to them by managers, engaging in violent acts and harsh language toward workers. Few Korean garment workers have not been hit and insulted. Although workers are familiar with the labor laws stipulating that these actions are illegal, their lack of human capital forces them to remain silent and to tolerate the abuse, for they know that better jobs are not available to them.

The most important aspect of the work team leader's power is the job of assessing workers' performance. Team leaders evaluate workers' attitudes, behavior, relationships with other workers, and other activities outside the factory, using a formatted document. The evaluation, which is scored and regularly reported to the supervisor, serves as the most important criterion for promotions and job rotations. Promotion can go only as high as work team leader, while job rotation typically means isolation from friends and sometimes is a signal of imminent termination.

Wages and Promotion

Production workers in the garment industry are paid by the hour and do not receive company welfare benefits. Monthly wages for production workers are composed of two parts, base pay and overtime pay (1.5 times base hourly pay). Garment industry workers receive the lowest hourly pay of all of Korea's manufacturing industries. The average monthly wage was US$419 in 1989, or 63 percent of the average wage in manufacturing as a whole and 82 percent of average textile industry wages. These ratios have remained stable over the years.

There are different promotion ladders for office workers and production workers. The two ladders mean that production workers do not expect to move to managerial positions, and such cases are extremely rare. It takes a production worker three to four years to become a team leader and five to seven years to become a supervisor. A supervisor is the equivalent of a section deputy in the promotion ladder for managerial workers, a position that usually requires three to four years for an ordinary clerk to attain. Supervisor is the highest position to which blue-collar workers can be promoted. These jobs are available to only three or four male skilled workers out of about one thousand employees in large firms. This system locks out most production workers, who are female. Many women quit their jobs with marriage, at the age of twenty-five or so. Garment workers have a high rate of turnover and the shortest job tenure of any of the manufacturing industries.

Restructuring of the Garment Industry

In the late 1980s the Korean economy faced important changes in its economic environment, which imposed serious constraints on the development model based on low wages and long hours of work. The first event was the wage hike imposed by the labor dispute of 1987; wage rates almost doubled in three years. This wage explosion limited Korea's comparative advantage in world markets. As the lowest-wage industry in manufacturing, the garment industry was particularly hurt.

The second event was pressure from the United States to appreciate the Korean currency. The Korean government could not resist the pressure, because the United States was the biggest customer of Korean exports. The value of the U.S. dollar in relation to the Korean won declined rapidly from 1985 to 1989. These circumstances had a devastating effect on Korean exports. Furthermore, the Korean government was pressured to lift various policy measures designed to control imports and protect domestic producers from foreign competition. Garments produced in China and other Asian countries became strong competitors, not only in world markets but also in the domestic market.

As their exports encountered difficulties in the global market, garment producers adopted several new strategies. First, they began to produce quality goods with their own private brands, for both the domestic and export markets.

Second, garment producers tried to move to less-developed countries or use workers from such countries in Korea. Capital flow from Korea to Southeast Asia and the Caribbean Basin was first motivated by the desire to evade quota restraints imposed by the United States. But as the pressure of domestic wage hikes became more intense, the search for low wages became urgent. Some garment producers have attempted to employ illegal immigrant workers from Southeast Asian countries, such as Bangladesh, Pakistan, the Philippines, Thailand, and Indonesia. Roughly one hundred thousand illegal immigrants worked in Korea in 1991. Some garment producers have opened plants in less-developed countries such as Indonesia, the Philippines, and Guatemala. Foreign direct investment by Korean garment manufacturers has increased rapidly; Korea has become the largest foreign investor in the Guatemalan maquiladoras. Korean garment firms have been accused of unfair labor practices and brutality in these countries (Peterson 1992).

Third, garment producers are reducing their production facilities in Korea, closing their factories, and seeking to shift to alternative businesses. Even when they have decided to continue in garment production in order to avoid labor disputes, many producers have reduced their factory size and shifted to subcontracting. The number of garment factories, the operation rates of the factories, the number of the garment workers, and the number of sewing machines have all declined since 1987 (Table 8.3).

Working conditions have also changed. The traditional, authori-

Table 8.3

Decline of Korea's Garment Industry, 1987–1991

Year	No. of Factories	Operation Rate (%)	No. of Workers	No. of Sewing Machines
1987	3,147	91.1	366,400	256,850
1988	2,591	85.7	334,300	280,000
1989	2,369	81.2	284,000	238,000
1990	2,041	79.4	198,800	220,100
1991	1,824	N/A	N/A	N/A

Source: Korean Federation of Textile Industries 1991.

tarian labor management has become less viable. As quality has been upgraded, the demand for skilled garment workers has increased sharply, leading to another wage increase. The production process is moving from assembly lines to the team system, and worker autonomy is markedly improving. Perhaps repressive labor practices in the garment industry will gradually fade away.

Toward Industrial Paternalism

Recent changes in the garment industry employment system have accelerated as capital responds to Korea's industrial decline and to the significant erosion of its competitiveness in world markets. Capital's attempt to deal with the industrial crisis is taking the form of a strategic shift from the mass production of cheap commodities to the production of a diversity of expensive goods. This move requires the transformation of workers' skills and the production process, which, in turn, has enormous influence on the employment system in the garment industry (Hoffman and Rush 1988). Of the many structural factors promoting change in the employment system of the garment industry, three stand out: a labor shortage and wage explosion, the rise of organized labor, and the development of state welfare provisions.

The number of workers in the garment industry has gradually declined, starting in 1988. This drop, most notable in the case of production workers, mirrors an overall trend in the manufacturing sector. The number of manufacturing production workers declined from 2,904,000 in 1988 to 2,680,000 in 1992. Garment workers dropped from 267,354 in 1986 to 125,000 in 1992. The reduction in garment industry employment is attributed to a labor shortage, accelerated by a shift to the service sector since the early 1980s. Workers are reluctant to take jobs in the garment industry because of the low wages and hard work. According to a report by the Economic Planning Board (EPB), workers in the service sector were paid 1.7 times higher than those in the manufacturing industries in 1989 (EPB 1990). Capital's response to the labor shortage in the garment industry has been to transform the production process by promoting automation and technological innovation. This change, in turn, has accelerated the rapid decline of employment in this sector, with a concomitant decrease in firm size. Without changes in managerial strategy, employers could not induce workers to join the industry; hence, employers have changed their attitude toward workers, becoming more benevolent. High wages are the most attractive inducement for workers.

Although wages in the garment industry are still the lowest in manufacturing, a wage increase, often described as a "wage explosion," has occurred. As mentioned above, wages in the garment industry almost doubled between 1985 and 1989. Korea's wage increases are in contrast to the situations in Taiwan and Thailand. The marked rise in wages generates great pressure on garment manufacturers in Korea, who have depended on low wages to maintain their competitive advantage.

The rapid increase in wages is not peculiar to the garment industry but is characteristic of manufacturing in general. Its impact is fatal to labor-intensive industries such as garment manufacturing, however, because of their reliance on cheap labor. In sum, the growing labor shortage and the wage explosion have revealed the limitations of an employment system based on low wages and long hours of work. The institutional rules of the previous system have lost their efficacy.

A second factor promoting change in the employment system is the rise of organized labor. Although organized labor has not been fully able to achieve its goal of democratizing labor relations, it has enhanced its power to negotiate with the state and with employers. Indeed, the rise of organized labor has had a great impact on the employment system in the garment industry.

Employers, who in the past hid behind the state, have been forced to talk with unions concerning wage increases, hiring and firing, and personnel management. In unorganized firms, employers have encouraged workers to reactivate the labor-management cooperative councils as a bilateral channel of communication between managers and workers. In order to cope with union demands, employers have reduced firm size, diversified their subcontractors, and replaced young female workers with married women, who are relatively more immune to union activities. Smaller firm size has also enabled employers to cut operating costs by avoiding state welfare provisions, which are applied only to employers with one hundred or more workers. Despite efforts to avoid unionization, it is now common for managers and workers to meet at the collective bargaining table—which was prohibited until 1987—and to reach a fair compromise on workers' demands. The rise in unionism in Korea will undoubtedly pave the way toward industrial democracy.

The third structural change is the development of welfare provisions as a means of placating discontented workers. By international standards, Korea has been a welfare laggard, its official ideology has emphasized "growth first and distribution later." The absence of state welfare programs and company welfare benefits for production workers distinguishes authoritarian patriarchism from industrial paternalism. For example, minimum wage laws were introduced only in 1988. Other important programs, such as pensions and unemployment insurance, are still under discussion. Nevertheless, employers are expanding fringe benefits to production workers in order to improve worker loyalty and reduce turnover. According to a recent survey of unions, union leaders are most attentive to increases in wages and fringe benefits, followed by improvements in working conditions (Park and Park 1991).

These recent changes in the employment system have altered labor relations at both the national level and the plant level. Above all, employers in the garment industry are concerned that institutional reform of the employment system will force them to introduce welfare benefits and to improve working conditions. In addition, technological upgrading and automation of the production process helps workers improve their job autonomy. The production of more expensive goods requires more skilled workers with the power to negotiate with employers over wages and working conditions. The growth of job autonomy and the decline of technical control at the workplace are significantly undermining the institutional basis of authoritarian patriarchism and instead are facilitating the introduction of industrial paternalism. An editor of *Monthly Garment,* in a recent interview in Seoul, presented an optimistic view of the gradual transformation toward industrial paternalism, noting the change of garment manufacturers in their managerial attitude toward workers and their eagerness to rationalize the industry. He emphasized repeatedly that growing numbers of employers recognized that "employers and workers are in the same boat." If this belated recognition is emerging in the garment industry, perhaps the industry will lead the way to industrial paternalism, as it led the way to authoritarian patriarchism in the past.

References

Aggarwal, Vinod K. 1985. *Liberal Protectionism: The International Politics of Organized Textile Trade.* Berkeley: University of California Press.

Cline, William. 1987. *World Trade in Textiles and Apparel.* Washington, D.C.: Institute for International Economics.

Economic Planning Board (EPB). 1990. *Labor Shortage and Policy* (in Korean). Policy pamphlet. Seoul.

Hoffman, Kurt, and Howard Rush. 1988. *Micro-Electronics and Clothing: The Impact of Technical Change on a Global Industry.* New York: Praeger.

Korean Association of Textile Industries. 1988, 1991. *Report on the Textile Industry* (in Korean). Seoul.

Korean Federation of Textile Industries. 1991. *Textile Year Book.* Seoul.

Korean Foreign Trade Association. 1990. *The Statistics of Foreign Trade, 1989.* Seoul.

Park, D. J., and Ki Seong Park. 1991. *Labor Unions in Korea* (in Korean). Seoul: Korean Labor Institute.

Peterson, Kurt. 1992. *The Maquiladora Revolution in Guatemala.* Center for International Human Rights at Yale Law School, New Haven, Conn.

Song, Ho Keun. 1989. "The State against Labor Segmentation: Union Wage Effects in the Manufacturing Industries." *Korean Journal of Labor Economics* 12:121–38.

———. 1991. *Labor Politics and the Market* (in Korean). Seoul: Nanam.

Uh, Soo Bong. 1991. *Structural Changes of Labor Markets and Policy* (in Korean). Seoul: Korean Labor Institute.

Chapter 9

The Philippine Garment Industry

Rosalinda Pineda Ofreneo

The garment sector in the Philippines "started as a basically subcontracting, reexporting industry where raw materials are shipped from abroad for processing (cutting, embroidery, sewing, etc.) and then reexported. Part of the production process goes into the factory, but the bulk is subcontracted to cottage-type producers" (*Philippine Trade and Development* 1975, 26). Since the late nineteenth century, and particularly since the early twentieth-century introduction of export-oriented embroidery manufacturing under U.S. colonial rule, the majority of garment-industry workers (in the traditional garment-producing areas of Rizal, Bulacan, Cavite, and Batangas) have been Filipino women and children (Jimenez 1986, 7–10). By 1919 embroidery had become one of the most successful U.S.-promoted industries in the Philippines; by 1931 embroidered articles were one of the country's top-ten exports (Aldana 1989, 35).

In the early days most of the exporting manufacturers were owned by U.S. firms, including the prominent New York City company Ollendorf and Feltman Brothers, which is still in operation today. Many of the era's Filipino entrepreneurs were women graduates of the Bureau of Education's School of Household Industries. U.S. exporters provided capital, designs, and sales outlets. These contractors (or *cabecillas,* as they were called) competed with one another in the search for cheap labor in the immediate suburbs of Manila.

After a short disruption of the industry during the Japanese occupation (1941–45), garment exports picked up again. The first postwar wave of foreign firms emerged in the 1950s; most were established by U.S. interests engaged in embroidery. The government encouraged industry growth with new legislation, including the 1961 Embroidery Law, the 1970 Export Incentives Act, the creation of export-processing zones (EPZs) in 1970, and the establishment of the Garments and Textile Export Board (GTEB) in 1979. The Embroidery Law was of particular importance because it allowed garment exporters to import duty-free raw materials from their foreign principals through bonded warehouses.

The second wave of foreign investment began in the early 1970s, when President Ferdinand Marcos's martial-law regime granted even more privileges to foreign firms with the Export Incentives and Investment Incentives acts. These second-wave companies were known as the BOI firms, after the Board of Investments that provided their registration. They operated bonded manufacturing warehouses, bought raw materials directly, and enjoyed "tax credits on import duties as well as double deduction on promotional expenses for exports and on shipping costs" (Aldana 1989, 41).

The third wave of foreign firms set up shop in the EPZs constructed in the mid-1970s. Many of them were "quota refugees" from Japan, Taiwan, South Korea, and Hong Kong—countries suffering from export restrictions imposed by the United States. By operating from Philippine EPZs, their exports to the U.S. market were considered Philippine exports and thus were able to make use of Philippine export quotas. The Philippine government waived many taxes for EPZ firms, including income taxes, import duties and taxes, export taxes and fees, local taxes and fees, contractor's taxes, wharfage fees, and branch profits remittance taxes. EPZ firms also enjoyed freedom from limitations on foreign ownership and employment of aliens, priority in the allocation of foreign exchange and financial assistance from government institutions, simplified export and import procedures, and exemption from inspection of imports. With all these advantages, the foreign firms posed a threat to local manufacturers, who were unable to match resources. From 1973 to 1980, the portion of Filipino-owned garment firms dropped from 82 to 49 percent (Aldana 1989, 44).

In 1975, garments became the first nontraditional Philippine export product to reach US$100 million. The value of garment exports rose steadily, reaching US$580 million in 1981. After a decline during the 1982–83 global recession, export sales rose to US$1 billion in 1987. The upward trend has been maintained, and in 1991 garment-industry exports were valued at more than US$2 billion (Fajardo 1980; *ITC Newsletter* 1985; *Manila Chronicle* 1986; *Philippine Development* 1976; Reyes 1989; GTEB 1990a).

Not surprisingly, the number of garment-industry jobs has grown by leaps and bounds. In 1984, there were approximately 148,000 workers in 20,255 registered firms, 97.8 percent of which employed between one and nine workers (*ITC Newsletter* 1985). In 1988, 24,496 garment firms were registered, employing 246,000 workers, only 35 percent of whom could be considered regular workers. In 1981, however, a more comprehensive study estimated employment at about 450,000 to 500,000 for homesewers working on a contractual basis, and 214,000 for factory and homeworkers (*Philippine Development* 1981, 11).

The Bureau of Women and Young Workers of the Department of Labor and Employment released estimates more attentive to age and gender issues, by including workers as young as ten years old, those who worked as unpaid family labor, and people with a job but not at work (because of temporary illness, vacation, strikes, etc.). Under these guidelines, the people employed by the textile, apparel, and leather industries totaled 747,000 in 1980, 778,000 in 1984, and 820,700 in 1989; females accounted for 72.7 to 75.1 percent of the workers (Bureau of Women and Young Workers 1989).

Structure of the Garment Industry: The Global Context

The structure of the Philippine garment industry derives from and is similar to that of the Western industrialized countries. Because relatively low investments are necessary, a large part of production is contracted to small-scale producers—preferably in the less-developed world—with low-cost labor (Plant 1981, 64). In the Philippines, subcontracting has become multilevel. Orders may come from a foreign principal in the United States, Japan, Australia, or Europe. To meet these orders, the Manila-based exporter subcontracts the work to provincial manufacturers or agents, who further farm out the jobs—all the way down to rural households. The higher the placement on the subcontracting ladder, the bigger the take, with foreign principals, exporters, suppliers, and big subcontractors extracting the most profit from the system. They have been able to keep production costs at a minimum, because of the supply of cheap labor and low capital requirements. Subcontracting also provides maximum production flexibility, enabling the increase or decrease of output according to fluctuations in demand.

The Subcontracting Pattern

The following case studies illustrate who gains and who loses from the subcontracting system. In the first case, Catton Brothers, a firm based in New York, engaged in the manufacture of infantwear under the brand names Catton Candy and Baby Care (Cabalu and Javier 1982). It sent semiprocessed raw materials to its main subcontractor in the Philippines (fictitiously named S. Garments), paying it a mere four pesos (P4.00; about US$.50 by the exchange rate at the time) for the labor cost of one baby dress. Aside from employing its own factory workers, S. Garments had forty or fifty subcontractors in Bulacan, Laguna, and Batangas; one of them was Tanjutco Garments. Tanjutco was paid P2.00 (US$.25) per baby dress; this firm employed seventy in-house workers and had agreements with fifty subcontractors in the neighboring towns of Baliwag, Hagonoy, Calumpit, San Rafael, Guiginto, and Santa Rita, who turned out 80 percent of total production. These subcontractors, who received P1.00 (US$.12) per dress, farmed out jobs to other subcontractors, aside from employing an average of six domestic outworkers each at the barrio level. Wages for these subcontractees amounted to only P80 (US$9) a week, or P320 (US$35) a month at the most. So the village girl who sewed the dress received less than 1 percent of Catton's final price of US$15 in a U.S. department store (Cabalu and Javier 1982).

The employers in this case study found the subcontracting system advantageous for several reasons. They were able to reduce the cost of production and hence operate profitably in highly competitive markets. They could adjust production to meet fluctuations in demand. And they could use capital more efficiently by avoiding excess capacity and by solving problems connected with limited facilities and resources. The workers found only one advantage: job creation. Many disadvantages were outlined, however, including "insecurity of employment, low wages, long working hours, pressure for productivity, and lack of social security coverage and other forms of social welfare and protection" (Cabalu and Javier 1982).

Another case study examined a subcontracting arrangement in a rural community (a barrio located in the northeast tip of Bocaue, Bulacan) (Aguilar, Ofreneo, and Amante 1983). The exporter/supplier, selling his wares to foreign principals, was a factory owner based in Metro Manila. Through a contact person, he would find subcontractors able to handle the work and would provide them with materials and designs. The subcontractor could buy or rent machines, hire workers directly, and have them work in his home. In addition, he could farm out other jobs to domestic outworkers. During the industry's peak season (September to December), sewers earned about P9.00 a day (about US$.65 by the exchange rate at the time), while embroiderers earned as much as P50.00 (US$3.60). This heavy demand sometimes meant work days of up to fifteen hours. Off-season workloads (and therefore incomes) typically dropped to one-third of peak levels, if there was even work to be had.

A more recent study focused on the middle portion of the subcontracting chain, the local subcontractors (Aguilar 1990). The company, acting as contractor/factory owner, was ranked 127 in the 1987 list of top one thousand Philippine corporations, and counted seven Filipinos among its twelve major stockholders. It handled sewing and packaging services for its foreign principals in the United States, Spain, and Germany, who in turn supplied product samples and raw materials, including cloth, thread, and accessories. The company employed a regular work force of 2,600 and during the peak period (August to February) hired an additional 300 short-term contractual workers and 220 temporary workers.

The contractor/factory owner subcontracted the sewing of shirts and pajamas to subcontractors in Metro Manila during the peak season. One such subcontractor, located at Novaliches, was a Chinese-Filipino businessman who paid his workers mainly on a piece-rate basis, when jobs were available at all. Quality-control supervisors from the contractor checked on the workers' output. All embroidery work on half-slips, nightgowns, chemises, blouses, and robes was likewise farmed out to subcontractors in Taytay and Pasig in Metro Manila as well as in the provinces of Bulacan and Cavite. One such subcontractor, located in Taytay, and one hundred regular, highly skilled workers paid on a piece-rate basis. Because he accepted subcontracted jobs from a major company, M. Greenfield, he could provide work year-round.

A fourth study examined the upper rungs of the subcontracting ladder, showing that transnational corporations (TNCs) use a variety of arrangements with different types of subcontractors (Aldana 1989). TNCs in developed countries (retailers, trading companies, textile and garment firms) have processing or licensing agreements with subsidiaries with or without their own plants, with other foreign firms/agents, with joint ventures, or with Filipino firms/agents.

Garment Firms by Category

In 1988 1,067 garment firms were included in the GTEB list of exporters. Of these firms, 21 percent accounted for about 90 percent of exports for the year. In 1990 the total number of garment exporters rose to 1,203. The thirty-five top exporters, with value of exports above US$10 million, accounted for almost 40 percent of total garment exports (worth US$1.816 billion). The ten U.S.-owned firms in the top twenty—Aris (1), Gelmart (2), M. Greenfield (5), Royal Undergarments (9), Philippine Apparel (10), Levi Strauss (11), Grandoe Philippines (12), Novelty (13), Barbizon or Philippine Lingerie (14), and Philippine Gloves (17)—had an 18 percent share of exports. If these firms are combined with the five other foreign-owned firms, the share of foreign firms' exports increases to 22 percent. In contrast, 100 percent Filipino-owned firms in the same group had only a 9 percent share. The top fifty garment exporters, all with exports valued above US$7.5 million, had exports with a combined value of US$847.7 million, representing 47 percent of the total. These figures reveal the high concentration ratios in the garment export industry that were so evident from 1973 to 1986, when the top 10 percent of export firms consistently accounted for 79 to 84 percent of total exports (Aldana 1989, 56).

In 1991 some three hundred manufacturers/exporters were members of the Garment Business Association of the Philippines (GBAP), whose establishment in 1968 was spearheaded by members of the Filipino-Indian community. Members accounted for 47 percent of the garment industry's total exports of US$1.86 billion. Its membership is classified into 89 large companies (with an authorized capitalization of P5 million and above), 103 medium-sized companies (with a capitalization of P1 to P5 million), and 78 small companies (less than P1 million). Mixed with manufacturers/exporters were a sprinkling of domestic producers, suppliers, buying agents, trading companies, and traders.

In 1980 the Confederation of Garment Exporters of the Philippines (CONGEP) was founded. This umbrella organization coordinated the Philippine Association of Embroidery and Apparel Exporters (PAEAE) (operating under the Embroidery Law), the Garment Manufacturers Association of the Export Processing Zone Authority (EPZA), and about fifty-three other corporations.

In 1991 forty-one garment firms were operating in the four export-processing zones: twelve in Bataan, six in Mactan, two in Baguio, and twenty-one in Cavite. Twelve more were expected to open in the future. Twenty of the forty-one were majority Filipino-owned. The rest were majority foreign-owned, with South Korea (ten) taking the lead, followed by Japan (six), and the United States, Germany, and Hong Kong (two each). The United Kingdom, Switzerland, and India had one each (Export Processing Zone Authority 1991).

Garment firms can be integrated manufacturers, involved in all aspects of garment production including the sourcing of raw materials, or they can be subcontractors who work on orders from a principal and who either produce whole garments or concentrate on specialized processes, such as embroidery, smocking, or crocheting (Williamson 1987, 25). Among the subcontractors, independents have access to more than one buyer, while subordinates depend mainly on one large customer.

Of the estimated two thousand subcontractors, about four hundred belong to GARSAP (Garment Subcontractors Association of the Philippines). Formed in 1988, GARSAP hopes to work with exporters and the government to find solutions to such problems as low prices, nonpayment by contractors or exporters, lack of capital, and inefficiently small size (Pamintuan 1990).

Market Trends and Problems

The garment industry of the Philippines also has a domestic component. Little has been written about the firms catering to the domestic market, except that they tend to be much smaller than the exporters. From 1970 to 1985 domestic clothing expenditures dropped, and capita consumption of clothing fell 70 percent (Lim, Andal, and Dangazo 1986, 248–49). This decline was related to falling real wages and the severe economic crisis of the mid-1980s. For 1986, the GTEB recorded garment-industry revenues of US$1,278 million, of which US$552 million (43%) represented domestic production. Estimates for subsequent years pointed to a growing export share, so that by 1991 the export market's share would increase to three-quarters of the total (Williamson 1987, 6).

For the export market, countries with markets protected by quotas have remained the biggest buyers, accounting for about 83 percent in 1991. Of these countries, the United States took the largest share, with US$1.134 billion, or 56 percent of total garment exports; the European Community placed second, with US$456 million (23%). Nonquota countries (Japan, United Arab Emirates, Panama, Hong Kong, Kingdom of Saudi Arabia, and others) represented 17 percent of the import market, valued at US$352 million.

In September 1991 the Philippine Senate terminated the U.S. military bases. Garment manufacturers were apprehensive, expecting that the decision would have an adverse impact on their access to the U.S. market. Fearing also that the proposed phase-out of the Multifiber Arrangement (MFA) would cause the collapse of the garment-export industry, garment manufacturers' organizations rallied for an extension of the U.S. military base agreement. Despite these fears, the bilateral textile agreement between the United States and the Philippines was extended to December 31, 1993, under even more favorable terms. The agreement allowed a 27 percent increase in volume of shipments. Apparel exports to the United States would grow by US$500 million in 1992, to US$1.6 billion, or 62 percent of total exports for the year.

The Philippine garment industry is faced with the problem not only of the size of the U.S. quota, but also of who gets to use the quota. The GTEB has investigated complaints of unscrupulous garment manufacturers conniving with Chinese and Hong Kong smuggling syndicates. The goal of these efforts was to pass Chinese-made garments as Philippine-made, in order to export to the United States under Philippine quota allocations (del Castillo 1990). This deception was one cause of the high use of jeans and trousers quotas, which prompted U.S. authorities to impose an embargo on Philippine exports of these products (GTEB 1990b, 5).

The state plays a prominent role, through the GTEB, in promoting and regulating the garment export industry. The GTEB was created in 1979 after the Multifiber Arrangement went into effect; its powers and functions include overseeing the implementation of the garment and textile agreements between the Philippines and other countries, approving quota allocations and export authorizations, and issuing export licenses. In 1982 the GTEB was empowered to monitor the operations of bonded garment manufacturing warehouses and to prevent smuggling (GTEB 1989b). The GTEB's power was further extended in 1983, when it was permitted to revoke quota and export authorization and to take over warehouses guilty of smuggling.

Some garment manufacturers and exporters have complained about the GETB's stringent rules and regulations. They want the board's role to be more promotional than regulatory, claiming that the Philippine garment industry is perhaps the most regulated in the region and yet has lagged behind its less-regulated neighbors in export performance, especially in nonquota markets (Tolentino 1990; Saludo 1990).

Foreign Control

The garment industry claims to be one of the biggest dollar earners in the Philippines, alternating with the electronics industry for the top dollar-earning slot in recent years. Its share of total exports steadily increased from a negligible 0.1 percent in 1970, to 4.4 percent in 1975, 8.7 in 1970, 13.4 in 1985, and 21.7 percent in 1990 (Lim, Andal, and Dangazo 1986; Cezar 1991). These figures, however, should not be taken at face value. According to a 1982 Ministry of Trade and Industry report, 70 percent of the raw-material components of total garment exports were imported and were merely processed in the Philippines before reexportation. If the cost of raw materials is subtracted from total earnings, only 30 percent of the value of garment exports could be considered net dollar earnings (del Castillo 1982). These findings were supported by the results of a GTEB survey, which showed that the country's top one hundred garment-exporting firms netted an average of only US$0.30 to US$0.35 for every US$1 worth of products they exported in 1984.

The Philippine garment industry is almost totally dependent on imported machinery, equipment, and supplies. Manufacturers must engage the services of foreign technicians to teach the operation of imported machines. The same is true for the local textile industry, which supplies as little as 10 percent of the fabric needed by the garment-export sector. So-called technology transfer agreements between foreign and local firms have been a farce, because most have involved only the use of foreign brand names, licenses, and machinery; there has been little transfer of comprehensive technological expertise, and rarely have research and development facilities been established. Foreign control is exercised not necessarily through equity holdings, but through access to supplies, technology, credit, and guaranteed markets. Overseas interests have dictated the fabrics and machinery to be used, the designs to be followed, and the amount to be produced through a principal-subcontractor relationship with local manufacturers. In fact, many of the garment firms in the Philippines have exhibited direct or indirect foreign control, largely by U.S. interests. Ten of the top twenty garment exporters in 1990 were almost 100 percent U.S.-owned.

In the Board of Investments' list of registered garment projects (as of September 30, 1991), those with U.S. equity numbered 29; they were concentrated in large projects costing more than P5 million. Those with other foreign equity were as follows: the People's Republic of China, 41; India, 38; England, 25; Taiwan, 19; Japan, 14; Hong Kong, 12; Korea, 9; and Singapore, 7. The size of firms varied by country. Others, with equity in fewer than five projects, were Canada, Israel, Australia, Germany, the Netherlands, Portugal, Egypt, France, Syria, Gibraltar, Liberia, Switzerland, Ireland, and Bangladesh.

Numerically, of course, Filipino-owned firms comprise the overwhelming majority, and although some have managed to enter the top export slots, they have not been the most dynamic sector of exports. Many of them act as subcontractors for the big foreign firms. In 1986 foreign exporters, such as Gelmart, employed 13 local subcontractors. Other foreign exporters that use local subcontracting include Novelty, 21; M. Greenfield, 43; Philippine Apparel, 45; Levi Strauss, 14; and Philippine Lingerie, 15 (Aldana 1989, 96). Filipino-owned firms come under foreign control because they are bound by contracts to supply principals abroad. For example, Remerco, which is 100 percent Filipino-owned, has a tie-up with Chiyoda Baby Dress Company of Japan and is the licensee of the U.S. underwear giant Lovable. Generally, companies that are mostly transnational or joint ventures receive more incentives and benefits than small local firms.

Thus, if one were to devise a ladder to show who has profited the most from the garment-export industry, at the very top would be the foreign principals, mainly transnational corporations with branches, subsidiaries, joint ventures, or subcontractors in the country; even some of the large Filipino exporters play only ancillary roles. Some analysts point to this structure as the essential weakness of the Philippines garment industry, in contrast to countries where domestic interests predominate, such as Korea, Taiwan, Hong Kong, and China. Because foreign-owned firms have chosen the Philippines mainly to exploit cheap labor and not to develop long-term backward linkages with local suppliers, the industry has suffered. Had Filipino firms taken the lead, use of domestic inputs would no doubt have been greater and a more meaningful integration of the garment-export sector into the domestic economy would have occurred. Rival garment exporters in the region, such as Thailand, Indonesia, and China, are overtaking the Philippines because they have robust textile industries to supply them with cheap but high-quality fabrics.

Impact on Labor

As mentioned earlier, cheap labor has been the Philippines' main attraction for the influx of foreign firms engaged in garment exports. In 1973, Filipino garment and textile workers earned an average of US$35.40 a month, while Korean workers received US$45.10, and Japanese workers, US$257.60 (Paglaban 1978).

The wage differentials remain large to this day, yet garment manufacturers still seek exemptions from wage increases. The 1992 minimum wage in the formal sector (Metro Manila) is equivalent to US$4.21 per day, which manufacturers claim exceeds wage rates in other ASEAN (Association of Southeast Asian Nations) countries. An overwhelming majority of garment workers does not receive even the minimum wage, because of working in tiny shops or being paid on a piece-rate basis. Of the 20,255 firms registered in 1984, more than 99 percent were small-scale, employing fewer than one hundred workers. Among these, 19,813 were micro and cottage industry–sized establishments, such as tailoring shops and backyard-type garment subcontractors, employing fewer than ten workers (*ITC Newsletter* 1985).

The World Bank has encouraged the growth of such microindustries, resulting in multilevel subcontracting. For example, a Manila-based supplier firm subcontracts jobs to provincial manufacturers or agents, who further farm out the work all the way down to the rural household. This pattern, of harnessing the cheap labor of the thousands of women at the bottom of the subcontracting ladder, is most pronounced in the garment industry. The new international division of labor interacts with the sexual division of labor, manifested in the gender segregation of the labor market. This segmentation has put women in low-wage, low-skilled, low-status, unstable, and unprotected jobs. At the same time, women have been mainly or solely responsible for household maintenance, childcare, and consumption within the home. "Women's work" is considered secondary, supplemental, repetitive, and monotonous, and conforming to the presumed characteristics and talents of women workers. The existence of women homeworkers in rural areas enables employers to pit them against urban workers. When factory workers unionize or go on strike, as happened at Greenfield and Uniwear, management threatens to shift, or actually does shift, work to homeworkers (Paglaban 1978).

Maintaining Philippine garment exports' global competitiveness in the face of strong rivals (Taiwan, Hong Kong, and Korea) as well as emerging ones (Thailand, Indonesia, and China), requires low wage levels and high labor productivity. To meet deadlines for orders from abroad, employers use methods ranging from forced overtime to suppression of work stoppages and strikes. Women workers have also been subjected to discrimination and sexual harassment as a form of labor control. The biggest problem faced by workers, however, is job insecurity due to unstable production orders.

Consequently, labor unrest has stalked the garment industry since the late 1970s. Strikes have been waged by workers even in the biggest exporting firms, belying initial speculation that perhaps working conditions and labor relations would be better in establishments able to afford higher wages and better conditions. For example, the workers of M. Greenfield, whose foreign principal is the U.S. firm Playknits, went on strike in April 1978, seeking reinstatement of union leaders and a return to a normal work schedule after the company had subcontracted work to piece-workers. The strike was broken by the Department of Labor and Employment, which issued a back-to-work order. Twenty strikers were arrested and two hundred others were suspended. In April 1989 the workers struck again to protest the dismissal of thirty union officers. The police and the firm's armed security guards dispersed them violently; twenty-two workers were injured, three were declared missing, and three female strikers were beaten.

Gelmart, a U.S.-owned firm, refused to pay the P120 monthly emergency allowance in 1977, claiming financial distress. This action prompted five thousand workers to go on strike and march to the Department of Labor and Employment. As a result, management suspended two hundred workers. In 1988 Gelmart workers went on a slowdown to protest the transfer of machines to subcontractors, a violation of their collective bargaining agreement.

Some six thousand workers of Novelty Philippines, owned by the U.S. firm Baby Togs, went on strike in April 1981 to protest the dismissal of union workers, the hiring of new workers in their stead, and the pressure put on union members to sign affidavits to avoid dismissal. Philippine Gloves, owned by Fownes Brothers and Company, another U.S. firm, was struck in February 1988 as some eighteen hundred workers protested against nonpayment of wages, subcontracting, and an illegal lockout. Two hundred striking workers were retrenched as a consequence.

Non-U.S. firms have also been affected by strikes. In 1985 workers at Triumph, a German transnational corporation, staged a two-month strike to win severance pay and other financial assistance for workers who were retrenched because of a drop in orders (Aldana 1989, 84–93). In 1989 they struck again on the issue of wage increases. Even the EPZs have not been spared, having witnessed at least twelve strikes since 1981. An analysis of Department of Labor lists from 1988 to 1990 showed the following: sixteen to eighteen firms had actual strikes; 150 to 158 strike notices were posted; and 74,434 to 179,794 working days were lost.

Homework in the Garment Industry

The garment industry is the largest employer of homeworkers.[1] These women, whose ages range from four to seventy-four, live in depressed and sometimes squatter communities in both rural and urban areas. Typically, they live with their extended families in households with below-poverty-line incomes. Most are elementary-school graduates, although a significant number dropped out of the primary grades. Husbands of these homeworkers are usually employed as part-time industrial workers in urban areas or as seasonal farmers and agricultural workers in rural areas. The inability of husbands (and, for unmarried women, parents) to earn a living wage has been one factor contributing to the rise of women homeworkers. Whether married or single, adult female homeworkers are burdened with household chores and childcare in addition to their paid labor. Because garment production lends itself more easily to homework than other industries, and can engage the help of other members of the family, many women—especially those in the traditional garment-producing areas of Bulacan, Rizal, Laguna, and some parts of Metro Manila—engage in garment homework.

Tradition plays a major role in homework for women, both in terms of the industry and in terms of the culture. The garment industry has always relied heavily on women. The export policies of the 1970s, which required abundant, cheap, skilled, and temporary labor, were best served by the employment of women. Socialization helps mold women for obedience, diligence, passivity, cooperation, and responsibility, as well as for performing their duties at home while trying hard to generate added income. Girls receive training by exposure to their mothers and other female family members engaging in needlework at home and in the neighborhood.

Homeworkers have managed to find some advantages to the job, including the opportunity for income generation while staying at home with children, flexible hours, and the ability to get work without first acquiring extensive skills and training. But they cite negative aspects as well, such as excessively low wages, instability of orders, and exploitative and abusive contractors and subcontractors. Other common problems include production expenses (buying thread and renting sewing machines); informality of production arrangements (homeworkers rarely have written contracts establishing employer-employee relations, so they lack many forms of legal labor protection); lack of employment alternatives; and lack of means to start income-generating projects or to improve productivity (e.g., through acquisition of motor-driven or high-speed machines). Together with these production-related problems, women invariably mention the double burden of paid work and household work; the lack of social services (particularly childcare); the absence of credit access, education, training, or markets; and a lack of awareness of their rights.

Garment homeworkers usually aspire to be either subcontractors or regular factory employees. Only those who have attained some knowledge of labor laws and of the similar conditions suffered by other homeworkers have expressed the desire to organize themselves to tackle the negative aspects of homework directly. For the majority of homeworkers, however, the isolation of their work inhibits this process.

Recently, homeworkers in the Philippines established an organization called PATAMABA (Pambansang Tagapag-ugnay ng mga Manggagawa sa Bahay [National network of homeworkers]), which is engaged in nationwide organizing, consciousness-raising, skills-training, research, and advocacy work. The network operates with the help of the International Labour Organization and other governmental and nongovernmental organizations, including the Association of the New Filipina (KaBaPa). PATAMABA has set up garment production cooperatives and has facilitated access to credit, marketing, and technological assistance.

Conclusion

The garment industry is the Philippines's chief nontraditional export sector, registering a consistently upward trend in dollar earnings since 1984. Industry leaders are optimistic that the country will be the garment growth center in the region in the mid-1990s, because the newly industrializing countries (Hong Kong, Korea, Taiwan, and Singapore) are expected to shift to high-tech industries as their workers' wages climb ever higher.

The Philippines has the advantage of highly skilled and low-cost labor, but rival countries in Asia are competing with it in this regard. One competitive disadvantage is the inability of the local textile industry to supply cheap and high-quality fabrics to the garment-export sector; in neighboring countries such as Thailand and Indonesia, textile industries are more developed. Moreover, the overall political situation in these countries seems to be more stable.

Historically, there has always been a high level of foreign, mainly U.S., control in the Philippine garment industry. Since the 1970s Korean, Hong Kong, Japanese, and Taiwanese interests have likewise come in to take advantage of lower wage levels in the Philippines and to make use of the Philippine quota in the U.S. market. The concentration ratio is high, with a few big firms taking the lion's share of total garment exports. The Philippines's dependence on the U.S. market makes its garment industry quite vulnerable. Dependence is also manifested in heavy reliance on imported raw materials, machinery, and designs.

Although the garment industry has generated many jobs, most are at the lower end of the industry where work is often irregular, unprotected, and extremely low-paid. Women workers predominate in the industry and are typically consigned to the poorest jobs. Workers' unrest has haunted the industry since the late 1970s, not sparing the biggest export firms. Unionization proceeds unevenly and exists mainly in the formal sector. Organizing is beginning at the bottom, however, with the homeworkers establishing their own network for greater visibility and empowerment.

Notes

Acknowledgments: This chapter is based on my ten-year research interest in the Philippine garment industry. It is also part of a long-term advocacy to empower women workers, especially those at the bottom of the subcontracting ladder. Special thanks go to Merceditas Cruz for research assistance, Mira Ofreneo for clerical support, and Rene E. Ofreneo for the use of his research files.

1. For further information, see my "Industrial Homework in the Philippines," part of a study sponsored by the International Labor Organization, Geneva; and my *Philippine Garment Industry and Its Homeworkers: Focus on Bulacan Province,* submitted to the Rural Women Homeworkers Project, International Labor Organization, Bangkok, 1989. Part of this work was published under the title "Garment Homeworkers in Bulacan: Views and Initiative," in *Practical Actions for the Social Protection of Homeworkers in the Philippines.* Bangkok: ILO, 1993.

References

Aguilar, Virginia Sinay. 1990. *Subcontracting, Employment, and Industrial Relations in Selected Philippine Export Manufacturing Establishments.* Manila: ILO-Japan-DOLE Multibilateral Projects.

Aguilar, Virginia Sinay, Rene Ofreneo, and Sophronio Amante. 1983. *Domestic Outwork Arrangements in the Footwear and Garment Industries in Selected Philippine Communities: Case Studies.* Quezon City: Institute of Industrial Relations, University of the Philippines.

Aldana, Cornelia H. 1989. *A Contract for Underdevelopment: Subcontracting for Multinationals in the Philippine Semiconductor and Garment Industries.* Manila: Ibon Databank Philippines.

Bureau of Women and Young Workers, Department of Labor and Employment, and National Statistical Coordination Board. 1989. "Development and Implementation of a Data Banking and Reporting System on Women and Young Workers." Table 6. Manila.

Cabalu, Helen Juliet F., and Beulah V. Javier. 1982. "An Evaluation of the Subcontracting Arrangement in a Garment Enterprise: A Case Study." Undergraduate paper, School of Economics, University of the Philippines.

Cezar, John P. 1991. "Wires, Petroleum Kick Gold, Timber out of Top Exports List." *Business World,* March 26.

del Castillo, Butch. 1990. "It's Time to Review GTEB Operations." *Manila Standard,* August 13.

del Castillo, Julie C. 1982. "The Integrated Export Development Strategy, Focus on the Garment Industry." *Business Day,* September 22.

Export Processing Zone Authority (EPZA). 1990. *Investment Incentives and Procedures.* Metro Manila.

Fajardo, Bimba. 1980. "We're Out to Clothe the World." *Times Journal,* November 4.

Garments and Textile Export Board (GTEB). 1989a. *Comparative FOB Value of Garment and Textile Exports.* Metro Manila.

————. 1989b. "Review of the GTEB Mandate." In "Final Report" (September), 1:52–56. In GTEB files.

————. 1990a. *Annual Report.*

————. 1990b. *Comparative FOB Value of Garment and Textile Exports.* Metro Manila.

ITC Newsletter. 1985. 1 (August): 1.

Jimenez, Ma. Elisa L. 1986. *Profile of the Philippine Garments Industry: Focus on the Subcontracting Arrangement.* Quezon City: Institute of Social Work and Community Development, University of the Philippines.

Lim, Manuel T., Sergio M. Andal, Jr., and Ropi S. Dangazo. 1986. *A Strategic Study for the Development of the Garment Industry in the Philippines.* Metro Manila: Center for Research and Communication.

Manila Chronicle. 1986. "800M Garments Exports Expected." December 10.

Paglaban, Enrico. 1978. "Philippine Workers in the Export Industry." *Pacific Research* 9:6.

Pamintuan, Florentino B. 1990. "Power Shortage Delays Garment Export Orders." *Business Star,* April 27.

Philippine Development. 1976. "Garments: From Rags to Riches," July 31, 21.

————. 1981. "The Embroidery and Apparel Industry: An Overview." 10(1): 11.

Philippine Trade and Development. 1975. "The Garment Industry: Growth, Potentials, and Prospects." August.

Plant, Robert. 1981. *Industries in Trouble.* Geneva: International Labour Office.

Reyes, Alice H. 1989. "RP Garments Industry Dressed Up for a Killing in the Export Market." *Daily Globe,* July 31.

Saludo, Noemi L. 1990. "A Close Look at the Garment Export Industry." *Philippines Free Press,* November 3.

Tolentino, Ernesto. 1990. "Garment Industry Wars on GTEB." *Manila Standard,* August 10.

Williamson, H. 1987. "Garment Industry: A Review of the Export and Domestic Industry with Proposed Strategies and Plans 1987–1996." Report in GTEB files, Manila.

Chapter 10

Thailand in the Pacific Rim Garment Industry

Richard F. Doner and Ansil Ramsay

Thailand has enjoyed one of the most rapid economic growth rates in the world. Between 1965 and 1989 only six other developing countries had higher annual growth rates of GNP per capita (World Bank 1991, 202–3). One of the major contributors to this growth has been the garment industry. From small beginnings in the late 1960s, it became Thailand's largest export earner between 1986 and 1990.[1] Even more impressive, Thailand now ranks among the world's top fifteen garment-exporting countries (GATT 1990, 66). Thailand is one of a handful of less-developed countries that has been able to break into the ranks of the world's major clothing exporters (Mytelka 1991, 135).

Industry Evolution and Structure

Thailand's garment industry did not begin to develop until the late 1960s. Domestic consumer demand for garments was limited, and there was "almost no development of a garment industry, even as an import-substitution type" (JICA 1989, C-5). Ready-made garments became increasingly popular in the early 1970s, as rising per capita income helped to create demand. When the garment industry first developed, it was divided into two parts. One was aimed at domestic demand, including border trade with Burma and Indochina, and one "was aimed from the start at exports" (JICA 1989, C-5).

Initially, most garment-industry production was for the domestic market, but since 1970 there has been a substantial increase in exports. The value of exports rose from US$51.3 million in 1975 to US$2,576.8 million in 1990. In 1989 more garments were exported than were sold domestically (*Bangkok Post Weekly Review,* July 2, 1990, p. 20). Part of this expansion may be attributed to the relatively dualistic market. There are approximately 18,000 garment manufacturers in Thailand (JICA 1989, 2:11), but rough estimates from the late 1980s suggest that only 1,100 to 1,400 companies produced garments for export; of these, approximately 50 companies accounted for 60 to 70 percent of total exports (Steele 1989, 11).

Sources of Garment Growth

Domestic Factors

Analysis of the domestic sources of the expansion of the Thai garment industry must begin with state-societal arrangements. The organization of the civil society and the state, and the institutional links between the two, influences a country's capacity to develop and diffuse new technology (Hart 1992, 255). Although corporatists and their critics disagree on the primary criteria of economic success, it is nevertheless clear that there are basic requirements for successful economic growth, especially for countries vulnerable to external shocks. First, there must be pressure on entrepreneurs to achieve dynamic efficiency; such pressures can come from powerful state agencies using macroeconomic policies and/or from intense competition among firms. Second, there must be the capacity to resolve the numerous cases of market failure occurring in the process of development. Whether one considers firms' abilities to capture externalities (positive interfirm side effects), or the availability of collective or public goods beyond the capacity or willingness of particular firms to provide, increases in productivity require institutional arrangements that must reconcile individual needs and capacities for the good of the industry or country.

In this context, it is apparent that features of the Thai political economy that have encouraged garment-industry growth up to the present have also raised obstacles for continued growth and economic expansion; these obstacles are addressed in a later section.

State Factors

The relative autonomy of central economic agencies, especially the Bank of Thailand and the Ministry of Finance, has played a central role in Thai economic growth. This autonomy has enabled the state to pursue steady macroeconomic policies, including a commitment to a stable currency, low inflation, and conservative borrowing. Thai businesses operate in a setting of economic stability lacking in many Third World countries. This relative autonomy—in conjunction with the rules restricting parliamentary intervention in the budget process—has also resulted in "hard budget" constraints, limiting political leaders' ability to support inefficient firms and projects through state funding. Such inclinations have been further constrained by the absence of bonanza sources of revenue. State support for inefficient firms has not been eliminated, but Thai policies are more limited than those of many less-developed countries. Firms are more likely to be vulnerable to market forces, encouraging innovation in seeking new production methods and markets. The relatively fragmented nature of the Thai state has allowed many competing firms to emerge in the garment industry and in other business sectors. Unlike President Ferdinand Marcos in the Philippines, no Thai leader has been capable of promoting particular "crony" firms while suppressing others. Finally, there are pockets of efficiency within state agencies where capable and innovative state officials have promoted growth.

In addition to these general features of the Thai state, specific state policies have promoted the growth of the garment sector. The Board of Investment (BOI) made garments a promoted industry in 1967. Firms promoted by the BOI "are exempted from import duties and business taxes on machinery and equipment"; they are also exempted from corporate income taxes for varying lengths of time (Tonguthai 1991, 4). The state has further assisted with export promotion by enacting several favorable policies, including tax rebates on imported fabrics, yarns, and sewing machines; low interest rates; and reimbursement of taxes on export sales. Export help has also been available through the Department of Export Promotion (DEP), a part of the Commerce Ministry. The DEP has worked effectively with the Thai Garment Manufacturers' Association (TGMA) to sponsor exhibitions of Thai garments in Thailand and in European trade fairs. The Commerce Industry cooperated with the TGMA in quota negotiations with importing Multifiber Arrangement (MFA) member countries (Tonguthai 1991, 4).

Societal Factors

The government's support for garment production has been enthusiastic but not very extensive; private-sector and labor efforts, as well as the relative openness of foreign markets, have proven to be more influential. The particular features of capitalist-class development in Thailand have contributed considerably to the industry's growth. The country's economic expansion has been led by a dynamic Sino-Thai business class unhindered by serious ethnic tensions. Many early entrepreneurs had considerable experience in textiles, access to textile expertise from Shanghai after World War II, and connections with garment producers in other Asian countries. Early capital accumulation by these entrepreneurs' agricultural export activities provided the basis for the growth of banking and manufacturing, including textiles and garments. As discussed later, large commercial banks and business groups provided financing and other organizational supports to the expanding textile industry. Despite the existence of banks and business groups, however, a high level of competition within this private sector and a relatively fragmented political system have allowed a constant supply of new entrants. Finally, a tradition of cautious macroeconomic management by central bankers has resulted in realistic and stable exchange rates supportive of garment exports.

The second societal factor contributing to the rapid growth of the garment industry is the availability of a large, poorly organized, and politically weak work force. The Japanese International Cooperation Agency noted that "the Thai garment industry at the present time relies solely on 'cheap wages' " (JICA 1989, C-37). To this day, a large percentage of the Thai population (compared to that of other Southeast Asian countries) is engaged in agriculture; as the land frontier narrows, a steady supply of workers seeks jobs in urban areas, an abundance contributing to the pervading low wages. The Thai government maintains tight control over labor unions, leaving them too weak to negotiate for higher wages. The textile industry has the highest density of labor unions in the private sector, yet in 1990 "only about 2.5 percent of textile firms were unionized" (Satitniramai 1992, 33). In the garment industry only 1 percent of the firms were unionized. Union organization is also hampered by Thailand's flexible labor market; many urban workers from the countryside return to their villages during periods of slack labor demand (Phongpaichit 1992, 49). This situation clearly weakens the basis for strong unions, in a pattern somewhat similar to that of Taiwan. The development of unions also is impeded by the lack of ties between political parties and subordinate groups.

The garment industry continues to employ an overwhelming majority of women, especially in sewing and finishing jobs. Their wages have improved since the 1970s; conditions remain poor in many smaller firms, however, with wages below the minimum and few if any benefits. A study in the mid-1980s found that when overtime work was included, wages in the garment industry were generally higher than the minimum wage, although there were large discrepancies among firms.[2] Export-oriented and large firms paid higher wages and provided better working conditions than domestically oriented, smaller firms (Yosamornsuntorn 1986). A 1990 survey of small garment firms found workers making 72 to 108 baht per day (approximately US$2.88 to US$4.32), when the minimum wage was 100 baht (approximately US$4.00). These smaller firms can be extremely dangerous places in which to work. In 1990 eleven women died when a fire began in a four-story shop-house factory and they were unable to escape because of steel window grids. The women had been working fourteen-hour days and sleeping in the factory (*Bangkok Post Weekly Review,* November 3, 1990, 1).

State-Societal Linkages

The textile and garment sector is marked by a mix of clientelist and more functionally based ties between state and society. In the 1950s and 1960s clientelist ties predominated. Sukree Photiratanangkun made use of such ties with military and civilian officials to build his TBI Group into the largest integrated textile and garment firm in Thailand. More recently, functionally based ties have evolved, as representatives of the state and industry associations have developed strong working relationships. One example is the team of officials that worked with textile and garment industry representatives to negotiate a new quota agreement with the United States in 1991. Such relationships have become increasingly institutionalized. The domestic quota-allocation system (described in a subsequent section) is another area of linkage that has led to the expansion of Thai garment exports.

State efforts focus on promoting exports, because officials have a direct interest in increasing exports for revenue reasons. In other areas, linkages are weak; in some cases, they are obstacles to industry growth. State subsidies to the garment industry are insignificant, and research and development assistance is nil. The Thai state does little to provide information to the industry about technological changes or marketing. In the efforts to find solutions to various collective-action problems confronting the industry (such as the shortage of skilled Thai engineers and technicians and the weak linkages between the textile and garment sectors), state contributions are meager. Solving these problems is left to other institutions. Finally, some remaining clientelist relationships, especially those providing protection for a monopolistic dyestuff sector, are roadblocks to the further development of the textile and garment industry.

In summary, state-societal arrangements in Thailand have contributed to the rapid growth of the garment industry through a distribution of power distinguished by a state strong enough to sustain a stable macroeconomic climate but not so strong as to privilege favored firms; a dynamic Sino-Thai business class with firm links to outside support, domestic banks, and increasing coordination with the state; and a labor pool that remains plentiful, poorly organized, and relatively cheap.

International Markets

Externally, changing world markets and exchange-rate shifts have encouraged garment-industry growth, with foreign investment playing a minor but possibly expanding role. The industry's rapid growth has depended in part on timing: Thai growth was accelerating just as increasing restrictions were imposed on established exporters. In the 1970s U.S. and European Community restrictions on garment imports from Hong Kong, South Korea, and Taiwan gave Thai garment producers an opportunity to expand their exports to these markets. A 1971 bilateral agreement with the United States cleared the way for rapid export growth by placing less restrictive controls—as compared to those on East Asian NICs—on Thai garment exports (JICA 1989, 2:2). Subsequent agreements with the United States (in 1975) and the European Community (in 1976) provided Thai garment makers with assured markets, encouraging them to expand production.

Thailand moved into garment exports as garment buyers from the United States and Europe were looking for "low processing costs the world over. The garment manufacturers of Thailand seemed to fit the bill" (JICA 1989, 2:64). In the 1970s textiles and clothing were "relatively labour-intensive industries in which technology was stable, goods were largely standardized, competition was based on price, and economies of scale were relatively important" (Mytelka 1991, 111). Thailand was well suited to compete under these conditions, and its garment-export industry has been shaped by them. Primarily, the industry depends on orders from foreign customers who do their own design and marketing. Wholesalers and department stores are the major buyers of Thai apparel, followed by mail-order companies and specialty stores (Melnichuk 1990, 91). Thai firms produce clothes for Nordstrom, London Fog, Yves Saint-Laurent, Marks and Spencer, Liz Claiborne, Esprit, Calvin Klein, and Pierre Cardin, among others (Melnichuk 1990, 92; Steele 1989, 12). These customers are the major source of garment producers' information about foreign markets.

Further growth for the Thai garment industry came with a major devaluation of the baht in 1984 and the upward reevaluation of Taiwan's and Korea's currencies in 1985. Currency shifts made Thai garments more competitive in world markets and encouraged NIC garment producers to begin relocating production abroad (Siriwatpatara 1989, 155). There was a big jump in Thai garment exports in 1986 and 1987 (JICA 1989, 2:24). Despite increased foreign investment in recent years, the garment industry remains largely in domestic hands (JICA 1989, 2:70). In a 1991 interview, Viroj Amatakulchai, president of the Thai Garment Makers' Association, estimated that the foreign share of the garment industry was 10 percent (interview in Bangkok, July 1991). One recent estimate of foreign affiliates' share of textile, clothing, and leather exports was only 11.4 percent (Sibunruang and Brimble 1990, 74).

With the gradual upgrading of Thai garments and the industry's efforts to penetrate the (nonquota) Japanese market, there has been an increase in Japanese investments in the Thai garment industry. Hong Kong garment manufacturers have also invested in Thailand (Lardner 1988; Steele 1989, 13). In these instances, in spite of Thai majority holdings, the plants "are run as integral parts of international producing groups, for which Hong Kong is merely one of a number of manufacturing locations serviced by centralised marketing departments" (Steele 1989, 13).

Growth through Exports: Quota and Nonquota Markets

State-society relations, changing world markets, and exchange rates have facilitated the rapid growth of the Thai garment industry, but they have not guaranteed export growth. Garment exporters must navigate within a complex global market divided into quota and nonquota components. Thailand's more important nonquota markets include the Middle East, eastern Europe, some African countries, and Japan. Quota markets include the United States, the European Community, Sweden, Norway, Canada, Finland, and Austria. Quotas have been regulated through a series of bilateral agreements within the Multifiber Arrangement. Sales to quota markets have required that Thailand, like all exporting countries, distribute quota rights among potential exporters. In our view, the Thai quota-allocation system has facilitated the country's garment exports. Although this system lacks transparency and promotes rent seeking, it provides security for large firms and encourages smaller firms to explore nonquota markets, sometimes by pursuing subcontracting agreements. The general pattern has been for large-scale garment exporters to export to the quota markets of the United States and the European Community, while small and medium-sized exporters have found niches in nonquota markets (Siamwalla, Wiboonchutikula, and Sathirathai 1989, 35; Siriwatpatara 1989, 197). The Thai quota system benefits large, existing exporters more than newer and smaller firms. Large exporters who had established a strong record of exports received the largest principal quotas when they went into effect. The residual quota system also benefits these exporters.

Major Thai garment exporters acknowledge that the quotas are beneficial (Siriwatpatara 1989, 96–97). As well as protecting them from domestic competition, the quotas implicitly discriminate against NIC garment exporters—some of the Thai exporters' main rivals. Without the quotas, gaining access to markets in the United States and the European Community would have been much more difficult (Suphachalasai 1990, 60). There was a clear test of this thesis in 1982 when Norway withdrew from the MFA and turned to a global quota system. Under this new arrangement, Thailand's garment exports to Norway dropped dramatically, as Norwegian importers chose to buy from suppliers in Hong Kong, Taiwan, and Korea (Siamwalla, Wiboonchutikula, and Sathirathai 1989, 38; Siriwatpatara 1989, 96).

The quota system has been tinkered with frequently since its inception, partly as a result of lobbying by disadvantaged firms and partly because of rent seeking by ministers of commerce. Rent seeking is encouraged by the lack of transparency in the system; residual quota allocations are kept secret, and access to this information is carefully guarded by Commerce Ministry officials—only the officials and the firms receiving the residual quotas know the details. Apparently, several ministers of commerce have used these quota rents to provide funds for their political parties. Despite efforts to modify the system, it remains largely intact, continuing to benefit large, well-established firms.

Smaller firms thus have limited opportunities to obtain quotas. Although their sale is illegal, quotas are bought, and their prices on the underground market are well known. In July 1992 the standard price was US$.28 per garment. The typical practice is for a small firm to find a buyer for its garments and then scramble to find a quota to export the order. This procedure allows small firms some access to the quota market outside normal channels, and in this sense corruption "works"; nevertheless, the system bias against small firms remains. Illegally bought quotas are good for only one season, and they are expensive, often costing 10 percent of the shipment's value. Some of the larger garment exporters have also begun to move into nonquota markets (Siriwatpatara 1989, 191). Garment exports to the Middle East, and more recently to eastern Europe, have increased dramatically. In 1991 Poland became the second largest importer of Thai textiles and garments in the world; in 1989 it was ranked twentieth (*Bangkok Post Weekly Review*, January 24, 1992, 14). Quota markets used to absorb 70 percent of Thai garment exports, but by 1990 these markets accounted for only 52 percent.

In the extremely competitive and volatile nonquota markets, where orders vary from year to year, Thai garment exporters have been challenged by several garment-exporting countries offering lower wages. To deal with these uncertainties, small and medium-sized firms have turned increasingly to subcontracting, a trend that has accelerated since 1987. Although some subcontracted products are destined for domestic sales, most are produced by smaller firms for nonquota markets and for border sales to Burma and Indochina. These are essentially commodity markets, in which the major competition comes from Bangladesh and other low-cost producers. Subcontracting affords access to cheap labor and allows smaller firms to handle overflow orders without making new capital investments that may be unused in the following year.

Unlike the case in Taiwan, subcontracting in Thailand generally does not involve satellite firms. In the modal pattern, a small factory does the more difficult work and then subcontracts directly to home workshops. The geographical scope of subcontracting in Thailand has expanded into the provinces. In one case, a firm sent a truckload of precut fabric to a village in the northeast overnight. Villagers met the truck in the morning, sewed during the day, and returned the completed garments to the truck, which arrived in Bangkok the following morning.

Problems Facing the Garment Industry

Thai labor costs have risen both absolutely and relatively compared to those in Caribbean and Asian countries (such as Indonesia, the People's Republic of China, and India). As the skills of workers in these countries improve, the challenge to Thailand will increase. If Thailand's garment industry is to continue to grow, it must move into higher value-added garments. To do so, it must overcome its major obstacles: insufficient linkages between the downstream garment sector and the upstream (dyeing, printing, and finishing) sectors, and labor problems, including rising costs and the dearth of skilled workers (JICA 1989, C-41).

Links between the textile and garment sectors in Thailand are weak. Thai garment plants lack sophisticated machinery and dyeing and printing capacities. Much of the fabric produced in Thailand is exported as gray cloth (undyed fabric), and its quality is not good enough for use in the domestic export industry. Thus Thai garment manufacturers—especially those manufacturing for export—must import much of their fabric (Tonguthai 1991, 22). These problems are in turn a function of several related factors, including high tariffs on machinery and dyestuffs due to rent seeking by protected interests, and revenue concerns of the Ministry of Finance.

The shortage of domestic fabrics also means that Thai garment producers cannot react rapidly to changing fashion trends (JICA 1989, C-32). These trends threaten Thai garment exporters who have built their plants with large numbers of machines and workers aimed at mass production. Few are equipped to provide small runs of high-quality, diverse products (JICA 1989, 2:37). Poor-quality textile supplies also hamper Thailand's trade with Japan. Japan imports only about 2 percent of Thailand's total garment exports, while the United States and European Community countries account for 21 and 30 percent, respectively (Siamwalla, Wiboonchutikula, and Sathirathai 1989, 34).

The rising cost of labor and the shortage of skilled workers pose a formidable problem for the industry. Without skilled personnel, Thailand is unable to manufacture higher value-added garments (Tonguthai 1991, 23, 29–31). Universities and vocational and technical colleges produce only 250 graduates annually with specialties in textile and clothing (Tonguthai 1991, 18).

All these problems contribute to Thai garment producers' considerable handicap in international competition. Thailand forfeits value-added by having to import textiles. There has been a "chronic excess of imports of textiles over exports" since 1983 (JICA 1989, 1:8).

Sustaining Growth: The Role of Institutions

Given rising labor costs and strengthening Asian competitors, continued reliance on cheap domestic labor will not sustain Thailand's garment-export growth. Thai firms are exploring two options: some search for cheaper labor in neighboring countries, and some—through improved domestic production—move into higher-quality goods. We focus on the latter option. In an effort to identify the institutions through which the industry might best seek to address these challenges, we proceed from the assumption that industry-specific transactions occur along a continuum of sectoral governance structures. These range from the neoclassical free-market ideal (standard arm's-length contracts among independent actors in competitive markets) to more collaborative and hierarchical arrangements among and/or within firms, in some cases involving state participation and leadership (Kitschelt 1991, 462). The question, then, is twofold: What arrangements should the Thai garment industry adopt to resolve the problems outlined above? What arrangements seem politically and organizationally feasible?

More Collaborative Arrangements

Historically, technology in textiles and garments has developed under governance structures prescribed by neoclassical free-market ideals. But global pressure for greater flexibility and domestic pressure for better linkages in Thailand have increased the need for more collaborative arrangements. The necessity of a quick response to external-demand changes with relatively small batches has encouraged Thai firms to search domestically for more readily accessible yarn and fabrics instead of imported goods. The move to domestic procurement has been further prompted by efforts to capture greater value-added in exports, to cut inventory costs, and to reduce the industry's trade deficit.

Increasing local fabric and yarn input for highly specialized goods will require greater information sharing among upstream, midstream, and downstream industries. It will also require that fiber, yarn, and fabric producers be encouraged and/or compelled to abandon immediate profits for long-term quality improvements for the overall good of the industry.

In sum, improving garment production and exports now requires decision makers to view garments as being inextricably linked to a broader textile/apparel "commodity chain" and to focus on reconciling the interests of each of the chain's components in light of market pressures. That means promoting attempts to resolve differences on tariffs, entry barriers, and the provision of public or collective goods (such as employee training and wastewater treatment).

Thus sustained growth requires market-based linkages to be supplemented by more collective efforts, whether involving business associations, public-private sector networks, or state support. The importance of extramarket institutions is confirmed not only by the experience of the more successful garment exporters, such as Korea and Taiwan, but also by that of the disappointing cases, such as the Philippines and Colombia.

Domestic Structuralism

The need for efficient governance structures does not guarantee their emergence; existing industry and governmental institutions have constrained the development of more efficient organizations. Not all of Thailand's preexisting institutions hinder the country's prospects for creating more efficient ones, however. On the positive side, Thailand has features that suggest the possibility for institutional cohesion and efficient responses to competitive pressures. The country is not riddled by the kind of ethnic divisions that weaken economic and political linkages in Indonesia, for example. And Thailand's private sector is noted for both large business groups with high levels of competition and low entry barriers for new entrants.

Business groups have shown a considerable capacity for both foreign investment and domestic upgrading. They have been helped by Thailand's large commercial banks, especially the Bangkok Bank. This bank has offered critical assistance with locating local engineering and managerial talent, organizing capacity-reduction agreements, and financing local firms' moves into mid- and upstream production.

Despite their impressive size, business groups have not been able to dominate public policy. The relatively fragmented nature of Thai political interests, described as a "moving equilibrium," has precluded their presenting the kinds of political rigidities stymieing textile and apparel growth in the Philippines and Colombia (Overholt 1988).

The state's traditionally low capacity and willingness for effective intervention, and the private sector's weak associational strength, present a less optimistic picture. Since the mid-nineteenth century fiscal stability has been the overriding concern of Thai leaders. Until the early 1980s revenue from diversified agricultural exports helped to maintain fiscal balances. There was little need for functional linkages between those controlling trade policy (in the Finance Ministry) and industry groups. The trade regime served to generate revenues rather than to promote linkages among upstream, midstream, and downstream firms. The capacity for effective intervention was also weakened by politicians' tendencies to view ministries as sources of largesse, rather than as opportunities to make sectoral production processes more efficient. The relatively low level of organization in the Thai private sector has also undermined the emergence of more efficient governance structures. Until the 1980s Thai business associations tended to be narrow and peak associations especially weak.

Non-Path-Dependent Learning

Herbert Kitschelt suggests that countries constrained by prior institutional endowments will develop new and more efficient governance structures only on rare occasions; events such as an economic depression, a loss in a major war, or a fundamental altering of a country's position in the international system are required to shake up existing institutional arrangements (1991, 469–70). Although this scenario captures the necessity of external pressure for change, we suggest that the shift out of path-dependent learning may be less cataclysmic and more mediated by domestic factors in the Thai case. More specifically, Thailand's potential for institutional innovation stems from its domestic vulnerability to losses of export revenues and its relative ethnic harmony.

Thailand's susceptibility to export-revenue loss seems to have accelerated the need for institutional and technological innovation. The early 1980s slump in commodity prices, combined with the country's traditional concern with fiscal stability, prompted the beginning of new tendencies within the broader political economy. These tendencies include greater concern with manufactured exports on the part of macroeconomic policy makers, strengthening of export-oriented private interests, private-sector associational growth pressing for export-promoting policy changes, and an expansion of nonclientelist discussion between state officials and business-associations (Laothamatas 1992).

These changes are uneven, but they are apparent in textiles and garments. The importance of exports has strengthened the position of garment firms vis-à-vis upstream groups, thus altering the power configurations among components of the commodity chain. The main apparel group, the Thai Garment Manufacturers' Association, has become increasingly active in attempting to improve the quality of textile inputs and in proposing needed tariff reforms to make the industry more effective in the global arena.

We do not wish to exaggerate Thailand's progress; the country still lacks a major textile technology institution of the sort developed by the early 1980s by Korea; nor does the Thai state have a functioning agency to coordinate this industry. Since 1980, however, the industry has clearly increased its organizational capacities. This mixed record highlights the importance of nonmarket institutions for reconciling individual interests with broader industry concerns. Whether Thailand's potential for achieving institutional innovation is realized depends on shifting political arrangements—factors beyond the scope of this chapter. We have argued that such innovation is necessary and that it is at least possible.

Notes

Acknowledgments: We are grateful for the help of Suphat Suphachalasai and Pawadee Tonguthai in writing this chapter.

1. Garments were surpassed by electronics as the top export earner in 1990 (*Bangkok Post Weekly Review,* January 3, 1992, p. 12).

2. In 1986 the average wage (including overtime) for the 206 workers interviewed was US$3.21 per day. The minimum wage at the time was US$2.66 (Yosamornsuntorn 1986, 58).

References

General Agreement on Tariffs and Trade (GATT). 1990. *International Trade.* Geneva.

Hart, Jeffrey A. 1992. "The Effects of State-Societal Arrangements on International Competitiveness: Steel, Motor Vehicles, and Semiconductors in the United States, Japan, and Western Europe." *British Journal of Political Science* 22(3): 255–300.

Japan International Cooperation Agency (JICA). 1989. *A Study on Industrial Sector Development in the Kingdom of Thailand: Second Year Final Draft Report.* Bangkok.

Kitschelt, Herbert. 1991. "Industrial Governance Structures, Innovation Strategies, and the Case of Japan: Sectoral or Cross-National Comparative Analysis?" *International Organization* 45(4): 453–94.

Laothamatas, Anek. 1992. *Business Associations and the New Political Economy of Thailand.* Boulder, Colo.: Westview Press.

Lardner, James. 1988. "Annals of Business: Global Clothing Industry." *New Yorker,* January 11, 39–73.

Melnichuk, Pawalpat. 1990. "Chasing the Rising Sun: A Study of Thai Garment Companies Exporting to Japan and the United States." Master's thesis, Cornell University.

Mytelka, Lynn Krieger. 1991. "Technological Change and the Global Relocation of Production in Textiles and Clothing." *Studies in Political Economy* 36 (Fall): 109–43.

Overholt, William H. 1988. "Thailand: A Moving Equilibrium." In *Thailand-U.S. Relations: Changing Political, Strategic, and Economic Factors,* edited by Ansil Ramsay and Wiwat Mungkandi. Berkeley: Institute of East Asian Studies, University of California.

Phongpaichit, Pasuk. 1992. "Nu, Nit, Noi, and the Informal Economic Sector in the Development of Thailand" [in Thai]. *Thammasat Economic Journal* 10(2): 33–52.

Satitniramai, Apichat. 1992. "The Formation of Labor Unions in the Textile Industry." Master's thesis, Faculty of Economics, Thammasat University, Bangkok.

Siamwalla, Ammar, Paitoon Wiboonchutikula, and Surakiart Sathirathai. 1989. "Fun and Games with Quotas: Thailand and the VERs on Cassava and Garments." Paper presented at the International Conference on Voluntary Export Restraints, Trade Policy Research Center, Washington, D.C., June 5–8.

Sibunruang, Atchaka, and Peter Brimble. 1990. "Foreign Direct Investment in Thailand: Recent Trends and Policy Issues." *Asia-Pacific TNC Review.* ESCAP/UNCTC Publications, series A.

Siriwatpatara, Kaewjai. 1989. "A Study of the MFA and Bilateral Agreements and the Effects of Quota Restriction on Thai Textile Exports." Master's thesis, Faculty of Economics, Thammasat University, Bangkok.

Steele, Peter. 1989. "Thailand's Garment Export Trade." *Textile Outlook International,* March, 8–25.

Suphachalasai, Suphat. 1990. "Export Growth of Thai Clothing and Textiles." *World Economy* 13 (March): 51–73.

Tonguthai, Pawadee. 1991. *Thailand's Textile and Clothing Industry: The Role of Women.* Vienna: United Nations Industrial Development Organization.

World Bank. 1991. *World Development Report.* New York: Oxford University Press.

Yosamornsuntorn, Amphan. 1986. "Wages and Working Conditions in the Garment Industry. "Master's thesis, Faculty of Economics, Thammasat University, Bangkok.

Chapter 11

The Garment Industry in Singapore: Clothes for the Emperor

Sara U. Douglas, Stephen A. Douglas, and
Thomas J. Finn

The rulers of modern Singapore inherited a tradition of entrepôt trade, a well-developed port, and a highly industrious population. This combination of assets led Singapore to export-oriented industrialization before any other country in the region (Ariff and Hill 1985). Not surprisingly, textile and apparel manufacture was a contributor to this process. The more crucial contributor, described below, has been an extraordinary set of state agencies. These agencies, operating in a context of continuous political leadership and highly centralized policymaking, are part of a process that ensures that in Singapore clothes (and in fact all industrial output) are indeed "for the emperor."

Scale of Production

In the 1960s and 1970s a variety of foreign-based transnational companies, including many textile and apparel manufacturers, entered Singapore's economy. Already searching for ways to avoid quota restrictions, enterprises in Hong Kong and Taiwan were attracted by Singapore's generous tax and export incentives, low labor costs, supportive (i.e., repressive) labor policy, inexpensive building sites, and excellent port facilities. Although usually obscured by high-output industries, the textile, clothing, footwear, and leather industries as a group contributed significantly to state economic planners' objectives both by relieving unemployment and by boosting the country's export statistics. This industry group accounted for only 6.3 percent of increased value-added and 5.3 percent of increased output in manufacturing, yet provided 14.8 percent of Singapore's new employment by sector and an export-output ratio of 56.1 percent in 1969 (Rodan 1989).

In 1970 Singapore's textile and apparel subsectors (of the textile industry or textile complex) were comparable in size; textiles produced 49.5 percent of total industry output and 49.7 percent of value-added, and apparel contributed 50.4 and 50.3 percent of output and value-added, respectively. Although garment production expanded, the growth of the textile sector slowed during the 1970s, dropping severely in the first half of the 1980s before beginning to regain strength. The average annual percentage decrease in output between 1981 and 1990 was 0.3 percent for textiles; apparel showed an 11.7 percent increase. By 1990 the sectors had become quite differentiated; textiles produced only 17 percent of total industry output and 18 percent of value-added (Department of Statistics, Singapore 1970–88, 1989–91).

The more capital-intensive textile production includes such activities as polymerization (production of manufactured fiber), spinning (yarns from both natural and manufactured fibers), yarn texturizing, weaving and knitting of fabrics, finishing of yarn and fabrics, and the manufacture of made-up textile goods except apparel (e.g., laces, braids, cordage, rope, twine, carpets, and rugs). Because of Singapore's limited resources, almost all fiber used by the textile industry must be imported. It is then processed in the spinning, weaving, and finishing operations that account for most of the textile sector's output.[1] Some establishments dye and finish imported gray goods. Mills in Singapore primarily produce knitted fabrics and printcloths of cotton and cotton-polyester blends used by domestic apparel manufacturers.

During the first half of the 1980s the industry contracted noticeably, partly because of a dwindling labor supply and rising labor costs. Production for export lagged behind imports. Perhaps the most remarkable and significant statistic bearing on textile production—and a compelling vindication of government policy—was the increase in value-added per employee, from US$1.1 million in 1970, to US$7.7 million in 1980, and to US$17.4 million in 1990.

For Singapore's apparel industry, output as a percentage of total manufacturing registered a moderate increase between 1970 and 1990, rising from 1.9 to 2.4 percent. This figure translated, however, into an impressive increase over that twenty-year period of 342 percent. Singapore's small garment-manufacturing companies employed slightly more than 28,000 persons in 371 establishments in 1990. Several Singaporean designers, having achieved name recognition for themselves and their labels, have established manufacturing companies and are trying to gain increased international recognition. They became successful largely by way of their own boutiques, as well as the support of local retail stores, shopping centers, and regional trade shows organized by the Trade Development Board.

Larger apparel firms, typically more capital intensive and export oriented, have engaged primarily in contract manufacturing for foreign companies. Value-added in this sector rose from US$7.7 million in 1970, to US$124.5 million in 1980, and to US$285.5 million in 1990. Over the same period, productivity per employee rose from US$2.8 million, to US$14.6 million, and to US$33.8 million in 1990 (Table 11.1).

The Textile and Garment Manufacturers Association of Singapore (TGMAS, an active trade association that represented approximately 230 manufacturers as of 1991), the Trade Development Board (TDB), and the Economic Development Board (EDB) were responsible for reducing the industry's reliance on labor and promoting high-value clothing. The TDB and EDB, usually acting on plans submitted by TGMAS, often provide financial support to industry-wide projects. The goals of these projects include increased automation and improved productivity, worker training, fashion design, and market development.[2] TDB and EDB, increasingly recognized as "business architects," are among the four state agencies that invest large sums of state money. This approach has held the private sector's domestic investment costs down. At the same time, the state has encouraged Singaporean companies to invest abroad. These circumstances help explain the decline in domestic textile and apparel net-investment commitments by an average annual percentage of 6.2 percent between 1981 and 1988. Fortunately, this decline was offset by foreign

Table 11.1

Principal Statistics of Singapore's Apparel Industry, Various Years

Year	No. of Firms (10+ Employees)	No. of Firms as % of Total Manufacturing Firms	No. of Paid Employees	Output Value (US$ millions)	Output Value as % of Total Manufacturing Output Value	Average Annual Wages (US$ millions)	Census Values Added (US$ millions)	Output per Employee (US$ millions)	Value-Added per Employee (US$ millions)	Average Annual Wage per Employee (US$ thousands)
1970	162	9.1	9,987	27.8	1.9	5.1	7.7	2.8	0.8	0.5
1980	374	11.0	27,188	396.4	2.6	70.4	124.5	14.6	4.6	2.6
1981	374	10.8	27,870	438.2	2.5	85.0	146.0	15.7	5.2	3.0
1982	406	11.2	28,608	434.1	2.5	95.0	152.3	15.2	5.3	3.3
1983	391	10.7	27,234	440.8	2.5	101.5	156.3	16.2	5.7	3.7
1984	387	10.5	25,710	509.3	2.6	111.2	171.1	19.8	6.7	4.3
1985	370	10.5	24,782	470.6	2.7	103.3	157.1	19.0	6.3	4.2
1986	371	10.7	24,842	570.5	3.3	102.2	166.2	23.0	6.7	4.1
1987	373	10.5	27,718	740.4	3.4	121.1	220.3	26.7	7.9	4.4
1988	379	10.2	29,081	860.3	3.1	137.2	257.1	29.6	8.8	4.7
1989	372	10.1	29,105	918.2	2.8	N/A	279.2	31.5	9.6	N/A
1990	371	9.9	28,086	950.1	2.4	N/A	285.5	33.8	10.2	N/A
Avg Annual % Change										
1970–80	11.9	1.9	15.7	120.5	3.3	116.4	137.9	38.3	43.2	38.2
1981–90	−0.1	−0.8	0.1	11.7	−0.4	7.7[a]	9.6	11.5	9.6	7.1[a]

Sources: Adapted from Singapore Department of Statistics, *Yearbook of Statistics,* various years. Data for 1989 and 1990 adapted from Singapore Department of Statistics, *Monthly Digest of Statistics,* April 1991 (Singapore: Singapore National Printers Ltd.).

Note: Conversion from Singapore$ to US$ is based on average annual exchange rates, Singapore Department of Statistics, *Monthly Digest of Statistics,* various years. N/A = Not available.

[a] Avg annual % change, 1981–88.

net-investment commitments, which make up the largest portion of investment commitments to the industry.

In the other Southeast Asian countries the textile complex constitutes one of the largest manufacturing sectors and is a primary contributor of export earnings, employment, and gross domestic product. In contrast, Singapore's textile and apparel industries account for less than 3 percent of the country's manufacturing output and have never contributed more than 6 percent of the country's exports. Although they are not so vital as some others to Singapore's national development, these industries complement the country's overall economic strategy, especially in the case of labor issues.

Labor

By the mid-1970s state authorities were boasting of successes in speeding the economy's progress toward less labor-intensive activities (Goh 1976). Rather than focusing on products, governmental policies emphasized processes, such as education, technical training, and labor management.[3] Programs in these and related areas have encouraged value-added and upmarket manufacturing, leaving standardized production to other countries that can perform more cheaply. These developments have led to a more automated domestic industry, attuned to such applications of high technology as electronic data interchange, color-matching technology, "responsive manufacturing," speed sourcing, unit production systems, and finishing modules. That is the case in plants in Singapore as well as in offshore, Singapore-owned plants (Braithwaite 1991).

In 1988 the average annual wage paid to employees in textiles was US$7,400, slightly less than the average wage paid to workers in all manufacturing industries (US$7,800); surprisingly, incomes in manufacturing were lower than in any other sector, including agriculture and fishing. In the labor-intensive apparel sector, however, the average was only US$4,700; workers prepared to accept such subpar wages were in short supply. Because textile and apparel enterprises typically employ a majority of female workers, however, these industries were able, for a while, to tolerate the labor shortage more easily than others. Female labor-force participation rose from 54 percent in 1970 to 81 percent in 1988 (Deyo 1991). But by 1989 even these industries were being squeezed by the continuing severe labor shortage, and by the end of 1988 foreign workers comprised 45 percent of textile and apparel employment (*Textile Asia* 1989a). These foreign workers consisted primarily of unskilled and semiskilled workers from Indonesia, Malaysia, and Thailand, and a much smaller number of skilled workers from Hong Kong. Successful implementation of the high-wage policy, in combination with one of Asia's lowest birth rates, had created a new social and political problem (Curry 1991).

Accordingly, the Ministry of Labour's decisions to restrict the use of foreign workers aroused concern among textile and apparel manufacturers. In 1989, in addition to an increase in the tax rate applied for the use of foreign workers, the maximum proportion of foreign workers that a firm could employ was reduced to 40 percent (*Textile Asia* 1989a). Although the limit was restored in mid-1991 to 45 percent, this situation was behind the TGMAS president's assertion that "the industry is going through radical structural changes" (*Far Eastern Economic Review* 1991f; *Textile Asia* 1991a, 204). The scarcity and high cost of labor had been evident for years; with the state's positive support, manufacturers already had begun shifting operations to Malaysia or Indonesia and, more recently, Laos. By mid-1991 more than half had established direct subsidiaries or subcontracting operations in Malaysia and Indonesia while concentrating on other, more service-related activities in Singapore (*Textile Asia* 1991b).

Labor costs have risen in spite of, not because of, the effectiveness of organized labor. Singaporean unions have not been easily formed, and 90 percent of them are affiliated with the government-controlled National Trade Union Congress (NTUC). Garry Rodan's opinion of the effectiveness of this control is widely shared: "Instead of unions exerting pressure on behalf of their members for improved conditions and remuneration, Singapore unions are an instrument of the government's social and economic management" (1989, 179).

Internationalization

As part of a national effort to respond to resource constraints (including but not limited to labor) and the prospect of continued increasing protectionism in industrialized countries, differential labor costs have made it easier for the government to persuade Singaporean companies to look abroad. "Arm's-length trade" is no longer the modus operandi (Wong and Ng 1991). Government-controlled companies have shown the way by investing heavily overseas. Small size and insufficient capital make it difficult for most garment companies to internationalize, especially into nonneighboring countries. The predominantly large companies that have done so (e.g., Wing-Tai, Lee Yin Knitting, Bodynits, and Chomel) have not limited themselves to manufacturing, engaging also in marketing, distribution, and retailing activities outside Singapore. Joint ventures and other types of entry and expansion strategies exist in the United States, Japan, mainland China, Hong Kong, and Australia, in addition to ASEAN (Association of Southeast Asian Nations) countries, among others.

This "Singapore International" policy helps to account for the country's emergence as a regional center for textile and clothing production and trade. The republic leads and services Southeast Asian countries in such areas as garment pricing, distribution, advertising, and sales-management functions that are closely associated with Singapore's pursuit of the status of regional leader in financial, communications, and transportation development. Government incentives are partially responsible for the greater variety of service offerings (such as technical training and regional research) that have recently emerged; joint ventures also have made a difference. The opening of the International Merchandise Mart in 1990, with majority holdings by Japanese retailer Yaohan and billed as the only one of its kind, encouraged several international buying houses either to move regional headquarters to Singapore (e.g., Levi Strauss) or to move a part of their operations (e.g., Polo Ralph Lauren). The Mart is designed to offer retail buyers one-stop shopping, with manufacturers' showrooms, warehouses, and a large exhibition hall for trade-promotion events all under one roof. The computer system at the Mart is compatible with Singapore's electronic data interchange network, the TradeNet System, which is designed to speed up processing of trade documents (*Textile Asia* 1990a). For the textile and apparel sector, the establishment of the Mart has reinforced the state's recent initiatives encouraging transnational companies to set up headquarters in Singapore. At the same time, the state continues to urge Singaporean companies to become transnational themselves (Chua 1991).

In an earlier period internationalization of the industry took the form of large quantities of direct foreign investment, and textiles and apparel were among the industries most affected by this influx of foreign capital and companies. By 1975 foreign firms were absorbing 76 percent of total manufacturing inputs, producing 71 percent of total output, and accounting for 80 percent of total investment commitments in manufacturing and almost 70 percent of manufactured exports. By the early 1980s the last figure, which is most pertinent to the government's export-oriented strategy, had reached 90 percent (Deyo 1991, 70). The largest investors in Singapore's apparel industry are Hong Kong and Taiwan; investments continue to emphasize subcontracting and, more recently, the establishment of regional offices in Singapore.

Trade in Textiles and Apparel

In 1986, at the outset of the Uruguay Round of trade talks, Singapore's acting trade and industry minister, Lee Hsien Loong, reminded the plenary session of the General Agreement on Tariffs and Trade (GATT) how extremely serious the talks were for his country. "For Singapore, a breakdown of the world trading system would not merely mean the loss of a few percentage points of GDP, it would be the end of our livelihood—a total economic disaster" (*New Straits Times* 1986, 11). This sentiment was reiterated by Singapore's new prime minister, Goh Chok Tong (Goh 1991). With total trade (domestic exports and reexports, plus imports) exceeding the country's gross domestic product by 300 percent—a ratio higher than that of any other country—free trade was and is Singapore's lifeblood. By 1990 the total trade/GDP ratio was 332 percent (*Far Eastern Economic Review* 1991b).

Domestic Trade Policy

Singapore always has been a free port par excellence. In recent decades, however, the island republic has initiated some protectionist policies intended to stimulate industrialization. C. Y. Lim has reviewed the imposition of these policies and their adjustment in relation to various phases of development (1988). For example, between 1960 and 1965—what might be called Singapore's import-substitution phase—tariffs were placed on certain products produced domestically (e.g., soaps, detergents, paints). Between 1963 and 1965, during Singapore's brief incorporation into the Federation of Malaysia, import quotas were imposed on 230 commodities. As Singapore moved from labor-intensive to more capital-intensive export promotion from 1972 to 1978, import quotas gradually were replaced by tariffs on many manufactured goods. Soon these tariffs too were gradually removed; during the 1980s most of those remaining were reduced to a maximum ad valorem rate of 5 percent (Lim 1988; Tay 1986).

While duties have been removed or kept at low levels for inputs necessary for export production, Singapore has maintained a low tariff on apparel. Even though the ratio of apparel reexports to exports is moderate (37% in 1990), the Free Zone Act (1966) is an essential component of Singapore's entrepôt textile trade strategy. The policy exempts from duty and quota restrictions imported items that are to be reexported or transshipped, and thus is consistent with Singapore's desire to provide regional storage and transshipment facilities (Tay 1986). Although industrial estates are well established there, Singapore, unlike many countries, has no designated export-processing zones that are physically separated from the local economy. In essence, the entire republic is an export-processing zone.

The near absence of protectionism in Singapore is partly a matter of political realities. Garment makers and others in the textile and apparel industry have been no more able than capitalists and entrepreneurs in other sectors to influence government policy and thus to obtain one or another form of state protection. As B. N. Tay has pointed out, neither industry groupings nor electorates appear to carry much weight in an opposition-less political system (1986).

Textiles and Apparel in the Balance of Trade

The extent and nature of globalization for the Singapore economy is further emphasized by several factors. Total trade increased steadily from US$16 billion in 1970 to US$113 billion in 1990 (Department of Statistics, Singapore 1970–88, 1989–91). Singapore had a trade deficit throughout the 1980s, reflected in data for 1990 showing that 46 percent of total trade represented exports, about a third of which were reexports (Department of Statistics, Singapore 1989–91). In 1983 the United States took over as the leading importer of goods from Singapore and has retained that position since then, taking 21 percent of the total in 1990; Malaysia, with 13 percent, and Japan, with 9 percent, follow. The leading category of goods and commodities imported into Singapore is crude petroleum (11% in 1990), followed by office machines (7%) and telecommunications apparatus (6%). Woven textile fabric imports represented 2 percent of total imports. Office machines accounted for 17 percent of Singapore's exports in 1990, followed by refined petroleum products (15%) and telecommunications apparatus (10%). Clothing made up 3 percent of exports in 1990, while woven textile fabrics represented 1 percent.

These data on the textile and garment trade, expressed as percentages of total trade, seem so small as to render the sector a negligible element of the Singaporean economy. That perspective has its limits: the significance of the figures becomes apparent when they are compared with those of other Southeast Asian countries—all of which are known as major suppliers in the global garment trade and in which textiles and apparel are a much larger portion of manufactures. In 1988 the value of apparel exports from Thailand was US$1,825 million; from Singapore, US$1,239 million; from Malaysia, US$831 million; from Indonesia, US$797 million; and from the Philippines, US$441 million (GATT 1989–90).[4] Generally, other Southeast Asian countries' apparel exports have grown more rapidly than Singapore's, but clearly Singapore has been a major participant in this trade.

Singapore imports (mainly from Taiwan, Japan, and Malaysia) a great deal of fiber, yarn, and fabric (colored and printed cotton and synthetics as well as gray goods); as a result, a trade deficit exists in textiles and apparel as a combined category. There is little doubt that Singaporeans produce more apparel than they consume. Moreover, the trade surplus in apparel is understated, because tourists account for a substantial portion of domestic clothing sales.[5] Since 1983 exports, especially clothing, have grown rapidly; clothing exports rose from US$477 million in 1983 to US$1,393 million in 1989. And as a direct result of increased exports, during that same period the textile and apparel trade deficit declined from US$417 million to US$93 million.

Almost two-thirds of Singapore's textile product exports are destined for the United States; about 90 percent of these exports is clothing. The U.S. share of Singapore's overall trade is proportionately not that large; according to the *Asia 1991 Yearbook,* it is 20.5 percent (*Far Eastern Economic Review* 1991b, 9). In 1990 U.S.-Singapore trade amounted to US$21 billion, and U.S. investors added US$9 billion to the Singapore economy (*Far Eastern Economic Review* 1991d).

As Trade and Industry Minister Lee's statement indicated, Singapore has been an active, highly supportive member of the GATT. The failure of GATT negotiators to conclude the Uruguay Round of table talks as scheduled (in December 1990, and again in April 1992) was an ominous development for Singapore and its ASEAN allies. Their position, as expressed in a statement issued by the ASEAN contracting parties (Indonesia, Malaysia, the Philippines, and Thailand) was one of alarm: "A failure of the Round will inevitably lead to mounting protectionism, unchecked unilateralism and inward-looking trade blocs—and those would certainly be detrimental to the trade interests and economic situation of the developing countries" (GATT 1992, 7).

Failure of the Uruguay Round negotiations has not yet produced "unchecked unilateralism," but at minimum it means continuation of the Multifiber Arrangement (MFA), the multilateral framework that has regulated trade in textiles since 1974. Singapore has been able to negotiate relatively satisfactory bilateral agreements with the United States, the European Community, Canada, Norway, and Sweden, enabling impressive apparel export expansion. Nevertheless, these arrangements entail tedious and costly quota-management processes. Singapore authorities prefer termination of the MFA and such associated restrictions as "voluntary" export restraints (i.e., quotas), as do their ASEAN colleagues. It has been argued, however, that without the MFA countries that are small producers (but, like Singapore, not the lowest price producers) will lose guaranteed access to profitable markets.

Legal and Institutional Framework

Singapore's apparel subsector can be described as small, reasonably robust, and subject to uncertainties that are built into the country's unique circumstances. One truly unusual feature of the Singapore economy, for example, is the remarkably high rate of savings. Between 1980 and 1988 gross domestic savings amounted to 41.8 percent of gross domestic product—a hefty chunk of resources that would represent a drain on economic activity and stability were it not for compensatory foreign investment. As long as direct foreign investment can be sustained, the savings (much of which is generated by the Central Provident Fund program) yield huge reserves from which the state can finance its interventionist activities as needed and position itself to play an even more extensive role in the economy in the event of crises.

Foreign investment in Singapore has received a boost from the travails of Hong Kong, as anxious investors anticipate the effects of the transfer of that island's sovereignty in 1997. Nevertheless, Singapore's elite has not relied on such serendipitous events in the development and execution of their export-oriented industrial strategy. Since about 1990, for example, they have been busy refining their latest major international thrust, the "growth triangle" concept. The garment industry is well suited to this approach, a sort of multinational platform linking Malaysia, Indonesia, and Singapore in an effort to capitalize on the regional division of labor while avoiding resource duplication and intramural competition. Whether or not the growth-triangle idea is successful in economic terms, it is indicative of the government's relentless efforts to cope with the changing global economic environment. And, not so incidentally, it addresses a continuously vital political issue: relations with neighboring nation-states.

Singapore's economic growth should not be mistaken for the outcome of natural and inexorable evolutionary processes, nor is it a demonstration of the virtue of laissez-faire economics. Most of the deliberate and vigorous policies that have shaped the textile and apparel industries are integrated into a larger and dynamic strategy. Although this strategy can be characterized by such central principles as "process over products," human resources and high wages, infrastructural development, and others, it also is manifested as an institutional and legal framework. The Ministry of Trade and Industry and other statutory agencies generally are responsible for implementing industry strategy and securing manufacturer cooperation. The Economic Development Board centralizes the supervision and planning of national industrial development and finances much research and promotional activity, as well as providing leadership to other semiautonomous boards and state corporations responsible to the cabinet.[6] Labour Ministry control of industrial relations is so tight that the 16 percent of workers who do belong to unions experience the same work-related constraints and opportunities as their nonunion peers.

Legislation affecting business activity is perhaps unavoidably complex. In addition to the generally expediting effects of Singapore's compactness, however, public authorities have made conscious efforts to simplify legal procedures and requirements. For example, a recently published comparison of the ease with which foreign executives can obtain temporary work permits in Asian countries placed Singapore as a close second behind Hong Kong (*Far Eastern Economic Review* 1992, 14).

Together with the National Employers' Federation, the Industrial Training Board coordinates the training of skilled workers. The National Wages Council, representing both employers and unions, is responsible for advising the government on annual wage increases. The Central Provident Fund Act, which mandates a compulsory worker contribution to a government fund to secure a lump-sum retirement payment, ensures that each employee has a stake in the regime's economic strategy. Statutes in the area of labor relations regulate workplace safety, child labor, undocumented workers, and so forth without imposing an undue burden on business.

"Without imposing an undue burden on business" is, in fact, a resounding understatement. Labor unions are closely watched, and disruptive activities, certainly strikes, are not tolerated. Confronted with recession in 1985, unions blithely complied with a wage reduction (*Far Eastern Economic Review* 1991b, 28). There is evidence that this sort of political control is an even more important attraction to overseas investors than the more specific inducements crafted by the government (Deyo 1991, 70). Former prime minister Lee Kuan Yew's tough-minded prioritization of economic and political stability, and even the government's sloganeering, obsessively consensus-building approach, can be seen in this light.

Conclusion

There is a downside to the zealously proactive orientation of the state. As Walden Bello and Stephanie Rosenfeld argue, the newly industrialized countries of East Asia, Singapore included, pay a high price in freedom for their economic achievements (1990). Whether or not this position is overstated, many observers agree that within Singapore's mostly well educated population there is a growing sense of unease, a suspicion that the wag's version of a national motto for Singapore, "Give me liberty or give me wealth," may be all too correct. Emigration, disproportionately concentrated in precisely the young and talented segment of the population that Singapore scarcely can afford to lose, is symptomatic. R. L. Curry estimates that emigration is up from about two thousand per year in the 1980s to five thousand in 1990 (1991, 20).

Short of provoking people to leave, it is likely that government heavy-handedness stifles creativity, frivolity, and the tinkering that seems to be the mother of technological invention. And the state's eagerness to denounce all criticism concerning human rights, whether originating inside or outside the country, is at least a little embarrassing to local intellectuals and international friends. State authorities may be awakening to this problem, as suggested by re-ported preliminary discussions of the need for a public rela-tions–oriented Singapore International Foundation and "Friends of Singapore" organization (*Far Eastern Economic Review* 1991e).

The degree of interdependence with the global economy also could be problematic. Singapore's industrial growth is married to business processes and trends that it does not own or even control; these factors are beyond the control of any one nation-state. Export demand, which had accounted for 90.5 percent of economic growth in 1988 and 77.8 percent in 1989, produced only 63.7 percent in 1990 (Chua 1991, 263).[7] Although exports to Japan and the European Community are increasing, Singapore, as we have noted, relies heav-ily on the U.S. market for garment exports; economic conditions in the United States were expected to have a direct and depressing effect on textile and apparel production in Singapore in 1991. Intensification of U.S. trade relations with Canada and Mexico and, more generally, the consolidation of three large transnational trading blocs, as forecast in many quarters, naturally are unwelcome to Singapore business interests and technocrats. Even the geographically less adventuresome growth-triangle concept is burdened with the political risks inherent in the pre-ASEAN tradition of rivalry and conflict within the region.

The actions and interests of investors, managers, and workers— not to mention consumers—in the garment industry receive secondary attention in this study: the role of the state is paramount. It is possible that a different method, especially a more microanalytic perspective, would reveal more autonomous and influential initiatives coming from within the industry. It would be interesting to know whether textile and garment interests in the private sector agree with the virtual parade of economists who have been calling for a reduction in the role of the state. Even the large continent of scholars from the National University of Singapore who participated in researching and writing *Policy Options for the Singapore Economy* adopted this position, however delicately (Lim 1988).

The gradual succession in leadership that is so much a part of contemporary Singaporean politics may encourage bolder efforts by such economic interests to promote new policies. But whether these interests really would prefer a more independent posture is doubtful. If Singaporean manufacturers of textiles and garments are to enjoy a sustained second industrial revolution, surely the state, through a purposeful set of programs as varied as growth triangles and labor co-optation, will have to continue to intervene. Because this intervention is costly and risky, observers and policy makers alike will be compelled to reassess the wisdom of propping up this particular industry.

Notes

1. Although yarn production typically has been low in Singapore, DuPont (of the United States) continues to increase its investments there, recently working on doubling the capacity of its Lyrca plant. Toray (Japan) has a 10 percent investment in this project. The majority of the output will go

to Taiwan, Thailand, and South Korea. This project brings DuPont's total manufacturing investment in Singapore to about US$465 million, which the company plans to increase by US$1.2 billion when a nylon plant is constructed, probably before the year 2000 (*Textile Asia* 1992).

2. Grants and projects of this sort frequently are reported in *Textile Asia*. For example, the July 1989 issue includes an article on a S$430,000 commitment by the EDB, TDB, and Wing Tai Garment Manufacturers to develop a computerized conveyer system for the industry (*Textile Asia* 1989b).

3. The effects of these and related programs on workers and their families are surveyed by J. W. Salaaf, whose sample includes garment-industry employees (1988).

4. In the same year, Singapore was second to Thailand among Southeast Asian exporters of textiles.

5. Singapore's receipts from foreign tourists in 1990 amounted to 10.1 percent of GDP, higher than in any other country in the region (*Far Eastern Economic Review* 1992, 55).

6. As an indication of the scope of the state's activity, government employment accounts for 20 percent of total employment (Salaaf 1988, 23).

7. For evidence that a trade recovery was a key element in the unexpectedly strong overall performance of the Singapore economy in 1991, however, see *Far Eastern Economic Review* 1991a and 1991c.

References

Ariff, M., and H. Hill. 1985. *Export-Oriented Industrialisation: The ASEAN Experience.* Sydney: Allen and Unwin.

Bello, Walden, and Stephanie Rosenfeld. 1990. *Dragons in Distress: Asia's Miracle Economies in Crisis.* San Francisco: Institute for Food and Development Policy.

Braithwaite, A. 1991. "Rising Giant." *Textile Asia,* October, 103–6.

Chua, B. H. 1991. "Singapore 1991: Celebrating the End of an Era." In *Southeast Asian Affairs 1991,* edited by S. Siddique and C. Y. Ng, 253–66. Singapore: Institute of Southeast Asian Studies.

Curry, R. L., Jr. 1991. "Singapore's Emerging Labor Shortage as a Constraint to Progress." *Journal of Third World Studies* 8(1): 6–24.

Department of Statistics, Singapore. 1970–88. *Yearbook of Statistics.* Singapore: Singapore National Printers.

———. 1989–91. *Monthly Digest of Statistics.* Singapore: Singapore National Printers.

Deyo, F. C. 1991. "Singapore: Developmental Paternalism." In *Minidragons:*

Fragile Economic Miracles in the Pacific, edited by S. M. Goldstein, 64–103. New York: Ambrose Video Publishing; Boulder, Colo.: Westview Press.

Far Eastern Economic Review. 1991a. "Against the Odds," July 11, 50.

———. 1991b. *Asia 1991 Yearbook.* Hong Kong: Review Publishing Co.

———. 1991c. "Fears Allayed," April 18, 62.

———. 1991d. "Modest Platform," October 31, 64–65.

———. 1991e. "Singapore Plans to Improve Image Abroad," March 7, 24.

———. 1991f. "Singapore Raises Limit on Imported Workers," October 24, 79.

———. 1992. "Briefing," February 13, pp. 14, 55.

General Agreement on Tariffs and Trade (GATT). 1989–90. *International Trade.* Geneva.

———. 1992. *GATT Focus* (January/February). Geneva.

Goh, Chok Tong. 1991. "Keynote Address by Mr. Goh Chok Tong, Prime Minister of the Republic of Singapore, Eighth General Meeting of the Pacific Economic Cooperation Conference, Singapore, 10 May 1991." *ASEAN Economic Bulletin* (Singapore) 8:95–98.

Goh, K. W. 1976. "A Socialist Economy that Works." In *Socialism that Works . . . the Singapore Way,* edited by C.V.D. Nair, 77–85. Singapore: Federal Publications.

Lim, C. Y. 1988. *Policy Options for the Singapore Economy.* Singapore: McGraw-Hill.

New Straits Times. 1986. "Free Trade, the Lifeblood of Singapore," September 19, 11.

Rodan, Garry. 1989. *The Political Economy of Singapore's Industrialization: National State and International Capital.* New York: St. Martin's Press.

Salaaf, J. W. 1988. *State and Family in Singapore: Restructuring a Developing Society.* Ithaca: Cornell University Press.

Tay, B. N. 1986. "Singapore: The Structure and Causes of Manufacturing Sector Protection." In *The Political Economy of Manufacturing Protection: Experiences of ASEAN and Australia,* edited by Findlay and R. Garnaut, 135–58. Sydney: Allen and Unwin.

Textile Asia. 1989a. "Regional Notes: Singapore," January, 92.

———. 1989b. "Regional Notes: Singapore," July, 128.

———. 1990a. "Regional Notes: Singapore," October, 145–46.

———. 1990b. "Regional Notes: Singapore," December, 101.

———. 1991a. "Regional Notes: Singapore," September, 204.

———. 1991b. "Regional Notes: Singapore," October, 72.

———. 1992. "Regional Notes: Singapore," May, 122.

Wong, P. K., and C. Y. Ng. 1991. "Singapore's Internationalization Strategy for the 1990s." In *Southeast Asian Affairs 1991,* edited by S. Siddique and C. Y. Ng, 267–76. Singapore: Institute of Southeast Asian Studies.

PART III

Mexico, Central America, and the Caribbean

Chapter 12

The Apparel Maquiladora Industry at the Mexican Border

Jorge Carrillo V.

The apparel industry played a leading role in Mexico's export ma-quiladora industry from the early 1970s until 1979, when the *Acuerdo Multifibras* (Multifiber Arrangement) was extended to Mex-ico. Protectionist restrictions were imposed for certain production processes (such as the cutting of fabrics, which was to take place only in the United States), effectively curtailing the industry's growth. The importance of this agreement was demonstrated by the high percentage of exports subjected to tariffs: 71 percent of the Mex-ican garment industry's exports to the United States were subjected to the rates fixed by the *Convenio Bilateral Textil* (Bilateral Textile Agreement) of the Multifiber Arrangement. The tariffs imposed by the United States on the Mexican textile producers were 6.8 percent in fibers, 9 percent in textiles, and 18.5 percent in apparel. In Canada the tariff percentages were 6.8, 6.2, and 15 percent, respectively. Ob-viously, Mexico is in an unfavorable situation regarding current tar-iffs and the ongoing tax-exemption process (Gaona 1992, 19). Although it is generally agreed that this state of affairs will change with the enforcement of the North American Free Trade Agreement (NAFTA), the apparel maquiladora industry has its own historic dy-namism, which ensures its independence from NAFTA.[1]

Characteristics of the Maquila Industry

The Mexican exporting maquiladora industry began in 1965 with the establishment of the government's Border Industrialization Program.

The program permitted tax-free imports of components to Mexico and exports of the finished products. This tariff reduction allowed transnational companies looking for lower production costs to relocate important production segments—most commonly, labor-intensive processes—to Mexico. The maquiladoras have been thought of as cost centers rather than profit centers, because the cost of production is concentrated in the host country, while profits are realized in the home country.

Generally, the maquiladora industry is assumed to be a homogeneous industrial sector, made up of firms with similar characteristics in terms of production, organization of labor, technology, and sociodemographic workers profiles. Although there was some truth in this assumption in the 1970s, two significant changes occurred in the 1980s. First, the various origins of capital (United States, Japan, Mexico) created a certain heterogeneity in the production processes and in industrial organization, such as the number of employees per plant, the levels of technology, and the suppliers' networks. Japanese plants usually have more employees than U.S. firms, which in turn have more than Mexican firms. The automated processes follow the same pattern: Japanese firms are more advanced than U.S. firms, and Mexican firms are at the low end. Industrial organization is most complex in Japanese companies; U.S. firms operate as subsidiaries; and Mexican plants operate as subcontractors.

Second, as companies moved new production segments to Mexico, a new generation of maquiladoras appeared, incorporating higher levels of technology and employing a more skilled labor force. Thus the concept of "maquiladora" was based on a specific tariff regime rather than on similarities in the structure and organization of production. Today a "maquiladora" plant can be totally or partially devoted to assembly or manufacturing activities, and it can even sell 40 percent of its production in Mexico. Therefore, the maquiladora industry is not an industry in itself but a system of special tariff treatments that promotes exports. Currently, it involves twelve productive sectors, among which the electronics, automotive-parts, and apparel industries are the most differentiated.

The exporting maquiladora industry is one of the most dynamic industries in Mexico. Its significance can be summarized as follows:

1. *Its relative importance in the national context.* The maquila

industry is the second largest national source of foreign exchange (US$5.3 billion in 1992), after oil (US$8.3 billion in 1992). As of 1991, it accounted for 20 percent of the economically active population working in the manufacturing industry, and it is expected to account for 25 percent by 1994 (CIMEX-WEFA 1992, table IV.1; Banco de Mexico 1993, table 2).

2. *Its actual and predicted growth.* The annual employment growth in the export maquila industry was 10 percent over during 1974–93 and reached 18.6 percent between 1984 and 1988—far exceeding employment creation in other sectors of the economy. The exporting maquiladora industry's economic behavior is closely related to the United States's economy. In 1981 there were 605 plants throughout the country; ten years later there were 1,933, and 2,856 are predicted for 1996. This significant growth in the number of plants paralleled increases in employment, from 131,000 employees in 1981 to 468,510 ten years later. The most important increase has been in value-added, which jumped from US$980 million to US$4.37 billion in the same period.

Traditionally, the maquiladora industry has been concentrated along the border. Nearly 71 percent of the total plants and jobs were located in that area as of 1992. Nevertheless, there has been a gradual increase in the importance of other areas. In 1981 88.1 percent of the total plants were located along the border, but this percentage will drop to 65.7 in 1994, and in the same period, border employment is expected to decrease from 88.9 to 66.6 percent of the total (CIMEX-WEFA 1992).

3. *Its industrial reorganization.* Previously, the exporting maquiladora industry was homogeneous, characterized by labor-intensive technology, low wages, and the absence of training, skills, technology transfers, and linkages within the Mexican economy. In recent years, however, the maquiladora industry has undergone a transformation. It is now characterized by several types of maquiladora plants with various degrees of technological innovation (equipment and processes), organizational innovations (geared toward quality improvement), changes in both the functional and communication hierarchies, and flexibility in collective agreements. In sum, the industry has made a variety of changes in an attempt to maximize the potential of technology and labor.

The Apparel Maquila Industry

Opinions vary regarding NAFTA's implications for the apparel maquiladoras in Mexico. Proposed econometric models show very dissimilar growth rates, depending on the statistical assumptions used. Other projections based on the behavior of exporting maquila industries indicate that, regardless of NAFTA, the apparel sector will show significant growth.

In 1981 there were 117 apparel maquiladora plants in Mexico, employing 18,060 workers and creating a value-added of US$100.2 million; a decade later these plants more than doubled their numbers, reaching 297 facilities, 43,830 employees, and a value-added of US$236.8 million. CIMEX-WEFA's econometric model projects 425 plants, 70,830 employees, and an investment of US$559.2 million for 1996, meaning an annual growth rate of approximately 10 percent (Table 12.1).[2] The economic recession in the United States hindered growth in 1990 and 1991, however, and a lower growth rate was expected to continue through 1992. For 1993, the employment growth rate has been double and foreign exchange earnings have been even more. The value-added, which includes wages, services, and expenditures for domestic raw materials, has maintained a 9.7 percent annual growth rate (even in 1989, a critical year for maquiladoras). Between 1981 and 1996 annual growth is expected to average 21.1 percent, a clear sign of the great dynamism in this economic activity. This optimistic projection can be explained by several factors: the historical growth of the industry, inflation control, the nominal depreciation of the peso, and the signing of NAFTA.

The incorporation of domestic raw materials has been very low. In 1981 national raw materials accounted for 1.04 percent of the total processes, and in 1991 the percentage rose slightly to 1.07, the projected average for the next five years (CIMEX-WEFA 1992). It should be noted that this result is not related to the Multifiber Arrangement: there was never much incorporation of domestic supplies in the twelve maquiladora industries along the border.[3] But because of NAFTA stipulations regarding rules of origin and the reduction of tariff exemptions, as well as the industrial reorganization begun in the mid-1980s, some sectors, including apparel, auto parts, and electronics, are expected to increase their incorporation of domestic inputs in coming years.

Table 12.1

Indicators of the Apparel Maquiladora Industry in Mexico

	1981	1991	1996 (est.)
Plants	117	297	425
Gross production (US$ millions)	340	800	1,820
Value-added (US$ millions)	100.2	236.8	559.2
Raw materials processed			
Value in US$ millions	0.247	0.567	1.273
Distribution (%)			
Domestic	1.04	1.07	1.07
Foreign	98.96	98.93	98.93
Workers			
Total number	18,060	43,830	70,830
Distribution (%)			
Production workers	88.3	84.9	83.0
Technicians	8.5	10.8	12.9
Management	3.2	4.4	4.1
Wages (US$/hour)			
Composition	1.64	1.44	2.15
Base	1.32	1.15	1.73
Fringe benefits	0.32	0.29	0.42
Distribution			
Production workers	1.50	1.14	1.80
Technicians	2.42	2.63	3.48
Management	3.55	4.27	5.21

Source: CIMEX-WEFA 1992.

Apparel plants are distinguished by the domestic origin of their capital; foreign ownership predominates in the other maquiladora sectors. Mexican capital constitutes a majority in 79 percent of apparel firms, with U.S. capital dominating in the remainder. Of the forty apparel plants in Tijuana, Ciudad Juárez, and Monterrey surveyed in 1990,[4] nine were fully owned by U.S. investors, seven were partially supported by U.S. capital, and the remainder were fully financed by Mexican capital.

Apparel manufacturing is a labor-intensive industry: in 48.5 percent of the plants surveyed, labor costs were 41 percent or more of the total production value. Nevertheless, there was a relatively important group (17% of the plants) in which labor costs accounted for less than 20 percent of the total production value. The average plant in 1990 had 175 employees, of whom 111 were production workers. Most workers were in small plants, though some plants had between 251 and 500 employees.

The use of technology in the plants varied according to the products being manufactured. In the apparel maquiladoras, the number of programmable units (a measure of the extent of "hard" technology—machinery and equipment) averaged 3.4 per plant. Variations in the incorporation of technology were demonstrated by the use of the "just-in-time" approach: 28.7 percent of the plants used this technique in only a few products (up to 20%); 54.8 percent used the technique in the majority of products (76% or more).[5]

During the 1980s the way work was organized began to change; there was a general shift away from the "Taylorism" of the 1970s, based on intensive and individual work, to a more flexible organizational approach, based on working in groups and increased responsibility. Flexible organization was defined by eight elements: problem diagnosis and solution, group production, quality circles, quality control, task turnover, multiskill, employment evolvement, and equipment maintenance. The reasoning behind the adoption of this technique was that the greater the labor participation in each of these elements, the greater the flexibility. There was a striking increase in the implementation of work teams (group production), encompassing 44.3 percent of the direct labor force, and employment evolvement (47.5%). This increase marked a fundamental change in work organization, leaving totally individualized activities behind. The survey data showed that 23.6 and 26.7 percent of workers were involved in task-turnover and multiskill groups, respectively; equipment maintenance accounted for 12.5 percent of labor. Quality circles accounted for 19.9 percent of the direct labor force; quality control, 7.8 percent; and problem diagnosis and solution, 6.4 percent.

Employment in the apparel maquila industries is dominated by direct production workers, who accounted for 88.3 percent of the total labor force in 1988 and 84.9 percent two years later. Technicians represented approximately 10 percent of the total work force and are expected to account for 12.5 percent by 1996. The apparel industry has shown a very stable employment allocation among the different categories, and these proportions will not change substantially, at least not before 1996.

One of the most striking features of the apparel maquiladoras is the relative increase in the percentage of employed technicians. Traditionally, the majority of workers have been women and youth (male and female), but there have been significant changes in the social characteristics of the labor force, including increased numbers of comparatively older personnel, males, and especially people with previous working experience. The criteria for worker selection has become more flexible.

An examination of the characteristics of production workers in the apparel and electronics sectors in the cities surveyed indicates how the apparel sector compares with other maquiladora industries (Table 12.2). In both sectors most workers are young; women constitute a majority; most women are childless; a majority have previous working experience; and most have completed only primary school. The most striking differences lie in the percentages of single workers (45.8% in apparel, 57.3 in electronics) and the average seniority (3.6 and 2.4 years, respectively).

The data on the sociodemographic profiles of production workers illustrate the problem of labor turnover. The monthly turnover rate in the apparel maquiladoras was 15.8 percent, compared with 10.5 and 9.7 percent in the electronics and auto-parts sectors, respectively. Between 1987 and 1989 the annual turnover rate of 28.5 percent was markedly greater than the employment rate of 12.5 percent. This discrepancy is explained by the fact that the border's work opportunities have not been limited to the assembly industries. In the external market, jobs in services and commercial work have abounded, both in the three surveyed cities and in the United States. Thus the exporting maquiladora sectors' labor problem is not a short-

Table 12.2
Characteristics of Apparel and Electronics Maquiladora Production Workers

	Apparel	Electronics
Male	23.15%	32.63%
Female	76.85%	67.37%
With children	36.42%	36.41%
Unmarried	45.81%	57.25%
With previous work experience	68.02%	60.31%
Average number of years in school	6.03	6.60
Average age	26.15	22.05
Average number of years at job	3.55	2.44

Source: Ministry of Labor and Social Security and El Colegio de la Frontera Norte, "Maquiladora Plants Survey: El mercado de trabajo e las actividades maquiladores," Tijuana, B.C., Mexico, 1990.

age of people with specific characteristics; the problem lies in whether they want to work in such industries and whether those who are employed there wished to remain.

The main difficulties for maquiladoras in the border area involve the lack of adequate infrastructure in the management of roads, services, transport, and toxic waste disposal, coupled with the deterioration of the meager infrastructure already in place. The severe scarcity of both skilled and nonskilled labor in border cities, especially Juarez and Tijuana, has also discouraged investment in the area. Several plants have relocated in central Mexican cities in search of the same benefits that led them to choose the border region during the 1960s. It seems likely that in the future, plants in Mexico's central states will grow more rapidly than those in the border area.

For all maquila industries, wages contracted considerably during the 1980s, dropping from US$1.64 per hour in 1981 to US$0.80 in 1987. Since then, wages have increased, but they have not yet equaled the levels of 1981. In 1991 the average wage for production workers was US$1.44 per hour (including benefits). Wages are expected to continue growing moderately, reaching about US$2.20 per hour in 1996 (see Table 12.1). In contrast to Mexican wage levels, the wages of production workers in Southeast Asian countries have increased more rapidly and on a more sustained basis (Table 12.3). By 1990 wages were 1.5 times more in South Korea and Mexico than in Mexico, and three times more in Taiwan.

Wages in the apparel industry are lower than those in other maquiladora activities, especially electronics (Table 12.4). In 1990 the average hourly wage (with benefits) for apparel workers was US$1.20, compared to US$1.57 in the electronics industry. The discrepancy can be explained by the relatively smaller sizes of the apparel plants and by the fact that apparel plants are predominantly Mexican-owned.

Mexican production workers receive food subsidies and productivity bonuses, which is common in work where payment is by the piece. In contrast to production workers' wages, which were lower than in any other sector, wages for administrators were slightly higher in the apparel industry than in other sectors.

Contrary to what one might expect, nonunionized plants have provided greater total compensation to workers than plants with

Table 12.3

International Wage Comparisons for Production Workers in Exporting Industries (US$/hour)

	1981	1983	1990
Mexico			
Excluding benefits	1.27	0.69	0.82
Including benefits	1.58	0.87	1.16
Taiwan			
Excluding benefits	1.08	1.12	3.31
Including benefits	1.12	1.16	3.45
South Korea			
Excluding benefits	0.74	0.82	2.13
Including benefits	0.88	0.96	2.62
Singapore			
Excluding benefits	1.09	1.19	2.10
Including benefits	1.65	1.84	3.07

Source: CIMEX-WEFA 1992.

Table 12.4

Average Hourly Wages and Benefits in the Apparel and Electronics Maquiladora Industries

	Apparel		Electronics	
	US$[a]	%	US$[a]	%
Total income	$1.20	100.0	$1.57	100.0
Wages	$0.65	54.1	$0.99	63.1
Benefits	$0.55	45.9	$0.58	36.9

Source: Ministry of Labor and Social Security and El Colegio de la Frontera Norte, "Maquiladora Plants Survey: El mercado de trabajo e las actividades maquiladores," Tijuana, B.C., Mexico, 1990.

[a]As of January 1990.

unions, which constituted about half the total in the three cities surveyed. Part of the explanation is that the bigger maquiladoras, the more economically influential firms, have used their resources to improve working conditions and thus avoid unionization. In the auto-parts industry, for example, the average hourly wage for production workers was US$2.27 in plants lacking a collective agreement, and US$1.85 per hour in plants with a collective agreement.

The survey found between twenty-one and twenty-eight different positions in the hierarchy of production and white-collar jobs in apparel maquiladora plants; nonskilled production jobs accounted for more than 87 percent of employment. Production workers generally enter at the lowest level in the hierarchy. Often employees were asked to work in a temporary capacity for a one- to three-month probationary period, after which they were given a permanent job.

Internal mobility opportunities were about the same in plants with collective agreements and those without. Seventy-two percent of workers above the first occupational level entered their job positions from outside the company, and the rest were promoted from within. Internal mobility was greater in plants where there were no collective agreements (31% of workers were promoted) than in those with collective agreements (24%).

There appear to be no specific criteria for deciding on promotions; typically, performance, attitude, and adherence to appropriate standards were cited. The predominant factors were efficient performance and a cooperative attitude.

Conclusion

Mexico's northern border's economic integration process suggests that industrial dynamism will continue during the next five years, with or without NAFTA.[6] The maquiladora industry has played a central role in this integration process. Since 1979 the apparel industry has maintained third place among maquiladora industries in generation of employment and foreign exchange; growth predictions are very positive for this sector.

Aside from its growth, changes in technology and in the organization of the work force help to explain the dynamism of the sector. Despite its generally labor-intensive, low-skill characteristics, the apparel industry has been affected by the structural changes experienced by all exporting maquiladora industries in Mexico since the early 1980s. In effect, two maquiladora sectors have emerged: one is more traditional, with greater use of labor and a lack of electronic machinery and just-in-time deliveries; the other is more modern, with greater use of programmable units and flexible organization approaches at work, and in which the share of labor in the value of the total product is less. Other changes include more advanced skills, a complex organizational structure, an increase in previous labor experience among female workers, and, after a substantial drop in the early 1980s, a relative improvement in income.

Nevertheless, working conditions in the maquiladora sector are still poor compared to those in the leading sectors. Furthermore, although income has risen because of the scarcity of labor in the border area, the shift of industries to new locations within Mexico could change that situation. Finally, apparel workers require further attention from the Mexican government on issues such as training, housing loans, and especially childcare facilities for the 37 percent of female workers with children.

Notes

Acknowledgment: I am grateful for the economic support of CONACYT in the writing of this chapter.

1. It should be noted that the export apparel maquila industry is productively and commercially independent from the domestic textile and garment industry, and even from the textile and garment-assembly plants located in the central region of Mexico. These other plants, also known as maquiladoras, existed long before the maquiladoras' export program. They are exclusively oriented to the internal market, and their costs and market structures are different from those of the export apparel industry.

2. The econometric model of CIMEX-WEFA is used here because it is based on the pattern of the maquiladora itself and incorporates the national economic context. All data are from CIMEX-WEFA 1992.

3. Use is particularly low in the electronics sector, where it dropped from 1.04 percent in 1981 to 0.74 in 1991.

4. This study is based on the results of a probability-sampling survey of electronics, automotive-parts, and apparel maquiladora plants in Tijuana, Ciudad Juárez, and Monterrey. The survey was developed by the Ministry of Labor and Social Security and El Colegio de la Frontera Norte and was conducted from late January to early March 1990. Two hundred ten questionnaires were distributed among selected maquiladora plant managers, enabling analysis of 358 plants. In the apparel sector, forty-four questionnaires were completed, which allowed analysis of sixty-eight facilities employing nine thousand workers. The sixty-eight plants made up the total apparel facilities in those three cities for that year and accounted for 30 percent of all apparel maquiladora facilities in Mexico.

5. The use of "just-in-time" in different percentages for different prod-

ucts in the same firm is explained by the differences in economies of scale and the temporality of the product.

6. This prediction does not mean that the growth of the apparel industry will be unaffected by NAFTA. The increase will be higher with NAFTA.

References

Albuquerque, F. C. De Mattos, and R. J. Fuchs. 1991. *Revolución technológica y restructuración productiva: Impactos y desafíos territoriales.* Buenos Aires: Colección Estudios Políticos y Sociales, ILPES/ONU, IEU/PUC, Grupo Editor Latinoamericano.

Alonso, H.J.A. N.d. "Crisis, sismos y microindustria doméstica del vestido: Estudio de caso en Netzahualcóyotl." *Serie Documentos de Investigación* 1:29–70. Mexico City: El Colegio de México.

Anderson, J. B. 1988. "Factor Substitution and Adaptation in the 'Off-Shore' Assembly Plants of Baja California." *Maquiladoras: Annotated Bibliography and Research Guide to Mexico's In-Bond Industry, 1980–1988.* Monograph series 24:9. San Diego: Center for U.S.-Mexican Studies, University of California, San Diego.

Anderson, J. B., and Roger Frantz. 1989. "Eficiencia en la industria del vestido en México." In *Reestructuración industrial: Maquiladoras en la frontera México–Estados Unidos,* edited by Jorge Carrillo V., 341–71. Mexico City: Consejo Nacional de Cultura and El Colegio de la Frontera Norte.

Banco de México. 1993. "Evolución de la economía mexicana en 1992." *Comerico Exterior* (Banco Nacional de Comercio Exterior), June.

Boon, G. K., and A. Mercado. 1990. *Automatización flexible en la industria.* Mexico City: Editorial Limusa-Noriega.

Bustamante, Jorge A. 1989. "Frontera México–Estados Unidos: Reflexiones para un marco teórico." *Frontera Norte* 1 (January–June): 7–24.

Carrillo, Jorge V., coord. 1991. *Mercados de trabajo en la industria maquiladora de exportación: Síntesis del reporte de investigación.* Tijuana: Secretaría del Trabajo y Previsión Social and El Colegio de la Frontera Norte.

Carrillo, Jorge V., and A. Hernández. 1985. *Mujeres fronterizas en la industria maquiladora.* Mexico City: Secretaría de Educación Pública and Centro de Estudios Fronterizos del Norte de México.

CIMEX-WEFA. 1992. *Maquiladora Industry Analysis* (Bala Cynwyd, Pa.), September.

Chávez, E. 1981. "Las empresas matrices de las maquiladoras mexicanas:

Dos estudios de caso de la industria del vestido." *Lecturas del CEESTEM.* Mexico City: Centro de Estudios Económicos y Sociales del Tercer Mundo.

Escamilla, N., and M. A. Vigorito. 1975. "El trabajo femenino en las maquiladoras de ropa." *Nueva Antropología* 18 (July).

Fernandez-Kelly, M. Patricia. 1983. *For We Are Sold, I and My People: Women and Industry On Mexico's Frontier.* Albany: State University of New York Press.

Gaona, Luis. 1992. "Transición de 10 años para liberar las cuotas textiles en el tratado." *El Economista* (Mexico City), February 12.

Gereffi, Gary, and Donald L. Wyman, eds. 1990. *Manufacturing Miracles: Paths of Industrialization in Latin America and East Asia.* Princeton: Princeton University Press.

González-Aréchiga, Bernardo, and José Carlos Ramírez. 1991. "Estructura contra estrategia: Abasto de insumos nacionales a empresas exportadoras." *Subcontratación y empresas transnacionales: Apertura y restructuración en la maquiladora.* Tijuana: El Colegio de la Frontera Norte and Friedrich Ebert Foundation.

Hanson, Gordon H. 1991. "The Economic Geography of Free Trade in Mexico: Evidence from the Apparel Industry." Paper presented at the seminar, Mercados de Trabajo: Una Perspectiva Comparativa, Tendencias Generales y Cambios Recientes, El Colegio de México, Mexico City, October 23–26.

Herzenberg, Stephen. 1991. *Continental Free Trade and the Future of the North American Auto Sector: Regionally Integrated High-Wage Production or Islands of Automation amid a Sea of Low-Wage Production?* Washington, D.C.: Bureau of International Labor Affairs.

Mendoza, Jorge. 1991. "La industria maquiladora en cifras." *Revista Expansión* 13(573): 36–45.

Oliveira, Orlandina, and García Grígida. 1989. "El significado del trabajo femenino en los sectores populares urbanos." *Estudios Demográficos Urbanos* 12: 465–93. Mexico City: El Colegio de México.

Richer, L. 1989. *Upgrading Labor-Market Information in Developing Countries: Problems, Progress, and Prospects.* Geneva: International Labor Office.

Chapter 13

Industrial Organization and Mexico–U.S. Free Trade: Evidence from the Mexican Garment Industry

Gordon H. Hanson

A North American free trade agreement represents the final step in Mexico's transition from import-substitution industrialization to export-led growth. Mexico's new development strategy assumes that low wages will allow firms to penetrate world markets. The country is counting on labor-intensive activities such as garment manufacturing for export success. In the garment industry, as in any industry, competitiveness is not determined by factor prices alone. Wages matter most in garment assembly, a low-skill, labor-intensive activity. But low wages are not enough to compete in world markets; garment firms need designs that reflect current fashion trends and marketing channels that provide linkages to foreign buyers. Design and marketing knowledge are acquired through experience.

Mexican garment manufacturers have two potential roles to play in the North American economy. One possibility is that Mexican producers will succeed as offshore plants, or maquiladoras. A second possibility is that Mexican firms will compete as integrated manufacturers, controlling their own design and marketing. The outcome matters crucially for the gains from trade that Mexico stands to realize. In the garment industry, assembly accounts for the most jobs, but design and marketing account for most of the value-added.

Between 1985 and 1987 Mexico eliminated most barriers to trade, bringing an end to four decades of import-substitution industrialization. The opening of the Mexican economy initiated a process of closer economic integration with the United States. To study the effect of Mexican trade liberalization on the country's garment industry, I used data drawn from ninety-five firm-level interviews, conducted between September 1990 and May 1991, with Mexican garment manufacturers, traders, and subcontractors, as well as published and unpublished government figures.

The organization and location of garment production are determined by the interaction between regional wage differentials and localization economies. Localization economies exist when the costs at which firms obtain industry-specific inputs decreases with the number of producers that share a location (Krugman 1990; Porter 1990). In garment manufacturing, external economies are most significant in marketing. Garment firms learn about frequently changing consumer trends by locating near other garment firms. External economies are weak or nonexistent in assembly, where low-skill work compels firms to locate in low-wage areas.

The presence of localization economies indicates that Mexico will play the role of a maquiladora in the North American garment market. Under the closed economy, production and marketing were highly concentrated in Mexico City. Over time, regional wage differentials caused firms to relocate production to outlying regions, but much of the industry's marketing activities remained in the capital. Free trade has exposed the Mexico City marketing center to competition with the larger, more efficient U.S. marketing centers in New York, Los Angeles, and Asian cities. For Mexico, competing against U.S. plants for garment-assembly work is easy, because of lower wages. Mexican producers, who previously served the domestic market, are becoming maquiladoras for U.S. firms. The conversion to maquila production does not necessarily mean that Mexico will suffer losses from expanded trade with the United States; gains from access to larger markets and improved product designs are likely to compensate for any losses from the conversion to offshore assembly.

Industrialization and Agglomeration

The distinguishing feature of garment manufacturing in Mexico is the geographic concentration of production and distribution. The pattern of agglomeration has evolved with the process of industrialization in Mexico.

Until the 1920s garment production in Mexico was carried out on a made-to-order basis. The individuals who pioneered the production of ready-to-wear garments were primarily Lebanese and Jewish immigrants, many of whom had been merchants in the old country and continued their trade after coming to Mexico. The sudden growth of Mexico City, brought about by the Mexican Revolution (1911–17), created the first mass garment markets in Mexico and made industrial garment production feasible (Walton 1977). Experience with fabrics gave the immigrant-traders an initial advantage in ready-to-wear garment production.

The newly established manufacturer-traders concentrated their shops in a few square blocks of downtown Mexico City, which became the nation's principal garment district. From this base the traders dealt with textile suppliers and garment retailers and distributed orders to subcontractors. In 1970 about 55 percent of garment-manufacturing jobs were located in the Federal District (the federal entity containing the capital). They remained concentrated in the capital until the 1980s (Table 13.1).

The newly established manufacturer-traders divided garment manufacturing into four vertical stages: fabric purchase, garment design, garment assembly, and marketing. They retained control over fabric purchase, design, and marketing, and divided assembly between their own shops and a large number of small subcontractors. In this arrangement, the manufacturer-trader kept skill-intensive

Table 13.1

Manufacturing Employment in Mexico, 1970–1988, by Region

	1970	1975	1980	1985	1988
All manufacturing					
No. employed (in thousands)	1,581	1,708	2,701	3,269	2,473
% in Federal District	55.4	50.8	44.7	33.2	29.2
% in border states[a]	6.9	10.1	9.6	11.2	16.4
Garments					
No. employed (in thousands)	98.5	102.4	144.0	146.8	173.3
% in Federal District	31.1	28.9	31.1	23.0	19.2
% in border states[a]	11.3	12.3	12.0	15.9	20.1

Source: Secretaría de Programación y Presupuesto, *Censo industrial,* various years.
[a]Baja California Norte, Sonora, Chihuahua, Coahuila, and Tamaulipas.

tasks in-house and subcontracted low-skill activities (Ghadar and Davidson 1987; Hoffman and Rush 1988). Fabric selection requires up-to-date knowledge of fabric trends and garment styles; garment design involves converting designs into workable patterns, grading patterns according to sizes, and cutting fabric into ready-to-assemble pieces (with minimal waste); and marketing requires established contacts with retailers. Garment assembly, which occupies 70 to 80 percent of garment workers, is a low-skill activity: the basic production unit is a single worker and a single sewing machine. Assembly workers become proficient after only a few months on the job.

The Mexican Industrial Census provides further evidence of the vertical organization of garment production. In 1981 Mexico had 12,199 garment establishments, employing 144,346 workers (SPP 1981). Only 250 establishments had one hundred or more workers; these large manufacturer-trader firms accounted for 43 percent of total garment employment. At the other end of the scale was a large number of small subcontracting establishments; 7,047 establishments did not employ remunerated labor, and another 2,186 establishments employed between one and five workers. The census reported that shops with five or fewer workers accounted for 11.6 percent of garment employment. The actual percentage, however, was most likely higher: many small shops do not pay taxes or comply with labor regulations and thus actively avoid government officials, including census takers.[1]

Production operations began to leave Mexico City as wage differentials emerged between the capital and outlying states. In 1970 average nominal garment-assembly wages in the Federal District were higher than in all other states, except the states of Mexico, which borders Mexico City, and Nuevo León, which by that time was already industrialized. Wage differentials between the Federal District and the states of Aguascalientes, Guanajuato, Jalisco, and Puebla were as large as two to one (Table 13.2).

Manufacturer-traders chose two different relocation strategies in response to regional wage differentials. Some firms relocated assembly to subcontracting shops in marginal neighborhoods and rural communities surrounding the capital. In this arrangement, the manufacturer-trader maintained design and marketing operations in the capital and transported cut pieces of fabric to subcontracting shops for assembly (Alonso 1991). The usefulness of satellite subcontract-

Table 13.2

Average Nominal State Wage as a Percentage of Average Federal District
Wage: Mexico's Garment Industry, 1970–1988

State	1970	1975	1980	1985	1988
Aguascalientes	53.9	72.7	75.0	83.7	71.2
Guanajuato	57.2	46.3	53.5	57.2	63.0
Jalisco	55.3	69.3	69.3	71.5	71.6
Nuevo León	98.1	96.5	89.3	94.9	80.2
Puebla	58.0	59.5	48.3	57.2	61.2
Tlaxcala	33.9	45.9	56.9	76.3	56.0

Source: Secretaría de Programación y Presupuesto, *Censo industrial,* various years.

ing communities proved to be short-lived. As Mexico City continued
to grow, it engulfed the surrounding communities where agglomerations of subcontractors were located, causing wages to rise in these
areas. One example is Nezahuacóyotl, a shantytown adjoining the
capital. The community was founded in the late 1960s; by 1975 it
was home to more than one thousand garment subcontractors employing five thousand workers. Ten years later the community had a
diversified local industry and many traders had begun to transfer
their subcontracting operations to more distant rural communities.

Other manufacturer-traders chose a more radical relocation strategy: they moved the entire production apparatus—design and assembly operations—to communities in outlying regions. These
pioneer firms were generally the first agents in their new locations
to produce for a broader industrial economy. Pioneers made two
types of initial investments in their new locations. They trained
workers in design, pattern-making, and fabric-cutting activities (all
requiring about two years of practice for workers to achieve standard
levels of productivity), and they organized machinists and subcontractors for assembly work. All individuals in the local garment industry worked for the pioneer in some capacity, and all local contact
with garment retailers and textile suppliers was through the pioneer.

As a result of industry relocation, the Federal District's share of
garment employment declined from 55.4 percent in 1970, to 44.7
percent in 1980, and to 29.3 percent in 1988. The majority of marketing activities, however, remained in the capital. In 1980 69.8 percent
of the wholesale trade in garments and textiles was conducted in the
Federal District (INEGI 1981).

The relocation of production by manufacturer-traders preserved its localized nature. New production centers grew up around pioneer firms, with firms specializing in the activity the pioneer brought to the region. Children's outerwear and industrial uniforms relocated to Aguascalientes; women's underwear relocated to Naucálpan; sweaters relocated to three communities in the states of Guanajuato, Mexico, and Tlaxcala; men's shirts moved to Tehuacán, Puebla; and women's outerwear moved to Guadalajara, Jalisco, and Monterrey, Nuevo León. Pioneers financed most local garment ventures with loans of equipment or machinery or by making former employees business partners. The pioneer firm in Tehuacán, Puebla, for example, currently has equity investments in a dozen local firms. A group of four pioneer families in Monterrey owns seven of the ten largest local garment factories and accounts for thirty-five local garment shops.

As the relocation of garment production proceeded, wage differentials between the Federal District and the new production centers fell. Wage differentials have been substantially reduced, although they have yet to be eliminated.

Over time, local firms have developed access to distribution channels independent of the pioneer. In some cases, firms in outlying regions have captured marketing activities from the capital, such as wholesale distribution of specific products, although the primary marketing center has not been fully supplanted. Guadalajara and Monterrey, for instance, have become regional distribution centers. This process generally takes a decade or more. Outlying agglomerations of garment producers ultimately shed the dominant firm–satellite firm structure, but the speed with which this transition occurs varies. In Aguascalientes and Guadalajara, for example, pioneer firms faded quickly into the background; in Monterrey and Tehuacán, pioneers dominated local production for several decades after their arrival.

The Offshore Assembly Enclave

An enclave of offshore assembly plants, or maquiladoras, has developed alongside the domestic industry. The plants are domestically owned and operated but rely on foreign firms for input supply, product designs, and access to foreign markets. Garment maquiladoras first appeared in the late 1960s but did not proliferate until the 1980s. Between 1980 and 1988 the share of national garment employment in maquiladoras increased from 12.9 percent to 20 percent. The expansion of maquiladoras was, until recently, concentrated along the Mexican-U.S. border (Sklair 1989).

The maquila arrangement closely resembles subcontracting in the domestic garment industry. U.S. firms undertake marketing and design activities, and subcontract assembly to maquiladoras. Maquiladoras have virtually no backward or forward linkages with the domestic industry. Raw materials are supplied by the foreign client firm. Between 1981 and 1988 domestic inputs accounted for an average of 0.25 percent of total inputs consumed by garment maquiladoras located along the border and 2.36 percent of total inputs consumed by those in Mexico's interior (INEGI 1989b). Foreign firms distribute assembled garments through their own marketing channels and export virtually all the output. The U.S. firms that engage in offshore assembly are primarily national retail chains, such as Sears and J.C. Penney, or firms with their own well-established national or regional labels, such as Haggar, Levi Strauss, and Warnaco (Waldinger 1986). Maquiladora production is concentrated in four products: men's pants (primarily jeans), men's shirts, bras, and underwear.

The border region's share of national garment employment increased from 6.9 percent in 1970 to 16.4 percent in 1988 (Table 13.1). This expansion coincided with an overall shift in manufacturing employment toward the border. The border's share of total manufacturing jobs increased from 11.4 percent in 1980 to 20.1 percent in 1988.

Policies in both the United States and Mexico encourage the development of maquiladoras. In 1965 the Mexican government initiated an official program to promote the expansion of an offshore assembly industry (Sklair 1989). The government waived foreign-ownership limitations for maquiladoras and exempted the plants from taxes and import duties. This basic package of incentives, with minor changes, has remained largely intact. To be eligible for tax breaks, maquiladoras must export their production. A presidential decree in 1987 reduced the export requirement from 100 to 80 percent, and a second decree in 1990 lowered the requirement further, to 50 percent (Ehrenthal and Newman 1988). In the United States,

Item 807 of the U.S. tariff schedule allows firms to engage in the offshore assembly of U.S.-manufactured components and pay import duties only on value-added abroad. In this arrangement, a firm imports components from the United States, assembles the components abroad, and exports the final product. If the firms used Mexican textiles, they would have to pay duties on the value of the entire garment.[2]

The Liberalization of Trade

In 1985 President Miguel de la Madrid announced that Mexico was joining the General Agreement on Tariffs and Trade (GATT). From 1985 to 1988 he initiated a series of reforms that drastically reduced most trade barriers. Trade barriers consisted of import tariffs and import-license requirements, both of which had been in effect—to varying degrees—since the 1940s. For garments, the production-weighted average tariff fell from 49.8 percent in June 1985, to 39.9 percent in June 1987, and finally to the new maximum allowable tariff of 20 percent in December 1987. Trade reform eliminated quantity restrictions. For garments, the coverage of import licenses as a percentage of domestic production was reduced from 100 percent in June 1985 to 88.8 percent in December 1985; it was eliminated entirely in May 1988.

Since these policy changes the domestic garment industry has stagnated. Between January 1987 and January 1990, domestic garment-industry employment increased by 0.16 percent, compared to a 2.7 percent increase in all manufacturing. Some of the stagnation of the domestic industry may be attributed to greater competition from imports. Garment imports increased from US$29.5 million in 1987 to US$214.8 million in 1989, and totaled US$183 million in the first eight months of 1990. In terms of domestic consumption, the import share rose from 5.3 percent in 1988, to 11.5 percent in 1989, and to 15 percent in 1990.

Mexico City is the point of entry for garment imports. Interview data suggest that many traders in the capitol's garment district have closed down their production activities to become importers.[3]

Few producers have succeeded in penetrating export markets, another reason for industry stagnation. Nonmaquiladora garment exports rose from US$52.7 million in 1987 to US$85.2 million in 1988 and decreased to US$68.3 million in 1989 (Table 13.3). For the first eight months of 1990 these exports totaled US$41.1 million—9.7 percent less than in the same period in 1989. Trade figures exaggerated the minimal export success of the domestic garment industry; a substantial share of nonmaquiladora garment exports is attributable to only a few large firms. The Secretariat of Trade and Industrial Promotion (SECOFI) provides a special classification for firms exporting more than US$3 million a year: of the 170 domestic garment firms currently listed as exporters, only 8 met these requirements in 1989. A lower bound for these 8 firms' total 1989 exports is US$24 million, or 27.1 percent of 1989 nonmaquiladora exports. Many of these large firms are current or former subsidiaries of transnationals.

The United States continues to be Mexico's principal trading partner. Between 1985 and 1989 Mexican garment imports from the United States increased from US$29.9 million to US$131.9 million; imports from the United States as a share of total garment imports fell from 89.1 percent in 1985 to 52.9 percent in 1990. Industry observers suggest that a large share of Mexican garment imports from the United States were manufactured in Asia and merely distributed by U.S. traders in New York and Los Angeles. Hong Kong is the most

Table 13.3

Mexico: International Trade in Garments, 1982–1990 (in 1985 US$ millions)

	Domestic Industry Imports I	Domestic Industry Exports II	Maquila Value-Added[a] III	Maquila Gross Exports[b] IV	Total Net Exports II + III − I
1982	161.723	20.697	67.338	196.128	−73.688
1983	9.282	13.571	50.909	217.521	55.198
1984	17.766	21.874	71.168	259.822	75.287
1985	33.546	16.695	71.878	238.131	55.027
1986	28.735	19.191	82.971	266.538	73.427
1987	29.485	52.630	100.868	299.954	124.013
1988	119.828	85.215	120.922	322.1 92	80.758
1989	224.990	68.263	160.325	496.281	3. 598
1990[c]	188.221	41.093	113.651	351.804	−35.431

Sources: Secretaraía de Comercio y Fomento Industrial, unpublished data; INEGI 1989b.
[a]Total exports less imported inputs.
[b]Total exports including imported inputs.
[c]January through August.

active new country in the Mexican garment market; its share of Mexican garment imports increased from 1.3 percent in 1988 to 22.4 percent in 1990.

The United States maintains quotas on Mexican garment exports under the Multifiber Arrangement (MFA). Recent Mexican-U.S. bilateral textile-trade agreements have made quotas more flexible. The current agreement, which was signed in 1988 and revised in 1990, allows Mexico to obtain quota increases on request for most goods. Quotas appear to be binding only for a few select products. From 1988 to 1990 average quota utilization rates were more than 60 percent in only four of the sixty-one product categories: overalls (112.9%), pants (102.1%), pajamas (88.6%), and shirts and blouses (80.9%).

In contrast to the anemic performance of the domestic industry, the garment-maquiladora industry is booming. Between January 1987 and January 1990 employment in the garment-maquiladora industry increased by 39.5 percent. Maquiladora exports have grown dramatically since the opening to trade, rising from US$300 million in 1987, to US$322 million in 1988, and reaching more than US$496 million in 1989. In 1989 value-added in maquiladora exports alone—total exports less the value of imported inputs—was 2.4 times nonmaquiladora garment exports. The overwhelming majority of Mexican maquiladora exports are destined for the U.S. market. The greater flexibility in U.S. quotas made this export expansion possible.

Most of the recent job growth in offshore assembly has taken place in interior Mexico, not along the border. The share of maquiladora employment in interior states increased from 20.9 percent in 1981 to 41.5 percent in 1988 (INEGI 1989b). Interview data suggested that the shift was the result of producers converting from domestic to offshore production. One example is the Tehuacán garment industry, in which firms have switched from subcontracting for Mexico City traders to offshore assembly for U.S. client firms.

Maquila conversion is not the only adjustment strategy evident in Mexico's garment industry. Interview material suggested that producers in a few agglomerations were coordinating efforts to adjust to the trade opening. These attempts are still in their formative stages and are limited to certain areas, but they demonstrate the variety of adjustment strategies. A common feature of coordinated adjustment has been the creation of new marketing channels, giving firms direct access to foreign buyers. Firms in the state of Aguascalientes, for example, created an export-trading company that serves as a vehicle for forming joint ventures with U.S. garment manufacturers. The trading company is jointly owned and managed by local firms. Firms in Guadalajara organized a trade fair to help local producers replace clients lost to imports. Profits from the trade fair are used to create a design center providing technical assistance to local firms. The intention is to make Guadalajara the next center for women's fashion in Mexico.

The principal government-sponsored initiative to help the industry adjust to trade liberalization is the Fashion and Design Center in Mexico City. The center was created through the joint efforts of the National Garment Industry Chamber and several government ministries. It offers firms the use of computer-aided design equipment and computerized cutting equipment. The goal was to enable small firms to work as a group and thus to produce large orders for foreign buyers. The new technology was intended to eliminate a perceived bottleneck between the design and assembly stages of production. The idea for the center came from a study by the Boston Consulting Group (BCG 1988). Neither BCG nor the government consulted the small firms that were the intended beneficiaries of the program. Most of these firms still use cardboard patterns of simple electrical cutting tools. The center has been in operation for two years. Its client base consists exclusively of medium-sized and large firms, none of which is exporting. The fee structure for computerized cutting favors large batches, and the facility requires 50 percent payment up front, making it prohibitive for small firms.

Industry Location, Vertical Organization, and Trade

Industry localization is a predominant feature of garment manufacturing. Localization is the rule in marketing activities, where proximity means access to information. In other garment activities, such as design and assembly, localization economies are weak or nonexistent (there are global constant returns-to-scale). For the various production activities, the divergence of technology creates conflicting locational imperatives. For marketing, localization economies compel firms to agglomerate; for other activities, firms are compelled to locate where factor costs are lowest. The resulting location patterns vary over the course of the development process in response to regional wages and changes in the underlying trade regime.

The Closed Economy

The development of the industry under the closed economy is characterized by two distinct stages.

Initial agglomeration. Under the closed economy, knowledge spillovers in marketing lead firms to agglomerate. Frequent changes in consumers' tastes in garments require firms to remain abreast of constantly shifting trends. Firms gain access to this information by locating near other firms. Access occurs indirectly through spying and imitation and directly through open communication between firms.

Knowledge spillovers are a widely cited characteristic of the garment industry (Lichtenberg 1960; Waldinger 1986). In a low-income country such as Mexico, style changes are less important than in industrialized countries; communication costs between locations are higher, however, because of poor telephone service and inefficient transportation systems.

Vertical separation and industry dispersion. Wage differentials between the trade center and the outlying regions cause the industry to separate. Firms move production, the labor-intensive activity, to low-wage regions and leave marketing concentrated in the initial agglomeration. Marketing knowledge gives traders a first-mover advantage, and they open periphery locations to production. In a given periphery location, a single trader assumes the role of pioneer. The pioneer makes front-end investments in training a cadre of design workers and organizing machinists for assembly.

Economic Integration

Trade liberalization has deepened the process of economic integration between Mexico and the United States. Integration changes the reference market for Mexican producers and has a dramatic effect on both the organization and location of production.

Vertical specialization. With localization economies in marketing, efficiency is determined by market size. Trade creates a pattern of vertical specialization in which the small country specializes in production and the large country specializes in marketing. Assembly is moved from the United States to Mexico, because of the lower wages south of the border. U.S. firms, given the larger size of the U.S. market, capture marketing activities from Mexico.

Industry relocation. International trade also leads to a relocation of production. Under the closed economy, border regions in Mexico played a small role in domestic garment production. With trade liberalization, the north became a natural assembly platform for marketing centers in the United States. Most U.S. garment firms doing business in Mexico are from the Los Angeles marketing center; Los Angeles is also the primary garment exporter to Mexico City. The small size of the Mexican market may not initially affect the balance between the New York and Los Angeles marketing centers, but over time it is likely that Los Angeles will emerge as the principal marketing center in the U.S., at least for a certain range of products.

North American Free Trade and the Mexican Garment Industry

Although the reasons discussed above explain localization in the domestic garment industry, many observers suggest alternative explanations for the expansion of offshore garment assembly in Mexico. Some attribute the growth of maquiladoras to existing policies, such as Item 807 of the U.S. tariff schedule, and suggest that maquila expansion will subside with the implementation of the North American free-trade agreement. This view confuses in-bond production with offshore assembly. Item 807 gives garment firms engaging in offshore assembly an incentive to use U.S. fabric; it implies nothing, however, about who should control design and marketing activities. If contacts with U.S. marketing centers were unnecessary, Mexican firms would participate in all aspects of off-shore production, not just assembly. They could take advantage of Item 807, Mexican fiscal incentives, and low Mexican wages by establishing a plant in the United States to purchase U.S. fabric and a second plant in Mexico to assemble garments. In reality, Mexico's role is limited to assembly. Mexican assembly plants depend on foreign clients to provide designs and market access.

Critics rightly note that a maquiladora-oriented development path contains several shortcomings. In garment manufacturing, assembly represents the least profitable link of the value-added chain; value-added by maquiladoras between 1981 and 1988 represented an average of 32.7 percent of the total value of maquila exports. Maquiladoras also face highly cyclical demand for their labor. When U.S. garment manufacturers face a downturn in demand, maquiladoras are laid off first. During the 1981–82 U.S. recession, employment in garment maquiladoras fell by 16.9 percent. Between June and September 1990, the early phase of the 1990–91 recession, garment employment fell by 2 percent, compared to a 6.1 percent increase during the same period the year before.

Is Mexico doomed to the task of offshore assembly in the North American market? Interview material suggested that there are gradations between the two extremes of pure assembly and integrated production and marketing. In the development of the domestic industry, producer agglomerations typically controlled design activities and, in some instances, part of the wholesale distribution process. What distinguishes the experience of domestic-producer agglomerations is that their participation in design and marketing was limited to specialized tasks. Specialization allowed them to coexist with a larger marketing center in Mexico City.

In the newly open economy, firms in Aguascalientes and Guadalajara appear to be following a similar strategy of specialized vertical expansion. Firms selected a highly value-added activity—in both cases, wholesale distribution—and attempted to capture the activity from larger, more-developed marketing centers. Currently, firms in Guadalajara are trying to use their accumulated experience in distribution to establish a design center. A common feature of the strategies has been the reliance on a regional trade association—in both cases, the local delegation of the National Garment Industry Chamber—to coordinate activities. These experiences suggest that coordination is a necessary component in the transition from assembly to higher value-added activities.

There appears to be a natural role for policy in coordinating actions to capture design and distribution activities from larger marketing centers. Indeed, the Aguascalientes export-trading company and the Guadalajara trade fair seem obvious candidates for replication in other regions. These initiatives were developed, organized, and implemented by Mexican firms. The only government-sponsored initiative, the Fashion and Design Center in Mexico City, is similar in scheme and intent to those in Aguascalientes and Guadalajara but has failed because the project coordinators neglected to consult the target population of firms. There remains little doubt that a role for policy exists; however, there remains a great deal of doubt about the government's ability to carry out the appropriate measures.

Conclusion

For Mexico, integration is a double-edged sword. It allows Mexican firms to gain access to new markets on a scale that was unattainable under the old regime. But the trade-off for improved market access is a loss of control over the production process. Access to U.S. markets requires Mexican firms to shift from vertically integrated manufacturing to assembly. Given the immensity of the U.S. economy, it is likely that the gains Mexican producers enjoy from having access to the U.S. market would swamp any losses from ceding marketing activities to U.S. firms.

There is a strong nationalist current in Mexico that equates offshore assembly with a loss in sovereignty. This view overlooks the regional disparities that were an inherent feature of import-substitution industrialization. Under the closed economy, Mexico City emerged as the country's principal industrial center. The process of geographic concentration in the capital peripheralized other regions in the country. Limited regional decentralization did occur, but it only served to move low-skill activities out of the capital. The North American free-trade agreement will transform the process of regional economic development in Mexico. Integration will convert the former center into a periphery region of the United States, while granting the northern region access to substantially better markets and technology. To call this a loss in sovereignty is not a nationalist perspective but a regionalist bias that favors the welfare of the center over the welfare of other regions.

Notes

1. An interview I had with a Mexico City subcontractor illustrates this point. After an hour-long interview, although it was clear that I was a for-

eigner, the subcontractor believed I was a government inspector; he expected me to ask for a bribe (the going rate is US$20).

2. In 1987 the U.S. weighted-average tariff on fabrics was 11.5 percent. Until 1990, firms using Mexican textiles to manufacture garments for export had to pay the 15 percent Mexican value-added tax. For domestic sourcing of textile inputs to be cost-effective, Mexican fabrics would have to cost an average of 26.5 percent less than U.S. textiles.

3. See also *Expansion*, April 17, 1991, 72–73.

References

Alonso, J. A. 1991. *Mujeres, maquiladoras e industria doméstica*. Mexico City: Siglo Veintiuno Editores.

Boston Consulting Group (BCG). 1988. *Sector textil*. Mexico City: Banco Nacional de Comercio Exterior.

Ehrenthal, D., and J. Newman. 1988. "Explaining Mexico's Maquila Boom." *SAIS Review* 8:189–211.

Ghadar, Fariborz, William H. Davidson, and Charles S. Feigenoff. 1987. *U.S. Industrial Competitiveness: The Case of the Textile and Apparel Industries*. Lexington, Mass.: Lexington Books.

Hoffman, Kurt, and Howard Rush. 1988. *Micro-Electronics and Clothing: The Impact of Technical Change on a Global Industry*. New York: Praeger.

Instituto Nacional de Estadística, Geografía et Informática (INEGI). 1981. *Censo comercial, 1981*. Mexico City: INEGI.

———. 1989a. *Resultados oportunos*. Aguascalientes: INEGI.

———. 1989b. *Estadísticas de la industria maquiladora de exportación, 1978–1988*. Aguascalientes: INEGI.

Krugman, P. 1990. *Geography and Trade*. Cambridge: Massachusetts Institute of Technology Press.

Lichtenberg, R. 1960. *One-Tenth of a Nation*. Cambridge: Harvard University Press.

Porter, Michael E. 1990. *The Competitive Advantage of Nations*. New York City: Free Press.

Secretaría de Programación y Presupuesto (SPP). 1966. *VIII Censo industrial*. Mexico City: SPP.

———. 1971. *IX Censo industrial*. Mexico City: SPP.

———. 1976. *X Censo industrial*. Mexico City: SPP.

———. 1981. *XI Censo industrial*. Mexico City: INEGI.

Sklair, Leslie. 1989. *Assembling for Development: The Maquiladora Industry in the U.S. and Mexico*. London: Unwin Hyman.

Waldinger, Roger D. 1986. *Through the Eye of the Needle: Immigrants and Enterprise in New York's Garment Trades.* New York: New York University Press.

Walton, J. 1977. *Elites and Economic Development.* Austin: University of Texas Press.

Chapter 14

Export Manufacturing, State Policy, and Women Workers in the Dominican Republic

Helen I. Safa

Since the early 1980s export-led development strategies have become increasingly popular in Latin America and the Caribbean, especially in the manufacturing sector. Although the Border Industrialization Program in Mexico is the best known and most important in terms of exports to the United States, other countries also have turned to export as a way of earning foreign capital and alleviating the current debt crisis, sometimes spurred by the neoliberal policies of the International Monetary Fund.

In the smaller countries of Central America and the Caribbean, exports have been the primary development strategy since incorporation into the world economy in colonial times. Starting in the 1960s, an increase in manufacturing (in addition to traditional agricultural exports such as sugar, coffee, and bananas) followed the "industrialization by invitation" strategy initiated by Puerto Rico a decade earlier. Import-substitution industrialization, which was designed in the postwar period to stimulate domestic industry in the rest of Latin America, never achieved great success in the Caribbean Basin, because of the lack of capital and technology in these countries (even more acute than that in the larger countries). The small size of these countries, combined with their low purchasing power, limited the possibilities of developing a viable internal market, which is critical for import substitution. In order to gain access to foreign markets, capital, and technology, Caribbean countries are dependent on transnational corporations.

In recent years, prompted by the debt crisis and growing unemployment, the competition among Latin American and Caribbean countries for foreign investment in export manufacturing has been intense. Governments have attempted to encourage foreign investment by lifting trade barriers and offering tax holidays, subsidized credit, export subsidies, and freedom from import duties on machinery and raw materials needed for production. Most Caribbean countries also allow unrestricted profit repatriation. Special export-processing zones were constructed—at public expense—for export-manufacturing plants, complete with water, electricity, roads, and so on. Thus the state has played a major role in fostering export manufacturing, often aided by the U.S. Agency for International Development (USAID), which in the 1980s made this a key development strategy throughout Latin America and the Caribbean (Joekes and Moayedi 1987). The U.S. Congress has attacked and restricted the USAID policy of financing and advertising free-trade zones; these actions were the result of U.S. labor unions' investigations into these practices and their consequent job losses for U.S. workers (Bradsher 1992, 5).

In addition to providing cost benefits to U.S. manufacturers, export manufacturing was viewed by the U.S. government as a way of improving the stagnant economies of Latin American and Caribbean countries while promoting political stability in the region (Deere et al. 1990, 154). Special tariff programs were instituted to promote the relocation of labor-intensive phases of manufacturing abroad as early as the beginning of the 1960s, through Items 806.30 and 807 (now known as Harmonized Tariff Schedule HTS9802.00.80) of the U.S. Tariff Code, which reduced duties on imports with U.S. components assembled or processed abroad. These items aided U.S. industry's competitive position by limiting U.S. tariffs to the value-added on goods assembled abroad, thus substantially reducing labor costs. Item 807 in particular provided the basis for the maquiladora plants under the Mexican Border Industrialization Program, as well as stimulating the growth of assembly plants in the Caribbean, where manufacturing exports grew rapidly during the 1960s and 1970s (Deere et al. 1990, 143–44). The Generalized System of Preferences, enacted in 1974, authorized the president to grant duty-free treatment to eligible products from Third World countries for a period of ten years, provided that at least 35 percent of the products' total value came from direct processing costs in those countries.

U.S. government support for export manufacturing in the Caribbean Basin was enhanced by the 1983 enactment of President Ronald Reagan's Caribbean Basin Initiative (CBI). Although textiles and garments are excluded from the CBI, because of opposition from U.S. labor, the United States has granted certain Caribbean countries special import quotas through the Guaranteed Access Levels (GALs) program, sometimes referred to as 807A. Under the GALs program, apparel imports to the United States have grown 76 percent each year since 1987, but they are limited to garments composed entirely of fabric made and cut in the United States (Deere and Meléndez 1992).

Partly in response to these various tariff incentives, U.S. investment in the Caribbean Basin between 1977 and 1982 was growing at a faster rate than in any other world region. According to a U.S. Department of Commerce survey released in 1988, the leading countries in terms of reported investments were the Dominican Republic, Jamaica, and Costa Rica, with 54 percent of the value of new investments of U.S. origin and 24 percent of Caribbean origin.[1] The remainder represented increasing Asian investment in the region, concentrated in the garment sector, through which Asian firms hoped to regain privileged access to the U.S. market (Deere et al. 1990, 169). The composition of U.S. investment in the region changed dramatically after 1984, largely because of sharp cuts in traditional commodities such as sugar in the Dominican Republic, bauxite in Jamaica, and petroleum in Trinidad. As a result, though mining and mineral products constituted more than half of U.S. imports from Caribbean Basin countries in 1984, manufacturing had supplanted those products by 1990 (Table 14.1).

The shift toward export manufacturing in the Caribbean Basin countries implies a profound restructuring of their economies: economic emphasis moved away from traditional commodities, which had been principal exports for many years, to providing cheap labor for U.S. light industry. Export manufacturing lessens the need to develop the internal market required by import substitution; on the contrary, the external market demand for export manufacturing requires the maximum reduction of production costs, principally wages, in order to compete effectively on the international level. In

Table 14.1

Composition of U.S. Imports from CBERA-Beneficiary Countries, 1984 and 1990 (in US$ thousands)

	1984		1990	
Sector	US$	Share (%)	US$	Share (%)
Agriculture/fishery	2,222.6	25.3	1,982.5	26.3
Mining/mineral products	4,459.2	50.8	1,520.0	20.2
Manufacturing	1,937.7	22.1	3,763.2	50.0
Other	162.2	1.8	259.5	3.5
Total	8,781.7	100.0	7,525.2	100.0

Source: U.S. Department of Labor, Bureau of International Labor Affairs, *Trade and Employment Effects of the Caribbean Basin Economic Recovery Act, Seventh Annual Report to the Congress,* Washington, D.C., 1991. Reproduced from Deere and Meléndez 1992, 70.
Note: CBERA = Caribbean Basin Economic Recovery Act.

fact, the availability of cheap labor appears to be the prime determining factor for investment; that helps to explain why most of the jobs generated through export manufacturing are for women, who previously represented a small percentage of the industrial labor force under import substitution.

In this chapter I focus on the socioeconomic consequences of export-led industrialization in the Dominican Republic, which, under the CBI, became the leading source of apparel exports in the Caribbean, with exports totaling US$516.9 million, or 2.6 times more than the total exports from other CBI countries in 1988 (Dauhajre et al. 1989, 97). The Dominican Republic is a classic case of recently initiated export manufacturing, with a total of 135,000 workers in 385 firms in 1991, corresponding to 4.4 percent of the economically active population (FundApec 1992, 30–32). The number of firms and workers in the free-trade zones rose spectacularly after 1983 (Table 14.2) and is directly attributable to currency devaluations mandated by the International Monetary Fund, which reduced the costs of labor and other expenses in the Dominican Republic to one of the lowest levels in the Caribbean. About three-fourths of these jobs are held by women, and most are still employed in the three original free-trade zones created before 1980. Because of the growth of export manufacturing, the value of exports increased 12.8 percent annually between 1983 and 1988—despite the sharp decline since 1982 of U.S. sugar import quotas and hence of the Dominican Republic's traditional sugar exports (Deere et al. 1990, 166).

Table 14.2
Growth in Employment in Dominican Free
Trade Zones, 1981–1991

Year	Number of Employees
1981	18,317
1983	19,255
1984	25,657
1985	30,902
1986	51,203
1987	72,735
1988	83,815
1989	122,986
1991	134,998

Source: Consejo de Promoción de Inversiones, Banco
Central, Consejo Nacional de Zonas Francas y Banco
Mundial. Reproduced from Fundapec 1992, table 1,
p. 30.

The garment industry, along with electronics, has been the area of
greatest expansion in export manufacturing in the Caribbean Basin.
Between 1983 and 1986 the region's textile and apparel imports to
the United States grew by an annual average of 28 percent, increasing to 39 percent in 1987. Most of the growth in the region's garment
exports is under Items 807 and 807a (GALs), with exports from the
Dominican Republic, Haiti, and Jamaica increasing by more than 20
percent annually during the 1980s (Deere et al. 1990, 167). In 1988
garments represented 78 percent of all manufacturing exports from
the Dominican Republic, with a total value of US$183.8 million, an
increase of 333.4 percent since 1981 (Dauhajre et al. 1989, 39–40).
By 1991 Dominican garment imports to the United States under 807
and 807a had risen to $781 million.

Export-led industrialization in the Dominican Republic, however,
has not led to self-sustained growth capable of generating more complex and capital-intensive forms of industrial production, as in East
Asia and even Mexico. Dominican state industrial policies favor foreign investment over domestic industry in the free-trade zones, and
U.S. import restrictions limit export-led industrialization to assembly operations. These assembly operations, requiring cheap, unskilled labor, resulted in a change in the industrial labor force from
a male-dominated economy based on sugar to a largely female labor
force based on light industry. This increased incorporation of

women into the labor force—although in dead-end, low-paid jobs—
has given Dominican women more economic responsibility and authority in the household, while men are increasingly marginalized.
These changes are illustrated in a 1981 survey of 231 women workers in the three oldest Dominican export-processing zones, and in
eighteen interviews conducted in 1986 with a subsample of women
working in the garment industry in La Romana, the oldest of the free-
trade zones.[2] Through these primary sources and secondary data, we
can examine the impact of export manufacturing in the Dominican
Republic, particularly on women workers, on both the national and
household levels.

State Policy and Export Manufacturing in the Dominican Republic

Garment and textile manufacturing commonly represent the first
stage of industrialization in both advanced industrial and developing countries, in reference to earlier forms of industrialization in the
nineteenth century as well as the more recently initiated export manufacturing. Developing countries have had a comparative advantage
in labor-intensive industries such as garment manufacture, which
require relatively low levels of capital and technology and an abundance of cheap labor, to be provided chiefly by women. The enclave
pattern of export-led industrialization in the Caribbean, however,
combined with low investments in research and development and
tariff regulations requiring the use of U.S. materials, has resulted in
few transfers of skills and technology to these developing countries;
together these factors have dampened rather than stimulated domestic production.

In a study of the Caribbean clothing industry, Peter Steele argued
that it "is the obvious intent of the U.S. administration to make it
impossible for participating countries to build up substantial apparel
industries which are not just offshore assembly operations for U.S.
contractors but self-sufficient manufacturing enterprises such as
those developed in the Big Three [Hong Kong, Taiwan, and South
Korea] and other major garment-supplying countries" (1988, 58). In
1986 60 percent of local costs in the Dominican Republic was spent
on wages and salaries, and only 4 percent was spent on raw materi-

als, most of which consisted of paper and other office supplies (Dauhajre et al. 1989, 51). In the Dominican Republic, most garment-manufacturing firms geared toward export are direct subsidiaries of U.S. transnationals, rather than domestic producers subcontracted to these foreign investors. In 1988, 63 percent of the export-processing firms in the Dominican Republic were owned by U.S. capital (10% were Dominican-owned), and in the last few years there has been increasing investment from Korea, Hong Kong, and Puerto Rico (Abreu et al. 1989, 76), although Dominican investment grew substantially from 1987 to 1990, constituting 40 percent of all new firms created during this period (FundApec 1992, 35). The garment industry's heavy dependence on U.S. capital, technology, and markets, and the lack of linkages to the domestic economy in all areas but labor, significantly reduces the industry's ability to generate growth and more complex, capital-intensive forms of industrial production, either in export processing or in the domestic economy, as it has in Asia. On the contrary, export manufacturing increases Caribbean dependence on the United States and contributes little to the general economic development of these small and open economies.

In the Caribbean, the state's principal role in export manufacturing is to create a favorable climate for foreign investment through investment incentives and wage and labor control. Few production workers are paid a fixed wage; instead, they operate on a piece-rate system. Most workers in Caribbean export-processing zones are entitled to the minimum wage, provided they can meet production quotas. Hourly wages vary considerably between countries and over time (and with fluctuations in currency exchange rates); in 1990 Dominican wages in export processing stood at US$0.50 an hour, among the lowest of any Caribbean Basin country (Table 14.3). To attract foreign capital, the Dominican state passed industrial-incentive laws providing tax holidays of eight to twenty years, exemptions from import duties, and no restrictions on profit repatriation (Deere et al. 1990, 145). Labor control has been achieved by outright repression or prohibition of unions in the Dominican free-trade zones, further increasing the vulnerability of workers.

Dominican economic policy was established by a "predatory state," set up by the dictator Rafael Trujillo, who ruled the country from 1930 to 1960. Trujillo's government legacy was followed by many of his successors. It included strong state intervention in the

Table 14.3

Minimum Wage in Selected CBERA-
Beneficiary Countries

Country	US$/Hour
Aruba	2.86
Bahamas	2.20–3.00
Trinadad and Tobago	2.14
Netherland Antilles	1.18–3.08
Antigua and Barbuda	1.10
St. Kitts and Nevis	1.08
Belize	0.87
St. Vincent	0.76
Dominica	0.75
Guatemala	0.75
Costa Rica	0.71–0.84
Panama	0.59–0.78
Dominican Republic	0.50
El Salvador	0.50
Grenada	0.48
Haiti	0.39
Guyana	0.38
Honduras	0.33
Jamaica	0.27

Source: USITC, *Annual Report on the Impact of the Caribbean Basin Economic Recovery Act on U.S. Industries and Consumers, Sixth Report, 1990,* USITC
Publication No. 3432, Washington, D.C., 1991. Reproduced from Deere and Meléndez 1992, 70.

Note: CBERA-Caribbean Basin Economic Recovery Act.

economy (in Trujillo's case, often in pursuit of personal gain), control of labor, and dependence on exports. Despite elections and lip
service to increasing democratic participation, the state continued
to serve the interests of the agrarian and industrial elite, with little
attention paid to the needs of the poor. Import-substitution industrialization and increasing sugar exports to the United States (replacing
Cuban imports after the revolution) did lead to considerable economic growth, particularly from 1969 to 1977, but unemployment
rates hovered above 20 percent, and in 1980 underemployment was
estimated at 43 percent. Income distribution has remained highly
unequal, with 10 percent of the population receiving more than one-
third of all income from 1967 through 1984 (Ramírez et al. 1988,
29–49). Though the public-expenditure levels in health and educa-

tion are generally low, there have been notable gains in these areas since the 1950s. From 1950 to 1980 illiteracy decreased from 57 to 25 percent, the gross general mortality rate was reduced 60 percent, and the infant mortality rate decreased 43 percent, while life expectancy increased from 43 to 61 years (Ramírez et al. 1988, 143). But with the onset of the economic crisis in the 1980s, which led to malnutrition and inadequate medical care, infant, child, and maternal mortality rates rose again (Whiteford 1990, 222).

The economic crisis and the 1983 imposition of IMF-mandated structural adjustment measures further reduced the state's control over the economy, as well as cutting the government services and personnel through which the state's largesse was commonly dispensed. The Dominican Republic's open economy made the country more vulnerable to changes in the balance of payments and rising interest rates on the debt, which grew to US$3,719.5 million in 1985, half the GDP (Ceara 1987, 22). Labor was also weakened by structural adjustment measures that resulted in higher levels of unemployment and inflation and lower real wages. Despite several increases in the minimum wage, the real hourly wage in the Dominican Republic in 1990 was estimated to be only 62.3 percent of that earned in 1984 (FundApec 1992, 32).

Starting in the early 1980s, the United States reduced sugar quotas for the Dominican Republic and other Caribbean countries, resulting in increased unemployment, particularly among men. The Dominican Republic accounted for roughly half the annual U.S. sugar quota from the Caribbean Basin, which dropped from an average 1.6 million tons in 1979–81 to 268,000 tons in December 1987. The decline in sugar exports also negatively affected foreign-exchange earnings and domestic growth in the Dominican Republic, because the value-added component of sugar is estimated to be as high as 90 percent, while for garments assembled from U.S.-made and -cut cloth it averages, at most, 27 percent (Deere and Meléndez 1992, 63–66).

Export manufacturing was designated to compensate for the loss of employment and foreign exchange in sugar production, and the abundance of low-cost female labor in the Dominican Republic attracted business. Manufacturing exports grew 307.4 percent between 1981 and 1988, to US$502.1 million, with textiles and garments averaging 35.8 percent of exports during this period. This increase was due to the growth of free-trade zones, not the domestic manufactur-

ers' exports, which actually declined during that period from 97 to
63.6 percent of total exports (Dauhajre et al. 1989, 38–39, 43). Domestic manufacturing is declining; it employed 12 percent fewer
workers in 1991 than in 1980 (FundApec 1992, 43). Few export-processing firms have used local materials, apparently because of poor
quality and high prices brought on by high import taxes and energy
costs; these circumstances have also harmed domestic manufacturing.

Export-Led Industrialization and Economic Development

Although the spectacular increase in Dominican export manufacturing was designed to alleviate unemployment and to produce badly
needed foreign exchange, neither goal has been adequately realized.
The jobs created in the free-trade zones have been primarily for
women and have contributed to their increasing participation in the
labor force. Male unemployment, however, which suffered because
of declining sugar production, has not been reduced. Women's
wages have been extremely low and have thus generated few demand linkages to the rest of the economy. Moreover, Dominican export manufacturing has been an increasingly inefficient generator of
foreign exchange: the value-added from free-trade-zone exports as
foreign exchange dropped from 45 to 25 percent from the late 1970s
to 1988. As a result, despite the fivefold increase in the total value of
exports from the Dominican free-trade zones, from US$117 million
(1987) to US$517 million (1988), the economy remained virtually
stagnant, with average GDP growth rates of only 1.1 percent per year
(Deere and Meléndez 1992). The fundamental reason is found in U.S.
trade policies, which reduced export manufacturing in the Dominican Republic (and throughout the Caribbean Basin) to low value-
added assembly operations. Because the tariff programs under which
most of these export manufactures (particularly apparel) enter the
United States mandate the use of U.S. materials, the dutiable portion
of 806-807 imports has not exceeded 32 percent of total import value
since 1985. Under the GALs program, the dutiable portion on apparel imports is even lower, 26 to 27 percent. If the costs to the government—of building infrastructure for the free-trade zones, of lost
fiscal revenues due to tax holidays, of the investor guarantees of un-

restricted profit repatriation—are included in the equation, then this form of export manufacturing appears unlikely to promote self-generating growth and development in the Dominican Republic.

Dominican Export Manufacturing and Female Labor

Female economic activity rates in the Dominican Republic more than quadrupled in thirty years, from 9 percent of total employment in 1960 to 38 percent in 1990 (Table 14.4).[3] Several factors in the development process favored this dramatic increase, including urbanization, the growth of the tertiary sector, and the rise in export processing. At the same time, the female population became more employable: educational levels rose, and fertility declined markedly (Duarte et al. 1989). Male labor-force participation rates dropped 10 percent from 1950 to 1960 (not in tables), reflecting men's growing marginalization in the economy.

In 1981 more than half the economically active women were in the tertiary sector—including white-collar and domestic-service workers—which then constituted the largest female occupational group. The percentage of women in manufacturing also grew so that now it is estimated that they constitute half of all industrial workers and three-fourths of all workers in the free-trade zones (Baez 1991, 16). Export manufacturing is now the most important source of urban employment for women, surpassing even domestic service, which until 1981 constituted the principle source of female employ-

Table 14.4

Female and Male Labor Force Participation Rates in the Dominican Republic, 1960–1990

	1960	1970	1981	1990
Female	9.3	25.1	28.0	38.0
Male	75.9	72.6	72.0	72.2
Both	42.9	48.8	49.5	54.7

Sources: National Office of Statistics 1966, 1985, and in edited tables from 1970 Census. 1990 figures from Central Bank of the Dominican Republic, survey of Labor Force, January–March 1990. Reproduced from Ramírez et al. 1988, 41 (table 11.18). The 1990 figures are taken from Baez 1991, 13.

Note: These figures include people ten years old and older who are employed or are actively seeking employment.

ment (Baez 1991, 25). Garment firms employing a largely female labor force have always predominated in the Dominican free-trade zones; in 1992 they constituted 67 percent of all firms (Consejo Nacional de Zonas Francas de Exportación 1992). Clearly, export manufacturing is a key component of Dominican development strategy and has had a major impact on women's incorporation into the labor force.

Women have become major economic contributors to the household, and in our sample of women workers in export manufacturing, 38 percent considered themselves the major economic providers. Juana Santana, for example, sustained her family of three children on her weekly salary of DR$57 (about US$20), covering food, rent, babysitter, and her own expenses such as transportation and lunch. Her partner drove a *público* (taxi) owned by his family but did not earn much. Juana received no financial assistance from the father of her two older children, who left to work in another town. She had worked for the same garment firm for eight years, despite complaints of forced overtime and delayed state-mandated pay increases. With three children to support, her husband's unstable income, and the high cost of living, she knew she had to continue working. Juana noted: "De todas maneras yo tengo que trabajar, sea en la Zona o por ahí en una casa de familia, de todas maneras, porque es que yo no puedo estar atenía al esposo mío. Porque lo que él gana no me da, para ayudar a la familia y para ayudar en la casa." (Anyway, I have to work, either in the zone or in a private home [as a domestic], anyway, because I cannot be dependent on my husband. Because what he earns is not enough, to help my family and to help me here at home.)

Juana's situation was typical of what many women workers in the free-trade zones faced: low wages, poor working conditions, lack of inexpensive and adequate childcare, few job alternatives, partners offering limited assistance or none at all, and an increasingly high cost of living. Export manufacturers have shown a preference for women workers, because they are cheaper to employ, less likely to unionize, and have greater patience for the tedious, monotonous work employed in assembly operations. Most women workers in the free-trade zones were young (three-quarters of the sample were under thirty) and had no previous work experience (two-thirds), which increased their vulnerability. In addition, 78 percent of the women sampled were rural migrants, more than half were married, and one-fourth were female heads of household, who carried the heaviest financial responsibility as principal or sole economic providers. Two-thirds of our sample had young children to support, increasing their financial burden.

Typically, workers' discontent has been expressed in turnover or eventual withdrawal, rather than through labor organizing. No unions operate in the Dominican free-trade zones (although they are not legally prohibited), and acknowledgment of workers' rights to association in free zones is included in the U.S. Generalized System of Preferences and as a criterion of eligibility under the CBI. The level of unionization in the country as a whole never represented more than 10 or 15 percent of the labor force, and unions have been plagued by fragmentation because of their ties to political parties (Espinal 1988).

Workers have been fired and blacklisted with other plants if discovered carrying out any union activity. Hilda, for example, was fired several years ago, along with sixty other women, for trying to organize a union in the factory where she and Juana worked. The woman received no support from the Ministry of Labor, and Hilda was blacklisted from working in any other factories in the free-trade zone. As the manager told them when they were fired: "La que se meta en sindicato sabe que va a perder su empleo aquí y no va a trabajar más en Zona Franca, porque ustedes saben que el peje grande come al peje chiquito." (Whoever gets involved in unions here knows she will lose her job and will no longer work in the free-trade zone, because as you know the big fish eats the little fish.) Seventy percent of the women workers who responded to this question in the CIPAF sample indicated that they were in favor of unionization; clearly, these workers were conscious of their exploitation and of the need to organize but felt helpless to do anything about it.[4] Workers knew they could be dismissed for any reason and that there were many other women waiting for their jobs.

The lack of support women receive from the Ministry of Labor has also deterred worker militancy. Women who have tried to take complaints of mistreatment or unjust dismissal to the Ministry of Labor have generally been rejected in favor of management. In the survey, 86 percent of the women in the free-trade zones claimed not to know of this office, and only 12 percent had presented complaints. As Luz, a twenty-six-year-old garment worker stated: "La Secretaría del Trabajo no se envuelve en defender a una de nosotras. O sea, ellos siempre se van a favor de los gerentes." (The Secretary of Labor does not defend one of us. That is, they are always in favor of the managers.) It is interesting to note that patriarchal notions of male superiority are reinforced by gender hierarchies recreated in the workplace, with male managers in control of female workers.

The economic crisis in the Dominican Republic has increased the demand and the supply of women workers. Inflation, unemployment, and decreasing male labor-force participation rates resulted in a reduction in real income and increased the need for additional members of the household to join the labor force. This need was made more acute by the cuts in government services mandated by structural adjustment, forcing families to spend more on medicine, health care, education, and other necessities (Cornia, Jolly, and Stewart 1987; Deere et al. 1990).

Although there have been several increases in the minimum wage to keep up with inflation, purchasing power has declined. Salaries have become so low in the free-trade zones that many workers have tried to earn extra income through a *san* or *rifa* (raffle) and have sold objects, including food, jewelry, watches, and cosmetics, to their fellow workers. Some managers have prohibited these activities, but many workers still engage in them. Hilda, for example, played *san*, although she knew the manager did not like it; she claimed: "Si yo viviera atenida a lo que me pagan en mi fábrica yo no pudiera sostener mi casa. Porque yo tengo cuatro hijos." (If I lived off what they paid me in the factory, I couldn't support my household. Because I have four children.) In the survey sample, about three-fourths reported income from outside sources, but it was chiefly from other household members who were working, rather than nonwage activities. The interviews made clear, however, that the high cost of living brought on by devaluation and the economic crisis necessitated the increases in informal economic activity. Most of the women's male partners had odd jobs in the informal sector, such as selling cooked food, driving cabs part-time, working at temporary jobs in construction, and participating in raffles.

Why have workers not protested? Many factors contribute to the lack of worker solidarity in export manufacturing, including the constant turnover among workers, their recent entry into industrial employment, their youthfulness, family responsibilities, high unemployment, and the dearth of job alternatives. But the principal obstacle to greater labor solidarity in the Dominican Republic is outright government repression. There have been several strikes in the free-trade zones, primarily over wage increases, and several attempts to set up labor unions. All efforts have been met by mass firings of the workers involved, as well as blacklisting in other plants, to intimidate other workers.

Although Dominican women workers have been relatively weak in the workplace and the polity, where workers' power must be exercised collectively to confront capital and the state, they have begun to assume more authority in the family. Such authority is derived from women's increased economic contribution to the household, which has taken on major significance in the light of growing male unemployment and its debilitating impact on a man's capacity to be the sole breadwinner. In short, it is not simply the fact that women are employed but the importance of their contribution to the household economy that gives them a basis of resistance to male dominance in the family.

A thirty-eight-year-old supervisor in the free-trade zones who lived alone, although she had eight children in three consensual unions, said she would not quit working, even if she found another man, because

> son hombres machistas. De que piensan de que si la mujer trabaja se va a gobernar demasiado, porque así es que se usa aquí en Santo Domingo. Se que cuando la mujer trabaja entonces ellos ven que es liberal, un poco más liberal, que no pueden hacerle mucha maldad y no pueden abusar. . . . Pero muchos hombres cuando la mujer no trabaja, la mujer tiene que esperar obligado, mal pasar, aguantarle al hombre muchas cosas. Pero cuando la mujer trabaja ya ahí cambia, porque estamos trabajando los dos. (They are *machistas.* They think that if the woman works, she will rule too much, because that's the way it is here in Santo Domingo. When a woman works, they think she is liberal, a little too liberal, that they can't mistreat or abuse her. . . . But many men, when the woman isn't working, the woman is obliged to wait, to have a bad time, to put up with many things from a man. But when the woman is working, then things change, because we are both working.)

This statement clearly demonstrates the subordination imposed on Dominican women who do not have paid employment.

Most women agreed that paid employment gave them greater le-
gitimacy in negotiations with their husbands, even if they considered the man to be the head of the household. In general, more
egalitarian relationships seemed to exist among couples who were
both working, were better educated, were long-time city dwellers,
married at a relatively older age, and were legally married rather
than living in consensual union. For example, Julia was recently
married in a civil ceremony at age twenty-four and was expecting
her first child. Both she and her husband worked in the zone, where
she had worked for seven years; she noted: "Yo diría que eso me
hace sentir más segura, porque ya yo misma manejo mi dinero y sé
en que lo voy a gastar y lo que me corresponde." (I would say that
[work] makes me feel more secure, because I manage my own money
and I know what I will spend it on and what belongs to me.) Most
married women could not count on their husbands for help with
housework and childcare, however, although some received assistance from their children and/or other female relatives, so they were
burdened also by the "double day."

Most of the changes in household authority patterns in the Dominican Republic have come about through a gradual process of negotiation, in which women used their increased economic contribution
to the household to bargain for greater autonomy and authority. But
many women still cling to the traditional notion of the man as the
head of the household. The high rate of consensual unions and of
marital instability, coupled with the pressures of the economic crisis, has heightened the women's insecurities and fears of challenging
male dominance. The crisis also has threatened the men's role as
provider. Thus, household authority patterns have been altered by
women's increasing labor-force participation and men's diminishing
economic role.

Conclusion

Four main actors appear to play critical parts in the promotion of
export-led industrialization: the state, foreign capital, local capital,
and labor, which includes an increasing number of women. In the
Caribbean, as in Latin America generally, foreign capital has the
dominant role, particularly in the form of direct foreign investment

by transnational corporations, which has long been the principal source of capital inflow.[5] Part of the explanation for this dominance lies in the historical hegemony of U.S. capital in the region, even in the export of primary commodities such as sugar in the Dominican Republic. U.S. economic hegemony has diminished the power of the local industrial elite, especially in the Caribbean, where small size and low purchasing power sharply limit the strength of the domestic market. The state and labor were further weakened by the economic crisis and structural adjustment measures, whereby the IMF largely determined the terms of trade, wage increases, currency exchanges, and even state development policy. As Barbara Stallings noted in an article examining the role of foreign capital in economic development, "in its extreme version, the issue at stake is whether the state's choice of development strategy determines the role of foreign capital or whether foreign capital determines development strategy" (1990, 80).

East Asian countries, such as Taiwan and South Korea, have opted for the first strategy, while the Caribbean and much of Latin America have fallen victim to the latter. The export-promotion strategies of these East Asian countries have been quite different from those in the Caribbean; they illustrate the importance of state policy in determining the growth potential of export-led industrialization (Gereffi 1990; Jenkins 1991). East Asian state policies relied heavily on government intervention in the economy, including control over foreign capital and technology; they cannot be seen as an example of free-market policies, as some have suggested. The state took a leading role in the shift toward more capital-intensive forms of export-led industrialization, including heavy investment in research, technology, and worker-training programs, and did not allow export-processing zones to dominate, as in the Dominican Republic. In this way, East Asian states prevented the dependency on the United States that Latin America, and especially the Caribbean, has experienced, and have been able to move into the second stage of high-tech, capital-intensive, export-led industrialization. Between 1980 and 1987 Korea and Taiwan maintained average annual growth rates of 8.6 and 7.5 percent, respectively, much higher than the average annual GDP growth rate of 1.1 percent in the Dominican Republic over the same period (Gereffi 1990, 11).

Labor was weak in both regions and under strong state control to ensure the political stability needed for foreign investment and economic growth. It could be argued that weak labor is necessary for the success of export-led industrialization, because low wages and an absence of labor unrest are critical components for international competition (Deyo 1986). That is one of the reasons women are favored as a source of cheap labor in both regions. Full employment in the more developed East Asian countries has contributed to greater domestic demand and, consequently, to some improvement in workers' bargaining power, wages, and working conditions (Lim 1990, 113). The success of the East Asian development strategy can be seen in the increasing labor shortages in more fully developed countries such as Taiwan and Korea; in contrast, export manufacturing has not led to any reduction in the characteristic labor surplus of the Caribbean Basin.

The increased incorporation of women into the labor force has had both positive and negative consequences. Dead-end factory jobs in the garment industry are hardly liberating for women and may only increase their burden, particularly if they are married and retain responsibilities for domestic chores. Nevertheless, Dominican working women appear to have greater authority over the budget and other household decisions as a result of their larger economic contribution, while the weakening of the man's role as principal breadwinner has contributed to a growing rate of marital instability and female-headed households (Safa 1990). Patriarchy is traditionally much stronger in East Asia and is reflected in the lower percentage of married women in the labor force.[6] In addition, the process of export-led industrialization has not diminished the need for male workers as it has in the Dominican Republic and other areas of the Caribbean. The East Asian emphasis on capital-intensive industrialization for the domestic as well as the export market has enhanced the incorporation of men into the labor force, enabling them to retain their economic control over the household.

Thus, the failure to generate more capital-intensive, high-tech jobs has limited the possibility for male employment as well as increasing the dependence on female labor. It also has restricted the possibilities for self-generating growth. This failure can be attributed, partially, to different state policies in the Caribbean and East Asian regions, in turn reflecting the general weakness of the Caribbean, because of its tradition of U.S.-dependent development. Limiting export manufacturing to mere assembly operations demonstrates the United States's conscious efforts toward maintaining trade policies that favor production and skilled jobs in the United States (in part to appease domestic labor interests). The United States's success in promoting this policy throughout the Caribbean Basin countries will only accelerate their total conversion into sources of cheap labor for U.S. entrepreneurs, increase their dependency on the United States, and guarantee a decrease in their capacity for self-generating growth.

Notes

1. During the 1970s export manufacturing in Haiti also grew at an average rate of more than 40 percent and employment rose to nearly forty thousand workers, but this trend was sharply curtailed after 1980 because of the political instability surrounding the ouster of President Jean Claude Duvalier (De Wind and Kinley 1988, 107–16).

2. The survey was conducted by CIPAF (Centro de Investigación para la Acción Feminina), a private Dominican women's research and action center, which kindly authorized use of these data.

3. The economically active population in the Dominican Republic includes all persons ten years old or older, including those over sixty-five. The 1990 figures are taken from a 1991 report by Clara Baez for the Inter-American Development Bank.

4. Twenty percent of the sample refused to answer this question, indicating the degree to which women workers in the free-trade zones are subject to antiunion intimidation.

5. Even in the larger and more advanced economies of Argentina, Brazil, and Mexico, the share of foreign firms in manufactured exports is greater in South Korea and Taiwan (Jenkins 1991, 221).

6. Gallin (personal communication) argues that married women make up an important segment of the huge subcontracting network in Taiwan but are not counted in official government statistics.

References

Abreu, Alfonso, Manuel Cocco, Carlos Despradel, Eduardo García Michael, and Arturo Peguero. 1989. *Las zonas francas industriales: El éxito de una política económica*. Santo Domingo: Centro de Orientación Económica.

Baez, Clara. 1991. *"Mijores y Desarrollo en la República Dominicana: 1990–91."* Unedited report prepared for Inter-American Bank, Santo Domino, Dominican Republic.

Bradsher, Keith. 1992. "Conferees Agree to Restrict Projects by A.I.D." *New York Times,* October 4, p. 5.

Ceara, Miguel. 1987. *Situacioã socioeconómica actual y su repercusión en la situación de la madre y el niño.* Santo Domingo: INTEC and UNICEF.

Consejo Nacional de Zonas Francas de Exportación, Secretaría de Estado de Industria y Comercio. 1992. *Cantidad de empresas operando en las diferentes zonas francas del país a marzo de 1992.* Santo Domingo, Dominican Republic.

Cornia, G., R. Jolly, and F. Stewart, eds. 1987. *Adjustment with a Human Face,* vol. 1. New York: UNICEF; Oxford: Clarendon Press.

Dauhajre, Andrés, Elizabeth Riley, Rita Mena, and Jose A. Guerrero. 1989. *Impacto económico de las zonas francas industriales de exportación en la República Dominicana.* Santo Domingo: Fundación Economía y Desarrollo.

Deere, Carmen Diana, Peggy Antrobus, Lynn Bolles, Edwin Meléndez, Peter Phillips, Marcia Rivera, and Helen Safa. 1990. *In the Shadows of the Sun: Caribbean Development Alternatives and U.S. Policy.* Boulder, Colo.: Westview Press.

Deere, Carmen Diana, and Edwin Meléndez. 1992. "When Export Growth Is Not Enough: U.S. Trade Policy and Caribbean Basin Economic Recovery." *Caribbean Affairs* 5:61–70.

De Wind, Josh, and David H. Kinley III. 1988. *Aiding Migration: The Impact of International Development Assistance on Haiti.* Boulder, Colo.: Westview Press.

Deyo, Frederic. 1986. "Industrialization and the Structuring of Asian Labor Movements: The 'Gang of Four.' " In *Confrontation, Class Consciousness, and the Labor Process,* edited by M. Hanagan and C. Stephenson. Westport, Conn.: Greenwood Press.

Duarte, Isis, Clara Baez, Carmen J. Gómez, and Marina Aríza. 1989. *Población y condición de la mujer en República Dominicana.* Estudio No. 6. Santo Domingo: Instituto de Estudios de Población y Desarrollo.

Espinal, Rosario. 1988. *Torn between Authoritarianism and Crisis-Prone Democracy: The Dominican Labor Movement.* Working Paper No. 116. Notre Dame, Ind.: Helen Kellogg Institute for International Studies.

Fundación Apec de Credito Educativo, Inc. (FundApec). 1992. *Encuesta Nacional de Mano de Obra.* Santo Domingo, Dominican Republic.

Gereffi, Gary. 1990. "Paths of Industrialization: An Overview." In *Manufacturing Miracles: Paths of Industrialization in Latin America and East Asia,* edited by Gary Gereffi and Donald L. Wyman, 3–31. Princeton: Princeton University Press.

Jenkins, Rhys. 1991. "The Political Economy of Industrialization: A Comparison of Latin American and East Asian Newly Industrializing Countries." *Development and Change* 22:197–231.

Joekes, Susan, with Roxana Moayedi. 1987. *Women and Export Manufacturing: A Review of the Issues and AID Policy.* Prepared for the Office of Women in Development, USAID. Washington, D.C.: International Center for Research on Women.

Lim, Linda. 1990. "Women's Work in Export Factories: The Politics of a Cause." In *Persistent Inequalities: Women and World Development,* edited by Irene Tinker, 101–19. New York: Oxford University Press.

Ramírez, Nelson, Isidoro Santana, Francisco de Moya, and Pablo Tactuk. 1988. *República Dominicana: Población y desarrollo, 1950–1985.* San José: Centro Latinoamericano de Demografía (CELADE).

Safa, Helen I. 1990. "Women and Industrialization in the Caribbean." In *Women, Employment, and the Family in the International Division of Labor,* edited by J. Parpart and S. Stichter, 72–97. London: Macmillan.

Stallings, Barbara. 1990. "The Role of Foreign Investment in Economic Development." In *Manufacturing Miracles: Paths of Industrialization in Latin America and East Asia,* edited by Gary Gereffi and Donald L. Wyman, 55–89. Princeton: Princeton University Press.

Steele, Peter. 1988. *The Caribbean Clothing Industry: The U.S. and Far East Connections.* Special Report No. 1147. London: Economic Intelligence Unit.

Whiteford, Linda. 1990. "A Question of Adequacy: Primary Health Care in the Dominican Republic." *Social Science and Medicine* 30(2): 221–26.

Chapter 15

The Maquila Revolution in Guatemala

Kurt Petersen

In 1984 few Guatemalans were familiar with the term *maquila*.[1] The Guatemalan Congress had recently passed legislation to lure foreign and domestic investment in this export-assembly industry, also known as *outsourcing* and *drawback*. But only the handful of young, ambitious exporters who fervently lobbied for the bill foresaw that within a decade the maquila industry would be the fastest-growing sector of the Guatemalan economy. When the law was passed, about six factories, all assembling apparel for export, employed fewer than two thousand workers. In a mere eight years this fledging industry expanded more than twenty-five times. By 1993 more than 275 garment maquila factories were employing more than fifty thousand workers who assembled nearly US$350 million in garments for export to the United States.

The boom in garment-assembly production is thrusting the term *maquila* into the everyday vocabulary of millions of Guatemalans and transforming the country's economic and social history. To most Guatemalans, the maquila represents the dozens of converted warehouses where young women and children labor long, monotonous hours sewing precut pieces of cloth into complete garments, which are immediately shipped to U.S. department stores. Large signs posted on the sides of these buildings, offering employment and "excellent" compensation to young women, mark their location. The labels McKids, Ralph Lauren, and Van Heusen indicate that the clothing is for U.S. consumers. Although the maquila industry accounts for only 3 percent of the total work force, its impact is more dramatic in certain geographical areas such as Guatemala City, Sacatepequez, and Chilmaltenango, where 5 percent of the total work force and 22 percent of the industrial work force is employed in maquilas (Instituto Nacional de Estadística 1990).

The maquila phenomenon is also changing the face of traditional agricultural villages far removed from the industrialized districts of the capital. Foreign investors, particularly Koreans, are constructing state-of-the-art maquila factories in rural areas. Santo Domingo, Chenacoj, for example, is a town of six thousand indigenous peasants, or *campesinos,* accessible only by a four-mile, winding, hilly road. For centuries, agriculture has governed the local economy and life in general; harvests from nearby fields and wages from migratory treks to enormous coastal *fincas* (plantations) historically have provided the sole means of sustenance. In 1989 a rival to this traditional way of life arrived in the form of a maquila factory. Today scores of young men and women gather in the town square daily at six in the morning to board old school buses that transport them to a one-thousand-machine, Korean-owned maquila factory.[2] There they operate sewing machines and irons, snip dangling threads from assembled garments, and box items for up to seventeen hours a day. When not staying over in the factory, the workers depart well after dusk. "Santo Domingo," said one of these workers, "will never be the same. The factory now controls our lives."[3]

Reactions to this disruption of social and economic life are mixed. Proponents of the maquila industry hail this phenomenon as a viable employment alternative to migratory harvesting and as an essential stage of industrial development. Critics argue that this "employment option" is a contemporary form of servitude in which fourteen-year-old girls work fourteen hours a day for a pittance. All commentators nevertheless agree that the maquila industry's impact on the lives and culture of the Guatemalan people is unprecedented.

Even progressive unionists are unsure how to respond. In the face of widespread poverty they are reluctant to condemn the enormous influx of employment, yet they want to expose those managers and investors who memorize the investment code but scorn the labor code. "If they [maquila factories] generate more work, that is fine, but what comes along is disrespect for the law and inhumane conditions," explained Byron Morales, a leader of a progressive labor federation, Trade Union Unity of Guatemalan Workers (UNSITRAGUA). "In theory this strategy is perhaps a good thing, but in practice it has achieved practically nothing. These are superficial answers, simply generating employment and bringing some foreign exchange into Guatemala but leaving the underlying inequities untouched."

In short, the penetration of the maquila into the daily life of hundreds of thousands of Guatemalans has been rapid, massive, and controversial. It is perhaps the most profound economic event since the attempted land reform of the early 1940s, abruptly terminated by a U.S. government–sponsored coup d'etat.

Private Sector and USAID-Managed Industry

Since the CIA-directed 1954 coup, Guatemalan central governments have had a nominal impact on economic growth. Although these unstable regimes have frequently published plans for economic development, the private business sector has retained de facto control over virtually every significant economic enterprise or decision in the last three decades and is responsible for more than 90 percent of economic activity. The maquila industry presents a rare moment of consensus between the private sector and the government concerning an economic strategy: both view the maquila as a necessary (and profitable) stage in Guatemala's industrial development.

This government–private sector consensus has generated a clear division of labor in the promotion of the maquila industry: the government promulgates maquila-incentive laws and formulates monetary policy, and the private sector implements the law and exploits the policies. Left alone, this arrangement might have fostered modest industrial growth. But the underlying cause for the remarkable explosion of the maquila industry has been the United States, through its highly influential and supportive Agency for International Development (USAID), the development arm of the U.S. State Department.

During the 1970s USAID elected to promote the maquila industry precisely because it was inoffensive and nonthreatening to the landed oligarchy. But rising political unrest, an unprepared USAID staff, and finally, the reduction of U.S. economic and official military assistance to Guatemala in 1977 (because of human-rights abuses that led to the withdrawal of the USAID mission) stunted full-scale implementation of the maquila strategy. It was nearly a decade later, when USAID returned to Guatemala in 1986, that a systematic campaign to champion the maquila industry was launched.

The Maquila Worker: Nontraditional Worker for Nontraditional Manufacturing

In their seminal study of worldwide assembly operations, Joseph Grunwald and Kenneth Flamm concluded, "A feature that seems to characterize all assembly activities is a predominantly female work force—an overwhelming proportion young and unmarried" (1985, 226). The workers in Guatemalan maquila factories uphold this classical portrait; most are girls and young women between the ages of fourteen and twenty-four. The vast majority are single and live with their parents at home, where their income helps to offset household expenses. Some of these young women have children outside marriage; others are recently married. At least four-fifths of the workers in Guatemala City's maquila factories are women.[4] In rural maquila factories, however, where more acute poverty and fewer jobs force indigenous men into the labor pool, nearly half the workers are men (most married with children).

The maquila worker is anomalous in the industrial work force. Male workers have historically dominated industrial employment, particularly in periods of industrial growth; in 1989 more than three-fourths of Guatemalan factory workers were men. Traditionally, young unmarried women have found employment as domestic workers, and even in times of expansive industrial production their participation was limited to cleaning the homes of the managers and industrialists. During Guatemala's rapid manufacturing growth in the 1960s and 1970s, female workers actually experienced a decline in industrial employment (Chinchilla 1977). By contrast, female workers are the work force of the thriving maquila industry; for the first time in Guatemalan history, female workers have taken the lead in industrial expansion.

Nevertheless, jobs are segregated by sex in most factories. In the city, sewing is almost exclusively the domain of female workers. "The work is more gentle, more appropriate for women. Men want to earn more, and the pay is very little in sewing," explained a manager from B y D Confecciones. Advertisements for operators frequently request only female applicants. Women also account for most of the "finishers," who cut threads and check seams before shipping. Male employees fill the packing, cutting, and ironing sections of the factory, as these tasks are considered more "strenuous" and consequently more appropriate for men.

Some personnel managers and owners assert that women not only are more dexterous but, just as important, are less inclined to be "troublemakers." These employers believe that women are more docile and respectful of authority than men and hence less likely to rebel. "Men are more likely to form unions. Women do not have this mentality," candidly explained an employer. "They are more prone to do what you tell them without questioning. It is a bonus that they are better sewers." In addition, preference for age and marital status further limits the available labor pool; owners almost unanimously desire young, unmarried women in order to capitalize on their availability, youthfulness, and endurance.

Health, Safety, and Working Conditions

Health and safety conditions in Guatemalan workplaces are a low priority for government agencies, employers, and many employees. Few workplaces provide protection from dangerous machinery and toxic chemicals or practice preventive medicine. Even unions have been known to sacrifice health and safety concerns in pursuit of improved material benefits. "With starvation at the doorstep of so many, we put our efforts into increasing what the worker takes home to feed his children. Negotiations over health and safety are a luxury," said a union official.

The lack of tangible government pressure, combined with a surplus of willing workers, creates vast opportunity for exploitation. Since health and safety improvements (such as better ventilation, more exits, clean bathrooms, potable water, adjustable chairs) result in increased costs—at least in the short term—most maquila owners consider them unnecessary.

Workers and owners agreed that few serious accidents occur in maquila factories. The simplicity of the shop floors—chairs, tables, and machines in straight rows—and the relatively safe machinery minimize most immediate, life-threatening industrial accidents. The most common injuries are pierced and cut fingers and hands, followed by fainting (due to prolonged sitting and heat exhaustion) and electric shocks and burns (from improperly rigged or overburdened electrical systems and burned-out machines).

Although serious industrial accidents are rare, the potential for cumulative health and safety problems is high. The intensity and longevity of work periods pose serious risks to worker health. The labor code states that workers are entitled to morning, lunch, and afternoon breaks, but no factories provide regular afternoon breaks, and in almost half the factories workers are forced to skip the morning break; many others choose not to take their breaks in order to increase output and income. As a consequence, tens of thousands of workers labor four or five hours consecutively, break for a half-hour and then return for five to ten more hours of continuous sewing.

The lack of adequate ventilation and protective masks means that workers are exposed to chemical fumes and dust from the cloth. Because there are no specific regulations limiting the chemicals used in garment and textile production, workers risk inhaling large doses of carcinogenic and other harmful substances such as formaldehyde. Dust from the cloth, particularly around the cutting machines, is a constant irritant for workers.

Every interviewed worker complained of headaches. Few workers can afford glasses, and so many are forced to squint to compensate for impaired eyesight. Workers also told of varying degrees of back and neck pain caused by the padless, wooden seats. "Sometimes when they will not let us go to the bathroom, I want to scream from the pain," commented a worker. Others expressed total fatigue. "When I leave at the end of the day, I care barely stand up," said a fifteen-year-old worker with eight months' experience in the factories. "Every part of my body hurts, but especially my arms and back. I thought I would get used to it, but so far the pain seems to be getting worse each day."

Because the industry has grown substantially only since 1988, it is difficult to determine the long-term effects of these unhealthful and unsafe conditions. The consequences of the maquila revolution for workers' bodies are unknown. On a larger scale, conditions are ripe for an epidemic of cumulative trauma disorders (CTDs), illnesses that plague workers in the garment industry in the United States.[5] Caused by repetitive motions, forced exertions, awkward postures, and vibrations, CTDs are illnesses of the musculoskeletal and nervous systems that involve damage to tendons, muscles, and nerves on the hands, wrists, elbows, arms, backs, or legs. The primitive factory conditions, the pressure to produce, and lack of rest periods in Guatemalan factories provide ideal conditions for this illness. One health and safety official in Guatemala believes that unless a dramatic restructuring of the workplace occurs immediately, "an entire generation of workers will be physically disabled by these illnesses."

In maquila factories forced overtime is probably the most flagrant labor-rights violation in the industry: overtime is always obligatory and rarely compensated for at the legally mandated rate. Most workers are required on pain of dismissal to labor at least two hours of overtime each day. The average work week of maquila workers ranges from fifty-five to sixty-five hours, with some workers claiming normal work weeks of eighty hours or more.

Operators labor until the doors are unlocked at the end of the day. Requests to leave the premises early are routinely met with very real threats of dismissal. To "humanize" the workplace and comply with the International Labor Organization's standard, the 1986 Guatemalan Constitution reduced the maximum work week from forty-eight to forty-four hours. Subsequent hours are considered overtime and must be voluntary, and the maximum work day may not exceed twelve hours. Despite this clear guideline, agents of the Labor Ministry's General Inspection of Labor Division consider violations of hourly limits the gravest and most common infringements of the rights of maquila workers. Employers defend their use of forced labor as a consequence of the volatile nature of the garment-assembly industry. The requirements of the apparel industry, they argue, vary according to seasonal and market demand, and hence factories need a flexible work force to meet these fluctuating production deadlines.

More than one hundred factories force employees occasionally or regularly to work through the night. Workers typically arrive in the morning and are then told that the regular shift is extended until midnight or later. Few workers object, as all know the consequence of dissent is dismissal. A short dinner break is provided for the catered meal of rice and tortillas. At midnight or later the machines stop, the lights are extinguished, and the workers scramble for a clean, warm place to rest. Cloth scraps and remnants become makeshift blankets, protecting them against frigid nights. Covered by cloth, the workers huddle together on the floor, or on a bench or table, and attempt to sleep until early the following morning, when they are awakened an hour before work for breakfast and a brief wash. Then the operation begins anew. It is not uncommon for factories, under pressure to complete an order, to force workers to work several nights in a row. In one factory two seventeen-year-old operators casually reported that during especially busy periods they worked straight through an entire week, never leaving the factory from seven in the morning on Monday until five in the evening the following Saturday.

"By far, the two largest pools of complaints from all workplaces we receive here are child labor and illegal dismissals of pregnant women," reported the subdirector of the Guatemalan Labor Institute (IGT). "When a maquila factory lets out for the day," commented a union organizer, "it looks more like a high school than it does a factory." Maquila factories have become notorious for their exploitation of child workers. Indeed, an estimated 10 to 50 percent of the maquila work force is under the age of sixteen. In factories outside the capital, as many as half the workers are minors, some as young as six years old.

The labor code prohibits employment of minors under fourteen years of age, except when it can be shown that the child will work in the capacity of an apprentice or that "extreme poverty" warrants the child's contribution to the family economy. In such cases, workers are required to demonstrate this proof to the IGT, which issues limited work permits. Economic reality dictates a less formal regime. According to census data, nearly 20 percent of children between twelve and fourteen are working to supplement their families' incomes (Instituto Nacional de Estadística 1988). The percentage increases dramatically with age.

Maquila employers consider pregnancy the greatest enemy to production. More than one-fourth of management representatives contended that women take advantage of their ability to get pregnant, entering the job market early in their pregnancy with the intention of obtaining the paid maternity leave. Most managers scrutinize and discriminate against female workers on the basis of their capacity to give birth, requiring them to produce medical proof they are not pregnant in order to be hired or, more crudely, in some cases simply not hiring any woman who has "the slightest lump or mound" on her stomach. Workers have no actual recourse when denied a job on this basis, because the labor code, though proscribing discrimination between married and unmarried women, does not forbid hiring discrimination based on pregnancy.

Labor inspectors report that sexual abuse of women employees by fellow workers and managers is rampant in Guatemala. Despite this regularity, the IGT receives fewer than ten complaints of sexual abuse annually. A combination of embarrassment, mistrust, cultural factors, fear of losing employment, and nearly impossible chances of successful prosecution keeps most complaints outside the formal system. Another explanation for the lack of complaints is a common belief that sexual abuse applies only to rape and violent molestation. Most workers seem to consider touching and fondling to be an annoyance, not abuse.

Although workers are very reluctant to discuss sexual abuse, evidence of widespread abuse surfaced in interviews. One woman claimed that she was raped by a supervisor and was then subsequently fired for pregnancy. Another reported constant advances from male supervisors and threats of reprisal if sexual acts were not performed. Several labor inspectors claimed that a few Korean factories had come to resemble brothels more than factories; allegedly, Korean supervisors at these factories forced women workers, under penalty of dismissal, to engage in sexual intercourse.

Management Paternalism

More than once, labor inspectors and other observers compared the control of the maquila managers over their employees to servitude. Workers more often likened the relationship to that of a teacher or parent and a child. "They [the management] treat us like little children. We cannot do anything without their permission. You have to raise your hand, just like in grade school. I feel like I am in school most of the time," complained a maquila worker. Although this feeling was more flagrant in Korean-managed shops, nearly every worker articulated feelings of inferiority arising from the treatment by managers and supervisors. In fact, maquila employers often do consider their role comparable to that of a parent. One Guatemalan personnel manager at a factory outside Guatemala City said: "I have to educate people to use the toilet, teach them how to use it; when you see the result of your work, you feel very comforted that you have done something for your people." At least one Guatemalan factory practices group punishment, in which everyone is penalized for the actions of a minority. In this shop someone wrote graffiti on a bathroom wall. When no one took responsibility for the act, the manager forced all the workers to share the cost of cleaning the wall. In another incident the cleaning boys allegedly left the water on in the bathroom overnight. When no one admitted guilt, all the cleaning boys were made to pay for the repair of the water damage.

Owners and managers consistently expressed the view that workers were incapable of controlling their actions and even their lives. "The workers have many problems in their homes. Many do not have water or electricity and have a very low salary," said a manager. "Usually, they have too many children. . . . Our aim is to make the workplace a better environment than the home. There is order here, something many are not accustomed to. It is not beautiful, but it is better than most of their homes."

Unionization and Workers' Right to Freedom of Association

Between 3 and 8 percent (depending on the source) of the economically active population in Guatemala belongs to functioning unions; in the maquila industry, as of March 1992, there were no active unions. Since the first maquila factory opened in 1984, the government has issued more than two hundred export licenses for maquila operations, but it has granted legal status to only two unions in the industry: for workers at Internacional Exportaciones S.A. (Inexport) and Pindu S.A. Today these two unions exist only on paper. In the summer of 1989 management at Inexport illegally discharged scores of union members, and the union collapsed when the government refused to reinstate the workers. The workers at Pindu are without a factory, as the owners, in the summer of 1991, relocated overnight to an unknown location outside the country. Dozens of groups and hundreds of individual workers have tried to organize unions in maquila factories without success. This failure does not imply a lack of will, docility, or widespread complacency; rather, it is a product of the government's inability or unwillingness to protect the workers' constitutionally guaranteed right to organize unions and to bargain collectively. Through both negligence and complicity, the government allows maquila employers to destroy workers' attempts at self-determination.

Both the labor code and the 1986 Constitution protect the right to associate, bargain collectively, and strike so long as all legal requirements are fulfilled. It is the opinion of most union officials that these "requirements" resemble burdensome obstacles more than legal safeguards. In contrast to the Labor Ministry's overbearing supervision of the process of union formation and recognition, its vigilance in regulating and sanctioning employer practices during union organizing drives is severely deficient. Guatemalan labor laws and their selective enforcement offer a paradise to the potential investor seeking to avoid intrusive government supervision of the operation of his business. "The Labor Ministry is like a little mosquito," confided a Guatemalan owner. "Sometimes a pest, but easy to swat away. We rarely worry about serious opposition from them. It is the workers themselves who create the problems."

Most workers interviewed indicated a substantial interest in forming and belonging to a union at their factory. Workers equated the presence of a union with job security, increased wages, benefits, and more dignified treatment. Almost unanimously, however, workers feared that serious attempts to organize would result in dismissal, if not physical violence. A pervasive belief that the employer would surely suspend or terminate production if a union should take root overshadows hopes of collective victory. In the maquila sector, this fear is compounded by the transient nature of the industry. With only machines to transport, factories can and will relocate if it is deemed necessary. "The companies will often say if you want to form a union, we will leave," a union federation official commented. "This is a direct threat to the worker who has economic needs. Out of fear, she opts to live with the problems of work because she wants to bring food to her home. Bare subsistence is better than nothing."

Employers fear unions in their factories more than any other man-made calamity, even coups. More than half of all managers answered that the "worst event or experience" they could imagine would be the presence of a union in their factory. When asked about whether his factory had a union, one manager in a large factory exclaimed,

No, thank God! At the moment our people are not educated enough to have labor unions. I have heard of some companies that have suffered the fate of labor unions, and they immediately go broke. It is not like other countries, when they have labor unions, they show that they want to work. They ask for a raise but they will work for it. Here, they ask for a salary increase and they want to work less. . . . I could work with a labor union because I understand what they are about, but not one from this country.

Harboring similar sentiments, most owners are willing to take extreme measures to prevent surges in the union activism in their shops.

Owners argue that their fear of unions is rational. Unions, they assert, especially Guatemalan ones, disrupt production and shift control to the workers. "This industry is very delicate and intolerant of disruptions," said Cardiz S.A. manager Carlos Arias, a U.S. university graduate. "Unions by their nature disrupt and, hence, must be avoided." The garment-assembly industry, as Arias notes, is a fragile, time-sensitive business; a contract not completed on time can jeopardize future business. Factories with a reputation for missing shipping deadlines generally have difficulty surviving. For management, all disruptions are insupportable.

In several highly publicized instances, employers have reacted to the rise of union activity with closure and relocation. "In Guatemala, there is a violent rejection of unions in most workplaces and especially the maquila industry," claimed a union organizer at UNSI-TRAGUA. Most employers are openly hostile toward real and suspected union agitators. Armed with this uncompromising determination, many managers are willing to implement a wide range of tactics, including dismissal, fragrant disobedience and manipulation of the law and its instrumentalities, threats and violence, and, if necessary, relocation of the factory. The dismissal of workers suspected of organizing is easily the most common and effective managerial tactic. Workers who are merely suspected of union propensities are routinely discharged with no legal recourse.

It is difficult for workers to have leverage or direct contact with the U.S. suppliers and jobbers from well-known brands such as OP, Levis, and Phillips-Van Heusen who contract nearly all the garment production of Guatemalan maquila factories. Since few of these labels have elected to invest directly in the maquila industry, most business is conducted and monitored through company representatives or independent agents located in Guatemala. The ten labels that maintain offices in Guatemala City choose the factories to contract, facilitate communication between the factories and the parent company, and oversee the quality of production through frequent visits to contracted shops. Other labels, such as Levis, regularly send specialists to train managers and operators. Smaller labels often work through brokers, mostly Guatemalan, who at any one time may represent four to eight different brands. These brokers are independent representatives, contracting, facilitating, and monitoring in exchange for a commission on sales.

Many workers report frequent visits of North Americans to their factories. Timeliness and quality, not working conditions or wages, are the primary concerns of these representatives and agents. When asked about the conditions in the factories, one manufacturer's representative replied, "Our job is to make sure the garments are produced on time and have the highest quality. We can suggest ways to improve production, but how the factories choose to meet our demands is none of our business."

The Entrepreneurs: Many Koreans and Guatemalans, Few North Americans

In a radical departure from the model of North American investors as the leaders of the industry, South Korean capital and owners have emerged as the undisputed giants of Guatemala's maquila industry. Although the fifty Korean maquila operations are a minority of the 275 total factories, these shops are generally larger (averaging more than 350 workers), use more advanced technology, and are more productive than their North American and Guatemalan counterparts. They account for nearly half of the maquila production (Korean Embassy figures and Vestex estimates, March 1992). Local capital has established more than 150 shops, but the great majority house far fewer than 150 workers. Locally managed factories are much less productive than Korean shops, because of less-experienced management and inferior machinery; in all, Guatemalan-owned factories account for approximately 30 to 40 percent of total production. Finally, U.S. investors, usually in joint ventures with local industrialists, maintain assembly operations in about eight larger factories, which assemble less than 10 percent of the garments for export. Other foreign investors include Israel and Germany.

Foreign investment was slow to enter the maquila industry. From 1984 to 1989 foreign capital controlled perhaps eight of sixty factories. Since 1989 North American investors have either invested or coinvested with Guatemalan entrepreneurs in about seven more plants. In comparison, Korean (including Korean American) investments have accounted for forty-four factories between 1989 and 1992.

A principal goal of USAID's maquila strategy is to entice foreign investment to Guatemala. From the agency's perspective, "foreign" means U.S., not Korean. In the region the primary goal of the Caribbean Basin Initiative is to encourage direct U.S. investment in production and distribution of nontraditional manufacturing and agricultural products.[6] The Guatemalan Nontraditional Exporters Association (GEXPRONT), for example, prints relevant incentive laws and promotional pamphlets in English and Spanish and distributes them to potential investors in the United States. But U.S. investors have bypassed direct investment in the industry.

Since 1989 Korean investors have seized leadership of the maquila industry. Korean transnational corporations (TNCs) have deposited more capital and constructed more factories in Guatemala than any other country in the region. Nearly all these factories have parent corporations or factories in Korea, from which the Guatemalan offspring receive advice, contracts, and experienced personnel. For the most part, the investors are middle-sized Korean firms, but several large transnational corporations, including Samsung, which has five factories, have invested in the industry.

The expansion of Korean assembly operations overseas results mainly from a rise in wages, labor unionism, and restrictive quotas within its domestic garment-assembly industry. The first Korean factory began operations in 1984, and by 1988 nine Korean factories were assembling garments. By March 1992, though the pace of investment had slowed, fifty factories were in operation, employing nearly twenty thousand Guatemalans. The Korean embassy in Guatemala acts as headquarters for individual Korean factories and as coordinator of the Korean investment campaign in the country and the region. As a result, individual Korean factories, while striving to maximize profits, are connected in the grand scheme to establish a Korean production structure in Guatemala.

As the lifesource of Korean factories, members of the Korean embassy staff are advocates, spokespersons, mediators, and consultants for individual Korean factories. The embassy micromanages the external, and sometimes the internal, affairs of these factories, which refer every question, concern, or dispute to the embassy for resolution. Korean administrators and supervisors rarely speak directly to Guatemalan officials or strangers before first checking with the embassy. In fact, the role of the embassy is so dominant that few Korean administrators arrive in Guatemala with even a rudimentary understanding of Spanish. "Besides the ambassador, they never speak with anyone outside the factory," said a U.S. embassy official. "With the embassy as their voice, they really don't need to learn Spanish."

The Korean factories' most distinctive feature is their fine-tuned system of repressive labor control. This system is designed to control totally the behavior and actions of workers. The practice is based on a logical and conventional premise: machine operators are only productive while seated and working. Management's task, then, is to hold operators in this productive position for as long as possible. "The most common reason for dismissal is disrespect for the company," explained the Korean personnel manager of Mi Kwang S.A. "We need people who cooperate; nonconformity is not tolerated." Disagreement with a supervisor—no matter how justified—is cause for immediate dismissal in Korean factories. Workers well understand this fact and choose more often than not to withhold their anger and frustration.

Guatemalan maquila owners are for the most part the young (in their mid-twenties to early thirties) sons of the wealthy landed elite. These entrepreneurs have strong ties and exposure to the United States. Most are graduates of U.S. or Guatemalan (private) universities, speak English fluently, and are highly motivated and confident. These men are hailed triumphantly by GEXPRONT and paternalistically by USAID as the "new breed of Guatemalan entrepreneurs," who have aggressively and altruistically assumed an active role in the economic development of their country, making money at the same time.

GEXPRONT and USAID officials frequently contrast the ethic of this new class of entrepreneurs with that of traditional business elites, members of the landed oligarchy, who inherited, as opposed to "earned," their wealth. In their view, the new class of Guatemalan businessmen is made up of progressive revolutionaries and explorers of unclaimed territory, youthful, determined, and well-intentioned entrepreneurs devoted to the improvement of their country. This characterization, however, requires comment. The maquila industry in Guatemala, as explained above, is an almost infallible business. As one maquila owner stated, "Any fool could make money in this business; it is just a matter of how much." Recent government policies to lure maquila investment, an "attractive" labor force, and low startup and operational costs ensure a healthy short-term profit for most maquila investors willing to accept the political risks, including political violence, unstable national governments, and a civil war against guerrillas. Most of the young men who enter the business flourish, despite minimal or no managerial experience. This widespread success may be more indicative of the maquila industry's high profit margin than the zeal and talent of Guatemalan entrepreneurs.

Despite significant exposure to the United States, Guatemalan maquila owners often lack strong contact with North American garment companies or their agents. Even fewer have consistent contacts or business that provide year-round work. As a consequence, employees have irregular working hours. It is commonplace for a Guatemalan factory to grant workers a "vacation" for several weeks, due to lack of work, and two weeks later require them to work nonstop several nights in a row to complete an order on time. Inexperience, along with the overzealousness of some, prompts owners to accept more orders than their workers are capable of completing on time under reasonable conditions and hours. Thus, workers are forced to labor for intolerably long hours, quality suffers, and shipments often are tardy. "Meeting deadlines," lamented one manufacturer's representative, "is the greatest problem of the maquila industry in Guatemala."

In addition to promulgating an array of incentive legislation, the Guatemalan government devalued the local currency to encourage exports and attract foreign investors, particularly in the maquila industry. The currency devaluation provides considerable benefit for maquila entrepreneurs. Because owner-investors are paid by U.S. buyers in U.S. dollars, but pay workers and local vendors in quetzals, the "floating" rate guarantees owners a sizable profit on sales.

Of course, these gains from devaluation might have been at least partially offset by parallel increases in wages. But wages in maquila factories have not kept pace, mainly because owners consider the government-instituted minimum wage a ceiling on compensation.

An Economic Miracle?

Many USAID, GEXPRONT, and Guatemalan government representatives proclaim that the explosion of maquila production is an economic "miracle." But it is not known how much of the reported $77 million generated in foreign exchange actually returns to Guatemala in hard currency.[7] Guatemalan law mandates that exporters deposit all payments for exported goods in an authorized Guatemalan bank, such as the state-operated Bank of Guatemala, where the dollars are converted to quetzals. Lax enforcement procedures and an official exchange rate set slightly below the actual free market rate, however, encourage many exporters to deposit in Guatemalan banks only the minimum amount of dollars necessary to pay expenses and employee wages. The remainder, sometimes constituting up to 40 percent of the total value-added, generally ends up in the United States. The actual gain of foreign exchange in many cases is limited to the expenses of the operation, while the profits pad North American bank accounts. On this profit drain, an industry consultant cynically commented, "More money goes to Miami banks than to Guatemalan ones." In addition to depositing profits in Korean banks, Korean investors contract Korean supervisory and administrative personnel to manage their shops, precluding Guatemalans from the most skilled, and hence most lucrative, positions in Korean maquila factories.

As long as these conditions remain, the contributions of maquila production to economic development in a country such as Guatemala are inherently limited. Despite the grandiose dreams of its promoters, the Guatemalan maquila strategy will likely fall far short of the hoped-for "economic miracle."[8]

Notes

1. In Guatemala *maquila* refers almost exclusively to garment-assembly production. Throughout this chapter I use maquila rather than *drawback, maquiladora,* or *outsourcing.*

2. An even more remote village, located an hour from the capital, El Tejar in the Department of Chilmaltenango, awaits a 90,000-square-meter Korean Free Trade Zone, aimed at employing more than ten thousand people in maquila operations.

3. Unless otherwise noted, quotations are from my interviews with maquila owners, workers, government officials, and other sources, conducted between March 1990 and March 1992.

4. This characterization is based on my interviews with workers, managers, and other interested persons. A survey of sixty maquila factories in November 1989 found that more than 70 percent of the workers were women, 65 percent of whom were unmarried (FLACSO 1990).

5. In an International Ladies' Garment Workers Union study of New York City garment workers, more than one-sixth of the one thousand respondents reported CTD symptoms (*Los Angeles Times* June 11, 1989, March 29, 1991).

6. Although encouraging U.S. investment is an explicit goal, the most significant incentive toward this end, a major tax break for investment in the region, was removed in the U.S. Congress before passage of the initiative.

7. Precise maquila production figures are not available, in large part because of severe deficiencies in data collection and an extremely secretive business community. Guatemalan government sources, the Bank of Guatemala, and the Economy Ministry's "One Stop to Export" consistently publish different export and import data. Apparently, the bank receives its figures from the customs agency, which is notoriously inefficient and unprofessional. "One Stop," on the other hand, merely tallies the export licenses it issues, but the value of these licenses is frequently manipulated by exporters. GEXPRONT, the main Guatemalan private-sector agency, periodically surveys owners on their operations. Unfortunately, usually fewer than half (and no Koreans) respond to these surveys, and there is no way to verify the responses. The most accurate source of export data is the U.S. Department of Commerce, which compiles import and export quantities by product. Because the United States receives almost all the maquila production from Guatemalan factories, this information provides a reasonable estimate of the overall growth of the industry.

8. For a more detailed version of this chapter see *The Maquiladora Revolution in Guatemala*, Occasional Paper Series No. 2, Orville H. Schell, Jr., Center for International Human Rights, Yale University Law School, 1992.

References

Chinchilla, Norma. 1977. "Industrialization, Monopoly, Capitalism, and Women's Work in Guatemala." *Signs: Journal of Women in Culture and Society* 3(1): 38–56.

Facultad Latinoamericana de Ciencias Sociales (FLACSO). 1990. "El desarrollo de la industria de la maquila en Guatemala: Estudio de casos de la occupación de la mano de obra feminina." December, 57–58.

Grunwald, Joseph, and Kenneth Flamm. 1985. *The Global Factory: Foreign Assembly in International Trade.* Washington, D.C.: Brookings Institution.

Instituto Nacional de Estadística. 1988. *Encuesta nacional sociodemográfica, 1986–87: Empleo total república* 2:107, 164.

————. 1990. *Encuesta nacional sociodemográfica, 1989: Empleo total república* 2:112.

Chapter 16

The Garment Industry and Economic Restructuring in Mexico and Central America

Norma Chinchilla and Nora Hamilton

The rapid acceleration of global economic integration and Latin America's profound economic crisis were two factors contributing to economic restructuring in Latin America during the 1980s. Economies characterized by production predominantly oriented to domestic (and, in the case of Central America, regional) markets shifted to production oriented to international markets. The garment industry has been profoundly affected by the international integration of production and the economic restructuring in individual countries.

The garment industry in Mexico, Central America, and the Caribbean is an important link in a three-cornered relationship among the United States, Asia, and Latin America. The region's proximity to the United States makes it a favorite site for U.S. offshore investment, which, since the 1960s, has included investment in the apparel industry. More recently, several factors, among them the elimination of the Generalized System of Preferences (GSP) for several Asian countries and the reduction of import restrictions through the Caribbean Basin Initiative (CBI), have combined with the region's proximity to the U.S. market to attract Asian capital to apparel and other industries.

In this chapter we address two questions: First, what has been the impact of international economic restructuring—particularly the new trade and investment links among the United States, Asia, and Latin America—on the respective economies in general and on the garment industry in particular? And second, what are the implications of these changes for the development of these countries and their integration into the world economy?

The Case of Mexico

Before the 1970s Mexican industrialization was largely based on import-substitution industrialization (ISI), that is, the domestic production of previously imported consumer goods (primary ISI), and eventually intermediate and capital goods (secondary ISI), for the domestic market. This model produced high levels of economic growth for more than three decades (from 1940 to the 1970s) but at the cost of increasing inequality. When the economy began to stagnate in the 1970s, the government, relying heavily on foreign loans, sought to expand production and especially to promote exports of manufactured goods and, increasingly, petroleum. This strategy temporarily forestalled the crisis but at the cost of a growing debt burden.

Before 1982 the garment industry shared in the "Mexican miracle" of rapid growth within a protected market (as well as some of the problems of uneven development). Clothing production is generally at the labor-intensive, low-technology end of the industrial spectrum, and firms are typically small or medium-sized, although a substantial proportion of workers are concentrated in a few large firms. Aside from the approximately two hundred thousand workers formally employed in garment manufacturing, a sizable number are in the informal sector, working at home or in small, unregistered workshops. Business leaders estimate that approximately 50 percent of the clothing firms and up to two-thirds of the workers are in the informal sector (Suarez 1992, 34–37).

Merchants or factory owners subcontract to informal workshops or homeworkers for several reasons: to deal with fluctuations in demand; to reduce production costs, particularly wages and benefits; or to avoid unionization by keeping firms small (firms of more than twenty workers are required to have unions). In contrast to workers in the formal industry, women who work in the home tend to be older, less educated, married with children, and from rural areas (Peña and Gamboa 1989; Beneria and Roldan 1987, 39).

Since the 1960s the garment industry has become decentralized.

Design, cutting, and assembly operations began to be relocated to regional cities—in part to take advantage of lower wages—and clothing began to be manufactured for export as part of the border industrialization (maquiladora) program. Established in 1965 as a means to hire rural migrants when the U.S. bracero program ended, the maquiladora program in fact provided employment for young women in labor-intensive industries (electronics, apparel, toys, etc.) that imported supplies and exported production to the United States (see Chapters 12 and 13).

The result was a divided garment industry. Border factories produced for export using imported materials, with few links (beyond wages) to the national economy. Factories and workshops in Mexico City and other regional cities produced for a protected domestic market, in some cases drawing on the labor of homeworkers, and using mostly Mexican-made threads and fabrics. Thus the domestic industry was integrated, but the high costs of inputs from the textile industry, which was characterized by an oligopolistic structure, high profits, and limited technological innovation, were passed on to the garment industry (Suarez 1992, 31, 33).

The petroleum- and debt-funded boom came to an abrupt end in the early 1980s when a series of events—an international recession, falling oil prices, a dramatic increase in international interest rates, a large and growing trade deficit, and massive capital flight—brought Mexico to the brink of financial collapse. In 1982 the Mexican government began a series of negotiations with foreign creditors and the International Monetary Fund (IMF) to reschedule debt payments. As elsewhere, agreements with the IMF entailed stabilization and structural adjustment programs to reduce or elminate budgetary and balance-of-payments deficits, requiring severe cutbacks in government spending, subsidies, and imports and resulting in unemployment and the forced closing of some firms. Real wages declined by an estimated 50 percent, and growing numbers of workers were forced into the informal sector. After four decades of growth Mexico experienced several years of negative growth in the 1980s, with sustained recovery beginning only in 1987.

Partly as a result of external pressures, the successive governments of Miguel de la Madrid (1982–88) and Carlos Salinas de Gortari (1988–94) undertook a drastic restructuring of the economy, including the privatization of state-owned firms and measures to encourage the return of flight capital and foreign investment. In 1986 Mexico joined the General Agreement on Tariffs and Trade (GATT), and various policies were introduced to facilitate trade and foreign investment, including the elimination of import permits, sharp cuts in tariffs (from up to 200% to an average of 9%), and the reduction of bureaucratic red tape for foreign investment, which in the past could cause delays of up to two years (Darling and Miller 1991). The Salinas government has also pushed negotiations with the United States and Canada for Mexico's entry in the North American Free Trade Agreement (NAFTA), which gives investors in Mexico the combined advantage of low Mexican wages and access to the U.S. market. Prospects of NAFTA and other government measures have led to increased investment in Mexico even before the effective date of implementation (January 1, 1994), although it is too soon to evaluate the extent and permanence of Mexico's recovery.

These changes have affected the Mexican garment industry in several ways. First, the decliine in purchasing power resulting from the sharp drop in wages in the early 1980s caused the closing of some firms, dismissals of workers, and various cost-cutting efforts, such as relocation and increased use of subcontracting. Employment and production began to recover by the end of the 1980s, although production levels remained behind those of manufacturing in general; in 1990 apparel production had not reached its 1981 levels (CA-NAINTEX 1992, 10–12).

Second, economic restructuring has increased the global integration of the garment industry. The maquila industry was the fastest-growing sector in Mexico during the 1980s, and garment production has been an important part of that growth (see Chapter 12). Many nonmaquila firms began to export, using imported fabrics and often imported designs, involving a trade-off between the loss of upstream activities (e.g., design departments) and the gain of enhanced quality and U.S. market access. Production for export also involves a trade-off between dependence on traders in Mexico City and dependence on U.S. manufacturers and retailers, such as Arrow Shirts, Levi Strauss, and Sears (see Chapter 13).

Third, the opening of trade facilitated the import of cheap clothing and textiles. Beginning in 1985, tariffs on imported textiles and garments were reduced from aproximately 50 to 20 percent (Darling 1992). Some domestic garment producers have taken advantage of the trade opening to import fabrics, making their products more competitive with imports. But this option is not available to many small producers, who depend on credit from the textile manufacturers (Darling 1992). Both textile and garment manufacturers have complained that the trade opening was too extreme and abrupt, not allowing them sufficient time to upgrade their industries, and has resulted in dumping and unfair trade practices, with some products priced below the cost of primary materials (CANAINTEX 1992, 25). Trade liberalization has also undercut the advantages of increased exports; while textile and garment exports to the United States increased 214 percent between 1980 and 1990, imports increased 500 percent (Suarez 1992, 63). One factor in this imbalance was the dramatic influx of products from several Asian countries and the United States (much of the latter having been first imported from Asia, especially the People's Republic of China, for export to Mexico). Some Mexico City traders have become distributors for Asian clothiing imported through the United States by relatives in New York and Los Angeles (Darling 1992).

In effect, the trade opening appears to have created a division within the domestic sector of the garment industry, between those manufacturers able to import high-quality fabrics and produce internationally competitive clothing for higher-income groups, and those who continue to depend on the less-competitive domestic textile industry for inputs. The fortunes of the latter depend in part on the apparel and textile industries' ability to pressure the goverment to provide further protection against low-cost imports and/or to obtain the necessary credit and technical resources to upgrade their industries.

Thus the effect of the 1980s' economic crisis and restructuring has been to increase the Mexican garment industry's international integration, evident in the growth of the border maquila industry and in the domestic industry's dependence on imported fabrics and designs and, in some cases, on the U.S. market. At the same time, domestic industrial integration, through the expansion of backward linkages among producers, has been inhibited by such factors as U.S. tariff Item 807 (now HTS9802.00.80) and import quotas, as well as problems of high costs and the domestic textile industry's inefficiency. Given these conditions, it is not clear that NAFTA will result in greater use of domestic textiles.

A possible countertendency can be found in the efforts of some regional manufacturers to promote greater integration within Mexico. The Cámara de Vestido de Aguascalientes, for example, has promoted several initiatives, including the establishment of a degree in industrial design at the state university, involving opportunities for new designers to participate in international events and make contacts with other specialists (Suarez 1992, 26–27). The ability of Mexican producers to reincorporate upstream activities at a higher level of efficiency and quality is an important factor in assessing the garment-assembly industry as an agent of growth.

The economic crisis and subsequent restructuring has weakened the position of organized labor. Traditional labor organizations suffered an erosion of their status within the hegemonic party and were unable to stem the large-scale dismissals and drastic wage cutbacks of the 1980s, thus diminishing their credibility among rank-and-file workers (Roxborough 1989, 102–6). Wages in the garment industry dropped dramatically in the early 1980s, from 18.6 to 4.7 percent of production costs between 1977 and 1988 (Carrillo 1990). In 1992 garment workers often received less than the minimum wage of US$4.00 per day (Darling 1992). Union activity has been discouraged, and union activists are often among the first to be fired when firms confront international competition by laying off workers.

The weakening of the traditional union structure has led to renewed efforts by independent unions and the formation of alternative organizations. In the aftermath of the 1985 Mexico City earthquake, garment workers formed the militant, independent Nineteenth of September union, initially to secure compensation for women whose jobs had been lost when their sweatshops were destroyed. Subsequently, the union expanded its goals to challenge the government-controlled CTM (Mexican Labor Confederation) for control of the garment firms. Resistance by government-controlled labor boards and factionalism within the union have undermined its effectiveness, but it has played an important role in the movement for independent and democratic unionization in Mexico (Carrillo 1990). Women in the maquila industries have also begun to organize on a broader basis, encompassing community as well as workplace concerns.

In sum, global changes in the garment industry, economic crisis, and restructuring have combined to increase the international integration of Mexico's garment industry, to weaken its domestic integration, and to deepen the division between those sectors linked to international markets and inputs and those dependent on domestic textiles and consumers. The economic recession and structural adjustment measures have also undermined the position of Mexican labor; the welfare of workers is now tied less to traditional unions and more to alternative unions and other organizations.

The Garment Industry in Central America

In Central America, ISI was implemented through the creation of a common market that linked five countries (Guatemala, El Salvador, Honduras, Nicaragua, and Costa Rica) through the elimination of trade barriers among them and the erection of common external tariffs. Trade among the five countries grew rapidly in the 1960s and more gradually in the 1970s, based largely on the export of industrial products to regional markets. During the 1960s, industrial production grew at a rate of 8.5 percent, and in the 1970s, at 6.4 percent. By the 1970s an increasing proportion of manufactured products was exported to markets outside the region (Guerra Borges 1989, 53, 55).

Industralization within the Central American Common Market was not without problems, however. Although all five countries experienced economic growth, initial inequalities between them were often aggravated, and Honduras left the common market after a war with El Salvador in 1969. Foreign corporations attracted by the protected regional market and government incentives predominated in certain sectors, and while intraregional exports of industrial products increased, imports of industrial inputs and machinery also grew. In some cases, industrialization consisted of last-stage assembly or the processing of imported parts. The growing trade deficit (resulting in part from declining prices of traditional commodity exports and increased oil prices, as well as imported industrial inputs) was a factor in efforts to increase exports (Chinchilla and Hamilton 1984).

The economic crisis affecting all of Latin America by the early 1980s was intensified by civil war in Guatemala, El Salvador, and Nicaragua, which had indirect effects in Honduras and Costa Rica. Both domestic and regional markets were reduced; intraregional trade declined from more than US$1 billion in 1980 to less than US$500 million in 1986. By the end of the decade governments in all five countries had embarked on economic stabilization and structural adjustment programs under the auspices of the IMF, the World Bank, and the U.S. Agency for International Development (USAID). Often these programs involved the reduction or elimination of subsidies, cutbacks in public spending and employment, privatization of state-owned enterprises, trade liberalization, and the reorientation of the economies to export-led growth, based on nontraditional exports to international markets, particularly the United States.

USAID encouraged a shift to nontraditional exports and established a series of institutions designed to promote and attract investment in the development of new agricultural and industrial exports. Exports to the United States were also encouraged by the Caribbean Basin Initiative (CBI), launched by the Reagan administration in 1983. The CBI allowed certain products duty-free entry into the United States but excluded key products such as sugar, shoes, and textiles. Investment in the garment industry was more directly affected by Item 807, which limited duties on goods assembled overseas from U.S. components. This measure enabled U.S. manufacturers to take advantage of cheaper labor overseas and thereby to compete more effectively with garment imports from developing countries (Steele 1988, 48, 53).

In 1990 the Bush administration announced the Enterprise for the Americas Initiative, a proposal for the ultimate creation of a trade bloc encompassing all of North and South America. In the meantime, the pending NAFTA agreement led to concerns that Mexico's direct access to the U.S. market would undercut the benefits of the CBI and draw investment from Central America to Mexico. These concerns provided an impetus to the languishing common market, with the reintegration of the market seen as a step toward negotiation with the United States as a bloc. Free-trade negotiations have also been undertaken by countries of the region, individually or collectively, with Mexico, Venezuela, Peru, and other Latin American countries.

Here we look at the implications of these changes for the garment industry in two countries, Costa Rica and Guatemala. Costa Rica, the smallest of the five original common-market countries, is unique in the region as a stable democracy with a relatively advanced welfare state. As of 1992 it led the other Central American countries in garment exports to the United States and was third in Latin America as a whole (behind the Dominican Republic and Mexico). Clothing exports from Guatemala, the largest country in the region, did not increase significantly until the late 1980s, but today Guatemala has the most rapidly growing clothing-export sector in Central America.

The Case of Costa Rica

As in the other Central American countries, the process of industrialization, including the production of textiles and clothing, accelerated in Costa Rica with the formation of the regional market during the 1960s and 1970s. During the 1970s the Costa Rican government made efforts to promote exports to third (nonregional) markets. In 1973 the maquila program was established, and U.S. brassiere manufacturers set up subsidiaries in Costa Rica for export to the United States, taking advantage of Item 807. By 1978 Costa Rica was exporting several "nontraditional" products, including industrial products, to the United States and other countries (Steele 1988, 46; De la Ossa and Alonso 1990, 17–18, 50).

Although Costa Rica avoided the civil strife that engulfed the region in the 1980s, it was profoundly affected by the international recession, the drop in international prices for traditional commodity exports, and growing oil prices. By 1981 Costa Rica also had one of the highest per capita debts in the world, and in 1983 the government launched a series of stabilization and structural adjustment programs under the auspices of the IMF and World Bank. USAID set up several agencies to promote investment and exports, including CINDE (Costa Rican Development Initiatives Coalition), established in 1983 to encourage the development of new exports, attract foreign investment, and assist in marketing. Beginning in 1985, CINDE launched an aggressive drive to promote foreign investment by setting up several offices abroad, primarily in the United States. Partly under USAID prodding, the Costa Rican government offered a series of incentives for exports. Aside from tax exemptions for maquila industries, free-trade zones were established throughout the country and export contracts provided various incentives for exports having at least 35 percent value-added in Costa Rica (USAID 1990, 25; De la Ossa and Alonso 1990, 29).

Between 1984 and 1991 Costa Rica's exports doubled, from just over US$1 billion to US$2.2 billion, and in 1992 (according to preliminary data) they reached US$2.5 billion (*Central America Report* 1993, 40). Apparel was among the most rapidly growing exports.

During the 1980s clothing was exported by three types of firms: a small number of domestic producers able to shift their focus from declining regional and domestic markets to Item 807 assembly operations for U.S. firms; subsidiaries of U.S. apparel makers; and investors from South Korea (hereafter Korea), Taiwan, and Hong Kong. During the 1990s European and Colombian investments have been drawn to nontraditional exports, including textiles and apparel. Locally owned companies tend to be relatively small; one exception is El Acorazada, which manufactures men's trousers and jeans. U.S. firms continue to account for about two-thirds of the total; in some cases, U.S. firms have moved from East Asian countries to Costa Rica. They dominate the manufacture of brassieres: companies with Costa Rican subsidiaries include U.S. Lovable Co., Warnaco, Maidenform, and Bali. U.S. firms also manufacture shirts (Colonial, Van Heusen, Arrow, and Hathaway) and trousers (Lee, Farrah, and Garan). Most of the Korean and Hong Kong firms have concentrated in knit shirts, sweaters, and blouses. Many foreign-owned subsidiaries are maquilas, but some of the Asian firms are involved in CMT (cut-make-trim) operations in free-trade zones. Nonmaquila industries tend to depend on imported fabric from East Asia (Steele 1988, 96–101).

In 1991 Costa Rica's apparel exports, principally pants and shorts, lingerie, and shirts, reached US$450 million, of which US$438 million went to the United States (Barquero 1992). Aside from contributing to employment and foreign exchange, the apparel industry has been responsible for limited technology transfers, such as the training of middle- and lower-level personnel and loans of equipment to the National Training Institute.

Costa Rica's success in shifting to nontraditional exports, specifically apparel, has had a down side. First, government expenditures on incentives for exporters have been expensive, reaching 8 percent of central government funds in 1990, and have primarily benefited a small number of foreign and domestic firms. The projected elimination of these subsidies could lead to a reduction in export activities (Barham et al. 1992, 55–56; Edelman and Monge 1993, 26).

Second, the dramatic increase in exports has been accompanied by an even more dramatic increase in imports—a consequence of trade liberalization. The result has been a growing trade deficit, from US$81 million in 1984, to US$306 million in 1989, and US$655 million in 1990 (De la Ossa and Alonso 1990, 53; *Central America Report* 1991a, 1991b). The growth in imports can be partly attributed to the increase in purchases of machinery and other inputs for the development of nontraditional agricultural and industrial exports. But consumer goods imports have also grown (including clothing, which increased by 64% in 1989), resulting in the closing of some factories producing for the domestic market (CEPAL 1990a, 6–8).

Third, conditions for workers in the factories are often far from ideal. Costa Rican workers are highly trained and skilled, and productivity is comparable to that of firms in the United States; thus garment producers rely on higher value-added products—rather than cheap labor—to be competitive. But although Costa Rican wages and benefits are high relative to other Central American countries, they are approximately one-fourth the U.S. minimum wage. In addition, Costa Rican labor officials have complained of labor problems in the textile and clothing sectors, and several factories were closed because of accusations of owners' abuses. Workers have been forced to work overtime without pay, on occasion working up to sixteen hours at a time, and there have been reports of physical abuse and sexual harassment. In some cases, workers have been forbidden to join unions and have been fired for efforts to organize. Unionization has also been discouraged by other factors, among them the rise of *solidarismo,* a movement with strong support from private business (including foreign corporations) which advocates a nonconfrontational approach to labor-management relations and has the effect of undercutting the Costa Rican labor movement (Daly and Reed 1990; Levitsky and Lapp 1992, 28).

The future of the garment maquila industry in Costa Rica is uncertain. Because wages and benefits are higher in Costa Rica than elsewhere in Central America, and the labor force is highly skilled, CINDE and government policy makers have shifted their emphasis to industries using a higher level of technology and skills. There have also been discussions about developing upstream and downstream activities in the apparel industry (Steele 1988; Wiegersma 1992).

To date, the chief beneficiaries of the nontraditional export success have been foreign and domestic producers and exporters. At the same time, structural adjustment programs have resulted in cutbacks in health care as well as other services; during the 1980s the percentage of families living in poverty increased dramatically (*Mesoamerica* 1991; *Central America Report* 1990; EIU 1991–92, 30; Edelman and Monge 1993, 26–28). Whether Costa Rica's export success can endure and translate into higher standards of living for the population as a whole remains to be seen.

The Case of Guatemala

As in Mexico and Costa Rica, the rapid expansion in Guatemala (during the late 1980s) of export-maquila production of clothing and textiles should be understood within the larger picture of economic crisis and restructuring. Like Costa Rica, Guatemala has historically strong domestic garment and textile industries. During the 1960s and 1970s Guatemala, like Costa Rica, exported garments and textiles to the Central American Common Market. Unlike Costa Rica, however, Guatemala's push for garment, fiber, and textile production for export occurred within the context of vast inequalities in income and land tenure, a weak institutional structure characterized by reluctance to enforce labor codes or protect union rights since 1954, and a government implicated in extensive political repression.

During the 1980s Guatemala experienced a severe economic crisis, caused by a highly restricted consumer market, growing levels of external indebtedness, and a severe decline in domestic and foreign investment, due to political instability and the counterinsurgency campaign. Between 1978 and 1986 some three hundred fifty factories closed in Guatemala, and others produced below capacity. As in Costa Rica, the World Bank and USAID pressured the government to reduce tariffs and reorient the economy to the export of nontraditional goods to the rest of the world. The rise of garment-export production emerged as part of an overall attempt at "industrial reconversion" and the promotion of nontraditional exports.

USAID assisted government and private-sector officials in drafting a more attractive law governing maquila assembly and offered assistance in developing institutions to promote it. Since the passage of the law in 1985, Guatemala has experienced what many consider a spectacular, even "miraculous," growth in garment production for export, almost all of it in maquila assembly factories or domestic workshops. Since the late 1970s the maquila industry has become the principal source of new formal employment, with the number of workers employed increasing fifteen times (AVANCSO 1992; Petersen 1992). From 1986 to 1991 the garment maquila industry grew at a rate of 75 percent a year; by 1990 garment exports were almost double the value of vegetable exports, the second-ranked product (US$52,858,400 compared to US$27,076,000). Clothing, textiles, threads, and fibers were the only nonagricultural exports on Guatemala's nontraditional list.

As in many other countries, maquila production in Guatemala is characterized by intensive use of labor and relatively low technology. The level of investment per factory is low, and production often occurs with preexisting machinery or at preexisting levels of technology. *Bobbin* magazine reported wages and benefit expenses per employee as $US0.45 per hour (1991). Lax enforcement of minimum wage standards, however, puts the average closer to US$0.22 to US$0.30 per hour. Labor constitutes an estimated 14 percent of value-added in maquila production. The size of the maquila factories varies greatly, ranging from ten to seven hundred workers; the majority have eighty to one hundred fifty machines, but the number of factories with five hundred to one thousand machines is increasing (Petersen 1992).

The maquila factories, most of which are located in the capital city, contract directly with large U.S. clothing companies (such as Liz Claiborne, Ocean Pacific, Van Heusen, Guess, and Calvin Klein) but often subcontract to smaller companies or, more frequently, to home workshops, usually in the rural areas, which have two or three sewing machines. San Pedro Sacatepequez, a largely indigenous town located only fifteen kilometers from Guatemala City, is probably unique in the degree to which its inhabitants depend on subcontracted sewing throughout the year, some for Asian-owned maquilas in Guatemala and others through a direct contract with Phillips Van Heusen, the U.S. company. An estimated six thousand people earn their living through this activity in a town that had, for two decades prior, supplied clothing to stores in Guatemala City, other parts of the domestic market, and El Salvador. Villages targeted by USAID reports as ideal for maquila production, such as San Francisco El Alto (Totonicapan province), appear to have resisted maquila production or subcontracting in favor of continuing their traditional contracting for Guatemala City stores or production for the southern Mexican market (AVANSCO 1992).

Guatemalan officials and private-sector leaders believe that Guatemala can become the leading maquila producer in Central America and the Caribbean. Since the return to civilian government in 1986, Guatemalan entrepreneurs looking for places to invest their repatriated capital have apparently embraced the strategy with enthusiasm. Even under the best of circumstances, however, there may be external limits to Guatemala's maquila garment-export potential. In April 1989 Guatemalan government officials were called to the United States to discuss restricting their exports of cotton pants and shorts. These "discussions" resulted in the first quotas imposed on Guatemalan maquila production, administered by the Chamber of Industry.

Even more important, however, for the long-term potential of garment maquila to generate backward linkages in the Guatemalan economy are the quotas and other government policies in the United States and Korea which restrict or discourage the use of Guatemalan-produced fabric. Guatemala's production of cotton and other fibers gives it some hope of becoming the potential "full-service maquila" to which Alvaro Colom, a main Guatemalan promoter of maquilas, and the USAID advisers optimistically refer in their speeches. Liztex, Guatemala's only full-service cotton mill and largest textile producer (with its own cotton plantations), reportedly supplies 2 percent of the U.S. textile market (Ramírez 1992).

Liztex is an exception to the rule, however, and Guatemalan inputs to maquila production remain very low (a little more than 10% of value-added, according to the Ministry of Economy). Reportedly, two-thirds of textiles used in Guatemalan maquilas originate in the United States, one-fourth in Korea and other Southeast Asian factories, and one-tenth in Guatemala or other Latin American countries. Korean-owned maquilas tend to use Korean fabrics because of a state-sponsored policy of finding new markets for Korean textiles (prompted in part by U.S. quota restrictions). Although the geographical proximity of Guatemala to U.S. firms might favor the use of Guatemalan textiles and fibers, the persistence of U.S. quotas has resulted in most maquilas using predominantly U.S. textiles and thread.

Clearly, since 1988 maquila has represented the most important transformation in the structure of manufacturing in the country and constitutes a new "accumulation pole." It is the most significant source of new formal employment and the only source of dynamism in industrial production, which was declining after two decades of growth. But the jobs created by the maquila have been unable to stem the rising tide of unemployment, in part because declining real wages and high inflation have meant that many more people per household need to look for employment. In 1989 alone the elimination of unemployment would have required the creation of 69,000 jobs, and the "neutralization of growth in underemployment" would have required 76,000 jobs; 22,000 jobs were actually created in the maquila (AVANCSO 1992). Wages and living standards are below 1970 levels, and malnutrition and misery are spreading at unprecedented rates. Thus, the "maquila miracle" exists in the midst of an economic disaster, whose end is not yet visible.

Conclusion

A comparision of Mexico and Central America reveals similarities as well as differences. First, export promotion did not begin in the 1980s; in all the countries examined, the promotion of new export products was an important part of the economic strategy by the 1970s. The maquila border-industrialization program for exports to the United States was established in Mexico in the 1960s, and U.S. firms began maquila operations in Costa Rica (and El Salvador) during the 1970s. What was new in the 1980s was the added pressure of the international recession, foreign debt, and international lending agencies. These factors, plus the shrinking of domestic and regional markets, led to a shift in strategies, from an attempt to combine export promotion with production for domestic and regional markets to a more narrowly focused goal of integration into the world, mainly the U.S., market.

Second, in Mexico, Guatemala, and Costa Rica, the focus on exports has been accompanied by trade liberalization and a corresponding increase in imports, including imports of consumer goods.

Clothing and textile manufacturers in all three countries have complained of the rapid pace of trade liberalization, the increase in cheap garment imports from Asia, and in some cases, unfair trade practices, such as dumping. Central American firms also object to imports of used clothing from the United States, as well as contraband clothing (CEPAL 1990b, 204).

These changes point to an apparent gulf between clothing industries producing for domestic and regional markets and those producing for export. While some domestic industries—such as El Acorazada in Costa Rica and some of the regional garment producers in Mexico—have made the transition to maquila production for export to U.S. markets, others, especially the small and medium-sized industries, produce exclusively for local and regional markets. In Mexico there appears to be a further division between domestically oriented producers that have access to imported fabrics and have been able to maintain or expand production oriented to a high-income clientele, and those dependent on the traditional textile industry for both inputs and credit.

In general, the export industry has grown significantly in all three countries, but those industries producing exclusively for domestic/regional markets have stagnated or even contracted. In Mexico some garment manufacturers and merchants who previously bought domestic products for distribution have shifted to import distribution.

Third, the growth of nontraditional exports, and specifically garment exports, has contributed needed foreign exchange in both Mexico and Central America, but value-added (beyond wages) and backward linkages in the garment-export industry appear to have been limited. Because much of export-oriented production is in the maquila industries (meant for export to the United States under Item 807), backward linkages are limited by definition, and value-added is restricted to wages for assembly operations. Asian producers operating in free-trade zones often import their own fabrics. Exporters argue that locally produced fabrics, with some exceptions, are not of sufficient high quality for export production. Markets are generally controlled by firms or agents in the targeted countries.

Nevertheless, there are important differences in the garment industry in these countries. In Mexico most of the maquila industries producing garments for export to the United States are Mexican-owned, while in Costa Rica approximately two-thirds are U.S.-

owned. In Guatemala about half are Guatemalan-owned, and most foreign-owned firms are Korean, but the Korean and U.S. firms are much larger (in terms of employment and investment) than the Guatemalan ones. One factor in the predominance of foreign-owned firms in Central America (in contrast to Mexico) has been the significant role there of USAID in the promotion of nontraditional exports, including garments, and its efforts to attract foreign investment to the region.

There are also differences in wages and benefits, which among the countries studied here range from US$0.45 in Guatemala to US$1.09 in Costa Rica (*Bobbin* 1991). At the same time, countries such as Costa Rica, at the higher end of the wage scale, may offer certain advantages, including a trained labor force and a relatively stable political climate. Even in these countries, however, wages are considerably lower than in the United States, and low-wage labor constitutes a major attraction for investment in the garment industry. Because traditional unions have generally been ineffective in protecting workers' rights in these industries, improvements in working conditions are likely to be limited.

In Mexico and Central America, garment manufacturing is an important part of the dynamic nontraditional export sector; in Costa Rica and Guatemala, it is the leading industrial export of this sector. The industry's dependence on the U.S. market, however, suggests that its future is tied to factors beyond the control of the respective countries, such as the health of the U.S. economy, the implications of NAFTA, U.S. trade relations with Central American and Caribbean countries, and developments in the global garment industry. In the meantime, trade liberalization has tended to undercut the domestic clothing and textile industries in several countries, while reliance on imported inputs has limited the impact of export industries on long-term economic development.

References

AVANCSO. 1992. *El significado de la maquila en Guatemala: Elementos para su comprensión*. Guatemala City.

Barham, Brad, Mary Clark, Elizabeth Katz, and Rachel Schurman. 1992.

"Nontraditional Agricultural Exports in Latin America." *Latin American Research Review* 27(2): 43–82.

Barquero, Marvin. 1992. "Textileros temen efectos del NAFTA." *La Nación* (San José, Costa Rica), August 21.

Beneria, Lourdes, and Marta Roldan. 1987. *The Crossroads of Class and Gender: Homework, Subcontracting, and Household Dynamics in Mexico City.* Chicago: University of Chicago Press.

Bobbin. 1991. "1991 8th Annual 807/CBI Comparative Analysis," November, 48–49.

CANAINTEX (Cámara Nacional de la Industria Textil). 1992. *Memoria estadística.* Mexico City.

Carrillo, Teresa. 1990. "Women, Trade Unions, and New Social Movements in Mexico: The Case of the 'Nineteenth of September' Garment Workers Union." Ph.D. dissertation, Department of Political Science, Stanford University.

Central America Report 1990. February 6. Guatemala City: Inforpress.

———. 1991a. February 22. Guatemala City: Inforpress.

———. 1991b. January 18. Guatemala City: Inforpress.

———. 1993. February 19, 40. Guatemala City: Inforpress.

CEPAL (Comisión Económica para América Latina). 1990a. *Notas para el estudio económico de América Latina y el Caribe, 1989: Costa Rica.* LC/MEX/R.230 (22 June).

———. 1990b. "Reconversión industrial en Centroamérica: Diagnóstico de la rama de confección de ropa." *Revista de la Integración y el Desarrollo de Centroamérica* 47 (July–December).

Chinchilla, Norma, and Nora Hamilton. 1984. "Prelude to Revolution: U.S. Investment in Central America." In *The Politics of Intervention,* edited by Roger Burbach and Patricia Flynn, 213–49. New York: Monthly Review.

Daly, Emma, and Cyrus Reed. 1990. "Labor Pains: The Other Side of the Export Story." *The Tico Times,* May 4, pp. 1, 9; May 11, p. 17; May 18, p. 5; June 8, p. 10.

Darling, Juanita. 1992. "Fears of Free Trade." *Los Angeles Times,* November 9, section D.

Darling, Juanita, and Marjorie Miller. 1991. "National Agenda." *Los Angeles Times,* October 22, section H.

De la Ossa, Alvaro, and Eduardo Alonso. 1990. *La promoción de exportaciones en los países centroamericanos.* San José, Costa Rica: Proyecto IEAP-FLASCO, Documentos de Trabajo, Doc. EQU.S. 1/90 (March).

Economic Intelligence Unit (EIU). 1991–92. *Nicaragua, Costa Rica, Panama.* London: EIU.

Edelman, Marc, and Rodolfo Monge Oviedo. 1993. "Costa Rica: The Nonmarket Roots of Market Success." *NACLA Report on the Americas* 26(4): 22–29.

Guerra Borges, Alfredo. 1989. "Industrial Development in Central America, 1960–1980: Issues of Debate." In *Central America: The Future of Integration,* edited by George Irvin and Stuart Holland, 45–66. Boulder, Colo.: Westview Press.

Levitsky, Steve, and Tony Lapp. 1992. "Solidarismo and Organized Labor." *Hemisphere* 4(2): 26–30.

Mesoamerica. 1991. San José, Costa Rica: Institute for Central American Studies. July–January.

Peña, Florencia, and José M. Gamboa. 1989. "Home-Based Workers in the Garment Industry of Mérida, Yucatán, Mexico." *Latinamericanist* 24(1).

Petersen, Kurt. 1992. *The Maquiladora Revolution in Guatemala.* Occasional Paper Series No. 2, Orville H. Schell, Jr., Center for International Human Rights. New Haven: Yale University Law School.

Ramírez, Werner. 1992. Interview, March 27.

Roxborough, Ian. 1989. "Organized Labor: A Major Victim of the Debt Crisis." In *Debt and Democracy in Latin America,* edited by Barbara Stallings and Robert Kaufman, 91–108. Boulder, Colo.: Westview Press.

Steele, Peter. 1988. *The Caribbean Clothing Industry: The U.S. and Far East Connections.* Special Report No. 1147. London: Economic Intelligence Unit.

Suarez, Aguilar, Estela. 1992. *La pequeña empresa en el proceso de modernización industrial y tecnológica en México. IIa Parte: La pequeña y mediana empresa en la industria del vestido.* Mexico City: CEPROMET.

U.S. Agency for International Development (USAID). 1990. *Promoting Trade and Investment in Constrained Environments: AID Experience in Latin America and the Caribbean.* AID Evaluation Special Study No. 69. Washington, D.C.

Wiegersma, Nancy A. 1992. "The Apparel Industry in Nicaragua and Costa Rica." Paper presented at the conference, The Flow of Capital, Labor, and Trade in the Pacific Rim Garment Industry, University of California, Los Angeles.

PART IV

The United States

Chapter 17

Labor Squeeze and Ethnic/ Racial Recomposition in the U.S. Apparel Industry

Evelyn Blumenberg and Paul Ong

Since the late 1960s the globalization of apparel production has reshaped the spatial landscape of the U.S. garment industry as well as the composition of its labor force. Foreign products have entered the United States and have captured a growing share of the U.S. apparel market by undercutting U.S. prices. Thousands of domestic jobs have disappeared as U.S. garment firms have found themselves unable to match their foreign competitors.

In a process analogous to the international search for low-wage labor, some U.S. firms have established operations in regions of the United States with abundant supplies of nonwhite workers. New sources of female workers, primarily immigrants and blacks, have been incorporated into the garment labor force. With their low wages, immigrant workers have preserved the garment industry, especially in the large coastal cities of Los Angeles, Miami, and New York. Much of the literature on the garment industry focuses on immigrants in these cities; scholars have often overlooked the substantial concentration of apparel production in the South, where a partial dismantling of racial barriers has resulted in rising numbers of black garment workers. By 1991 Latinos and blacks comprised 20.5 and 15.4 percent of the industry's work force, respectively (U.S. Bureau of Labor Statistics 1992).

To understand the dynamics of the U.S. garment industry, it is necessary to examine the incorporation of new sources of labor at the regional level. Specific historical and institutional factors inherent in particular regions have determined how quickly firms have been able to adjust to changing economic conditions. Using the pre- and post-1970s as an organizing vehicle, we analyze three distinct regional patterns in the development of the U.S. garment industry: the decline of apparel production in New York, the stagnation of the industry in North Carolina, and the continued expansion of the industry in California (Figure 17.1). We begin with an overview of the U.S. industry.

Import Competition and U.S. Apparel Production

The opening of U.S. apparel markets to international competition is a relatively recent historical phenomenon. Imports grew from only 2 percent of the U.S. market in 1960, to 30 percent in the latter part of the 1980s (U.S. Bureau of Competitive Assessment and Business Policy 1970, 1990). Imported garments have penetrated the U.S. market through lower prices; a significant share of foreign-made goods comes from low-wage nations with lower production costs (including transportation expenses) than the United States. While lower wages provide the comparative advantage, the volume of imports is tied to the pace of industrialization in Third World nations. During

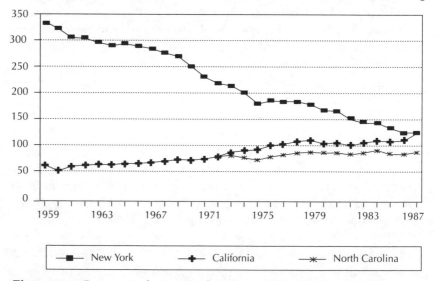

Figure 17.1 Garment Industry Employment by State (in thousands)

the 1970s, as export-driven development spread to an ever-increasing number of countries, the magnitude of foreign competition in the U.S. market increased. As the industrializing countries' wages began to rise, a new tier of garment-producing nations emerged to replace those countries unable to compete successfully in the rapidly changing international market.

Government policies—in the form of quotas and tariffs— attempted to slow the rate of market penetration of foreign goods, but these efforts were only nominally successful. Tariffs added to the final price of imports and reduced foreign competitiveness; quotas, such as those mandated by the Multifiber Arrangement (MFA), restricted garment and textile imports to the United States. Despite these legislative endeavors, imports continued to flood the U.S. market; political and economic forces hindered the passage of more stringent import restrictions. Because the administrations of the 1980s were dominated by advocates of free trade, there was no serious intervention during this critical period for trade relations. The government's limited role was endorsed by consumers who personally benefited, through lower prices, from foreign imports. Moreover, existing quotas failed to reduce the flow of imports to the United States; firms located in countries that had reached their quotas easily shifted their production to countries excluded from U.S. trade agreements.

A comparison of apparel prices relative to those of other goods demonstrates the market pressures on U.S. garment firms. The ratio of the two sets of prices remained fairly stable from 1950 to 1970; between 1970 and 1985, however, relative prices of apparel fell dramatically and then leveled off. Apparel prices (in real dollars) dropped by approximately one-quarter between 1972 and the late 1980s (U.S. Office of the President 1991, 351). Price competition placed U.S. producers under tremendous pressure to reduce production costs, and consumer prices fell while the imports' market share continued to rise.

Labor has borne much of the burden of the apparel industry's adjustment to imports. The demand for domestic labor is a derived one, directly linked to the underlying demand for the product. During this period of intense competition, substitutable foreign goods shifted the demand for domestically produced goods downward, and with it the derived demand for domestic labor. The garment industry fared poorly compared to other manufacturing sectors, although these too were hurt by the opening of the U.S. economy. During the 1970s and 1980s, manufacturing employment stagnated, but it did not experience a secular decline, as did garment employment. Total apparel employment peaked in 1973 at 1.43 million and declined to 1.03 million in 1991 (U.S. Bureau of Labor Statistics 1991, 1992). Experienced apparel workers were disproportionately affected by plant closures and permanent labor-force reductions. During the Reagan economic recovery of the mid- and late 1980s, the number of displaced workers declined significantly, particularly in manufacturing. Unfortunately, this decline did not occur in the apparel industry, where the number of displaced workers increased from 132,000 to 141,000 during the 1980s (Herz 1991, 3–9). These figures may even be biased downward, as they included only those workers who had three or more years of tenure with a firm; most apparel workers do not stay with firms for long periods of time, largely because of the inherent instability of the industry.

Those workers who managed to hold onto their jobs experienced lower wages and harsher work conditions. Eroding in strength, garment unions were unable to protect wages. With few effective institutional barriers to prevent competitive economic outcomes, market conditions established a new equilibrium, one that included lower wages. Real wages in the apparel industry grew secularly through the 1950s and 1960s and peaked at more than US$8.00 per hour (in 1990 dollars) in the late 1960s (U.S. Bureau of Labor Statistics 1984a). Since the 1960s wages have fallen; by 1991 they had dropped to US$6.50 per hour (U.S. Bureau of Labor Statistics 1991, 1992).

Not only did workers suffer declining wages and job losses; they also were forced to work harder. Employers pushed workers to increase output without extending work hours or raising wages. Before the early 1970s productivity in apparel grew at a much slower pace than that in the total nonfarming business sector. After the early 1970s, at the very time the economy encountered what was termed the "productivity crisis," output per garment worker grew to an accelerated pace. This growth can hardly be attributed to the introduction of new technology or other capital investments, because production techniques (except at some large firms) remained unchanged. Increasing output per worker was largely achieved through greater work effort, or "sweating."

To some extent, changes in employment, wages, and productivity have been distorted by the underreporting of work. Seeking to avoid government regulations, a noticeable segment of the industry has operated as part of the underground economy. Because cities with thriving underground economies—such as Los Angeles and New York—comprise only a small percentage of the total apparel industry, national figures are not likely to be significantly affected. Adjustments in the specific numbers, however, would only strengthen the conclusion that garment workers, always a low-wage labor force, have been forced to accept lower wages and deteriorating working conditions.

The Decline of New York's Apparel Industry

Until recently, clothing and New York were spoken of in one breath; the city had been the center for garment production, garment wholesaling, fashion, and design. Requiring little more than workers, a place to set up shop, and a few sewing machines, the New York garment industry expanded during the 1800s and early 1900s, providing jobs for the flood of newcomers to the United States and generating opportunities for entrepreneurship. The garment industry absorbed the influx of immigrants—predominantly Jews, Irish, and Italians—who sought economic inroads into the U.S. labor market.

The growth of apparel production in the Northeast stalled early, as institutional changes interfered with the ability of firms to maximize their profits. The passage of the Immigration and Naturalization Act of 1924 restricted the flow of immigrants, thereby limiting the available labor supply to New York producers. Unions gained an early stronghold in the industry and, with the use of strikes, maintained significant bargaining power. Finally, land values and rents began to rise. Producing garments in New York became too expensive for some firms; those with ample resources relocated to other regions of the country, while many resource-poor firms were forced out of business.

Like the U.S. garment industry itself, unionism in apparel manufacturing originated in New York. At the beginning of the nineteenth century tailors formed some of this country's first labor organizations and participated in many of the industry's earliest strikes. Almost a century later workers founded two of the industry's principal unions: the United Garment Workers of America and the International Ladies' Garment Workers Union (ILGWU). The ILGWU and other garment unions gained strength in the aftermath the famous 1909 strike known as the "Uprising of the Twenty Thousand," in which more than fifteen thousand female shirtwaist workers sought better working conditions (Seidman 1942, 102–4). Fearing competition from other, nonunionized sectors of the industry and threats to production, especially during the world wars, management grudgingly accepted trade unionism (Seidman 1942, 315–16).

The unions' hold on the garment industry persisted into the postwar period, contributing to New York's declining competitiveness. Union members campaigned actively to protect wages, often at the expense of employment. In 1971 84 percent of workers in the men's and boys' shirts and nightwear sector of the industry worked for shops where the majority were covered by union contracts (U.S. Bureau of Labor Statistics 1973). Roger Waldinger reported that even after unions successfully organized garment workers in states such as Pennsylvania and Massachusetts, New York workers earned wages 33 percent higher than newly organized workers in other northeastern states (1986, 70). In response to rising costs and regional competition, New York apparel employment dropped 83 percent from 1947 to 1970, falling from 417,100 to 249,200 workers. From 1950 to 1970 this contraction of apparel employment affected many firms, regardless of size. The number of firms with fewer than four employees declined by 59 percent, and the number of firms with more than one hundred employees dropped by 31 percent (U.S. Bureau of the Census 1952, 1972). Although many large firms were able to relocate, smaller firms, lacking such resources, simply closed their doors.

With rising foreign competition during the 1970s, New York's industry continued to decline. In contrast to previous years, however, loss of employment was accompanied by declining wages. From 1972 to 1987 average hourly earnings dropped from a high of US$10.27 to US$8.16 (in 1990 dollars); 1987 hourly wages were US$0.35 lower than they were in 1950 (U.S. Bureau of Labor Statistics 1992, 1991, 1989, 1984a) (Figure 17.2).

Labor unions and other institutions that had traditionally protected wages were no longer able to do so. Union membership de-

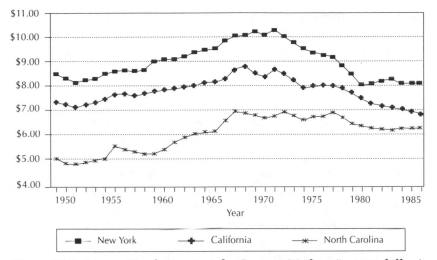

Figure 17.2 Average Hourly Earnings for Garment Workers (in 1990 dollars)

clined, and with it the unions' ability to negotiate and enforce strong contracts. In 1974 the unionization rate among producers of men's and boys' shirts and nightwear was 87.3 percent; it dropped to 82.8 percent in 1981 and 75.8 percent in 1987 (U.S. Bureau of Labor Statistics 1976, 1982, 1988b). Fragmentation of the industry into smaller units or across neighborhoods made it next to impossible to establish and enforce union controls. This weakness is especially problematic in an industry in which the mobility of labor and the limited life of most contracting firms make rapid response imperative. As a consequence of these changes in the industry, union-mangement relationships deteriorated. Labor leaders had difficulty limiting the use of contracting factories and enforcing standardized piece rates (ILGWU 1983, 76).

The apparel industry also experienced a spatial and ethnic transformation that reinstated labor-surplus conditions and enlarged the pool of immigrant entrepreneurs. Beginning in the late 1960s Chinese immigrants were arriving in New York City at the same time as the industry's aging work force was preparing to retire. By 1979 316,000 Chinese immigrants had migrated to the United States, 20 percent of them to New York (ILGWU 1983, 45). Chinese immigrants, many of them unskilled workers with little previous work experience, provided New York City factories with ample supplies of cheap labor. With the financial support of family and friends, some

Chinese immigrants were able to establish their own contracting shops. Between 1970 and 1982 the number of Chinese-owned firms in New York's Chinatown increased from 102 to 420 (ILGWU 1983, 42).

The profusion of Chinese immigrant entrepreneurs was closely related to the changing structure and function of New York's apparel industry. In recent years many large firms have abandoned New York. In 1970 there were seventeen firms with five hundred or more employees; by 1989 this number had fallen to nine. Accompanying the change in firm size has been a shift in the type of apparel produced. Previously, the New York producers most commonly manufactured dresses, coats, and suits, products for which demand was declining. Beginning in the 1970s, and coinciding with the change in industrial structure, New York apparel producers began manufacturing sportswear (ILGWU 1983, 33–34; Waldinger 1986, 89–103). Changes in fashion demand made small, flexibly organized firms better able to compete in the highly uncertain and differentiated sportswear market (ILGWU 1983, 34–39; Waldinger 1986, 89–122). Moreover, the minimal capital investments required to enter into sportswear production provided immigrants with opportunities for ownership.

Despite the transformation of garment production in New York, the industry has continued to lose apparel employment; in fact, the average annual loss in employment in recent years has outpaced the rate of employment loss in the years following World War II, a period when wages were still rising. From 1970 to 1987 New York's garment industry lost an average of 2.8 percent of its jobs annually; from 1947 to 1969 the average loss was significantly less, at 1.5 percent (U.S. Bureau of Labor Statistics 1984a, 1989).

Growth and Stagnation in North Carolina

In contrast to New York's garment industry, apparel production in the South grew rapidly during the postwar years until the early 1970s. Improved transportation systems increased the ability of firms to locate production sites away from the Northeast (Waldinger 1986, 55). Freed from locational constraints, firms were lured southward by supplies of cheap female labor, access to raw materials, and government-sponsored economic incentives. One of the primary reasons for southern relocation was the surplus of available laborers, former agricultural workers whose jobs were lost in the disruptive industrialization process (Cobb 1984, 84).

Not only were these workers cheap; they were also unorganized. By the 1930s the ILGWU had only one thousand workers below the Maxon-Dixon line (Cobb 1984, 89). Because the profits of the labor-intensive firms in the South depended exclusively on securing cheap wages, these firms actively resisted unionization. Cobb, in describing the antiunion sentiment of the South, quoted one southerner as stating that employers blocked unionization by using "everything from holiness preachers to rednecked deputy sheriffs, from the Bible to the bullwhip" (1984, 90). State governments vigorously opposed unionization efforts, believing they represented a major threat to the industrialization process of the region; by 1954 every southern state (except Louisiana and Oklahoma) had enacted right-to-work legislation, making it illegal for employers to require union membership as a prerequisite for employment (Cobb 1984, 93). Some had even more restrictive ordinances against unionization. Not surprisingly, unions had little success in the South. In 1971 only 28 percent of employees in firms producing men's and boys' shirts worked in shops where a majority of the workers were covered by union contracts; by 1988 this percentage had declined by almost one-half (U.S. Bureau of Labor Statistics 1973, 1988a).

Back-end linkages with textile producers also made the South a likely location for apparel production. By the mid-1920s North Carolina had surpassed Massachusetts as the leading textile-producing state in the nation (Falk and Lyson 1988, 5). Southern garment production not only attracted firms from the Northeast; it also developed indigenously through the increasing integration of textile and apparel production (Wood 1986, 174).

Northern firms were encouraged to relocate by "the selling of the South," a phrase coined by Cobb to describe the role of state governments in promoting industrial development (1984, 31–50). Desperate to attract industry to their communities, southern localities offered large economic incentives to those firms willing to locate within their jurisdictions. These incentive packages included provisions for industrial-revenue bond financing, assistance in the recruitment and screening of industrial employees, sponsorship of

industrial development authorities, subsidization of building construction loans, and land giveaways to incoming businesses (Falk
and Lyson 1988, 21).

Large-scale industrial investment in the South began as early as
the 1920s. Some firms relocated their entire operations to the South;
others simply opened southern satellite plants while maintaining
strategic control functions and/or marketing operations in New York.
The migration escalated during World War II, when the demand for
apparel products grew, and persisted into the 1970s. Garment factories developed in the countryside adjacent to small towns, taking advantage of the available labor pool of white, rural women. Between
1950 and 1970 apparel employment in the southern states (excluding Florida) more than doubled; in North Carolina it expanded by
248 percent, from 19,719 to 68,572 (U.S. Bureau of the Census
1952, 1991).

The rise of the southern apparel industry came to a halt in the
1970s, when foreign competition escalated and the once-excess supply of female labor in the South disappeared. In the face of growing
market pressure from global competition (Avery and Sullivan 1985,
34–44; Leonard 1986, 16–19), capital turned to black workers as a
new source of cheap labor in an effort to lower production costs
even further.

Changes in racial norms as a consequence of the civil rights movement combined with a tight southern labor market to open employment opportunities for southern blacks, especially in manufacturing
industries where blacks historically had been excluded. In the early
years of southern history, between 1870 and 1900, many skilled
workers in Greensboro, North Carolina, were black; they worked as
brickmakers, carpenters, foundry workers, and railway employees.
This racial division of labor changed after 1900, when blacks were
excluded from these same occupations and were systematically replaced by white agricultural workers. White men left the fields to
work in the lumber, woodworking, and furniture industries; similarly, white women left the farm to work in the tobacco, textile, and
garment factories. During the pre–World War II period southern economic development proceeded along occupational lines delineated
by race (Cunningham and Zalokar 1992, 551–54; Cobb 1984, 83–84;
Heckman 1990, 243–44). Black workers were predominantly concentrated in agriculture or in service jobs, such as janitorial and do-

mestic servant work. When blacks were hired in the manufacturing sectors, they seldom secured production jobs, but rather were assigned to jobs considered distasteful to white workers (Cobb 1984, 84).

This racial division of labor continued into the post–World War II period and was reflected in the garment industry. From 1940 to 1960 black workers comprised approximately 5 percent of total apparel employment in North Carolina (Wrong 1974, 40). Elaine Wrong traced the role of state policies in excluding blacks from the benefits of industrial growth. State employment agencies, replicating the pattern of racial segregation found in the textile industry, did not place black workers in apparel plants unless specifically requested to do so. Moreover, state and local government officials often furnished manufacturers with factory facilities; in return, they secured promises of jobs for white constituents (Wrong 1974, 43).

Since the 1960s the economic position of blacks has improved, largely because of the weakening of racial restrictions on hiring. By confronting racist practices through legislation and acts of civil disobedience, the civil rights movement contributed to increases in black wages as well as blacks' entrance into jobs held predominantly by white workers; the wage differential between southern blacks and whites declined form 38.5 percent in 1965 to 12.6 percent in 1975 (Heckman 1990, 242–46). While the wage gap between black and white women continued to be greater in the South than elsewhere in the country, southern black women's relative wages increased considerably between 1960 and 1980 (Cunningham and Zalokar 1992, 551–54). Moreover, after almost a century of excluding blacks from manufacturing employment, southern firms began to hire black workers.

As a consequence of the changing racial order, the percentage of black garment workers in North Carolina jumped; U.S. census data showed the proportion of black apparel workers rising from 5 to 16 percent between 1960 and 1970, with the upward trend continuing into the 1980s. Black workers comprised 25 percent of the garment labor force by 1980 and 28 percent by 1990 (U.S. Equal Employment Opportunity Commission 1990). The increase in the percentage of black southern garment workers was not unique to North Carolina but occurred throughout the South, with the Deep South experiencing the greatest increase in the percentage of black workers (Table

17.1) By the 1970s blacks were represented in the garment trades in proportions greater than their percentage in the population.

The admittance of black workers into the garment industry has perpetuated the historical legacy of low southern wages. In 1987 southern garment workers earned an average of US$6.25 an hour (in 1990 dollars), a wage 23 percent lower than that of New York workers (U.S. Bureau of Labor Statistics 1989). Although migration from the frostbelt to the sunbelt has waned in recent years, the preservation of lower-than-average apparel wages has given the southern garment industry temporary stability.

Nonetheless, apparel employment in some southern states has declined since about 1970 while only moderately increasing in other states. From 1970 to 1989 Arkansas, Mississippi, South Carolina, Tennessee, Texas, and Virginia lost garment employment; during this same period apparel employment in Georgia, Kentucky, and North Carolina grew. Total employment in the southern apparel industry has stabilized, but there is rising concern among industrialists and scholars that foreign imports will erode southern apparel production as it has in the Northeast (Avery and Sullivan 1985, 34–44; Leonard 1986, 16–19). As in the case of New York, it is unclear how much longer southern wages, even with the incorporation of black workers, can compete against the low wages paid by foreign firms.

The California Garment Boom

Apparel production in California seems to be the national exception. Employment in California's garment industry has grown steadily since the 1920s. By 1924 Los Angeles had emerged as the fourth

Table 17.1

Black Workers in the U.S. Southern Apparel Industry (in Percent)

State	1970	1990
Alabama	11.5	25.2
Georgia	19.2	35.9
Mississippi	13.6	44.6
North Carolina	16.7	27.8
Tennessee	6.8	9.3

Source: U.S. Equal Employment Opportunity Commission 1970, 1990.

largest garment center in the United States (Laslett and Tyler 1989, 19). California's apparel manufacturing expanded in the years directly following World War II, and the rate of employment growth in the state's industry also rose in the 1970s and 1980s, a trend shared by no other major apparel-producing region of the country. From 1950 to 1970 apparel employment grew from 53,000 to 74,000 workers; the pace of growth doubled from 1970 to 1989, when employment increased by 80 percent, expanding from 74,000 to 133,300 (U.S. Bureau of the Census 1952, 1972, 1991). As of 1989, garment employment in California had outstripped garment employment in every other state; nearly three-quarters of California apparel workers are employed in Los Angeles (U.S. Bureau of the Census 1991).

The success of the California apparel industry is largely the consequence of three interrelated factors. First, California has experienced an unprecedented increase in immigration, unmatched by any state in the country. Second, California's industry is unique in its lack of unionism. And finally, the state's apparel industry has developed lucrative product lines and adopted an industrial organization that insulates manufacturers from legal responsibility for labor.

A burgeoning supply of immigrant workers emerged in the late 1960s. Legal immigrants added 19 percent to the U.S. labor force from 1970 to 1980, an immigration rate comparable to that of the late 1800s and early 1900s (Morales, Ong, and Payne 1990, 223). The primary destination for a large percentage of these new immigrants was—and continues to be—California. During the 1980s 34.5 percent of all immigrants to the United States (2.3 million) settled in California, more than twice the number (14.2%) that settled in New York (Center for Immigration Studies 1991). California claimed 45 percent of all Asian immigration to the United States, while the mid-Atlantic states received only 17 percent. The percentage of recent immigrants in Los Angeles was 169 percent larger in 1980 than in 1970, because of substantial increases in Mexican and Asian immigration (Morales, Ong, and Payne 1990, 226). In 1970 Mexicans and Asians comprised 28 and 12 percent, respectively, of the new immigrants to Los Angeles; by 1980 these figures had doubled, to 43 and 24 percent, respectively (Morales, Ong, and Payne 1990, 226).

As a result of immigration, California has experienced a dramatic recomposition of its labor force, a transformation that has altered the composition of the garment industry. These changes are readily apparent in Los Angeles: In 1970 74 percent of all Los Angeles workers were non-Hispanic whites and 8 percent were of Mexican descent. By 1986 the non-Hispanic white labor force had dropped to 49 percent, while workers of Mexican descent had risen to 24 percent of the work force (Morales, Ong, and Payne 1990). From 1970 to 1986, therefore, the population of Mexican and Asian women—the demographic group most likely to be employed as garment workers—doubled. Data from the U.S. Census Bureau show that the California garment industry, at the time of World War II, was composed almost entirely of non-Hispanic white workers (86%); as of 1980, 24 percent of the workers were non-Hispanic white and the remainder were Latino and Asian (50 and 18%, respectively). These figures included workers from all occupations; Latinos and Asians comprised an even higher proportion of all production workers. In the late 1980s the racial and ethnic composition of the industry changed even further: Latinos comprised 75 percent of all garment workers. Blacks have been noticeably absent from the postwar apparel industry in California; according to U.S. census figures, they constituted only 8 percent of the industry's employees in 1950 and 5 percent in 1980. Because of these demographic shifts, California employers have had easy access to cheap labor.

Even the Immigration Reform and Control Act of 1986 (IRCA), a law prohibiting employers from hiring undocumented aliens, failed to restrict the supply of labor to the industry in the late 1980s (Sherwood-Call 1989, 53–63). IRCA sanctions were less than fully effective in curtailing the employment of undocumented workers. Moreover, California already had a well-established pool of reserve labor. Between 1989 and 1991 garment employment continued to grow, particularly in Los Angeles. An August 1991 survey by California's Employment Development Department found 79 garment-industry job openings and 254 applicants registered by the agency's field offices; only 10 of 139 employers reported experiencing labor shortages.

While large supplies of immigrant workers have created the potential for low wages, the lack of union organization has prevented labor from protecting wages. Historically, unionization in Los Angeles has been weak, and it has grown weaker in recent years. From 1970 to 1983 city-wide unionization rates in Los Angeles fell from 32 to 21 percent (Morales, Ong, and Payne 1990, 226). Industrial wage surveys of the garment industry for 1982 reported that not one of the more than thirteen thousand workers employed in women's and misses' dresses in the Los Angeles metropolitan area worked in an establishment where the majority of workers was covered by a union contract (U.S. Bureau of Labor Statistics 1984b). As late as 1987 there was no unionization in the men's and boys' shirts and nightwear sector of the industry in the Pacific region (U.S. Bureau of Labor Statistics 1988a).

Industrial structure and the changing work-force demographics have created barriers to effective labor organizing (Laslett and Tyler 1989, 88–92). The ILGWU has had difficulty organizing the newer, highly fragmented sportswear sector of the industry. Numerous small contracting shops are more troublesome to organize than larger manufacturers. Moreover, these small shops are often established as temporary operations, emerging in one location, going out of business when forced to sign union contracts, and then reemerging in other locations within the city under new names.

Foreign-born workers' apprehension with respect to institutional intervention also has hindered labor organization. Often employers have threatened to report undocumented workers to the Immigration and Naturalization Service if they engage in activities perceived as challenging management's authority. From 1953 to 1970 Communist leaders and their supporters were ejected from the ILGWU, causing the union to lose "some of the most dedicated and militant organizers in the industry, particularly when it came to organizing ethnic or racial minorities" (Laslett and Tyler 1989, 88–92). Although the new leaders were as dedicated to organizing workers as were previous union leaders, the leadership body has been disproportionately comprised of white males, who have had difficulty involving the growing numbers of Latina workers.

As in New York, the reliance on low-wage labor has shaped both the product choices and industrial organization of California' apparel manufacturing. Throughout this century California's apparel industry shifted from the highly skilled production of suits, cloaks, and dresses to the largely low-skilled manufacture of sportswear. In the years after World War II the rise in demand for casual wear—inexpensive blouses and dresses, swimwear, and so on—accelerated the shift to the production of sportswear (Laslett and Tyler 1989, 61–62). Changing product demand has been represented by the

growing number of firms that produce women's, misses', and ju-
niors' outerwear. In 1954 39.5 percent of all establishments in California manufactured products for this sector of the industry; by 1987
the share had increased to 66 percent. Concomitantly, California lost
firms in other areas of the industry, including men's and boys' suits
and coats, men's and boys' furnishings, women's and children's undergarments, and girls' and children's outerwear.

The industrial organization of California's garment industry rests
on the region's immigrant labor supply. Small, independent contractors meet the needs of sportswear manufacturers, whose operations
can be divided into separate functions and parceled out to numerous
operators. Most of the Los Angeles contractors are Asian entrepreneurs who, in turn, rely on the labor of Latino production workers.
This fragmented structure enables large manufacturers to pass the
financial risks of fluctuating product demand to small contractors.
More important, it allows manufacturers to avoid legal problems associated with subminimum wages, poor working conditions, and the
infraction of labor standards. Asian and other contractors are thus
left in "middlemen positions," where labor and union conflicts are
most likely to occur.

Although any one of these characteristics—large-scale immigration, weak unions, and industrial organization—does not ensure a
growing and prosperous apparel industry, the particular set of conditions unique to California seems, at least until recently, to have protected the state's garment industry from decline. With the help of
cheap labor from Latin America and Asia, California's garment industry has become a highly specialized and agglomerated regional
apparel-production center and continues to grow.

Conclusion

The globalization of apparel production into the developing nations
and the corresponding growth of apparel trade have hurt U.S. workers. Capital has attempted to overcome the "import threat" not only
by seeking cheap offshore labor, but also by incorporating new domestic sources of low-wage labor. In New York, higher-than-average
wages have perpetuated the pattern of job loss despite the recent
incorporation of Chinese immigrant labor. In North Carolina, the ero-

sion of institutional barriers and restrictive racial norms have unlocked a new labor pool: black female workers. The influx of these workers into southern apparel production has maintained extremely low wages and has forestalled industrial decline. Finally, the growth of California apparel production has been largely driven by the unrivaled influx of low-wage labor from Latin America and Asia. Despite geographic variation in industrial strategies, capital in all three regions has transformed the garment industry through an ethnic/racial recomposition of the work force.

Evidence from New York, North Carolina, and California suggests that the restructuring of U.S. apparel manufacturing has not yet reached its conclusion. The very logic of capitalism that prompts firms to seek new sources of cheap labor has engendered a convergence of working conditions between the Third World and the United States. While the long-term future of U.S. apparel production may depend on the ability of manufacturers to compete on the basis of characteristics other than price (such as style, quality, and flexibility), the industry's immediate future rests on the further erosion of wages and working conditions and the continued incorporation of a low-wage, black, and immigrant work force.

References

Avery, David, and Gene D. Sullivan. 1985. "Changing Patterns: Reshaping the Southeastern Textile-Apparel Complex." *Economic Review of the Federal Reserve Bank of Atlanta* 70 (November): 34–44.

California Employment Development Department. 1991. *Garment and Hospitality Industries Survey.* Garment and Hospitality Industries Special Report. Sacramento

Center for Immigration Studies. 1991. "State by State Immigration in the 1990s." *Scope* 9 (fall/winter): 14–15.

Cobb, James C. 1984. *Industrialization and Southern Society, 1877–1984.* Lexington: University of Kentucky Press.

Cunningham, James S., and Nadja Zalokar. 1992. "The Economic Progress of Black Women, 1940–1980: Occupational Distribution and Relative Wages." *Industrial and Labor Relations Review* 45 (April): 540–55.

Falk, William W., and Thomas A. Lyson. 1988. *High Tech, Low Tech, No Tech: Recent Industrial and Occupational Change in the South.* Albany: State University of New York Press.

Heckman, James J. 1990. "The Central Role of the South in Accounting for the Economic Progress of Black Americans." *American Economic Review* 80 (May): 242–46.

Herz, Diane. 1991. "Worker Displacement Still Common in the Late 1980s." *Monthly Labor Review* 114 (May): 3–9.

International Ladies' Garment Workers Union (ILGWU), Local 23–25. 1983. *The Chinatown Garment Industry Study.* New York: ILGWU and New York Skirt and Sportswear Association.

Laslett, John, and Mary Tyler. 1989. *The ILGWU in Los Angeles, 1907–1988.* Inglewood, Calif.: Ten Star Press.

Leonard, James C. III. 1986. "The Southeast's Textile/Apparel Trade and the Import Threat." *Economic Review of the Federal Reserve Bank of Atlanta* 71 (January): 16–19.

Morales, Rebecca, Paul Ong, and Chris Payne. 1990. "New Entrants into the Los Angeles Economy." *Transnationale Migranten in der Arbeitswelt* 22: 223–50.

Seidman, Joel. 1942. *The Needle Trades.* New York: Farrar and Rinehart.

Sherwood-Call, Carolyn. 1989. "Undocumented Workers and Regional Differences in Apparel Labor Markets." *Economic Review of the Federal Reserve Bank of San Francisco,* winter, 53–63.

U.S. Bureau of Competitive Assessment and Business Policy. 1970. *U.S. Industrial Outlook.* Washington, D.C.: Government Printing Office.

———. 1990. *U.S. Industrial Outlook.* Washington, D.C.: Government Printing Office.

U.S. Bureau of Labor Statistics. 1973. *Industry Wage Survey: Men's and Boys' Shirts and Nightwear, October 1971.* Bulletin 1794. U.S. Department of Labor. Washington, D.C.: Government Printing Office.

———. 1976. *Industry Wage Survey: Men's and Boys' Shirts and Nightwear, June 1974.* Bulletin 1901. U.S. Department of Labor. Washington, D.C.: Government Printing Office.

———. 1982. *Industry Wage Survey: Men's and Boys' Shirts and Nightwear, May 1981.* Bulletin 2131. U.S. Department of Labor. Washington, D.C.: Government Printing Office.

———, 1984a. *Employment, Hours, and Earnings, States and Areas, 1939–1982.* U.S. Department of Labor. Washington, D.C.: Government Printing Office.

———. 1984b. *Industry Wage Survey: Women's and Misses' Dresses, July 1982.* Bulletin 2187. U.S. Department of Labor. Washington, D.C.: Government Printing Office.

———. 1988a. *Industry Wage Survey: Men's and Boys' Shirts and Nightwear, June 1987.* U.S. Department of Labor. Washington, D.C.: Government Printing Office, March.

————. 1988b. *Industry Wage Survey: Women's and Misses' Dresses*. U.S. Department of Labor. Washington, D.C.: Government Printing Office.

————. 1989. *Employment, Hours, and Earnings, States and Areas, 1972–1987*. Bulletin 2320 (March). U.S. Department of Labor. Washington, D.C.: Government Printing Office.

————. 1991. *Employment, Hours, and Earnings, United States, 1909–90*. Bulletin 2370 (March). U.S. Department of Labor. Washington, D.C.: Government Printing Office.

————. 1992. *Employment and Earnings*. U.S. Department of Labor. Washington, D.C.: Government Printing Office.

U.S. Bureau of the Census. 1952. *County Business Patterns, 1950*. U.S. Department of Commerce. Washington, D.C.: Government Printing Office.

————. 1972. *County Business Patterns, 1970*. U.S. Department of Commerce. Washington, D.C.: Government Printing Office.

————. 1991. *County Business Patterns, 1989*. U.S. Department of Commerce. Washington, D.C.: Government Printing Office.

U.S. Equal Employment Opportunities Commission. 1970. *Job Patterns for Minorities and Women in Private Industry*. Employment Analysis Report Program. Washington, D.C.: Government Printing Office.

————. 1990. *Job Patterns for Minorities and Women in Private Industry*. Employment Analysis Report Program. Washington, D.C.: Government Printing Office.

U.S. Office of the President. 1991. *Economic Report of the President*. Washington, D.C.: Government Printing Office.

Waldinger, Roger D. 1986. *Through the Eye of the Needle: Immigrants and Enterprise in New York's Garment Trades*. New York: New York University Press.

Wood, Phillip J. 1986. *Southern Capitalism: The Political Economy of North Carolina, 1880–1980*. Durham, N.C.: Duke University Press.

Wrong, Elaine Gale. 1974. *The Negro in the Apparel Industry: The Racial Policies of American Industry*. Report No. 31. Philadelphia: University of Pennsylvania Press.

Chapter 18

Recent Manufacturing Changes in the U.S. Apparel Industry: The Case of North Carolina

Ian M. Taplin

Competitive pressures in an increasingly globalized marketplace are proving to be problematic for apparel production in North Carolina. As discussed in other chapters in this volume, since the late 1960s the U.S. apparel industry has faced intensified competition from a host of low-cost manufacturers in newly industrialized countries (NICs). Capitalizing on an abundant supply of low-wage labor, production in these countries has been aimed at the mass apparel market in the United States—precisely the segment that is most vulnerable to cost fluctuations.

Logically, one might assume that much of the domestic production of mass-market apparel goods would move overseas to low-cost labor sites, but that is not the case. Tariff and quota restrictions effectively protect much of domestic production, often at the expense of domestic apparel retailers and importers (Scott and Lee 1991). Domestic manufacturers, particularly those in California and the Northeast—where more fashionable women's clothing manufacturing takes place—successfully employ wage-depressing tactics using immigrant labor; but women's wear production is characteristically one of smaller-batch, nonstandardized items. In the large-batch, standardized product lines—such as knit products, outerwear, and men's and boys' shirts—that make up much of the mass market, economies of scale, new technology, and low-cost domestic labor allow U.S. manufacturers a productivity and cost advantage over imported goods. As production of these items is disproportionately found in the South of the United States, it is useful to examine the conditions in that region, together with product-cycle details that facilitate domestic manufacture. Although it is not possible to generalize from the case of North Carolina, industry trends in this state illustrate the salient characteristics of domestic firms' strategies.

Apparel Production in North Carolina

Apparel manufacture existed in the South before World War II, but it was after the 1950s that sustained in growth occurred. The South was particularly successful attracting manufacturers of standardized items for which large firms (more than 250 employees) were natural sites for volume production. Cheap labor, high levels of productivity, and favorable institutional forces made the area desirable for many manufacturers seeking lower production costs (Wright 1986). In fact, many southern states built economic development programs around a pro-business and anti–organized labor position that has been crucial to the area's comparative advantage (Cobb 1984; Falk and Lyson 1988).

In the 1960s the South began to upgrade its transportation system, especially by building interstate highways, making the region even more attractive, because goods were more easily shipped to retail centers in other areas of the country (Waldinger 1986). Backward linkages with an established textile industry in the region proved to be a further asset, speeding up the delivery of bulky piece goods and enabling many of the larger apparel manufacturers to coordinate production with local textile firms (OTA 1987).

Intermittent, and generally unsuccessful, attempts at unionization have enabled employers to maintain a quasi-paternalistic control over labor through a combination of repression and poverty, reinforcing the worker's acknowledgment of the prevailing power structures (Schulman 1983; Leiter 1986). In the absence of alternative rural job possibilities, such employment practices have continued largely unchallenged.

Men's and boys' shirt manufacture illustrates these general trends. In 1990 three-fourths of the industry's workers were located in the

Southeast (mainly Alabama, Georgia, North Carolina, and Tennessee). Average hourly earnings for sewing machine operators in this region were 89 percent of those in the mid-Atlantic region. Other nationwide comparisons revealed that occupational pay levels were 5 to 20 percent lower in nonmetropolitan than in metropolitan areas and typically 10 to 35 percent lower in nonunion than in union plants (U.S. Department of Labor 1992, 1).

North Carolina is representative of the South in that apparel manufacturing grew after World War II and is currently more likely to be found in large firms with standardized product lines. In 1939 there were fifty-three apparel establishments employing 6,487 workers; by the late 1940s those numbers had practically tripled; they continued to increase until 1987, when there were 780 establishments employing 78,500 workers (Table 18.1). There has been a steady growth in both employment and the number of establishments in men's and boys' furnishings and women's and children's undergarments from the 1940s through the early 1970s, stabilizing during the 1980s. In 1987 43 percent of North Carolina's apparel workers were employed in these segments of the industry, a proportion that has remained fairly constant since 1947, when it was 40 percent. In each case, a product line of highly standardized and less fashionable items lends itself to large-volume production systems and economies of scale that are best realized in a large factory setting.

Although classified separately from apparel, knitting mills have witnessed a similar pattern of growth in large firms.[1] One of the distinguishing characteristics of this sector, however, is its high rate of capital expenditures relative to apparel. For instance, in 1987 new capital expenditures per knitting mill production worker were approximately four times that for men's and boys' furnishings (US$2,482 and US$662, respectively), and three times that for apparel in general (US$829). These figures are indicative of the more automated nature of production in the knit-goods sector. Wages are higher in knitting mills than in other apparel sectors, largely because of the higher value of marginal productivity rates. In 1987, for example, knitting mills' average hourly wage was US$6.53, compared with US$5.54 for apparel (U.S. Department of Commerce 1987).

The standardized volume production of these three sectors contrasts with the more fashionable and volatile women's and misses' outerwear sector. This sector witnessed a secular increase during the

Table 18.1

Apparel and Knitwear Establishments in North Carolina, 1947–1987

	1947	1954	1958	1963	1967	1972	1977	1982	1987
Total apparel									
establishments	144	207	243	372	473	559	702	732	780
Employees	16,644	21,364	29,378	47,243	64,600	79,100	77,100	77,500	78,500
Men's and boys' furnishings (SIC 232)									
establishments	45	62	68	88	113	122	141	145	138
Employees	5,500	8,800	10,900	16,600	22,600	23,100	21,600	20,000	23,100
Establishment employment mean	122	142	160	189	200	189	153	138	167
Women's and misses' undergarments (SIC 234)									
establishments	13	27	32	70	102	149	213	201	201
Employees	252	1,910	3,400	6,600	10,400	15,100	17,400	19,400	13,600
Establishment employment mean	19	71	106	94	102	101	87	97	68
Women's and children's undergarments (SIC 234)									
establishments	19	39	48	59	57	64	65	64	61
Employees	1,200	4,700	6,300	9,400	9,900	12,400	11,600	9,900	10,500
Establishment employment mean	63	121	131	159	174	194	178	155	172
Knitting mill (SIC 225)									
establishments	457	529	570	641	631	739	700	637	583
Employees	49,685	60,313	62,186	68,203	80,600	N/A	N/A	80,500	81,300
Establishment employment mean	109	114	109	106	128	N/A	N/A	126	139

Source: U.S. Department of Commerce, *Census of Manufactures,* North Carolina, various years.

Note: N/A = not available.

same period, and although the number of establishments remained fairly constant during the 1980s, employment declined 30 percent, from 19,400 to 13,600 workers. The shift to a smaller average establishment size has mirrored the national trend in women's wear: the average establishment employs thirty-four workers, and 60 percent employ fewer than twenty. In 1947 95 percent of North Carolina's apparel employees were production workers; by 1987 the figure was 86 percent. The historic preponderance of women in the apparel labor force, primarily working as machine operators, has continued. In 1987 80 percent of textile, apparel, and furnishing machine operators in North Carolina were women (135,887), of whom 36,171 were black (U.S. Department of Commerce 1987). Again, these figures are consistent with national industry averages, the only difference perhaps being the higher-than-average participation by black females in the labor force in southern apparel.

If one includes the labor force in knitting mills, it is clear that the majority of workers in North Carolina have been employed in large firms in the mass-production, standardized-goods sector. This employment and production norm is indicative of broader regional southern trends. In entering such market niches where production efficiencies could be attained through economies of scale, manufacturers in this region capitalized on pools of low-wage, semiskilled labor. The persistence of regional wage differentials between the South and Northeast, lower operating costs, and rising productivity levels combined to make North Carolina in particular, and the South in general, an attractive site for domestic production. In the same way that the Northeast and California have used ethnicity to isolate workers and to keep wages depressed, southern manufacturers have located firms in rural areas and small towns, hiring women and then blacks to realize comparable levels of isolation.

Responses to Import Penetration

The growth of clothing imports since the 1970s imposed competitive pressures on southern manufacturers; the low-wage NICs often concentrated on the lower-cost, mass-market products of the type produced in the South. Rising labor costs, a rise in the value of the dollar against foreign currencies, sluggish domestic market growth, and high interest rates that stifled capital spending through the early 1980s combined to impose further pressures on domestic manufacturers (Avery and Sullivan 1985). In response, many southern manufacturers sought ways of better organizing an existing and sometimes smaller labor force, automating production whenever possible, and improving coordination between backward (textile companies) and forward (retail outlets) linkages. Such changes have often produced high rates of productivity increases similar to those reported by Mark Sieling and Daniel Curtin in a study of the national men's and boys' suits and coats sector (1988).

Although apparel is a labor-intensive industry in which close to 80 percent of the employees are production workers, the cost of materials can be as much as 60 percent of total costs, whereas labor accounts for only 25 to 30 percent. Not surprisingly, manufacturers are as concerned with reducing material wastage and rationalizing material flow as they are with reducing labor costs. Since the late 1970s many southern firms have explored ways of reducing production costs through technological innovations and organizational changes in the work process. Positioned in the standardized, large-volume product market, they have been better able to mechanize facets of the production process than firms in the more volatile women's wear sector. When mechanization has not been feasible, manufacturers have relied on restructuring work organization to enhance the productivity of the existing labor force.

To study these strategic responses, I conducted interviews in 1991 with eight North Carolina manufacturers.[2] All the firms had, to varying degrees, introduced new technology or reorganized work systems.

Technological and Organizational Changes

Most firms have sought ways to reduce costs —by cutting material wastage, minimizing inventory periods, speeding production, and reducing the number of defective products—in response to the heightened competitive environment. Such changes, representative of the strategies adopted by large firms in the region, have three dimensions.

First, microelectronic technology has been introduced into garment preparation, facilitating speedier transmission of design information to manufacturing (OTA 1987; Kazis 1989). Second, sewing tasks have been partially automated and production monitored through computerized tracking systems (Riley 1987). Third, team-production systems—reorganizing workers as an alternative to the traditional batch system—have been introduced (AAMA 1988).

Changes in Garment Preparation

Computer-aided design (CAD) and computer-controlled cutting (CCC) have been introduced in the production stages, where much of the fabric wastage occurred (Hoffman and Rush 1988). CAD systems permit designs to be transferred easily to video display terminals (VDTs) for markers to arrange jigsaw-like for pattern cutting. Such systems can reduce fabric wastage for patterned items by as much as 25 percent.

CCC systems can also reduce wastage but are limited by the lack of speed and flexibility of the reciprocating knife that performs the actual cutting. It is also difficult for such machines to cut large bundles of cloth, hence slowing down movement of the product from the design/grading stages to actual garment assembly. Some firms, however, have overcome this problem by redesigning the work flow, cutting items in smaller bundles and then transferring them immediately to the assembly stage. Such a system depends on reorganized work stations and just-in-time inventory and supply systems; only two of the firms in the sample had successfully managed this reorganization. In this respect, CCC technology has outpaced the material-handling capacity of the assembly process.

Changes in Garment Assembly

With the exception of knitting mills, firms have been less successful in transforming garment assembly through automation, largely because fabric manipulation has proved difficult to mechanize. Some peripheral operations, such as pleating, hemming, needle positioning, and thread cutting, have been automated, but as yet nothing has replaced the sewing machine as the primary assembly tool (Shepherd 1987).

Larger firms have found some success with general-purpose machines for which specialized attachments permit easily reconfigured production by semiskilled workers (Riley 1987, 80). One of the firms interviewed used dedicated machines (in this instance buttonholers and collar assemblers) for their high-volume items for which standardized production runs lasted more than one year. Because sewing machines are worker-paced rather than automated, however, most efforts to rationalize work have focused on an increased regulation of the worker.

Five of the firms in the sample had introduced computerized tracking systems (electronic point-of-entry systems, or EPOS) that facilitate easier recording of employee work tasks and permit the manufacturer to track the product through the inspection stage and on to the retailers. Designed to respond to buyer-driven pressures from retailers, EPOS have also proved particularly useful as a form of microelectronic surveillance of assembly workers.

In moving away from mechanical engineering systems to microelectronic processing, firms have often found it necessary to reorganize the work force to accommodate the "total systems" basis of such technology (OTA 1987). In other words, the benefits of microelectronic applications in one area of the production process can often only be realized by complementary applications in related areas. There is no better example of this than the attempts to rethink the traditional "bundle" system of materials handling.

Restructuring the Work Process

Until recently, the bundle system—in which garment components are cut and packed in bundles of twenty-five to thirty parts and then sent to the sewing floor for assembly—proved to be the major impediment to rationalizing product flow in the factory. Such a system resulted in the slow movement of goods through production, with an item taking weeks before it was finally assembled. Efforts to improve the throughput of the product and reduce the amount of time spent in inventory have focused on unit production systems (UPS) and modular sewing (AAMA 1988). Nationwide, evidence of success in inventory reduction in men's and boys' shirts manufacture can be seen in a decrease in the value of year-end inventories as a percentage of materials' costs (from 32.6% in 1977 to 27% in 1987). Little change is evident in the ratio of inventory to workers for the industry as a whole, except for large firms (in excess of 250 employees), where the value of year-end inventories per production worker fell from US$7,613.64 in 1982 to US$5,525.71 in 1987 (U.S. Department of Commerce 1987). This finding suggests that large firms, where many of the changes described in this chapter occur, have more successfully managed inventory reduction than their smaller counterparts.

In UPS, computers balance the work flow as individual components are shipped to operators working alongside a transporter. Bundles are eliminated, as single garments are brought to workers at work stations and then returned to the overhead transporter for shipment to the finishing area. It is an assembly line that intensifies work and imposes a technological pacing on workers, who remain isolated (Bailey 1993). Of the four firms in the sample interviewed that had experimented with such a system, however, all had abandoned it because they could not manage the product flow efficiently enough.

The modular manufacturing concept, which borrows heavily from Japanese auto manufacturing, uses teams of cross-trained workers organized into small groups (modules) that together assemble an entire garment. Bundles are shipped to work stations, where each worker performs a particular task before passing it on to the next worker for a separate task. Using decicated sewing machines, sewing operators repeat standardized tasks, yet their pay is based on group productivity norms. Such group pressures have proved effective in increasing productivity levels and enhancing product quality. The system also speeds the flow of the product and reduces work-in-process inventories. Four of the firms in the sample had such a system and found it successful in meeting their production quotas and cost imperatives.

Intensification of Labor

Changes of the type described above are costly, with payoffs frequently related to increases in market share or niche marketing strategies (Rosen 1984). Such changes are more likely to be successful when made part of strategies that combine cost cutting and manufacturing a high-quality branded good at a low price. This particular strategy has been central to the recent successes of Sara Lee, one of North Carolina's major apparel and knitwear firms. In all the firms, such changes were seen as a necessary part of restructuring to meet the flexibility demanded by enhanced overseas competition.

The three largest firms in the sample reconfigured production in the mid-1980s to take advantage of the new technological possibilities. Each pursued strategies designed to increase its market share so that improved profits would come from an increase in the volume of unit sales. Such changes involved a reorientation of some managerial functions and a reorganization of production workers.

Managers in each of the three firms said they were required to focus more attention on speeding the product through the production process, reducing the number of defects, and integrating formerly separate work practices. Line managers were given greater responsibility for determining production methods but also were made accountable for "inadequate" increased throughput achievements. Several complained about the ambiguity of their current responsibilities, brought about because their evaluation was often based on a "best-case scenario"; it was incumbent on them to motivate the teams of workers so that preestablished quota goals could be met. This task proved difficult, because not all the workers in the teams were capable of working at optimum levels, and absenteeism and labor turnover disrupted the team setting.

Another managerial complaint focused on managing the passage of goods through production. The bundle system provided a buffer preventing a backlog of work or supplies in one area from adversely affecting overall production schedules. Modular systems, however, require a managed flow of materials that resembles just-in-time systems and reduces inventory. This flow takes the slack out of production but simultaneously limits the lead time for products. The plant manager of a men's and boys' shirt manufacturer employing seven hundred workers commented: "It's a real nightmare sometimes, trying to balance small orders that have just come in with ongoing production that seems to get done much faster than in the past. We used to suffer from backlog; now we produce goods so fast they back up in the loading area. Scheduling more variations in the input side with greater quantity in the output is what drives me crazy."

That same manager also complained about other areas outside production that had not fully embraced the flexibility mandates; purchasing was singled out for particular blame. He said that while production had moved toward implementing a just-in-time system, purchasing operated on a just-in-case method. Not only did it affect his ability to coordinate production; it also contributed to competitive tensions between departments of the same firm. A similar situation had developed at one of the other firms in the study.

It is among production workers that some of the most dramatic changes have occurred since the introduction of modular sewing or attempts to accelerate production. The team system, usually with ten workers to a team, has allowed work-in-progress to be cut by as much as 90 percent, with products turned around in two to three hours. Production quotas are established for the teams, and workers in the team are paid a base rate for meeting the quota. Any production in excess of the quota is rewarded by payment that is a proportion of the base rate (10% production in excess of the quota equals an additional 10% of the base rate payment).

Quotas and team personnel are determined by the managers. A short training period for all workers who move to team production is required, primarily to introduce the concept of self-directed work. This training was seen by management as essential if workers were to be weaned away from the atomistic piece-rate system. As teams become accountable for meeting standard quotas as well as agreed-on group production in excess of these quotas, productivity pressure on individual workers is displaced from managers to a more abstract group norm. This change is clearly beneficial to management, providing it can create self-directed work teams that will strive for wage increases based on increased self-exploitation.

Workers in each of the teams are cross-trained to perform a series of different tasks within the team. But the cycle of tasks (hemming, collar attachment, etc.) has remained standardized and repetitive with little, if any, opportunity for individual worker discretion. Managers in all but the smallest firm said that few workers were trained in all the tasks because, as one manager glibly noted, "we could not afford a bunch of such skilled cross-trained workers; they'd be off at AT&T or IBM doing programming or something at $11 an hour!"

Labor turnover and absenteeism were problems cited by managers of four of the firms interviewed. In part, such problems are a reflection of tight labor markets, with unemployment rates of 2 to 3 percent in the Piedmont region of North Carolina during the late 1980s. Attracting employees willing to work for wages that are low relative to what they might earn in adjacent metropolitan areas appears to be proving somewhat difficult, especially for the smaller firms that cannot offer the more lucrative benefits packages provided by the larger firms.

Absenteeism has proved to be particularly disruptive for modular systems. One manager (in a firm with nine hundred employees) complained of absenteeism rates that amounted to approximately 3 to 5 percent of the work force daily, with workers often using allotted sick days for holidays. When that occurs, "floaters" (workers not assigned to a permanent team) substitute for missing workers, but they lack the social integration necessary to be committed to group production norms. Consequently, production quotas suffer.

It seemed that firms with one hundred to two hundred fifty employees were best able to integrate employees into teams and to instill a sense of long-term responsibility to the workings of that team. The three sample firms in this size range all had lower levels of turnover and absenteeism than the two larger firms. Since its introduction in 1985, modular manufacturing had proved especially beneficial to one women's and childrens' undergarment firm employing 175 workers. The plant manager claimed that with modular team systems,

> workers internalize the work effort that is team-induced. We encouraged the election of team leaders but made sure each team had several workers who were both popular and productive. That way, we stacked the productivity cards in our favor. Since then, it's been a great success; labor turnover is down to less than 2 percent; productivity is up, as is quality. The latter is especially important because we have been able to cut the number of people in inspection and put them into production and coordination tasks.

With little training and virtually no new technology, skills have been merely reconfigured and productivity increases have been predicated on labor intensification.

In each of the firms interviewed, management had successfully cultivated an atmosphere of instrumental paternalism. In comparison to the largely immigrant labor force in California and New York, which earns depressed wages in sweatshop conditions, the workers in my North Carolina sample fared quite well.[3] The worker-management adversarialism of the type found in some manufacturing industries was conspicuously absent here. Management capitalized on this acquiesence, seeking through work reorganization and a benign "worker empowerment" the means to improve the efficiency of employees without resorting to increased overt supervision. As one assistant manager said, "the new systems better utilize existing workers, making task performance more standardized without me having to constantly check up on them." And the shift supervisor of a knitting mill employing 620 workers added:

> With most of our workers not graduating from high school, it's been difficult to devise systems that would match their skill levels. Some are great workers and we should pay them more. Others don't give a damn, are lazy, and we should pay them less. Modular's been good because it evens them all out. Essentially, the good now monitor the bad. We can now stop worrying too much about whether or not [sewing machine operators] are going to do the correct job and concentrate on getting smooth production.

The sample's other knitting mill (employing nine hundred workers in hosiery production) had not introduced modular systems. Instead, it used a modified batch system that was part of a quick-response manufacturing strategy. It had automated the weaving and knitting process, using computer-controlled systems to inspect for flaws, but sewing was done manually. The workers were paid on a piece-rate system except those whose work was machine-paced. The highest-paid received US$8.50 an hour; the lowest, US$5 to US$6 an hour. The labor force was generally older (average age of forty-two) than workers in the other firms.

This particular plant was the most labor intensive and least technologically sophisticated of the twelve plants belonging to its parent company. It produced goods for the company's specialty markets (high-fashion products), which required customized manufacture that prevented standardized volume production. In the other eleven plants, a smaller labor force (approximately five hundred employees per plant) produced the same volume of goods per plant. In these plants, all facets of the production process had been mechanized, with workers employed in machine-maintenance work, as operators, and in finishing and packaging tasks. Workers received an hourly wage between US$5 and US$8 an hour, depending on length of service and experience.

In each of its plants, the company used EPOS to track daily sales of its product by approximately 50 percent of its vendors. This practice allowed the company to supply basically on demand for the retail stores electronically linked with it. Cutting down on inventory and reducing the labor component in production had dramatically reduced variable costs for this firm. In fact, one manager told me that raw material costs as a percentage of total costs had risen from 40 to 55 percent since the extensive automation of production ten years before. He also emphasized that quality had improved with automation; hand sewing results in a less durable product, whereas automated sewing provides consistency, predictability, and easier tracking and rectification of flaws.

With the exception of one firm in the sample (a men's and boys' sportswear manufacturer employing 120 workers), all had introduced automated cutting machines; five had CCC systems. Because garment preparation involves more skilled (and therefore more costly) workers, firms have attempted to improve their efficiency or reduce the numbers of such operatives. Efforts have focused on the handling and cutting of materials because these functions are very labor intensive. Both the women's and children's underwear firms, for example, used warp knitting machines that simultaneously knit and separate lace bands used in underwear. Electronic eye sensors and pneumatic edge-guidance systems release the machine operator from manually feeding and guiding the product, enabling him or her to focus more attention on inspection for flaws and other tasks. This technology reduced the number of workers needed in garment preparation while improving the quality of the finished product.

New Technology and Routinized Work

The trends illustrated in these examples tell us something about large apparel firms' efforts to cope with heightened competitive pressures. Although the industry is engaged in the active generation of new "demands" (for example, new fashion items), from the standpoint of one firm fashion changes are more or less exogenous. As price-takers, therefore, most firms seek ways of containing production costs, becoming more flexible in their response to market volatility, and pursuing increasingly segmented markets. Larger firms, with standardized product lines that permit economies of scale, have retained their competitive edge by innovating technologically and organizationally so they can better coordinate production with the changing demand imperatives.

We have seen how new technology and reconfigured work facilitate the control and coordination of workers through a combination of microelectronic monitoring and performance-based, group-mediated incentive systems. The associated work reorganization has embedded the control of semiskilled workers into group-based norms of self-exploitation in which gender segmentation remains paramount. Current employees can be trained to work in the new work teams, but the skills required of them are not cognitively greater than for their original operating tasks. That enables firms to keep labor costs low by continuing to hire from traditional apparel labor pools. It also means that these firms do not compete for workers with the better-paid jobs in the service and manufacturing sectors that are proliferating in the metropolitan counties of the South, attracting the more-skilled workers (Falk and Lyson 1988).

Together these changes have enabled firms to speed the flow of goods through the manufacturing process. Firms can monitor performance rates *and* the quality of that performance without recourse to more confrontational forms of personal supervision. Such productivity-enhancing strategies are based on a judicious combination of new technology and old worker-control ideologies that maximize the benefits and acknowledge the constraints of local labor markets. There is no evidence to suggest that managerial decisions regarding the organization of production are a departure from Fordist conceptions of the labor process. Worker input into decision making is limited, an excessive reliance on women and minority workers persists, and union avoidance is paramount. New machines and work practices remain, therefore, inextricably linked to extant labor process organization.

Notes

1. Knitting mills are distinguished from apparel companies because they are more fully integrated operations, weaving or knitting fabrics for manufacture, whereas apparel companies manufacture from purchased fabrics.
2. Interviews were conducted with plant managers and supervisory per-

sonnel at two knitting mills manufacturing hosiery, two women's and children's underwear firms, three men's and boys' furnishing firms (one manufacturing shirts, two manufacturing sportswear), and one women's and misses' outerwear firm. All were located in North Carolina, employed more than one hundred workers, and had been established for more than twenty years.

3. The 175-employee women's and children's undergarment firm paid the highest wages (approximately US$9 per hour in 1991), had the most stable labor force (an average employment period of eight years for the work force as a whole), and had the lowest annual labor turnover rate (less than 1%) of the sample interviewed.

References

American Apparel Manufacturers Association (AAMA). 1988. *Flexible Apparel Manufacturing.* Arlington, Va.: Technical Advisory Committee, AAMA.

Avery, David, and Gene D. Sullivan. 1985. "Changing Patterns: Reshaping the Southeastern Textile-Apparel Complex." *Economic Review of the Federal Reserve Bank of Atlanta,* November, 34–44.

Bailey, Thomas. 1993. "Organizational Innovation in the Apparel Industry: Strategy or Technique." *Industrial Relations* 32(1): 30–48.

Cobb, James C. 1984. *Industrialization and Southern Society, 1877–1984.* Lexington: University of Kentucky Press.

Falk, William W., and Thomas A. Lyson. 1988. *High Tech, Low Tech, No Tech: Recent Industrial and Occupational Change in the South.* Albany: State University of New York Press.

Hoffman, Kurt, and Howard Rush. 1988. *Micro-Electronics and Clothing: The Impact of Technical Change on a Global Industry.* New York: Praeger.

Kazis, R. 1989. "Rags to Riches." *Technology Review,* August/September, 42–53.

Leiter, Jeffrey. 1986. "Reactions to Subordination: Attitudes of Southern Textile Workers." *Social Forces* 64:948–74.

Office of Technology Assessment (OTA). 1987. *The U.S. Textile and Apparel Industry: A Revolution in Progress.* OTA-TET-332. Washington, D.C.: U.S. Department of Commerce.

Riley, S. 1987. "The Industrial Revolution: Our Time Has Arrived." *Bobbin,* April, 67–89.

Rosen, R. 1984. "A Study of Market Segmentation and Target Marketing." *Hollings Apparel Industry Review.*

Rothstein, Richard. 1989. *Keeping Jobs in Fashion: Alternative to the Euthanasia of the U.S. Apparel Industry.* Washington, D.C.: Economic Policy Institute.

Schulman, Mark. 1983. "Systems of Control over Labor in Rural Textile Communities: The Case of the American South." *Rural Sociology* 2:295–301.

Scott, Robert, and Thea Lee. 1991. *Reconsidering the Benefits and Costs of Trade Protection: The Case of Textiles and Apparel.* Working Paper No. 105. Washington, D.C.: Economic Policy Institute.

Shepherd, Jacob. 1987. "Mechanizing the Sewing Room." *Bobbin*, May, 93–96.

Sieling, Mark, and Daniel Curtin. 1988. "Patterns of Productivity Change in Men's and Boys' Suits and Coats." *Monthly Labor Review* 3(2): 25–31.

U.S. Department of Commerce. 1987. *Census of Manufactures, Industry Series.* Washington, D.C.: Government Printing Office.

U.S. Department of Labor. 1992. *Industry Wage Survey: Men's and Boys' Shirts.* Washington, D.C.: Government Printing Office.

Waldinger, Roger D. 1986. *Through the Eye of the Needle: Immigrants and Enterprise in New York's Garment Trade.* New York: New York University Press.

Wright, Gavin. 1986. *Old South, New South.* New York: Basic Books.

Chapter 19

Immigrant Enterprise and Labor in the Los Angeles Garment Industry

James Loucky, Maria Soldatenko, Gregory Scott, and Edna Bonacich

The increasing globalization of the U.S. apparel industry is most visible in expansion of overseas assembly and production of garments for import back to the United States. In a more subtle concomitant movement, the garment industry in the United States has become reliant on immigrant labor, oftentimes from the very countries where U.S. firms are active. Immigrants from Latin America and Asia now predominate in the garment sectors of many U.S. cities. In New York, many Chinese and Dominicans are employed, while Chinese and other Asians prevail in San Francisco (Waldinger 1986). In Los Angeles, Mexican women have long been a majority of the garment work force, which today increasingly includes immigrant men and workers from Central America and Asia.[1]

The movement of people from developing to developed countries, including into garment work, can be understood in part as a product of the dislocations created by the enormous transnational movement of capital (Cheng and Bonacich 1984; Light and Bonacich 1088; Sassen 1988). Economic dislocations occur as transnational enterprises displace people from peasant agriculture and other economies without fully absorbing them into new labor pools. Political dislocations occur as authoritarian or militaristic regimes encourage the entry of foreign capital and protect privilege. Often this process is accompanied by war, which serves as an additional motivation for exodus.

The processes of globalization and immigration are clearly linked.

The U.S. apparel industry is especially attracted to immigrant workers because of the need to address low-wage competition from imports—competition that ironically is generated by the U.S. industry itself through its overseas production. Immigrant workers, particularly the undocumented, are often the only ones available to work at the low wages that U.S. apparel manufacturers feel compelled to offer to maintain competitive local production.

In this chapter we consider the role of immigrants in Los Angeles's garment industry in detail. We draw on ethnographic observations in garment shops and interviews with workers, mainly from Mexico and Central America, to explore the great employment insecurity and harsh working conditions associated with garment work. These accounts also reveal, however, how people in such situations respond so as to increase their power and ultimately their degree of control over the future.

Immigrants and the Los Angeles Apparel Industry

The emergence of Los Angeles as a global manufacturing and trade center is inextricably linked to growing numbers of Latin American and Asian immigrants, whose cheap labor fueled the region's dynamic economic growth. With the rising competitive threat posed by low-wage labor in other countries, firms in Los Angeles, and throughout the United States, have become ever more reliant on inexpensive, usually immigrant, laborers to do the work at home, while also shipping more production abroad. Of an estimated 120,000 garment workers in Los Angeles, up to 80 percent are Latin American immigrants, mainly from Mexico but also from Guatemala and El Salvador. The rest are mostly Asian immigrants, including Chinese, Vietnamese, Koreans, Thais, and Cambodians.

From the start, garment work has been a major entry point for immigrants in Los Angeles. Drawing on this large labor pool, while attracting buyers to lines of casual sportswear that became known as "the California look," the city became the fourth largest garment center in the country by 1924 (Laslett and Tyler 1989, 19). Since the mid-1950s the transfer of the apparel industry to Los Angeles has accelerated, even as garment employment and production declined elsewhere in the nation. As production became increasingly oriented to the middle of the mass market, the industry underwent a widespread switch to section production, enabling firms to cut costs while remaining responsive to fashion trends. For workers, the almost total conversion to piece rates meant a corresponding downward pressure on wages and job security. These rapid changes led firms to contract with a growing number of smaller shops, those able to concentrate on specific lines and items or to specialize in particular steps in producing a garment. By the 1980s traditional "inside" shop manufacturing accounted for less than 15 percent of apparel production in Los Angeles (Laslett and Tyler 1989). The proliferation of contractors and subcontractors operating small, nonunion shops is reflected in an expanding geographical spread of the industry. Shops now extend east and south of the traditional garment district near the city center, and the number of shops in nearby Orange County has mushroomed in recent years.

Today there are about five thousand apparel firms in Los Angeles County, although the precise number is unknown because many operate underground. The apparel industry in the Los Angeles region, which represents three-quarters of the California industry (Sherwood-Call 1989), produced about US$9 billion worth of apparel at the wholesale level in 1991, according to sales volume estimates by Fabric Marketing Researcher, a New York consulting firm.

With its cheap domestic work force, Los Angeles is likely to continue to be a major apparel manufacturing center. Many of Los Angeles's manufacturers (including industry giant Bugle Boy) have production facilities overseas, mainly in Asia. The Los Angeles industry also takes advantage of its proximity to Mexico, which has emerged as a significant site for garment outsourcing from the United States. By staying in Los Angeles, however, the industry can capitalize on quality control and timing for its more fashion-sensitive production which, given the need for quick response to changes in demand, is not easily exportable.

The Los Angeles garment industry is generally organized around the principle of contracting. Manufacturers design clothing, purchase the textiles, and sell finished goods to retailers, but contract most sewing and some cutting operations. The advantages to manufacturers of the contracting system are numerous. First, they have considerable flexibility and can turn to contractors when needed. By maintaining stable relationships with a core group of contractors and hiring others on the fringe to deal with sudden changes in demand, manufacturers are better able to deal with the highly seasonal and erratic nature of the industry.

Contracting also externalizes labor, separating it from the rest of production. Manufacturers need not deal with recruitment, training, and maintenance of a stable work force, but can turn over all the functions of labor management to contractors, who end up serving much like the labor contractors in agribusiness. Contractors provide work space, sewing machines, thread, and the labor of small teams of workers to perform tasks that are completely specified by the manufacturer.

A third advantage to the manufacturer is that contractors can be pitted against one another. Contracting shops tend to be small, require little capital to open, and have many immigrants ready to enter the business, giving manufacturers a tremendous advantage in bidding labor prices down to a bare minimum.

Finally, the contracting system enables manufacturers to disregard labor standards in the sewing factories. If U.S. or California labor codes are violated, manufacturers can turn a blind eye and claim that another, totally independent business is responsible.

Under the contracting system, then, manufacturers obtain their sewing very cheaply while leaving many of the problems connected with the apparel industry to immigrants contractors.[2] At the same time, the competition inherent in a system based on labor-intensive assembly, fashion volatility, and finishing small batches with quick turnarounds is intense. Multiple bids, verbal contracts, sudden cancellations, and markdowns by manufacturers are common. Up to one-third of garment contractors in Los Angeles go out of business in any given year. Driven by deadlines and small margins, contractors often respond by slashing wages and pressuring workers to increase speed and efficiency.

Immigrant Contractors

The proliferation of small contracting firms that produce specialized items for larger manufacturers is encouraged by relatively easy entry and low overhead. These conditions have always attracted entrepreneurs, many of them immigrants. Some rise from the ranks of workers, while others arrive with sufficient capital to start contracting. By coding the ethnicity of state garment license holders, we found that Latinos comprised 35.5 percent and Asians 51 percent of all garment-firm owners in Los Angeles. Koreans (19.2% of all owners) were the most well established ethnic group in the industry, as their concentration in the heart of Los Angeles's garment district suggests. Korean shops appear to be larger than others, thereby accounting for a higher proportion of employment.

The growing presence of immigrant entrepreneurs has increased the number of small operators. In 1970 firms with fewer than four employees comprised 17 percent of all firms. By 1989 the percentage of firms with fewer than five employees had grown to more than 31 percent. Reflecting the increase in the proportion of small firms, average firm size also declined, from a high of thirty-two employees per firm in 1970 to twenty-seven per firm in 1988 (U.S. Department of Commerce, selected years).

There is often an ethnic difference between contractors and workers in Los Angeles. The proportion of Latinos is much higher among workers, while the proportion of Asians is higher among contractors. Consequently, we frequently find Asian contractors employing Latino workers.

The low wages and poor working conditions maintained by contractors are, in large measure, imposed by the manufacturers. The presence of an intermediary stratum of contractors distances manufacturers from workers, who perceive only contractors as being to blame for their plight. In this sense, garment contractors perform a classic "middleman minority" function, becoming scapegoats for an entire oppressive system that they did not create (Bonacich and Modell 1980).

Perhaps because they are so prevalent, Asian contractors are singled out as being overly demanding when garment workers discuss their work. As one Central American worker explained, "Koreans squeeze out even the last drop. They even want you to work on Sunday. But if they see you doing a lot of work, they say the company reduced the price [piece rate]. And they know if you don't have papers and can't complain." In other cases, particularly when contractors and workers are of the same ethnicity, relations are characterized by paternalism. Employees, especially those who are undocumented, can work for even lower wages and under poorer conditions in such shops on the grounds that the contractor is "doing them a favor" by providing a job at all.

Two cases help to illustrate some of the issues regarding immigrant contractors. Arriving in Los Angeles from Guatemala in the mid-1970s, Pascual began working as a sewing-machine operator for various Asian and Latino contractors. Using savings and borrowed money, he purchased four machines in 1984. With his wife and children working beside him, he began by subcontracting from a Korean, who paid him poorly, as his was a small, new outfit. He slowly added machines and operators and now has more than thirty machines. His employees are from Mexico, El Salvador, and Guatemala, and most know him through social networks. Today Pascual himself subcontracts portions of lots his firm cannot finish. He sends out ironing to a Mexican woman who has set up a small shop in rented space in the same building and has gotten worker referrals and equipment loans in turn.

Workers regard Pascual as fair. Still, contract deadlines are passed on to the workers in the form of pressure to work longer hours, such as during lunch. Once, when a quality control agent for a jeans company criticized the stitching, Pascual's manager immediately warned the workers that it could mean no further work. During seasonal slowdowns and when contracts are few, workers are let go or get less work.

Another firm was recently launched by three brothers from another Guatemalan community. Their immediate concerns involved raising capital and garnering contracts. Needing machinery, insurance, and a place to rent, they pooled the US$20,000 they had saved over four years and purchased fourteen machines. One brother, who had learned English in night school, visited various companies each day, some on the basis of classified ads. From some the brothers received samples, which they duplicated. Securing a few small contracts allowed them to hire several countrymen and other walk-ins from El Salvador, Mexico, and Taiwan. They have been poorly paid, however, since their firm is considered both inexperienced and small, and several contracts were terminated because the firm was a day or two late with delivery. The brothers accept the small margins they make, out of necessity, but worry that as more production moves to Mexico, it will be tough to stay in business.

Garment Work

Most garment work in Los Angeles involves section work, with garments passed from one manually controlled machine to another in a chain. Section work is directly linked to the rapid expansion of smaller shops, where workers' leverage against poor working conditions is particularly weak.

The increase in contracting, described as a reemergence of sweatshops, is associated with a deterioration of labor standards in this industry (U.S. General Accounting Office 1988). The average hourly pay of garment workers in Los Angeles is officially given as US$6.62, the lowest average pay for any industry in the county (U.S. Department of Labor 1991). This figure includes experienced workers, who make a good deal more than the average, but omits workers who are employed in the underground economy. Real average wages are much lower; many workers do not make the minimum wage of US$4.25 an hour. Few employers make up the difference if piece-rate pay falls below minimum wage, or pay time and a half for overtime work, though they are legally required to do so.

The two most frequent grievances expressed by workers relate to cuts in piece rates and unsteady hours. As workers become more skilled and boost piece-rate earnings, many employers reduce the prices paid per piece, thereby keeping the average pay rate low. Both the seasonal nature of the industry and its fashion volatility lead to wide swings in workloads; workers may labor six days a week when production is heavy, or scarcely if at all when orders are down.

Many garment workers have experienced nonpayment of wages or fictitious deductions from paychecks. They are sometimes made to punch time clocks, which record official, though fictional, hours. Quite often they are paid in cash, bypassing all records. Workers may not mind avoiding taxes, but they also miss the protections associated with paying into funds such as Social Security, unemployment insurance, and workers' compensation. In fact, garment workers rarely receive any benefits. Few get paid vacation time, sick leave (or guarantee of reemployment after recovery), or health benefits.

Along with hours and wages, health and safety conditions vary widely. Many contracting shops are in old buildings where ventilation is poor and fire danger is exacerbated by the presence of flammable fabric, crowded quarters, and blocked-off exits. Most small shops lack lunchrooms, and bathroom visits may be discouraged by filthy conditions, if not more directly by disapproving contractors.

Instances of child labor also occur in this industry, but homework is far more common (Fernandez-Kelly and García, 1989). Although it is illegal for workers to sew in their own homes, some contractors nonetheless require workers to take sewing home at the end of the day. Sometimes workers solicit homework as a means of increasing their earnings.

However uninformed they may be about their legal rights, workers generally know when they are being cheated, and the hardships of their lives are unmistakable. Garment workers often labor in an atmosphere of fear—of deportation or of losing their jobs. For people struggling to survive in a large and expensive city, the threat of job loss serves as a formidable sanction against complaining or engaging in efforts to alleviate harsh conditions. Nevertheless, workers respond to the conditions inherent in this industry in a variety of ways. As we shall see, these often represent attempts to gain more control over adverse situations, and sometimes they are successful.

Garment Workers

Besides the dominant presence of immigrants, the social characteristics of Los Angeles garment workers are variable, but a few generalizations can be made. Unlike the case in many developing countries, the Los Angeles garment labor force is not confined to single, young women. One finds women of all ages. Many are married and have children, and as primary or shared heads of households they must work in order for their families to survive. As one of the industries that continues to hire undocumented workers despite the employer sanctions of the Immigration Reform and Control Act of 1986 (IRCA), the apparel industry seems to be attracting undocumented men as well as women. Today the proportion of men working in the industry may be as high as 40 percent.

Many garment workers do not speak English well. Although that is not a deterrent in obtaining garment employment, language can be a factor in exploitation within shops. However, some workers may be able to leave the industry when they master English, particularly if they have other skills or credentials.

Garment work is, of course, not unskilled. A few enter with some facility, particularly women who have sewn clothes at home. But most need some training, which is achieved by paying to practice in a sewing school or during an on-site trial period that is generally not compensated. Experienced workers can attain incredible speeds and earn two or three times the minimum wage. But sewing skills are not readily transferrable to other occupations, making it difficult for workers to leave the industry. A lack of options, rather than a lack of skills, appears to be the primary barrier facing most immigrant workers concentrated in this entry-level industry (Soldatenkó 1992). Both the options and the constraints experienced by garment workers are illustrated by the profiles of several workers.

Jesie Martinez, now seventy-eight years old and retired, came to Los Angeles as a child from a Mexican border town. She followed an older sister into the garment industry after being denied other employment, despite having taken business courses and holding a high school diploma. She began as a sewing-machine operator and then moved into sample making, which required accuracy rather than speed. Jesie recalls Mexicans working alongside eastern Europeans, Italians, and blacks during the 1930s and 1940s and the strength of the garment union in many of the shops where she worked. At one point she tried to enter suit-making because it paid better, but says she was repeatedly blocked because she was Mexican. Jesie also recalls how manufacturers turned to contracting and section work during the 1960s. This system forced workers to take lower piece rates and made unionization more difficult.

With their earnings, Jesie and her sister were able to buy a home. She continued as a sample maker, earning more from manufacturers than she would have with contractors. After twenty years with one firm, she quit after it relocated and she was robbed while waiting for the bus. She found a job closer to her home but was told there was no more work after she refused the employer's demands to take work home. To this day she enjoys sewing and takes pride in what she produced, but she says it was always hard work.

Alicia Gonzalez was thirty-three when she left Mexico City, where she had worked as a sewing-machine operator before setting up a small shop that designed and sewed slips. In Los Angeles, she lived with friends, who helped her to find a job sewing zippers. After developing speed and accuracy, she obtained a better-paying job through other friends and worked on sewing skirts for several years. Complications from the birth of her only son forced her to quit work for three years. When her health improved, she resumed working in a series of shops, most of which were unionized until the 1960s. She quit in the early 1970s, however, after the increase in contracting had driven down prices for sewing to such a level that she would make nearly as much solely from retirement benefits.

Alicia recalls how tough and competitive garment work was. It required sitting at a machine and working nonstop without looking at the clock. Every morning she rose early to repeat the routine. Alicia suffered from high blood pressure, arthritis, and glaucoma, though she does not attribute these ills directly to garment work. At least once, because she was skilled, Alicia was told that she was making too much money and would be paid less per piece. She could not understand this complaint, since she knew that her productivity increased the earnings of her boss. She also reports that workers would not let others know what they were earning. Although Alicia feels the work has always been too demanding, she believes that conditions in the industry today have deteriorated to a point that no one can make a living sewing anymore.

When Berta Contreras and her husband and child came from Mexico in 1976, they moved in with relatives because they had no money. Her husband found a minimum-wage job in a factory, and Berta went door to door looking for work. Eventually, a small sewing contractor from Mexico offered her work where she could learn without being paid. Once she had mastered the blind stitch, Berta began to earn US$100 a week. The family was able to move to an apartment and slowly began acquiring furniture.

Berta became very skilled but could not earn even the minimum wage with the piece rates that were being paid. For a while she took a second job in a doughnut shop. She then turned to cleaning houses during the day while sewing garments at home at night, although piece rates for homework were very low. Berta says that she was often so exhausted in the evenings that she would rather sleep than eat. Eventually, her husband got a better-paying job, while Berta started a small contracting shop in her backyard, setting up six sewing machines and an ironing board. She registered with the state and paid employees better than minimum wage, but her business survived only seven months.

Today Berta, now forty-two, works as a quality controller for a manufacturer during the day and sews gowns and patterned squares for quilts at home at night. She takes classes to learn new skills and has become very artistic in making wedding ornaments and sewing sequins. But although she makes more money than she would as a housecleaner or if sewing only for a contractor, she must still maintain multiple jobs to support her family.

Elbia Sanchez arrived in Los Angeles in the late 1970s from El Salvador. She had worked as the neighborhood seamstress and as a receptionist and had also gained valuable survival skills by selling food out of her house. In Los Angeles, Elbia first worked as a live-in domestic worker, but most of her earnings went to pay rent for a room she shared with a friend on weekends. She next worked in a factory that made bicycle ornaments and was able to send money home to her family. When the factory closed, she turned to sewing work and has worked for contractors and subcontractors ever since.

Elbia has been cheated out of wages many times. ONce she labored for a whole weekend, from early morning until late at night. When she showed up on Monday, the contractor had moved out, and she was never able to get the money she was owed.

Like many workers, Elbia faces the problem of affordable childcare. This situation led her to take on homework, in which she buys and cuts material, sews garments, and sells them to a store. She has sought employment with a manufacturer but has found only more poorly paid work with contractors.

Power and Resistance in the Garment Workplace

Little is known about immigrant garment workers' thoughts and feelings about the world of loudly humming overlock, single-needle, buttonhole, and ironing machines in which they invest long hours of poorly compensated labor. The nature of the contracting and piece-rate systems of garment production in Los Angeles entails the exercise of seemingly inexorable authority and dominance within many garment shops. The most potent leverage that owners and managers have, of course, is the ability to terminate a worker's position in the factory. Protesting reduced piece rates or increased workloads is unlikely if it means being fired, either immediately or at one's first mistake following a complaint. Interviews and observations however, illuminate some of the complicated subtleties by which domination is resisted both in the face of power and behind the scenes in ways that contribute to an increase in workers' control over their situation.

Language is a primary means by which garment owners and managers dominate the organization of the work day. Verbal abuse is especially common at the subcontracting level, where "unproductive" workers hear harsh orders and derogatory remarks about their work or even their race, gender, or appearance. A frequent complaint is that everyone is shouted at for mistakes made by any one worker. Talking among workers is usually prohibited. Silence is often enforced by managers who stalk the floor and single out "talkers," lest they slow production or exchange information about wages or treatment.

In an industry that is so ethnically stratified, the absence of a shared language serves further to isolate and subordinate mainly Latino workers from employers, who are often Asian. This language disparity makes it hard for workers to communicate about something they do not like, and it helps owners to avoid intimate contact with workers and the threat to authority such contact might imply. Language does, however, also offer opportunities for unanticipated resistance or even advancement by workers who are able to understand and communicate in the language of their employers. One worker who knows some English reports being treated more kindly by a particularly abusive owner. In this case, language not only helped her resist being exploited but also may have led her employer to try to defuse or manipulate her potential ability to inform and empower co-workers. Other workers suggest that "selective understanding," when beneficial, may help garment workers to deflect verbal attacks and retain a greater measure of self-respect.

Garment workers are subjected to further physical and emotional atomization through spatial separation from one another. The linear alignment and noisy machines create a workplace inhospitable to conversation. Contractors also customarily restrict physical movements of workers and may also rely on workers to cooperate in "snitching" on one another, in return for favored treatment. Thus, both geographic control and the uncertainty and competition characterizing relations among workers constitute means by which workers are forced to labor long, repetitious hours at their machines in silence.

For their part, many workers try to achieve facility with various machines, since that can translate into higher wages as well as greater physical mobility within the factory. Those able to use a wide range of machines and to perform more than one task possess multiple skills that are transferable to other firms. With earnings from garment jobs, other workers purchase sewing machines to do sewing brought home from the factory or to turn out everything from reusable diapers to fashionable jackets. Ultimately, some workers are so successful in accumulating both skills and savings that they set up contracting operations themselves.

With today's accentuation of quantity and standardization over quality and intricacy, men may be given more opportunity to learn to operate different machines. The benefits, if there ever were any, of the ideology that women possess a "natural" dexterity for performing delicate work, have been supplanted by the need for endurance in long hours of repetitive procedures. This requirement, accompanied by a concept of women as physiologically unable to match men in such strenuous tasks, has resulted in a transformed sexual division of labor in which women workers are still less well off than men. Although differences in treatment ultimately depend on particular manager-worker interactions (which include female garment workers being the objects of sexual domination or sexualized favoritism), greater license for men to move about the shop and consequently to accumulate knowledge of various machines provides them with more earning power. Compounded by home and child responsibilities that envelop women, this gendered imbalance of opportunity is contributing to the end of the "female majority" in the garment industry.

These observations indicate some of the entangled ways in which language, spatial features of production, and surveillance are used to install competition and fear in the labor process. The result is a landscape of work that pits garment workers against owners and managers, as well as one another. As one worker observed, "at the factories you have to work hard to beat your own friend in order to succeed." Nevertheless, workers' situations and struggles are fluid and complex as well; closer attention to what workers say and do is certain to reveal further the informal, almost imperceptible ways in which garment workers survive in an industry notorious for its drudgery and exploitation.

Conclusion: The "Third World Within"

In Los Angeles, as throughout the Pacific Rim, garment workers make significant contibutions to the production of clothing yet garnish little in the way of wages or security of employment. This disparity raises questions of whether there is enough surplus generated by this industry to sustain better wages and working conditions, and what workers themselves can do to better their situation. In the garment industry, beneficiaries included owners and stockholders of manufacturing firms, retailing firms, and financial agencies that provide credit to the industry, as well as owners of real estate rented to contractors, contractors themselves, and the well-paid managers and professionals associated with the industry. But because both profits and accountability are dispersed and to a great extent hidden, workers are at a great disadvantage. Essentially, they are at the bottom of a diffused, competitive system in which they bear the brunt of deadlines and the squeezes of small margins that are passed sequentially from retailers to manufacturers to contractors.

An array of programs exists to uphold the rights of workers and to prevent them from falling below a decent minimum in wages and labor standards. Nonetheless, the role of the state in this regard is undercut in several respects. First, in California, the labor commissioner has neither the personnel nor the resources to investigate violations properly. Even if someone is caught, that business often simply closes and reopens elsewhere or under a different name. Efforts to pass a joint liability bill that would hold manufacturers responsible for law violations in contracting shops face strong opposition from manufacturers (Soldatenko 1992).

Second, federal immigration laws give an obvious advantage to employers and hurt undocumented immigrants and workers in general. The employer sanctions of IRCA appear not to have seriously affected apparel production in Los Angeles. The industry's size, fluidity, and increasing geographical spread make enforcement inherently difficult, and both employers and employees have made key adjustments to get around IRCA's provisions (Loucky, Hamilton, and

Chinchilla 1990). IRCA does appear to have contributed to a general decline in conditions for garment workers, however. The law's main result has been a general reduction of piece rates for everyone. Employers assume that those lacking work authorization will do whatever is demanded in order to keep a job, driving the base pay down for all workers. One machine operator conceded, "It's getting worse everywhere. Where we would get twenty-three cents [a piece], now it's twenty-one cents. But since they can find others [to work], we accept the pay. We don't have other options." For other workers, there has been more pressure to take on homework.

Some have argued that problems generated by undocumented immigration can be stemmed by either sealing the border or creating overseas assembly plants. If employment opportunities in this industry serve as a magnet for immigrant workers, it is asserted that transferring those opportunities to developing nations, particularly in the Caribbean and Central America, should provide immigrants with less incentive to leave their homelands, while U.S. employers will be able to get the work done without encouraging immigration. If, as we argue, however, the forces that create immigration are in part generated on the U.S. side of the border, the premises on which such policies are based can be questioned. Instead of stemming emigration, the development of overseas assembly plants may actually enhance it. If the dominant pattern of industries such as apparel is simply to shift assembly abroad, with little linkage to either local or overall national economic development, there is no reason to believe that the emigration of workers who remain unemployed in their homelands will not continue. Maquila and immigrant workers may increasingly become the same people, moving between countries depending on where garment operations are set up.

The situation of garment workers in Los Angeles is remarkably similar to the situation of garment workers in the less-developed countries to which the industry has migrated. For this reason, immigrant workers in Los Angeles are sometimes described as a "Third World within." The creation of such a sector within a highly developed city shows the effects of globalization; by putting a downward pressure on wages in this industry, globalization pushes Los Angeles producers to turn toward the most exploitable work force they can find: undocumented immigrants. Meanwhile, globalization also dislocates people in their homelands, creating an emigrant work force seeking jobs in developed countries such as the United States, even if they cannot establish legal residence. Finally, globalization helps to create a group of immigrant entrepreneurs eager to find a niche between capital and labor.

These consequences of globalization contribute to the tremendous class and ethnic tensions that have become so prominent in Los Angeles. The garment industry has many features exemplifying these tensions, and its dynamics help to explain why parts of the city exploded in April 1992.

Ultimately, the solution to these problems cannot be found in Los Angeles alone. Globalization allows capital to pit workers against one another all over the globe. The only far-reaching way workers can empower themselves is through the development of an international labor movement. All garment workers, no matter where they are, suffer from low wages and poor working conditions. They need to work together to combat these conditions: the evolution of global capital requires the concomitant evolution of global labor.

Notes

1. Each of the authors of this chapter has independently conducted research on aspects of the apparel industry in Los Angeles. Loucky has worked with Central American garment workers and has studied the impact of IRCA (Loucky, Hamilton, and Chinchilla 1990). Soldatenko conducted in-depth interviews with Latina workers (1992), as did Scott (1992). Bonacich has studied the overall structure of the industry (1992).

2. It should be noted that contracting locally bears a strong resemblance to Item 807 and maquiladora production; on both cases, an independent contractor organizes the sewing for a manufacturer. The only differences are the location of the enterprise and the tendency for mass-produced items with low fashion content to be produced outside the country and for season-driven items requiring short lead times to be contracted within Los Angeles.

References

Bonacich, Edna. 1992. "Alienation among Asian and Latino Immigrants in the Los Angeles Garment Industry: The Need for New Forms of Class Struggle in the Late Twentieth Century." In *Alienation, Society, and the*

Individual, edited by Felix Geyer and Walter R. Heinz, 165–80. New Brunswick, N.J.: Transaction.

Bonacich, Edna, and John Modell. 1980. *The Economic Basis of Ethnic Entrepreneurship: Small Business in the Japanese American Community.* Berkeley: University of California Press.

Cheng, Lucie, and Edna Bonacich, eds. 1984. *Labor Immigration under Capitalism: Asian Workers in the United States before World War II.* Berkeley: University of California Press.

Fernandez-Kelly, M. Patricia, and Anna M. Garcia. 1989. "Hispanic Women and Homework: Women in the Informal Economy in Miami and Los Angeles." In *Homework: Historical and Contemporary Pespectives on Paid Labor at Home*, edited by Eileen Boris and Cynthia R. Daniels, 165–79. Urbana: University of Illinois Press.

Laslett, John, and Mary Tyler. 1989. *The ILGWU in Los Angeles, 1907–1988.* Inglewood, Calif.: Ten Star Press.

Light, Ivan, and Edna Bonacich. 1988. *Immigrant Entrepreneurs: Koreans in Los Angeles, 1965–1982.* Berkeley: University of California Press.

Loucky, James, Nora Hamilton, and Norma Chinchilla. 1990. *The Effects of the Immigration Reform and Control Act on the Garment, Building Maintence, and Hospitality Industries in Los Angeles.* Washington, D.C.: Division of Immigration Policy and Research, Department of Labor.

Sassen, Saskia. 1988. *The Mobility of Labor and Capital: A Study of International Investment and Labor Flow.* Cambridge: Cambridge University Press.

Scott, Gregory. 1992. "The Everyday Politics of Domination and Resistance: An Ethnographic Inquiry into the Local Production of Garments for the Global Market." Master's thesis, Department of Sociology, University of Southern California, Santa Barbara.

Sherwood-Call, Carolyn. 1989. "Undocumented Workers and Regional Differences in Apparel Labor Markets." *Federal Reserve Bank of San Francisco, Economic Review*, winter, 53–63.

Soldatenko, Maria. 1992. "The Everyday Life of Latina Garment Workers: The Convergence of Gender, Race, Class, and Immigration Status." Ph.D. dissertation, Department of Sociology, University of California, Los Angeles.

U.S. Department of Commerce, Bureau of Census. Selected years. *County Business Patterns: California.* Washington, D.C.

U.S. Department of Labor, Bureau of Labor Statistics. 1991. "Current Employment Statistics." Unpublished data provided by California Employment Development Department.

U.S. General Accounting Office. 1988. *Sweatshops in the U.S.: Opinions on Their Extent and Possible Enforcement Options.* Washington, D.C.

Waldinger, Roger D. 1986. *Through the Eye of the Needle: Immigrants and Enterprise in New York's Garment Trades.* New York: New York University Press.

Conclusion

Chapter 20

The Garment Industry, National Development, and Labor Organizing

Edna Bonacich, Lucie Cheng, Norma Chinchilla, Nora Hamilton, and Paul Ong

This chapter draws on the previous chapters as well as on discussions at the Conference on the Globalization of the Garment Industry in the Pacific Rim.

The garment industry has been a factor in the economic development of several countries, particularly those of East Asia. Before we discuss the industry's role in development, however, it is important to distinguish among different meanings of *development*. Development is often defined in terms of macroeconomic indicators, such as rate of growth, level of investment, and increase in exports. It can also be defined in normative terms that encompass not only growth but the relatively equitable distribution of the benefits of growth among the population. Here we define *development* as the emergence and expansion of an efficient, integrated productive structure characterized by increasing levels of productivity, with the understanding that the primary goal of development is a rising standard of living for the entire population. This standard includes basic rights to health, education, housing, and employment, which in turn involve decent wages and working conditions. Ideally, such goals are incorporated in development strategies, but in fact their inclusion is generally a function of the organization and activism of affected sectors of the population. Thus, the organization of workers and other sectors is necessary to ensure that development achieves the goal of higher standards of living.

The Global Garment Industry and Development

Because of its dynamic and global nature, the international garment industry seems to be incompatible with national development goals. Development strategies imply planning and thus some level of stability; the global garment industry is highly volatile and unpredictable, subject to constant modifications in the rules of international trade—policies over which developing countries have little control (such as GSP, GATT, and MFA)—and frequent shifts in production sites, in efforts to lower costs and guarantee market access. Some of the largest companies, such as Liz Claiborne, have products manufactured entirely through arrangements with independent suppliers (three hundred in the case of Claiborne), with no one supplier producing more than 4 to 5 percent of total output. Some companies lease rather than own properties in other countries and operate without contracts. While these features maximize flexibility for the companies, they add to the instability of the apparel industry as an instrument of growth.

Nevertheless, several East Asian countries have been able to take advantage of the international garment industry as a step in the development process. It can provide an entrée to international markets, foreign capital, and technology. It can contribute to foreign exchange through export earnings and generate additional resources for development. It also provides employment, a particular benefit for labor-surplus countries.

In East Asia, the garment industry has also contributed to an integrated productive structure, moving into the development of upstream (design and cutting) and downstream (market) activities, as well as the development of backward linkages with the textile industry. Taiwan, for example, switched from imported cotton to domestically produced synthetic fiber between 1966 and 1973. Higher value-added can also be obtained through product upgrading. In response to the Multifiber Arrangement, Taiwan shifted to new product lines with higher value-added; Thailand did the same in response to rising labor costs. Increased labor costs have also led several countries, including South Korea, Taiwan, and Hong Kong, to shift to offshore production in other Asian countries.

Mexico, Central America, and the Caribbean have experienced some of these benefits, but often they come with costs arising from structural adjustment programs imposed in the context of the debt crisis. The rapid growth in garment exports has contributed to foreign exchange, but this gain is sometimes offset by increased imports, including imports of cheap apparel, for example, in Mexico and Central America. This enclave pattern of investment has meant limited transfers of skills and technology, particularly in the Caribbean. In most of these countries, as well as the Philippines, the export-garment industry seems to have advanced little beyond the category of an offshore maquila industry.

It should be pointed out, however, that several of these countries had already achieved a relatively high level of economic development (on the basis of industrialization for the internal market) before embarking on an export-led growth strategy. Most of them have a garment industry that produces for domestic or regional markets, or both, and in some cases draws on domestically produced textiles. But often these textile industries have become inefficient from overprotection, so that garment manufacturers producing for export prefer to rely on imported fabrics. Garment and textile production for domestic markets has suffered also from the increased availability of cheap imports with trade liberalization.

Several factors may help to account for the apparent differences in the role of the garment industry in the Asian countries and in Latin America. Though all the countries examined are dependent on foreign markets, and some are dependent on foreign investment, Mexico, Central America, and the Caribbean have a unique relationship with the United States as part of its sphere of economic and political influence. This relationship provides certain advantages: proximity to the U.S. market and special provisions, such as the Caribbean Basin Initiative (CBI) and the free-trade agreement with Mexico, have made these countries particularly attractive as sites for offshore investment. But foreign investment and subcontracting have often meant that initiatives taken by foreign companies and governments are in the interests of foreign industry rather than domestic growth. Thus, while measures such as tariff Item 807 have provided access to protected U.S. markets, requirements that inputs be imported (and in the case of apparel, that fabrics be designed and cut in the United States to take advantage of guaranteed access levels) have tended to discourage the development of upstream activities and backward linkages within the host country.

Timing may be an additional factor. The earlier shift to export-oriented industrialization of several East Asian countries enabled them to take advantage of an expanding international economy; more recently, exports have confronted contracting markets and growing protectionism in developed countries. During the 1980s several of the Latin American economies (and that of the Philippines) were weakened by the debt crisis and severe recession, leading to greater intervention by the International Monetary Fund (IMF) and other lending agencies, including the Agency for International Development (USAID) in the Caribbean and Central America. Structural adjustment measures proposed by these agencies include economic and especially trade liberalization, which have the effect of opening the economies to cheaper imports and increasing balance-of-trade deficits even when exports, especially garment exports, are growing.

Whatever the merits of trade liberalization as a policy, it is contrary to the strategy pursued by several East Asian countries. In fact, a perhaps critical distinction between the two sets of countries has been the presence in East Asia of domestic institutions with sufficient control over their national economies to devise and implement long-term growth strategies; at the same time, such institutions must be sufficiently flexible to respond to international signals and domestic challenges by shifting to new types of products, new markets (and/or expanded production for domestic markets), new sites of production, and new industries. In several countries the state has played such a role, particularly through autonomous research and development organizations modeled on MITI (Ministry of International Trade and Industry) in Japan. In Korea, for example, not only are exports heavily subsidized, but the government has made selective use of protective tariffs to promote specific industries for limited periods of time. In Singapore and Taiwan as well, the apparel industry, along with other industries, has benefited from substantial state economic intervention.

Such planning and flexibility have required a certain degree of autonomy both from the domestic private sector and from foreign capital and institutions: to a large extent, the governments in Korea and Taiwan have been able to determine which industries would be protected and where foreign capital would be welcomed and where excluded. In some cases, the state in Latin American countries has also played a strong developmental role, which has been used to create space for domestic capital in the context of a strong foreign presence. Latin American governments, however, appear to be much more subject to pressures from private capital, both domestic and foreign—one factor in the continuation of high levels of protectionism beyond the point necessary for industries become competitive.

It may be argued that the Latin American countries are simply at an earlier stage in the process of export-led growth and that they too will be able to advance to higher value-added activities and a more integrated industry. In Mexico, agglomerations of garment producers have taken steps to establish upstream activities. Costa Rican policy makers have recognized that their country's comparative advantage lies in its educated and skilled labor force and are concentrating on higher value-added products. Nevertheless, the Latin American countries, as well as second- and third-tier garment producers in Asia, confront higher levels of global competition and protectionism than the East Asian countries at an earlier period, and the export-led path to development remains an uncertain one.

Even the Asian NICs face domestic and international challenges to the continued success of their model. One of the effects of development is the increased strength of certain sectors of private capital that are able to penetrate the state and, in effect, undermine its autonomy. Thus the ability of state institutions to guide the development process may be more limited in the future.

Moreover, the North American Free Trade Agreement (NAFTA) could cause a shift from the cross-Pacific alignment between the United States and Asia to a regional alignment between the United States and Latin America. To the extent that Asian export production is dependent on U.S. markets, such a realignment raises significant questions regarding the future of the export-led model.

Labor Organizing and Development Goals

The challenges posed by the global garment industry for labor organizing are formidable. In the first place, the nontraditional export model tends to look on "cheap and abundant" labor as a major resource for developing countries. Legal wages are less than US$0.50 per hour in Guatemala and El Salvador; actual wages may be even lower. Cheap labor has been a major factor in the shift of Korean industry to offshore production in Asia and Latin America, as well as in the move of U.S. companies to open plants in Central America and the Caribbean.

The identification of low-wage labor as a major attraction for foreign investment, and foreign investment as a dominant strategy for development, means that there is an intrinsic contradiction between development and labor organizing, leading to a correlation between export-oriented industry and labor-repressive policies. U.S. companies seeking to open plants in Central America, for example, were allegedly assured that they would not have to deal with unions. Producers in Taiwan and Korea have stated that the absence of unions is their major criterion in selecting countries for investment. There is also to some extent a conflict between workers, who suffer from low wages, and consumers, who benefit from the availability of inexpensive clothing.

The fact that production workers are found in the most competitive and least profitable segment of the apparel industry operates as a further brake on wages. In this buyer-centered industry, profits are concentrated in marketing and, to the extent the industry is globalized, in the advanced industrial countries. Within the United States, contractors and workers are squeezed while major profits accrue to design, engineering, and marketing.

Labor organizing is additionally discouraged by the structure of the apparel industry, which is often dispersed into small shops, with contracting (often at several levels) and homework leading to further fragmentation of the labor force. Legislation to the effect that unions must be permitted in shops employing a certain number of workers has reinforced the tendency toward small workshops, as in Mexico. In Asia, many of the small shops employ chiefly relatives. Women employees are often purposefully used to keep labor flexible and cheap.

Other efforts to undercut unions range from prohibitions against unions (often illegal but nonetheless practiced, especially in the Caribbean and Central America), to "solidarismo" (an industry-subsidized policy of collaboration between industry and workers, which has obtained a following in Costa Rica and other Central American countries), to industrial paternalism, as in Korea. State control of major labor organizations (as in Mexico and Singapore) has also undermined the effectiveness of labor. Unionization is, of course, even more dramatically threatened by the international nature of the garment industry, which pits U.S. workers trying to retain their jobs and wages against workers in other countries desperately in need of even low-paying jobs.

Conditions affecting workers, both positive and negative, often stem from circumstances beyond their control, such as labor shortages or surpluses and rural-urban migration. Thus workers in Korea, Taiwan, and Thailand, among other places, benefited from wage increases during the 1980s, reflecting labor shortages as well as labor organization and militancy. Wages dropped sharply in several Latin American countries during the same period, as a consequence of unemployment resulting from the economic crisis and structural adjustment programs. The improvements for workers in Asia could be reversed if, as is feared there, NAFTA leads to the loss of jobs. This situation pits Asian workers against those of Mexico and other Latin American countries, again undermining the potential for cross-regional labor organizing.

The problems of the garment industry (and other international industries) have led to a basic reconceptualization of labor organizing. Although some U.S. unions have supported protectionism, especially in the context of NAFTA, others oppose protectionism because it makes workers compete against one another. Several strategies have been developed to improve working conditions globally.

First, it is recognized that labor movements must become social movements, going beyond strictly workplace issues and linking them to other concerns, such as environmental and minority issues. One example is provided by workers in industries along the U.S.-Mexico border who have organized to combat pollution in the region. Mexico's Nineteenth of September movement has attempted to redefine workplace issues to include gender, workplace democracy, and broader concerns. The ILGWU has developed Justice Centers in Los Angeles, San Francisco, and New York in an effort to build community-based unionism. Other examples are La Mujer Obrera in El Paso and Asian Immigrant Women's Advocates in Oakland.

Second, efforts are being made to establish certain minimum international standards for labor in areas such as workplace safety. U.S. labor and human-rights organizations have used a provision of the U.S. Generalized System of Preferences (GSP), requiring respect for the rights of labor, to try to enforce labor rights in Guatemala. After several years, the U.S. Congress agreed to open an investigation into alleged violations of labor rights which could lead to the suspension of access of Guatemalan products to the U.S. market. The social charter of the European Economic Community represents an attempt to protect labor rights in the context of economic integration, and pressures from labor organizations and their supporters led to the inclusion of some safeguards for labor under NAFTA, although these are far from adequate.

Third, workers and their supporters have put pressure on the headquarters and retail outlets of transnational businesses, as well as on governments. For example, a U.S. group known as the Guatemala Labor Education Project, under the auspices of ACTWU (the American Clothing and Textile Workers Union), has helped workers in Guatemala fight for union rights by putting pressure on companies such as Phillips Van Heusen; tactics include letter-writing campaigns to company headquarters and to retailers that carry their products. The group has also urged supporters to write letters to the Guatemalan labor minister and to the Korean Embassy in the case of a Korean contractor in Guatemala known to abuse and underpay workers. This organization promotes the distribution of leaflets, boycotts, and putting pressure on the U.S. government to suspend the GSP for Guatemala.

Ultimately, workers and their supporters must find new ways to organize at the international level. Capital is organized at this level, and the globalization of production means that decisions are increasingly made with little input by labor and other affected populations. Because international competition in effect pits workers against one another, a situation often encouraged by nationalistic campaigns on the part of industry and government, cross-national and cross-regional labor organizing is extremely difficult. Nevertheless, efforts are being made to develop international networks and cross-national unionization training. An example of such a network is the women's organization Mujer a Mujer. A great deal more effort and resources need to be put into these projects.

Conclusion

The establishment of an export-oriented apparel industry does not automatically translate into national development or better standards of living for a country's population. Structural conditions may exert positive or negative influences on prospects for development. A key element appears to be the existence of a "developmental state" or other institutions (e.g., business associations) capable of strategic planning and flexible response to international and national challenges. Depending on circumstances, the development of backward linkages (textiles, fibers), upstream activities (design, cutting), downstream activities (marketing), or higher-quality products can help to transform an export-oriented industry into higher productivity and growth for a country's economy as a whole.

Finally, for higher productivity and growth to translate into better working conditions as well as higher standards of living for the entire population, labor and other affected groups must be organized. Effective organization may require the incorporation of new concerns (such as environmental standards), new constituencies (consumers, immigrants, human rights organizers), and new strategies and tactics (such as international consumer boycotts). Most important, the globalization of industry requires labor and other groups to look beyond national boundaries and to organize internationally in order to have an effective voice in decisions affecting them.

List of Contributors

Richard P. Appelbaum is Professor of Sociology at the University of California, Santa Barbara.

Evelyn Blumenberg is a Ph.D. candidate in architecture and urban planning at the University of California, Los Angeles.

Edna Bonacich is Professor of Sociology and Ethnic Studies at the University of California, Riverside.

Jorge Carrillo V. is a full-time researcher at El Colegio de la Frontera Norte, Tijuana, Mexico.

Chi-Fai Chan is Senior Lecturer in Marketing and International Business at the Chinese University of Hong Kong.

Lucie Cheng is Professor of Sociology at the University of California, Los Angeles, and Visiting Professor of Urban Studies at National Taiwan University, Taipei.

Norma Chinchilla is Professor of Sociology and Director of Program in Women's Studies at California State University, Long Beach.

Richard F. Doner is Professor of Political Science at Emory University, Atlanta.

Sara U. Douglas is Associate Professor of Consumer Sciences at the University of Illinois, Urbana-Champaign.

Stephen A. Douglas is Associate Professor of Political Science at the University of Illinois, Urbana-Champaign.

Thomas J. Finn is a practicing attorney and consultant to numerous U.S. and Southeast Asian companies.

Gary Gereffi is Associate Professor of Sociology at Duke University.

Nora Hamilton is Associate Professor of Political Science at the University of Southern California, Los Angeles.

Gordon H. Hanson is Assistant Professor of Economics at the University of Texas, Austin.

Ho-Fuk Lau is Senior Lecturer in Marketing and International Business at the Chinese University of Hong Kong.

Seung Hoon Lee is Professor of Economics at Seoul National University, Seoul, Korea.

James Loucky is Associate Professor of Anthropology at Western Washington University in Bellingham.

Rosalinda Pinedo Ofreneo is Professor of Social Work and Community Development at the University of the Philippines, Metro Manila.

Paul Ong is Associate Professor in the Graduate School of Architecture and Urban Planning at the University of California, Los Angeles.

Mei-Lin Pan is a Ph.D. candidate in sociology at Duke University.

Kurt Petersen is Education Director of the United Farm Workers of Washington State.

Ansil Ramsay is Professor of Government at St. Lawrence University, Canton, New York.

Helen I. Safa is Professor of Anthropology and Latin American Studies at the University of Florida, Gainesville.

Gregory Scott is a Ph.D. candidate in sociology at the University of California, Santa Barbara.

Maria Soldatenko received her Ph.D. in sociology at the University of California, Los Angeles in 1992.

Ho Keun Song is Professor of Sociology at Hallym University, Kangwon-Do, Korea.

Ian M. Taplin is Professor of Sociology at Wake Forest University, Winston-Salem, North Carolina.

David V. Waller is a Ph.D. candidate in sociology at the University of California, Riverside.